HITLER'S PARATROOPERS IN NORMANDY

HITLER'S PARATROOPERS IN NORMANDY

THE GERMAN II PARACHUTE CORPS IN THE BATTLE FOR FRANCE, 1944

GILBERTO VILLAHERMOSA

FRONTLINE
BOOKS

First published in Great Britain in 2019 by
FRONTLINE BOOKS
An imprint of
Pen & Sword Books Ltd
Yorkshire - Philadelphia

ISBN 9781848327719

A CIP catalogue record for this book is
available from the British Library

Typeset in Palatino Roman
Printed and bound by TJ International

Pen & Sword Books Ltd incorporates the imprints of Pen & Sword
Archaeology, Atlas, Aviation, Battleground, Discovery,
Family History, History, Maritime, Military, Naval, Politics,
Social History, Transport, True Crime, Claymore Press,
Frontline Books, Praetorian Press,
Seaforth Publishing and White Owl

For a complete list of Pen & Sword titles please contact

PEN & SWORD BOOKS LTD
47 Church Street, Barnsley, South Yorkshire, S70 2AS, England
E-mail: enquiries@pen-and-sword.co.uk
Website: www.pen-and-sword.co.uk

Or
PEN AND SWORD BOOKS
1950 Lawrence Rd, Havertown, PA 19083, USA
E-mail: Uspen-and-sword@casematepublishers.com
Website: www.penandswordbooks.com

Contents

Introduction

In June 1944, American and British forces fighting desperately to establish a foothold on French beachheads and then break out of Normandy's formidable hedgerows, the confining bocage, found themselves opposed by a diverse array of Wehrmacht formations. These ranged from elite German Army panzer and Waffen SS divisions to run-of-the-mill Army regular, reserve and static infantry divisions fighting alongside Luftwaffe (German Air Force) Field Divisions, and even 'Eastern' battalions consisting of Russian, Georgian and Central Asian soldiers.[1] Fifty-eight German divisions, numbering approximately 1,873,000 men, guarded the coasts and interior of the Netherlands, Belgium and France against an attack.[2] The severely debilitated Luftwaffe and Kriegsmarine, the German Air Force and Navy, were all but absent from the air and sea battle, leaving the ground forces to fight almost unsupported.[3] Among those formations defending in France, as part of *Oberbefehlshaber West*, or OB West (Armed Forces Command West), were a host of new formations raised to meet the expected Allied invasion. These included the newly formed First Parachute Army Headquarters, II Parachute Corps

---

1. The SS was part of the Wehrmacht until the attempt on Adolf Hitler's life on 20 July 1944. After that date it was raised to equal status with the Wehrmacht.
2. Wilt, *The Atlantic Wall*, p. 128.
3. The First U.S. Army estimated, prior to the battle, that the German Air Force could deploy some 1,350 aircraft, including almost 700 single and twin-engine fighters and fighter-bombers, on D-Day and the German Navy more than 300 ships of all classes, including eleven destroyers and as many as sixty Motor Torpedo E-boats. See *First United States Army Report of Operations 20 October 1943 – 1 August 1944*, 'Annex No. 1 Initial Joint Plan,' pp. 14–15.

Headquarters, and all or elements of the 2nd, 3rd, 5th, and 6th Parachute Divisions belonging to Herman Göring's Luftwaffe. Except for the 2nd Parachute Division and its subordinate 6th Parachute Regiment, these formations were so new that they didn't appear on the latest edition of the *Order of Battle of the German Army*, prepared by the U.S. War Department in February 1944 for the use of troops participating in the invasion.[4]

Hitler had concentrated his hard-fighting Fallschirmjäger, his 'Hunters from the Sky', in Normandy and the Cotentin peninsula over the course of the previous year to meet the long-awaited Allied assault on the French mainland. He intended to use them as elite infantrymen in the upcoming battle, fighting alongside his elite panzer divisions, to help contain the American and British beachheads. The Führer, like most of his field marshals and generals, believed an Allied landing in France was inevitable and that the invasion and the battle that followed would decide the outcome of the war and the fate of the Third Reich. Having proven themselves to be an iron shield in defensive battles in Russia, North Africa, Sicily, and Italy, Hitler had ordered a dramatic increase in their numbers in 1944. Some, such as General der Fallschirmtruppe Eugen Meindl, General der Fallschirmtruppe Hermann Bernhard Ramcke, Generalleutnant Richard Schimpf, Major Friedrich August Freiherr von der Heydte, Oberleutnant Martin Pöppel and Obergefreiter Karl Max Wietzorek, were still the top-notch Fallschirmjäger they had been when they had had stormed Scandinavia, the Low Countries, the Corinth Canal, and Crete in 1940. Most, however, were relatively newly trained paratroopers, fresh from jump schools in Germany and France. Still others were paratroopers in name only. Splendidly trained and equipped, and with varying levels of combat experience, they were expected to play a major role in stopping the Allied assault in France and driving the invasion forces back into the sea.

The German II Parachute Corps was the Wehrmacht's second largest parachute formation of the war and played a pivotal role in the fighting in Normandy between 6 June and 31 August 1944. Later it would play an equally important role in the final defence of the Third Reich as the heart and soul of the First Parachute Army. Yet no history, official or otherwise, has ever been written of Eugen Meindl and his elite Fallschirmjager.

---

4. War Department, *Order of Battle of the German Army. February 1944* (Washington D.C: Military Intelligence Division, February 1944). Only the 1st and 2nd Parachute Divisions and their subordinate formations are listed on page 111.

Furthermore, information on the II Parachute Corps and its parachute divisions in north-west Europe is equally hard to come by, especially in the English language. Yet the fighting abilities of the German parachute divisions were rated by senior Wehrmacht and American commanders only after Germany's elite Army and Waffen SS panzer divisions. The British War Office *Pocket Book of the German Army*, published in September 1943 and utilised by British officers at Normandy, lauded 'the hard battle training, physical fitness and esprit de corps of the German paratrooper'.[5] And the U.S. War Department's World War II classified *Handbook on German Military Forces*, published in 1945, after the Americans had gone toe-to-toe with Hitler's Fallschirmjäger in France, noted: 'the German Air Force Parachute Division is believed to be the strongest type of the various infantry divisions', emphasizing: 'one may generally consider the present Air Force Parachute divisions as especially carefully selected, well trained, and equipped crack infantry divisions'.[6]

The German II Parachute Corps was born of necessity. The Third Reich's strategic situation in the summer of 1944 on the eve of the Allied landings in France bordered on the desperate. In the air, the US and British air forces were ravaging Germany's major cities and factories day and night, pummelling her major industrial centres, devastating her transportation and communications networks, disrupting the production of German weapons of war and ammunition, destroying tens of thousands of apartments and homes, and displacing millions of workers. On the ground, the Red Army had recovered from the calamitous defeats of 1941 and 1942 and was hurling westward at breakneck speed advancing on the Third Reich and Berlin. As they advanced ever forward, Stalin's soldiers were mauling their Wehrmacht opponents viciously and, despite their own appalling losses, devouring German formations faster than they could be replaced. In the Mediterranean, the Americans and British had succeeded in knocking Italy out of the war. With thirty-four Italian divisions on occupation duty in Greece, Yugoslavia, and southern France neutralised, Hitler was forced to replace them with thirty German divisions sorely needed on other battlefronts. General Mark Clark's Fifth Army had captured Monte Cassino in Italy and was on the verge of seizing Rome. Mussolini's centre of power would fall on 5 June, the day before the Allied invasion of France. It was the first major European capitol to fall

---

5. War Department, *TM-E 30-451 Handbook on German Military Forces*, p. 107; British War Office, *Pocket Book of the German Army*, 1943, p. 102.

6. War Department, *TM-E 30-451 Handbook on German Military Forces*, p. 107.

to the Allies. At sea, the Allies had emerged triumphant from the Battle of the Atlantic, inflicting heavy losses on Hitler's U-boats and applying their maritime superiority on all fronts. It was the Allies' air and maritime supremacy that would form the foundation of the Allied amphibious landings in France.

Yet the Third Reich in 1944 was still a formidable foe. Despite heavy losses on all fronts, the strength of the Wehrmacht was almost nine and a half million men, with more than six and a half million serving in the *Heer* (German Army) and another almost two million serving in the Luftwaffe. It was this fighting dynamo that the Allies would have to battle in France if they were to bring about the end of Hitler's Third Reich. As they would soon discover, to first their astonishment and later to their chagrin, Nazi Germany still possessed immense reserves of manpower (including more than eleven million foreign workers and slave labourers), resources, and production capability, along with internal lines of communications and, most importantly, the will to continue the fight. All this translated into a remarkable ability to rapidly and efficiently regenerate combat power against the Allies at the most critical times and places, prolonging the fighting to the bitter end.

Along with the German Army's elite and hard-hitting panzer formations, Hitler's paratroopers were the Third Reich's spear and shield in the Second World War. In the early years of the war they had been in the vanguard of Nazi Germany's offensive strategy, the tip of that spear, thrusting their way into Scandinavia, Holland, Belgium, the Balkans and Crete. Despite Hitler's victory in the Mediterranean in May 1941, the horrendous losses of the German airborne forces during the Battle of Crete had devastated their ranks. British Prime Minister Winston Churchill observed presciently that the tip of the German spear had been shattered. More importantly, the battle of Crete, along with heavy infantry losses in Russia, caused Hitler to reconsider the role of his elite paratroopers. No longer believing that strategic surprise using airborne troops was possible, he sought another role for his most elite soldiers. Their determination and defensive successes on the battlefields of Russia, Tunisia, Sicily and Italy confirmed them in their new role as Hitler's hard-edged and unbending shield. There they would earn their reputation as skilled, tenacious and fanatical defenders committed to preventing the Allies from ever reaching the Third Reich.

Although Hitler's paratroopers fought with distinction in Russia, North Africa, and Sicily, Italy was the first theatre in the war in which multiple parachute divisions of elite Fallschirmjäger were brought together under a single airborne command, the I Parachute Corps. At

Anzio, elements of the I Parachute Corps and its 4th Parachute Division formed the foundation of the initial German defence against the Allies. Later, as additional Wehrmacht formations were directed toward the American and British beachhead, the I Parachute Corps formed the right flank of the German line. The Fallschirmjäger's reputation as an elite defensive force was sealed in blood at Monte Cassino, between January and May 1944. There paratroopers of the 1st Parachute Division played a pivotal role in defending the ancient monastery, preventing the Allies from breaking through the Gustav Line and seizing Rome. Between January and May 1944, the Allies suffered 45,000 casualties during four assaults against Monte Cassino, while inflicting 30,000 on the Germans. It was only after the fourth assault on the position in May 1944, when the Americans and British committed some twenty divisions along a 20-mile front, that the Allies were finally able to throw the Germans off Monte Cassino and open the road to Rome. For Hitler and his Third Reich, the battle of Monte Cassino was the epitome of the courage, skill, and tenacity of the German Landser (the Wehrmacht equivalent of 'G.I.') and his Fallschirmjäger brother, fighting together, shoulder to shoulder, and holding their ground to the bitter end against the superior numbers and overwhelming firepower of the Americans, British, Canadians, Australians, New Zealanders, French, Poles, and even Italian Royalists.

For the Germans, the battle was an important strategic lesson, a precursor of things to come when the Allies finally invaded France and approached the borders of the Third Reich. The Führer and many of his generals believed that their qualitatively superior Werhmacht commanders and soldiers could fight the quantitatively superior, but strategically unimaginative and methodically ponderous Allies, to a standstill and win. Henceforth, Hitler would commit his paratroopers to bolster the defensive efforts of less elite Wehrmacht infantry formations, inflict maximum casualties on the advancing Allies, bleed them dry, and delay the Allied advance into Nazi Germany. Just as German Army soldiers had 'corseted' the less elite fighters of the Austro–Hungarian Empire on the Eastern Front in the First World War, Hitler's paratroopers would strengthen run-of-the-mill German infantry formations in France, infusing an element of steel into their defensive prowess. This delaying strategy would buy time to create new formations and manufacture new Wunderwaffen that, if produced on a large enough scale, would transform the very nature of the war. These 'wonder weapons' included ballistic rockets, cruise missiles, jet fighters, guided air-to-air and surface-to-air missiles, biological and chemical weapons, and improved types of submarines, tanks, artillery pieces and anti-tank guns. Germany's new formations and weapons would, in turn, create new military options by inflicting massive casualties and equipment losses on the Western Allies, facilitating the ability of the Wehrmacht to defeat or even split the Americans from the British, leading to outright victory, or at the very least a political settlement. Perhaps Hitler and his field marshals believed they could win the war and end it outside of the borders of the Third Reich, as had happened at the end of the First World War, when the Führer had served in the German Imperial Army.

The intent of this book is not to recount the history of the German Fallschirmjäger in the Second World War. That subject has been covered by other authors, in both German and English. I have addressed it in some depth in my own, *Hitler's Paratrooper. The Life and Battles of Rudolph Witzig* (2010).[7] Nor is it to retell all aspects of the story of the Allied invasion of the Normandy, whose success heralded the downfall of the Third Reich. The history of that critical turning point in the war has been recounted many times and continues to be retold. Indeed, new books on this subject continue to provide fresh and valuable insights into an old and decisive battle.[8] My focus here is on the Luftwaffe's II Parachute Corps, its commander, General der Fallschirmtruppe Eugen Meindl, and subordinate formations in Normandy from the Allied invasion on 6 June to the end of August 1944. Meindl was the epitome of the senior German airborne commander in the Second World War. Tough, experienced, and aggressive, Meindl cared deeply for his troops. Yet the shortcomings of the Wehrmacht and its leadership at Normandy were all too clear to him during the second battle for France in 1944. Nonetheless, Meindl's II Parachute Corps fought with bravery and tenacity for almost three months against the Americans, before being forced to fall back in the face of Allied air supremacy and overwhelming field artillery, superior Allied infantry and armour operations, and the collapse of weaker German units on its flanks. Trapped with the bulk of the German Seventh Army in the Falaise pocket, Meindl and his paratroopers maintained their discipline and were selected by the Commander in Chief of OB West to lead the German breakout to the east. That they managed to do so, despite suffering grievous losses, while so many around them died or surrendered, is a testament to their dedication and fighting ability.

---

7. See Gilberto Villahermosa, *Hitler's Paratroopers. The Life and Battles of Rudolph Witzig* (London: Frontline Books, 2010).

8. See for example Mark Reardon's new and extremely insightful *Defending Fortress Europe. The War Diary of the German 7th Army in Normandy, 6 June to 26 July 1944* (Bedford, Pennsylvania: the Aberjona Press, 2012).

Sufficient German and English language sources exist, including a plethora of first-person German monographs and narratives, along with U.S. and British intelligence reports, to construct a relatively complete and accurate chronological narrative of the Wehrmacht's Fallschirmtruppen in Normandy in 1944. Space, however, limits our coverage. This book will thus focus on the major battles of II Parachute Corps, 6th Parachute Regiment, and 3rd and 5th Parachute Divisions in Normandy. It will only touch on the 6th Parachute Division, which was committed too late to the Normandy battle to make any significant impact. Finally, it will complete the story of Hitler's paratroopers in France by discussing General der Fallschirmtruppe Hermann Bernhard Ramcke's 2nd Parachute Division at Brest. Ramcke's Fallschirmjager in Brittany never came under Meindl and his II Parachute Corps.

The heroes of the II Parachute Corps at Normandy and in the Falaise Pocket were first and foremost the officers and men of Generalmajor Richard Schimpf's hard-fighting 3rd Parachute Division. Considered by both Allies and Germans alike to be the Wehrmacht's pre-eminent parachute formation, it was at the centre of the most important battles of the Normandy campaign. 'The greater per centage of its troops were very young and thoroughly indoctrinated with Nazi ideology,' stressed the authors of the First U.S. Army After Action Report for Normandy, concluding, 'They could be counted on to fight very well, perhaps even better than the SS units.'[9] The largest infantry formation in Normandy, 3rd Parachute Division, defended first the approaches to St-Lô by mid-June and then the city itself by mid-July. Seizure of St-Lô was a prerequisite for the American breakout of Normandy, a fact recognised by the Germans. After the collapse of the Wehrmacht front in Normandy and the encirclement of two German armies at Falaise, the 3rd Parachute Division led the breakout to the east that allowed thousands, perhaps tens of thousands, of officers and soldiers to escape back to Germany. The official *OKW (Oberkommando der Wehrmacht – German Armed Forces High Command) War Diary* for the period called the II Parachute Corps' breakout from the Falaise pocket 'one of the great feats of the campaign' and stresses that during that operation 'the 3rd Parachute Division distinguished itself above all'.[10]

Another notable parachute unit at Normandy was the 6th Parachute Regiment, which fought as an independent formation, separate from its

---

9. HQ U.S. Army, 'After Action Report. 6 June 1944 – 1 August 1944', p. 19.
10. Schramm, *B-034 OKW War Diary: The West (1 April–18 December 1944)*, p. 113.

parent unit, the 2nd Parachute Division. The 6th Parachute Regiment was first attached to the German Army's 91st Luftlande (Air Landing) Division in the Cotentin peninsula during the initial fighting in Normandy. Major Friedrich August Freiherr von der Heydte and his Fallschirmjager were in the thick of the battle on D-Day, fighting paratroopers of the 101st Airborne Division even as they landed with their parachutes and in gliders. Because its commander in Normandy cooperated closely with his American captors after the war and attained high rank in the post-war Bundeswehr and the German government, von der Heydte and the 6th Parachute Regiment have received lavish attention and praise in English language histories. However, a close scrutiny of the unit's combat actions and its commander on D-Day at Viervielle, at St-Côme-du-Mont, and then at Carentan, where the regiment was defeated by American paratroopers, calls into question the accuracy of its post-war reputation. Even so, the 6th Parachute Regiment redeemed its standing somewhat in the last week of July, when it held Sainteny and Sèves Island against the veteran U.S. 90th Infantry Division.

Committed piecemeal to the Normandy battles after other Wehrmacht units suffered heavy casualties, Generalleutnant Gustav Wilke's 5th Parachute Division was the first Fallschirmjager formation not to receive parachute training. While its ranks included veteran paratroopers, especially among its commanders and NCOs, most of its soldiers were poorly trained and equipped. Denigrated by veteran Fallschirmjager such as Major von der Heydte and even by the Seventh Army Chief of Staff, *Oberst* Max Pemsel, 5th Parachute Division fought with considerable valour and boldness on Hill 122 and Mont-Castre on the approaches to St-Lô and later, alongside the elite Panzer Lehr Division up to Operation Cobra, the U.S. breakout from Normandy. Together, 6th Parachute Regiment, along with the 3rd Parachute and 5th Parachute Divisions, managed to hold their own and delay the American breakout from Normandy at St-Lô and Monte-Castre.

The formation and training of Generalleutnant Rüdiger von Heyking's 6th Parachute Division was interrupted by the Allied invasion at Normandy, making it the weakest of the Fallschirmjäger divisions in France in terms of leadership, personnel, and heavy equipment. One of its regimental commanders was a battled-hardened veteran of combat in Greece, Crete and North Africa. The other was an 'outsider', a former cavalry officer and Luftwaffe General Staff officer, who had never commanded German ground forces, let alone a parachute regiment. The 6th Parachute Division was committed too late to the Normandy campaign to have any significant impact on the battle.

General der Fallschirmtruppe Hermann Bernhard Ramcke's 2nd Parachute Division defended Brest in the Brittany peninsula, ensuring the port's complete destruction before surrendering. The harbour was desperately needed by the Allies and the actions of Hitler's paratroopers at Brest seriously crippled the logistical sustainment of the American and British armies, slowing their momentum as they advanced toward Germany.

Together, the Luftwaffe's parachute formations in France played a major role in condemning the Anglo–American armies to a slogging advance through the bocage. Although the Fallschirmjäger failed in their mission of defeating and containing the Allies indefinitely, Hitler's paratroopers succeeded in winning sufficient time for the Führer and the German High Command to move newly created formations and armaments to the West Wall, temporarily halting the Allied advance in September 1944, and prolonging the survival of the Third Reich.

The history of the German II Parachute Corps in Normandy provides valuable insight into the Wehrmacht's desperate and eventually futile battle, despite years of expectation and preparation, to first contain the Allied landings in the face of devastating air support and naval and artillery fire, then to destroy them by panzer-centric counter-attacks, and finally to escape encirclement and complete destruction by fast-moving Allied armoured and mechanised spearheads emulating the very best of the German blitzkrieg tactics of the early 1940s. Hitler and his field marshals expected the invasion and even believed themselves prepared for the Allied assault on France. They had not, however, anticipated either the sheer magnitude of the Allied assault nor the relentless air and naval firepower, which crippled their forces long before they could come to grips with the invaders. Indeed, only four days after the invasion, Field Marshal Erwin Rommel, the senior German field commander in Normandy with the most experience fighting the British and Americans, wrote of the 'immensely powerful, at times overwhelming, superiority of the enemy air force'.[11]

Nor did the senior leaders of the Wehrmacht and Waffen SS expect the hard-fighting U.S. infantry nor fast-moving American tank tactics that shattered their front at St-Lô, advancing rapidly into the depths of France and behind the German lines, robbing Hitler and his generals of the ability to staunch the immense and growing rupture in their lines. What emerges is a history of the Wehrmacht in France as uneven in its leadership,

---

11. Liddell Hart, *The Rommel Papers*, pp. 476–477.

composition, and quality as it had been three years earlier when it had invaded the Soviet Union, with an even more dysfunctional strategic leadership and fighting without the benefit of substantial air or naval support. This story of the Germans at Normandy then is predominately that of Hitler's ground forces battling together to prevent defeat. Despite the competition between the two organisations at the highest level of command, unit leaders at the operational and tactical levels often found common ground during the fighting. Standing shoulder to shoulder and transitioning, seamlessly, under each other's command, they were able to maximise their fighting potential.

The opening two chapters of this book detail the II Parachute Corps and Hitler's paratroopers in France prior to and on D-Day, providing an overview of the organisation, personnel, equipment, and deployment of all parachute formations in Normandy up to 6 June 1944. In war, numbers matter. Larger formations can cover more ground, in the defence or the attack, bring more weapons to bear, sustain more casualties, and remain in combat longer. Hence, the emphasis in the first chapter on the number of personnel and weapons in the Fallschirmjäger formations in France in 1944. Their size and armaments made them foes to be reckoned with. As Soviet leader Joseph Stalin is purported to have said: 'Quantity has a quality all of its own.' Because they were among the largest infantry formations in Normandy (and because sizeable replacements were not available), the German parachute divisions and regiments remained in combat without respite. Three chapters cover the 6th Parachute Regiment at St-Côme-du-Mont, Carentan, and Sainteny and Sèves Island. Two chapters tell the history of the 3rd Parachute Division at Hill 192 and at St-Lô. One full chapter is devoted to the 5th Parachute Division at Hill 122 and Mont-Castre. Another chapter relates the 2nd Parachute Division's dogged defence at Brest. The last chapter returns to Meindl and his beleaguered II Parachute Corps at Falaise as they struggled to survive and lead the German Seventh Army out of the Allied encirclement.

Hitler's paratroopers in Normandy were among the first and last of the Wehrmacht forces in France to successfully battle the Americans. They fought on every battlefront, alongside average German infantry divisions, such as the 77th and 352nd Infantry and elite Waffen SS divisions, like the 17th SS Panzergrenadier, 2nd SS-Panzer, and the Panzer Lehr. The last was considered the most elite Wehrmacht formation in France. The Fallschirmjäger, who considered themselves elite infantry, preferred fighting along the elite panzer troops of the Waffen SS. Their story is told not only from the perspective of the German commanders and paratroopers who fought the Americans, but also from the point of view of the American officers and soldiers who battled them. The latter provides a more accurate account of not only whom and what the elite German units faced in battle, but how they acquitted themselves. Their U.S. opponents ranged from elite paratroopers of the 101st Airborne Division, who fought Major von der Heydte's 'Lions of Carentan' from the first day of the invasion, to regular G.I.s and tankers of the 2nd, 29th, 30th, 83rd and 90th Infantry Divisions and the 6th Armoured Division, who faced the 2nd, 3rd, 5th and 6th Parachute Divisions in Normandy and Brittany. In the end, battered ceaselessly by American airpower and artillery, attacked continuously by U.S. infantry and tank formations, and bereft of air cover, replacements, and sufficient ammunition and equipment to continue the battle, Hitler's paratroopers in Normandy, like most of the Wehrmacht in France, were unable to hold the line any longer. Those who didn't fall at St-Côme-du-Mont, Carentan, Hill 192, Mont-Castre or St-Lô, perished during Operation Cobra following the American breakthrough at St-Lô, Falaise, Mons and Brest.

Foreword: 'Fierce but Fair'

'I am no writer and have no intention of trying to win a petty medal for detailed description,' wrote Eugen Albert Max Meindl, a former General der Fallschirmtruppe in Hermann Göring's Luftwaffe. At the time he wrote those words, however, in July 1946, Meindl was simply prisoner A451668 in Prisoner of War Camp No. 11 in Bridgend, Wales. The war in Europe had ended more than a year earlier and Meindl, the former Commander of the German II Parachute Corps in north-west Europe, was still being held by the Allies. He had been approached by members of the European Theatre of Operations Historical Section to answer yet another series of what must have seemed to him to be never ending inquiries on the conduct of the war. This time the questions were on the role of his corps in Operation Cobra, the First U.S. Army's breakout from Normandy. Major Kenneth W. Hechler, a United States Army Infantry Reserve officer and member of the European Theatre of Operations Historical Section, had previously interviewed Meindl and found him less than willing to cooperate fully. 'I recall distinctly that General Meindl took a rather light-hearted attitude toward the issues presented to him,' remembered Hechler. 'It is evident from his written report that he is deliberately attempting to be funny rather than necessarily to be accurate in his report.'

A Baden-Württemberger from south-west Germany, Eugen Meindl did not suffer fools gladly. By his own admission, he could be an extremely serious, difficult and even overbearing individual. Yet Meindl was one of the Luftwaffe's most talented commanders and highly decorated officers with a tremendous wealth of combat experience garnered in Poland, Denmark, Norway and Crete. Born on 16 July 1892 in Donaueschingen, a small town in the Black Forest, Meindl had joined the Artillery arm of the German Imperial Army in July 1912 as a fahnenjunker, or officer candidate. A natural athlete, he excelled in a country and an army that valued sports and athletics. He was an accomplished mountain climber and guide, with the initial conquests of several mountain peaks, as well as an excellent skier and horseman.[1] Klaus Meindl, who followed in his father's footsteps by joining Germany's Fallschirmtruppe and later served under Eugen Meindl in Russia and Normandy, recalls that on his father's commissioning in 1911, the elder Meindl had to pay 10,000 Marks to bring his two horses with him and provide for their feeding. He recalled that his father served as a balloon observer and was shot down three times. By the end of the conflict, Eugen Meindl has been decorated with the Iron Cross 1st and 2nd Class, the Tuerkischer Halbmond erster Klasse (Turkish Half-moon First Class), and the Hausorden von Hohenzollern or Hohenzollernscher Hausorden (the House Order of Hohenzollern), an order of chivalry awarded to military commissioned officers and civilians of comparable status, which ranked between the Iron Cross 1st Class and the Pour le Mérite. According to the younger Meindl, only his father's youth prevented him from being decorated with the Pour le Mérite, Prussia's highest order of merit in the First World War.[2] In light of his stellar war record, it is not surprising that Eugen Meindl was selected for the Reichswehr, Germany's post-war armed forces.

Like most senior officers in Hermann Göering's Luftwaffe and Fallschirmtruppe, Eugen Meindl was a member of the Nazi Party. The German Air Force was the most politicised of all the Wehrmacht's armed services and it was almost impossible for any officer to attain general officer rank without being a Nazi. Although we know a great deal about Eugen Meindl's service during the Second World War, much of it in his own words, we know very little about his attitudes toward the Nazi Party and Hitler's policies of Lebensraum (military expansion to win living space in the east) or Die Endlösungextermination (Final Solution) of the Jews. Not surprisingly, Meindl does not mention these in his writings. We must conclude that as a member of the Nazi Party, Meindl like so many other senior leaders of Hitler's Wehrmacht, was a supporter of Hitler, certainly in the early days when the armed forces of the Third Reich were overrunning Scandinavia, Europe, North Africa and the Mediterranean, and the Soviet Union, and his policies. Like most Nazi officers, however,

---

1. 'General der Fallschirmtruppe Eugen Meindl', *Fallschirmjäger-Lehrkompanie Normandie 1944*, www.fjr6.com/FJ-LEHR/fjlehrkompaniecom/2006%20 Pages/2006%20Meindl.htm. Accessed 6 September 2013.

2. 'General der Fallschirmtruppe Eugen Meindl', *Fallschirmjäger-Lehrkompanie Normandie 1944*, www.fjr6.com/FJ-LEHR/fjlehrkompaniecom/2006%20 Pages/2006%20Meindl.htm. Accessed 6 September 2013.

he probably began to distance himself from Hitler and the racial policies of the Third Reich once it was clear that Germany could not win the war.

During the inter-war period Meindl served in various staff positions and artillery units. At the beginning of the Second World War he participated in the Wehrmacht's invasion of Poland in 1939 as commander of a mountain artillery regiment, earning the Iron Cross 2nd Class. He then served on the Western Front until he was transferred to play a major role in the invasion of Denmark and Norway. On 7 June 1940, he volunteered to jump into Norway, although he had no previous parachute training, to reinforce Generalmajor Eduard Deitl's beleaguered 3rd Gebirgs (Mountain) Division. Following military operations in Norway he was decorated with the Iron Cross 1st Class and also authorised to wear the Narvik Shield. In September 1940 Meindl assumed command of the Luftland-Sturmregiment (1st Parachute Air-Landing Assault Regiment), which became known as Assault Regiment Meindl, after its commander. Promoted to generalmajor in January 1941, he was named Führer der Kampfgruppe West (Commander Battle Group West) during the airborne invasion of Crete. On 20 May, while leading his Assault Regiment and the Battle Group onto the island, he was badly wounded by machine gun fire, forcing him to temporarily hand over command to Oberst Hermann Bernard Ramcke. Although not able to lead his men, Meindl still took part in the assault on the key Maleme airfield and was recognised for his bravery and awarded the highly prestigious Knight's Cross to the Iron Cross on 14 June 1941.[3] The award was bestowed 'for exceptional personal bravery having a decisive effect on the outcome of a battle'.[4]

The same year that Eugen Meindl was decorated with the Knight's Cross his son, Klaus, followed in his father's footsteps by joining the Fallschirmjäger at the age of sixteen. Klaus was assigned to the 1st Squad, 1st Platoon, 1st Company, 1st Battalion of the Hildescheim-based Assault Regiment. He attended his jump training at Braunschweig and also qualified as an assistant glider pilot for the regiment's air group. Both Klaus's company and battalion commanders, Oberleutnant Egon Delica and Major Walter Koch, were legendary paratroopers, having recieved the Knight's Cross during the German airborne assault on Eben Emael in May 1940. When Klaus joined the Assault Regiment, it was commanded by

---

3. Hildebrand, 'Eugen Meindl', *Die Generale der deutschen Luftwaffe 1935-1945*, pp. 372–373; Dixon, 'Eugen Meindl,' *Luftwaffe Generals*, pp. 67–68.
4. SHAEF, 'Knight's Cross of the Iron Cross', *German Medals and Decorations*, p. 3.

his father. 'I absolutely got nothing for free!' he professed. Klaus and his father had the distinction of being the youngest and oldest paratroopers in the unit.[5]

In February 1942, Meindl's command was upgraded to divisional strength and transferred to the Eastern Front. There Meindl was given command of an additional five Luftwaffe field regiments.[6] These were created after the invasion of Russia in June 1941, when the Wehrmacht faced a shortage of ground troops and German commanders were forced to use Luftwaffe airbase and rear echelon personnel as ad hoc infantry to first defend installations and later against partisan units. In early 1942, seven Luftwaffe field regiments were formed and, after hasty infantry training by paratroop instructors, were sent to Russia. Eventually the role of these formations would grow to encompass even limited offensive operations.[7] Meindl's command played a major role in breaking through the Red Army forces encircling the Cholm Pocket and breaking into the town. For their part in the 105-day battle, he and his soldiers received the Cholm Shield.

In October Meindl returned to Germany as the Commander of the XIII Flieger (Air) Corps. It was during this period that he was asked by Hitler to supervise the formation of twenty-two new Luftwaffe Field Divisions. A highly experienced commander and skilled organiser, Meindl played an especially valuable role in the organisation and training of these divisions, initially created to support the ground war in Russia. Although he envisioned them, once fully trained and equipped, as a strategic reserve for the Eastern Front, Hitler had other thoughts and the Luftwaffe Field Divisions were committed to battle almost as soon as they were organised, thus squandering what Meindl believed to be immense defensive potential. 'Imagine what could have been achieved if my ideas had been followed committing these divisions together, instead of individually, as a strategic reserve, or in the spring after they had completed their training,' he remembered bitterly. 'Their piecemeal commitment resulted in terrifically high casualties without any success.'[8]

---

5. 'General der Fallschirmtruppe Eugen Meindl,' *Fallschirmjäger-Lehrkompanie Normandie 1944*, www.fjr6.com/FJ-LEHR/fjlehrkompaniecom/2006%20 Pages/2006%20Meindl.htm. Accessed 6 September 2013.

6. Dixon, 'Eugen Meindl', *Luftwaffe Generals*, p. 68.

7. Ruffner, *Luftwaffe Field Divisions*, pp. 6–7.

8. Meindl, *B-401 II Parachute Corps*, p. 27.

In July 1943, Meindl was promoted to generalleutnant. On 5 November 1943 he was appointed Commanding General of the II Parachute Corps, which had been formed from the XIII Flieger Corps. By February 1944 the corps had come under the control of OB West in Paris. Meindl was promoted to General der Fallschirmtruppe on 1 April 1944 and his command was subordinated to Friedrich Dollman's Seventh Army.[9]

Now, at fifty-four years old and with the war lost, Meindl was a prisoner of war and suffering from the multiple wounds he had received years earlier, including a bullet through the chest during the airborne invasion of Crete in May 1940. Having survived Normandy he had continued to fight for Hitler until he was taken prisoner, still commanding his beloved II Parachute Corps, on 25 May 1945 in Holland. He had watched this elite formation, manned by his cherished paratroopers and his own son, destroyed several times over in bitter, almost nonstop fighting between June 1944 and May 1945. No matter what he and his paratroopers had tried, they had been unable to stem the Allied onslaught in the west for very long after the Normandy landings. A deluge of American and British bombs, rockets and naval and artillery shells and a flood of Allied tanks and infantry had forced Hitler's Fallschirmjäger in Normandy relentlessly backward until they could no longer hold. And so, in the end they broke, although they were among the last of the Wehrmacht in Normandy to do so. Writing about the German armed forces' retreat following its defeat at the hands of the Western Allies in the second Battle of France, Meindl remembered bitterly:

> It was a pitiful sight ... not to be described in words! Dissolution and panic! And in between, my paratroopers, with contempt in their eyes – fulfilling their duties in an exemplary way! In tatters ... in many cases wounded ... dead beat and starving ... but despite all still carrying their weapons, very often two or three, still on the job, ready to help one another in need.[10]

Like his fellow German generals in captivity, Meindl no doubt had serious misgivings about working on military–historical issues in an Allied Prisoner of War camp. These would have been not only of a purely practical nature, occasioned, for example, by faulty memory, the lack of

---

9. Dixon, 'Eugen Meindl,' *Luftwaffe Generals,* p. 68.
10. Dixon, 'Eugen Meindl', *Luftwaffe Generals,* p. 68; Meindl, *A-923 II Parachute Corps. Part II. Northern France,* p. 39.

access to primary documents, maps and members of his staff, but perhaps even more of a psychological nature. First was the fact that captured German officers were supplying their former enemies with material of a military–historical nature based on their own knowledge and experience, even though the war was over. This ran contrary to everything they had been taught, to their loyalty to Germany and each other. One of Meindl's fellow German general prisoners called the situation 'unique in all history'.[11] Second was the fact that the monographs produced by Meindl and his fellow captives were regarded, according to the directives of the Inter-Allied Control Council, as 'militaristic', and were therefore banned in post-war Germany and could not be published. At the same time other writings labelled as 'militaristic' were purged from German libraries and bookshelves. As a result, there was great doubt among those who participated in the 'interviews' that an objective account of the war they had just gone through would ever be possible. Many believed that the Allies would never permit it. Additionally the same captive Wehrmacht general wrote that 'the daily recurring depressive knowledge that many of our colleagues were arraigned for trial before foreign military tribunals for their activities during the war, and have been, or are being sentenced by these tribunals, that others are continually being handed over … or live in expectation, and that these also have to expect court martial proceedings against them before enemy military tribunals.' Finally, was the knowledge of post-war Germany's 'immeasurable misery' that continued years after the end of the war. And while Meindl and his colleagues languished in captivity, their families suffered even greater deprivations. 'Added to this,' recorded former General der Flak Artillerie Wolfgang Pickert, who had commanded the German III Flak Corps at Normandy during the Allied invasion, himself a prisoner of war, 'is my own penniless family, vegetating in want and privation.'[12] In comparison, Pickert, Meindl and their fellow German generals were relatively well housed, fed and cared for in Allied POW camps.

Many were held at least initially at the British interrogation centre at Trent Park, a long-term confinement centre of senior German officers. The facility was a magnificent estate located in the low hills around Enfield, in the north of London. 'Great lawns with marble statues, glorious woodland with cedars and great oaks. A golf course, large swimming pool, a fine

---

11. General der Flak Artillerie Wolfgang Pickert, *B-597 III AA Corps in the Normandy Battles*, p. 2.
12. Pickert, *B-597 III AA Corps in the Normandy Battles*, pp. 2–3.

pond with wild ducks,' was how detainee Generalleutnant Erwin Menny, a recipient of the Knight's Cross and the former commander of the German 84th Infantry Division at Normandy before being captured by Allied troops, described the centre in his diaries. Unknown to its inhabitants, all the rooms, including common spaces, were bugged and it was hoped that the relaxed environment would encourage its high-ranking population to engage in frank private discussions and reveal secrets. German prisoners were lodged in a mansion with the most senior occupying one or two rooms and the remainder sharing a room. Each room was furnished with a bed, cupboard, commode, table and chair, and comfortable sofa. The furnishings and hot running water made captivity pleasant and German detainees indicated they were very satisfied with the accommodation.[13]

Not all captured German generals, however, fared as well as Meindl:

> I have been in detention for investigation for a whole year (in a prison for criminals), with four men in a small cell nine metres square. The only place to sleep is on the floor, with one hour of exercise daily in a 25-metre square high-walled court, and 200 grams of cornbread and one liter of vegetable soup with meat or fat per day and a few meager additions weekly, and subjected to a strict regime of a convict. That is my treatment.

So wrote Hermann Bernhard Ramcke on 9 July 1947 from a French prison in Rennes. Like Meindl, Ramcke was a General der Fallschirmtruppe. Unlike Meindl, he was also a fanatical, diehard Nazi, hardcore anti-Semite, and a blatant racist. Ramcke was nonetheless a legendary Fallschirmjäger and considered one of the bravest German soldiers of the war. Almost single-handedly he had turned the tide of battle at Crete in 1940 in favour of the Germans, snatching victory from the jaws of defeat when he led the 'Do or Die' assault that captured Malame airfield and broke the back of the British defence. He was one of the most decorated officers of the war and one of only three Luftwaffe officers to wear the Knight's Cross with Oak Leaves, Swords and Diamonds, instituted by Adolf Hitler on 15 July 1941 and personally awarded by the Führer. A recipient had to first be a winner of the Knight's Cross, and then the Knight's Cross with Oak Leaves, and then the Knight's Cross with Oak Leaves and Swords. Ramcke was also a recipient of the Iron Cross 1st and 2nd Class, each with a bar (indicating a second award) and the Baltic Cross 1st and 2nd Class,

---

13. Neitzel, *Tapping Hitler's Generals*, 18–22.

awards he won as a sailor in the German Imperial Fleet during the First World War.[14] He boasted to his British captors after the war that his book *Vom Schiffsjungen zum Fallschirmjager General* (*From Cabin Boy to Paratrooper General*), published by the Wehrmacht publishing house in 1943, had earned him some 800,000 Reichsmarks, a small fortune for the time.[15] Ramcke, the first commander of the German 2nd Parachute Division in February 1943, had commanded the elite formation again during the battle for Normandy. He was being held by the French for multiple war crimes committed by his troops while also serving as Commander of Wehrmacht forces in the Brest Fortress in Brittany during the summer of 1941. The German paratrooper general had ensured that his forces had completely demolished the port before surrendering it to the Allies, thus undermining the logistical sustainment of the Allied armies at Normandy for months to come and complicating their advance on the Third Reich. It was his defence of Brest that earned him the Third Reich's second highest award (the highest being the Grand Cross of the Knight's Cross, awarded only to Hermann Göring.)

Ramcke was described by British intelligence officers as 'inordinately vain' and with 'a most extensive knowledge of distorted history; ambitious, ruthless yet naïve, an opportunist.'[16] The charges for which he was being held by the French included murder, arson, and looting by his forces at the Brest Fortress. He wrote from his French cell:

Additionally, are the emotional tortures regarding the distress of my country and the great worries about our suffering and hungering families. Four boys, out of my seven children, are thought to have tuberculosis due to malnutrition. I lost all my estate in the Russian Zone of Occupation. My wife and children were only barely able to save their lives. Six out of the eight male next of kin died in battle. No pension or support is paid to my family, because as a [former Wehrmacht] general I belong to the 'damned militarists'. I accept all this as a fate imposed on us by God. But often one asks himself, whether this treatment, which I share with millions of German countrymen two-and-a-half years *after* the [end of the] war is compatible with the fundamental

---

14. Dixon, *Luftwaffe Generals*, pp. 31–32.
15. Neitzel, 'General der Fallschirmtruppen Bernhard Ramcke', *Tapping Hitler's Generals*, p. 309.
16. Ibid.

democratic principles for which the great nations of the west carried on the war.[17]

And in a British prisoner of war camp in England for Wehrmacht senior officers where their every word was being recorded, the unrepentant Ramcke was heard to say to his fellow prisoners: 'In the eyes of the people here I am branded "a diehard Nazi". I wonder if I shall *ever* get home?'[18]

Eugen Meindl was no doubt wondering if *he* would ever get home. He had been held as a prisoner of the Allies and had not seen his home or his family for almost two years. It is one thing for a soldier to endure years away from his home and family while at war; it is quite another thing to do so long after that war had ended. Moreover, Meindl had first been interviewed repeatedly as Commander of the II German Parachute Corps at Normandy, including in January 1946 and then again in April of that year. The former General der Fallschirmtruppe no doubt soon tired of being asked the same questions while still held in captivity. In the opinion of a series of U.S. Army interviewers, he stopped taking the sessions seriously. Finally, it is clear from reading his work that Meindl was indeed angry and bitter, and perhaps even a bit afraid. After all, many officers of Hitler's Wehrmacht were branded as criminals and prosecuted and punished for their complicity in war crimes. Meindl, like so many of his colleagues, was no doubt left wondering if he too would end up at the end of a hangman's noose.

The modern historian, however, finds very little that is truly distorted in Meindl's accounts of the war, as reflected in the manuscripts he produced for the Foreign Military Studies series. The former commander of the II Parachute Corps clearly comes across as flippant and sarcastic at times, and at other times even as extremely angry and bitter. Reading his manuscripts one senses a great deal of frustration, but certainly little that would cause one to question his recollection of events. Much of his resentment is aimed not at the Allies and their soldiers, but at Adolf Hitler and his former superiors in the Luftwaffe and the German High Command. And, criticisms notwithstanding, in the end General Meindl did produce what even his critical American interviewers called a 'voluminous manuscript'

---

17. Correspondence from Herman Bernard Ramcke, Rennes, France, July 9, 1947 to Colonel (Retired) Troy H. Middleton, Louisiana State University', U.S. War Department War Crimes Office, Judge Advocate General's Office, File No. 100-852, Hermann Bernard Ramcke.
18. Neitzel, *Tapping Hitler's Generals*, p. 107.

on the II Parachute Corp's role in Normandy. Perhaps the stubborn Baden-Württemberger, like so many of his imprisoned colleagues, had finally come to the realisation that the quickest path home lay in cooperating with his captors. It is perhaps appropriate then to allow General der Fallschirmtruppe Eugen Meindl to open this history of his II Parachute Corps at Normandy in his own words:

> I am no writer and have no intention of trying to win a petty medal for detailed descriptions. I would only stand well as an officer for my faultless soldiers in order that history will faithfully reflect their behaviour and fighting qualities … It is quite certain that the II Parachute Corps did not make the task of the conqueror any easier and I do not believe that our fierce but fair methods of fighting will furnish any excuse for stamping us as 'criminals'… For six weeks, II Parachute Corps prevented an enemy breakthrough at St-Lô and in the process disabled many tanks and planes. In my opinion, this can be regarded as a success, even if it did not save the situation on the whole, but only delayed the inevitable … It might be true that the II Parachute Corps had more than fulfilled all that had been expected of it, but at what a price!! I am ready, therefore, to step forward at any time and vouch for the bravery of the troops under my command, taking full responsibility for what I might say. Following my fundamental principle 'Save as much blood as you can', I went as far as my concept of soldierly honour would permit and many – more than few – owe their lives to me. And if it is true that here and there I have had hard things to say about this or that German operation, I insist that this is not black heartedness on my part but only recognition that even a great military nation has to obtain experience, if only to confirm conditions long known. And anyone bearing on his shoulders the weight of two years at the front may be deemed to have learned something during the period of his life.[19]

---

19. Meindl, *A-923 II Parachute Corps. Part II. Northern France*, pp. 1–2; Meindl, *B-401 II Parachute Corps*, pp. 42, 48.

Acknowledgements

This book would not have been possible without the assistance of my closest friend and fellow U.S. Army Historian, Lieutenant Colonel (Retired) Mark J. Reardon, a published author and authority on the U.S. and German armies in the Second World War and at Normandy. Mark graciously responded to all my requests for assistance with endless encouragement and insightful and extensive commentary and information on all aspects of this book. He freely shared his extensive collection of Normandy related primary and secondary U.S. and German sources and photographs with me, translating key German documents. Volker Greisser, a former German Army soldier and paratrooper and author of *The Lions of Carentan. Fallschirmjager Regiment 6. 1943–1945*, provided me with dozens of photos of Hitler's paratroopers in Normandy from his own collection. Historian George Nafziger provided me with a complete order of battle of German parachute forces in the Second World War, along with monographs on hedgerow tactics and German assault gun formations. Historian Joseph Balkowski provided me with photographs of General Hermann Ramcke at Brest and graciously allowed me to cite from his book. *From Beachhead to Brittany. The 29th Infantry Division at Brest, August–September 1944*. Norwegian historian Arve Robert Pisani also allowed me to use information from his excellent book *Bocage. The Battle of Normandy*. Bobby Sammons of MilSpecManuals.com provided me with dozens of primary source war operations and intelligence reports and documents, and expedited their delivery to me. The staff of the Rosendale Library in New York requested rare, primary source war documents for me that were critical to the success of this book. As a result, my cup once again runneth over.

As always, my wife Natalie and our three sons offered me endless assistance, encouragement, and inspiration. Natalie proof-read and edited every chapter expertly. And, like their grandfather and father before them, all three of our sons have served or are serving their country as American soldiers. This history of elite German paratroopers in the Second World War was written in the shadow of two young, elite, American paratroopers, both combat veterans. Finally, I owe a debt of gratitude to my publishers, Frontline Books in London, and especially to my editor, Kate Baker, for encouraging me to build on the story of the German Fallschirmjäger I began in *Hitler's Paratrooper*.

List of Maps

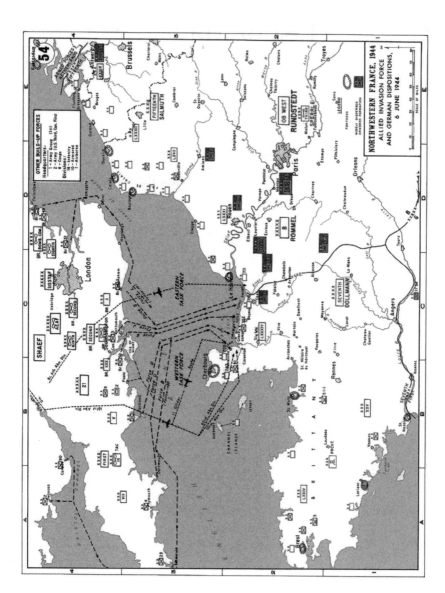

Map 1. Northwestern France 1944 (U.S. Army)

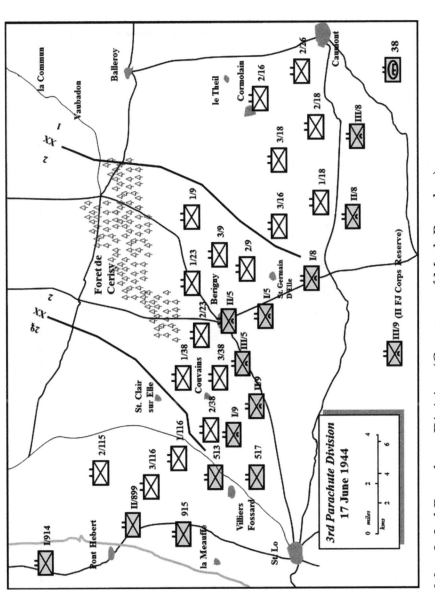

Map 2. 3rd Parachute Division (Courtesy of Mark Reardon)

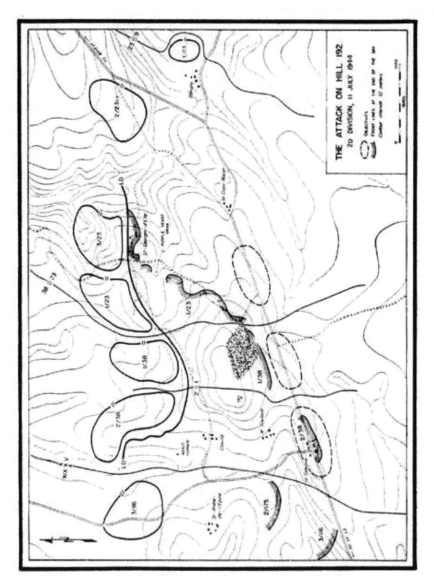

Map 3. Hill 192 (U.S. Army)

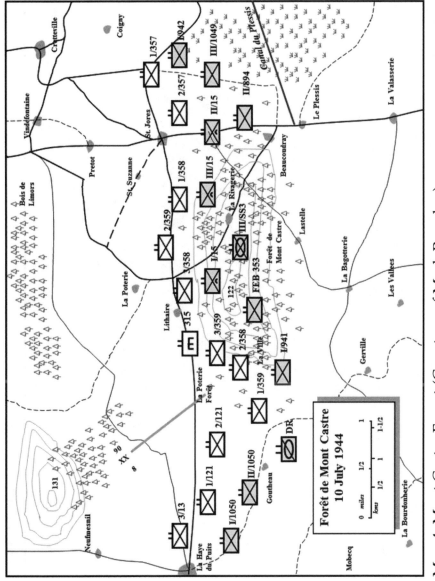

Map 4. Mont Castre Forest (Courtesy of Mark Reardon)

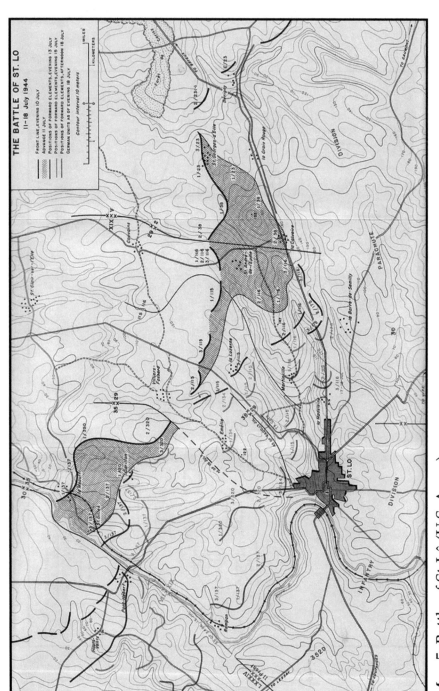

Map 5. Battle of St-Lô (U.S. Army)

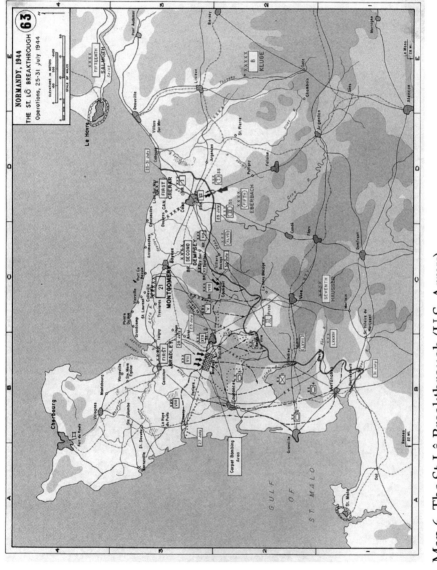

Map 6. The St-Lô Breakthrough (U.S. Army)

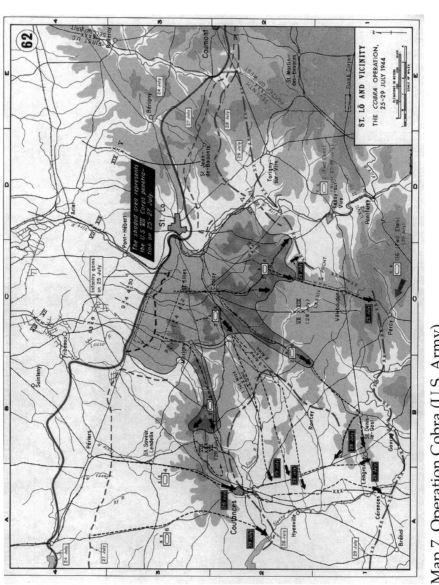

Map 7. Operation Cobra (U.S. Army)

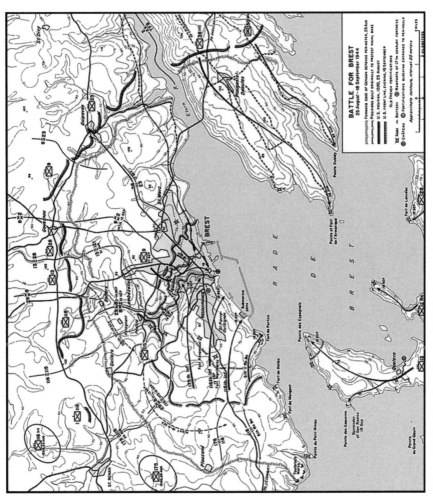

Map 8. Battle for Brest (U.S. Army)

Chapter 1

Hitler's Paratroopers in Normandy

In 1944 the best infantry divisions in the Wehrmacht belonged not to the German Army but to the Luftwaffe. These were the elite parachute divisions subordinated to the OKW. Until the fall of 1943, Reichsmarschall Hermann Göring's senior Fallschirmjäger headquarters had been the XI Fliegerkorps, commanded by Generaloberst Kurt Student, the father of the German Fallschirmtruppe. The corps was comprised of 1st Parachute Division at Avignon and 2nd Parachute Division at Arles in France. Later that year, Göring proposed a programme aimed at building up Germany's airborne forces to two parachute armies numbering 100,000 men by the end of 1944. In the light of the military manpower shortages facing the Third Reich at the time, Hitler was quick to accept. The two parachute armies were to be an elite arm, equal in status to the SS units in recruiting, armament, equipment, and training.[1] Left unsaid was the fact that these new formations would compete with the depleted divisions of the German Army for manpower, equipment, and weapons.

On 5 November 1943 the High Command of the German Air Force (OKL, Oberkommando der Luftwaffe) ordered the establishment of a series of higher headquarters to command and control the Luftwaffe's expanding parachute forces. The first of these was the Fallschirm-Armeeoberkommando (Parachute Army High Command), which was formed from XI Fliegerkorps on 1 May 1944. The Commander in Chief was the former Commanding General of the corps, Generaloberst Kurt Student. The fifty-four-year-old Student was a recipient of the Knight's

---

1.   Oberst Frhr. Von der Heydte, *MS # B-839 A German Parachute Regiment in Normandy (U.S. Army Historical Division, 1 July 1954)* cited in Gordon A. Harrison, *United States Army in World War II. The European Theatre of Operations. Cross Channel Attack* (Washington: Centre of Military History, 1989), p. 238;

Cross, which he was awarded for the successes of his airborne forces in their assaults on Eben Emael and Holland in May 1940, and the Golden Pilots Badge with Diamonds, presented to him personally by Göring. Student had been badly wounded in Rotterdam and required eight months of convalescence to fully recover. Upon his return to service, he took over the formation and command of the Air Landing Corps formed from the 7th Flieger Division and the German Army's 22nd Division. For reasons of secrecy, the corps was designated the XI Flieger Corps. Student had been instrumental in persuading Hitler to use his Fallschirmtruppe on a massive scale to seize the island of Crete from the British. Despite the success of Operation Merkur (Mercury), however, his paratroopers had suffered horrendous losses. 'I miscalculated when I proposed the (Crete) operation, and my mistakes caused me not only the loss of very many paratroopers – whom I looked upon as my sons,' admitted Student later, 'but in the long run led to the demise of the German airborne arm which I had created.' The heavy losses suffered by his Fallschirmjäger caused the Führer to dispense with further large-scale parachute operations. 'Of course, you know General, that we shall never do another airborne operation,' Hitler told Student. 'Crete proved that the days of the parachute troops are over. The parachute army is one that relies entirely on surprise. In the meantime, the surprise factor has exhausted itself.'[2] Instead, Hitler, had decided to use his Fallschirmjäger as elite defensive troops. They had proved their mettle on the Eastern Front, in North Africa, Sicily and in Italy, and the leader of the Third Reich planned on expanding them and committing them as select ground forces in the defence of France. As for Student, Hitler was critical of his commander of parachute forces, telling his entourage: 'Every time I tell him to do something, he takes minutes to think it over. He is a complete dull oaf but does his work splendidly. It's just that he is terribly slow.'[3]

---

2. Georg Tessin, *Verbänd und Truppen der deutschen Wehrmacht und Waffen-SS im Zweiten Weltkrieg 1939–1945*, Band I (Osnabrück: Biblio Verlag, 1979), p. 356; Karl Friedrich-Hildebrand, 'Kurt Student', *Die Generale der deutschen Luftwaffe 1934–1945*, Band III (Osnabruck: Biblio Verlag, 1992), pp. 363–365; Franz Kurowski, 'Generaloberst Kurt Student', *Knight's Cross Holds of the Fallschirmjäger* (Schiffer Publishing, 1995), pp. 233–235; French L. MacLean, *2,000 Quotes from Hitler's 1,000-Year Reich* (Schiffer Military History, 2007), p. 324; Major General Anthony Farrar-Hockley, *Student* (New York: Ballentine Books, 1973), p. 101.
3. MacLean, *2,000 Quotes from Hitler's 1,000-Year Reich*, p. 153.

Located at Nancy in France, First Parachute Army was put at the disposal of OKW, the High Command of the German Armed Forces. Its tasks included (1) official care of all parachute units on all fronts and on the home front; (2) training and deployment of all replacements for the parachute forces; (3) further development of parachute and air-landing tactics; and (4) a command and control headquarters if more than a single parachute corps should be utilised at any one time. The new parachute army was to include a parachute demonstration regiment, a heavy rocket launcher battalion, a bicycle battalion, an engineer battalion, and a signals battalion (later expanded to a regiment). These formations received the unit designation '21'.[4] First Parachute Army Troops would continue to grow, adding a flak regiment and a flak machine gun battalion.[5] An army staff augmented by specialised staff sections for planning the use of transport and glider aircraft and the development and training of airborne units in parachute and landing tactics, a Luftwaffe Technician's section, and a Meteorologist section added another approximately 3,000 personnel. Student's new headquarters joined 'without prejudice to its subordination to the High Command of the Luftwaffe' the OKW Reserve. At the end of July 1944, Student moved to the Berlin–Wannsee area, with elements of his general staff, quartermaster and adjutancy sections, to be able to personally exert influence on Hitler regarding the setting up of new projects related to his Fallschirmtruppe.[6]

All parachute troops were subordinated to the First Parachute Army, even if they were fighting under the command of other services, especially the German Army. This included all parachute training and replacements units, as well as all parachute schools. Among these formations were three parachute training regiments (though not all were fully formed), four parachute schools (each with a battalion of cadre, located at Stendal, Wittstock and Braunschweig in Germany, and Maubeuge near Paris), two air-landing schools (at Stendal and Hildescheim), two weapons schools (at

---

4. Tessin, *Verbänd und Truppen*, Band I, p. 356; Schacht, *MS # P-154 1. Fallschirmarmee, Mai bis August 1944*, p. 2.
5. Generalmajor Burkhart Müller-Hillebrand, P-154; *1. Fallschirmarmee, Mai bis August 1944* (U.S. Army Historical Division, 27 April 1954), p. 4; C.S.D.I.C, 'S.I.R. 1055 CS/480 Uffz Deiser 'The Parachute Army, 14 September 1944', RG 165, NARA II.
6. Schacht, *P-154 1. Fallschirmarmee*, p. 2.

Gardelegen and Paderborn), and a parachute packing school (at Oppeln).[7] To the delight of Student, these numerous formations were brought together for the first time in the summer of 1944 under a newly designated Commanding General for Parachute Training and Replacement Units and Inspector General of All Parachute Forces, General der Fallschirmtruppe Paul Conrath with its headquarters at Berlin-Wannsee. The First Parachute Army HQ also managed two storage depots located in Germany (one for weapons and equipment, another for chemical warfare gear).[8] Officially, the Hermann Göring Parachute Armoured Division was also subordinated to First Parachute Army, but this was only on paper.[9] Historian and Student biographer Major General Anthony Farrar-Hockley estimates that the commander of First Parachute Army had some 160,000 men from the Luftwaffe and Heer at his disposal by the beginning of the Allied invasion in June 1944.[10]

The same order that created First Parachute Army also officially created two parachute corps headquarters. II Parachute Corps, formed from the I Luftwaffe Field Corps on 1 February 1944, was the first Fallschirm-Armeekorps (Parachute Army Corps) established. Commanded by General der Fallschirmtruppe Eugen Meindl and based in France, its subordinate elements included a reconnaissance battalion, an assault gun battalion, a corps' artillery regiment, an anti-aircraft regiment, and a signals battalion, all with the unit designator '12'. I Parachute Corps was formed a month later, on 1 March 1944, from the II Luftwaffe Field Corps. Commanded by General der Fallschirmtruppe Richard Heidrich and based in Italy, its organisation mirrored that of I Parachute Corps and all its subordinate formations had the unit designator '11'. Also authorised at the same time was the formation of the 3rd, 5th, and 6th Parachute Divisions. These new formations were meant to augment the combat capabilities of the Wehrmacht at a time when the German 1st and 4th Parachute Divisions were heavily engaged in the ground war in

---

7. C.S.D.I.C, S.I.R. 1055 CS/480 Uffz Deiser 'The Parachute Army, 14 September 1944', RG 165, NARA II; War Department, *Special Series No. 7 Enemy Airborne Forces* (Washington D.C: Military Intelligence Services, December 2, 1942), p. 20.
8. C.S.D.I.C, S.I.R. 1055 CS/480 Uffz Deiser 'The Parachute Army, 14 September 1944', RG 165, NARA II.
9. Schacht, *P-154 1. Fallschirmarmee*, pp. 2–4; Hildebrand, 'Paul Conrath,' *Die Generale der deutschen Luftwaffe 1935–1945*, pp. 167–168.
10. Farrar-Hockley, *Student*, p. 134.

4

Italy, while the 2nd Parachute Division was fighting for its life in Russia. The 3rd Parachute Division was ordered formed at Rennes in Brittany on 1 February 1944. The location was later changed, however, to Brest. Its three major subordinate formations included 5th (a new unit), 8th and 9th Parachute Regiments. All combat support and combat service support divisional formations received the unit designator '3'. The 4th Parachute Division began forming on 1 February 1944 near Venice with 10th, 11th, and 12th Parachute Regiments and the unit designator '4'. The 5th Parachute Division began forming near Reims on 1 March 1944 with 13th, 14th and 15th Parachute Regiments and the unit designator '5'. Later, in June 1944, the 6th Parachute Division was ordered formed near Amiens with 16th, 17th, and 18th Parachute Regiments and the unit designator '6'.[11] Of these new parachute divisions, OB West received the 3rd and 5th Parachute Divisions and the 6th Parachute Regiment (from the 2nd Parachute Division). Both the 3rd Parachute Division and 6th Parachute Regiment were described in the United States' Army's official history of the Normandy campaign as 'first-rate fighting units.'[12]

To facilitate the formation of each division and provide them with a corps of seasoned paratroopers, the 3rd and 5th Parachute Divisions each received a Stamm-Bataillione (cadre battalion) from the 2nd Parachute Division, while the 4th Parachute Division received one from the 1st Parachute Division. The same order called for the formation of a fourth parachute school, a paratrooper leadership school (for 200 officers and 400 NCOs), two parachute training regiments with three battalions each, and a parachute replacement battalion.[13] Much was expected of the Luftwaffe's parachute formations in France. All were reportedly manned with volunteers and morale and firepower were considered excellent. This, however, was far from the reality and the parachute formations varied greatly in their quality.

II Parachute Corps

II Parachute Corps headquarters was formed around Melun, south-east of Paris. There it trained the new units that were to make up one of the Third Reich's largest parachute formations at the time. German corps-level

---

11. Tessin, *Verbänd und Truppen*, Band I, p. 356.
12. Schacht, *P-154 1. Fallschirmarmee*, pp. 3–4; Harrison, *Cross Channel Attack*, p. 238.
13. Tessin, *Verbänd und Truppen*, Band I, p. 356.

organisations were normally command and control headquarters with no combat units assigned on a permanent basis. A normal Wehrmacht corps headquarters consisted of just over 1,000 personnel, with the Corps Staff numbering 195 personnel and Headquarters Troops (service and support units) adding another 738. The remaining personnel normally consisted of a mapping department, military police and auxiliary staff. Infantry corps (Armeekorps) formed the backbone of the German Army, with each normally commanding two to three infantry divisions. The command structure, however, was flexible with respect to the number of divisions assigned as well as to parent army assignment based on operational requirements. Corps were frequently switched from the control of one army to another as the tactical situation dictated. Armies might normally command two to four corps, and in some cases as many as seven. During the war, the German Army fielded infantry, panzer, mountain, reserve infantry, reserve panzer, artillery, cavalry, and even a Cossack corps.[14] The German Air Force fielded four Luftwaffe Field Corps (I–IV) as command and control elements for its twenty-two Luftwaffe Field Divisions. The creation of parachute corps in 1943 was a first for Hitler's Wehrmacht and indicative of the pressing need for ground combat forces and commensurate headquarters to make up for the heavy losses on the Eastern Front. Just as the number of corps varied per army, so did the number of divisions assigned to each corps, and during the Normandy campaign, Meindl would find himself commanding one to four divisions at any one time.

Like many German higher-level formations, II Parachute Corps possessed a unique organisational structure. Its components included the 12th Parachute Reconnaissance Battalion, 12th Self-Propelled Assault Gun Battalion, 12th Artillery Regiment, 12th Flak Regiment and 12th Signals Battalion. This was more than an attempt at empire building on Göring's part. The light airborne troops had to be capable of conducting high-intensity offensive and defensive operations and required the heavy

---

14. Telford Taylor, *March of Conquest: The German Victories in Western Europe 1940* (New York: Simon and Shuster, 1958), p. 18. Cited in French L. MacLean, *Unknown Generals. German Corps Commanders in World War II* (Biblioscholar, 2012), Chapter 3. 'The German Corps System', Kindle. The number of corps grew throughout the war. On 6 June 1944 the Wehrmacht's order of battle included seventy-three Army corps, including fifty-two assigned to various Army headquarters. Total Army corps strength peaked in January 1945 at seventy-seven.

weapons to do so. All subordinate units, except 12th Flak Regiment located in Germany, were in or around Melun. The authorised strength of II Parachute Corps, excluding attached divisions, numbered 8,951 personnel. However, by the beginning of June it was still at 3,363.[15]

According to General Meindl, 12th Parachute Reconnaissance and 12th Signals Battalions were fully manned, well equipped, and consisted of trained paratroopers. Ideally the assault gun battalion and artillery and flak regiments would have provided the corps with tremendous anti-aircraft, anti-armour and anti-personnel firepower. However, while at 80 per cent of authorised strength, these units were still being reorganised and lacked essential weapons and equipment. Meindl notes that 30 per cent of the Corps Train (service and supply units) was comprised of qualified paratroopers and its subunits were also well equipped. As for the 3rd Parachute Division, between 70 and 75 per cent of the division's personnel were qualified paratroopers and its component units had between 30 to 70 per cent of their equipment authorised. Meindl reported in a post-war interview that the remaining personnel of II Parachute Corps were undergoing parachute training at the German jump school at Wahn. He added that a number of the 3rd Parachute Division's subunits, including the 12th Parachute Reconnaissance Battalion, had been trained in the use of troop-carrying gliders and were available for use as airborne troops.[16]

The II Parachute Corps commander failed to mention in his post-war interviews 2. Fallschirmjager Ersatz und Ausbildungs Regiment (2nd Parachute Replacement and Training Regiment). Two of the regiment's battalions were in Brittany. The third was located just south of Cherbourg. The regiment numbered approximately 1,000 to 2,000 personnel, had no equipment, was short of uniforms and was considered 'poorly trained'. The low level of readiness of this formation prevented it from fulfilling its training mission. This necessitated Meindl sending his non-jump qualified personnel to Germany for parachute training. Nonetheless, the regiment would play an important role during the Battle of Normandy by

15. General der Fallschirmtruppen Eugen Meindl, *MS # B-401 II Parachute Corps (Dec 1942–24 Jul 1944)* (United States Army Historical Division, May 1946), p. 1; Niklas Zetterling, 'II. Fallschirm-Korps,' *Normandy 1944. German Military Organisation, Combat Power and Organisational Effectiveness* (J.J. Fedorowicz Publishing, 2000), p. 150.

16. Meindl, *B-401 II Parachute Corps*, pp. 8.

providing parachute infantry replacements for 2nd Parachute Division's 6th Parachute Regiment.[17]

For tactical purposes, II Parachute Corps, along with 3rd Parachute Division and later 5th Parachute Division, was directly subordinate to Rommel. 'On Rommel's orders, 3rd Parachute Division was moved to the centre of the Brittany peninsula in the middle of March 1944 in order to be ready to repel any large-scale enemy airborne landing,' remembered Meindl. The Noires Mountains and the hills of Brittany were considered ideal for enemy airborne operations by the Germans and were weakly occupied at the time. II Parachute Corps staff, Corps' troops and 5th Parachute Division were also moved to Brittany shortly thereafter with the same mission.[18] Neither 3rd nor 5th Parachute Divisions in France were equipped with parachutes.[19]

In theory, each German parachute infantry division was composed of a regimental headquarters company; three parachute infantry regiments (each with three parachute infantry battalions, a 120mm or light artillery company, and an anti-tank company); a parachute artillery regiment (with one medium and two light artillery battalions); a parachute anti-aircraft battalion (with two heavy and two light anti-aircraft companies); a parachute 120mm mortar battalion (with three 120mm companies); a parachute anti-tank battalion (with one motorised and two self-propelled anti-tank companies); a parachute engineer battalion (with three parachute engineer companies); a divisional services battalion (consisting of supply, administrative, medical, maintenance, military police, and field postal units); and a reconnaissance company (made up of three parachute infantry platoons, a machine gun platoon, and a light artillery platoon). Total authorised strength for the division was 15,976 men. Of these, less than 10,000 were considered front line combatants. However, in German parachute formations all officers and soldiers were trained and expected to fight.[20]

The 1944 parachute division was equipped with tremendous firepower. Fallschirmjäger units were usually very well equipped and had access to the best weapons of the Wehrmacht. German paratroopers were among the

---

17. Zetterling, 'II. Fallschirm-Korps', *Normandy 1944*, pp. 150–151.
18. Meindl, *B-401 II Parachute Corps*, p. 9.
19. Harrison, *Cross Channel Attack*, p. 239 25n.
20. War Department, *TM-E 30-451 Handbook on German Military Forces* (Washington, D.C: Military Intelligence Division, September 1943), pp. 107–108.

first combat units of any army to use assault rifles and recoilless weapons in combat. They also readily employed the best of several foreign-made small arms. The German airborne division's vast and hard-hitting arsenal included more than 3,000 submachine guns, more than 900 light machine guns, eighty heavy machine guns, 125 81mm mortars, sixty-three 120mm mortars, twenty flame-throwers, twenty 88mm dual-purpose anti-tank guns (extremely lethal in the anti-armour role), some forty towed or self-propelled dual-purpose 20mm anti-aircraft guns, and almost 100 75mm and 105mm motorised or self-propelled light and medium artillery pieces. The German parachute division was authorised more than 2,000 motor vehicles, and almost 400 motorcycles for reconnaissance and transportation.[21]

Most of Hitler's paratroopers in France were armed with either the Mauser Kar 98L carbine or the MP-40 submachine gun. The Mauser was the standard shoulder weapon of the German Landser. Bolt-operated and with a five-round magazine, it was accurate and reliable. Moreover, it fired a powerful 7.92mm round, the standard German military rifle and machine gun ammunition. Originally designed for the Fallschirmtruppen, the iconic MP-40 submachine gun fired 120 to 180 rounds per minute and was in general use among the Wehrmacht's ground forces by 1944. Simple in construction and reliable, it had a maximum effective range of 200 yards. A few Fallschirmjäger in Normandy carried the technologically advanced, but problematic, 7.92mm FG 42 Fallschirmjägergewehr (Paratrooper Rifle). Another weapons specifically designed for the Luftwaffe's parachute forces, it was intended to provide them with superior firepower over their opponents. First produced in 1942, this ground-breaking, all-metal gun featured an acutely slanted pistol grip and a ten- or twenty-round box magazine mounted on the left side of the weapon, which fired 750 to 900 rounds per minute. Others carried the Gewehr G-43, a self-loading rifle with a ten-round magazine. Finally, a select few carried the MP-43, MP-44, or StG-44 assault rifle, capable of firing 550 to 600 rounds per minute. Standard sidearms included either the Luger or Walther 9mm pistols, with the latter replacing the Luger by 1944. German Fallschirmjäger were also armed with several different types of hand grenades, including the Model 1924 and Model 1939 Stick Hand Grenades (Stielhandgranate, called 'the potato masher' by the Allies) and the Model 1939 Egg Hand Grenade (Eierhandgranate). The former had a range of approximately 15 yards, while the latter were smaller and could be thrown considerably further.

---

21. Ibid.

German paratroopers also carried various types of smoke grenades and flares for obscuration or signaling purposes.[22]

Crew-served weapons included two light machine guns and three different types of mortars. Reliable and robust, the MG-34 could fire 800 to 900 7.92mm rounds a minute, while the new and improved MG-42 delivered a stunning 1,200 rounds a minute.[23] The Model 1936 50mm light mortar fired a three-pound high-explosive round more than 550 yards, while the Model 1934 81mm medium mortar fired a seven-pound shell almost 2,000 yards. A lighter, shorter version of the latter, developed in 1942, could still throw the standard 81mm ammunition some 1,200 yards. Finally, the Model 1942 Heavy 120mm mortar, virtually an exact German copy of the standard Red Army weapon, could fire four different types of high-explosive rounds 6,600 yards. The Fallschirmjäger also deployed two different types of recoilless rifles, the 75mm L.G. 40 and the 105mm L.G. 40. They were the first military force in the world to do so. Light for their calibre, these weapons, which fired high-explosive, armour-piercing and hollow charges, nonetheless weighed 320 and 855lb respectively and required a prime mover for mobility. Both packed a lethal punch and could destroy armoured vehicles at relatively close range. Developed for airborne operations, these weapons were augmented by the Model 1936 75mm Mountain Howitzer, which could be broken down into eleven loads, the heaviest weighing some 250lb. It could fire an almost 13lb high-explosive or hollow charge more than 10,000 yards. Some airborne formations were equipped with the Model 1940 105mm Mountain Howitzer, capable of throwing a more than 30lb shell almost 14,000 yards.[24] These weapons – reliable, accurate, and hard-hitting – were

---

22. War Department, *Special Series No. 14. German Infantry Weapons* (Washington, D.C: Military Intelligence Division, 25 May1943); Karl Venltzé, *German Paratroopers. Uniforms and Equipment 1936–1945. Volume II: Helmets, Equipment and Weapons* (Berlin: Zeughaus Verlag, 2016), pp. 243–25; Chris McNab, *German Automatic Rifles 1941–1945. Gew 41, Gew 43, FG 42 and StG 44* (Oxford: Osprey Publishing, 2013), pp. 21–26; Alejandro De Quesada, *MP 38 and MP 40 Submachine guns* (Oxford: Osprey Publishing, 2014), p. 36.
23. Chris McNab, *MG 34 and MG 42 Machine guns* (Osprey Publishing, 2012), pp. 17, 20.
24. War Department, *Special Series No. 14. German Infantry Weapons*; War Department, *TM-E 30-451 Handbook on German Military Forces*, Chapter VIII.

the foundation of the Wehrmacht's victories in Europe and Russia. They would be put to good use in the hedgerows of Normandy and Brittany by Hitler's Fallschirmjäger.

Each German parachute division was organised, manned and equipped differently due to shortages in trained personnel, equipment and armaments, and even motor vehicles. By mid-1944, standardisation of weapons, equipment and even uniforms in Hitler's Wehrmacht, let alone his Fallschirmtruppe, was problematic. Some of Hitler's paratroopers wore either the regular M-35, M-40 or M-42 Stahlhelm steel helmet, the iconic symbol of the German Landser. Others had the much sought-after round and thickly padded M-38 paratrooper helmet, a truncated version of the M-42 without the neck shield. This helmet, commonly worn with a cloth cover, became increasingly hard to find as the war progressed. The same holds true of the camouflaged and waterproof Fallschirmjäger Type III Jump Smock, worn over the uniform and under the equipment. The paratrooper trousers were quite long and loose and grey in colour, with pockets on the sides of the thigh. Finally, the boots were of heavy leather with thick rubber soles. They laced up on the sides and extended some way above the ankle, where the trousers were tucked into them. The most important and coveted uniform item was the parachutist's badge, a diving eagle, golden coloured with a swastika in its claws, in a wreath of oak and bay of oxidised silver colour. This was worn low on the left breast. Each Fallschirmjäger also had an identity disk and a camouflaged identity card.[25]

3rd Parachute Division

The backbone of II Parachute Corps was Generalleutnant Richard Schimpf's 3rd Parachute Division. A Bavarian, Schimpf had served as an infantryman on the Western Front during the First World War, earning both the Iron Cross 1st and 2nd Class. He transferred to the Luftwaffe in 1935 after training as a pilot and later served on the Luftwaffe General Staff during the German invasion of the Low Countries and France. In December 1941 he was made commander of the Kiev Air District in Russia and served as Chief of Staff of the Kharkov Air District. In September 1942 he took command of the Luftwaffe Field Division Meindl, the first German Air Force division-size formation formed. Later Schimpf went on to lead the 21st Luftwaffe Field Division. In February 1944 he assumed command

---

25. War Department, *Special Series No. 7. Enemy Airborne Forces*, pp. 25–28.

11

of the 3rd Parachute Division 'The ranks of the 3rd Fallschirmjäger looked upon their commander, Richard Schimpf, as a god,' reported one First U.S. Army assessment of the 3rd Parachute Division and its commanders, based on interrogations of its paratroopers. 'Schimpf, for his part, expected his men to live by his motto: a paratrooper dies in his foxhole.'[26] Oberst Max Josef Johann Pemsel, Chief of Staff of Generaloberst Friedrich Dollman's Seventh Army in Normandy, called Schimpf 'a highly qualified officer with a technical career and practical parachute experience.'[27]

The initial organisation of the 3rd Parachute Division was ordered by the Luftwaffe High Command in October 1943, within the area of Châlones-sur-Marne, Bar-le-Duc and Joinville fixed as its place of assembly. The division headquarters were at Joinville. When the 2nd Parachute Division was sent to Russia the following month, the division's 6th Parachute Regiment was left in Germany to serve as the cadre for the 3rd Parachute Division.[28] 'In order to have this valuable Division near the expected invasion front line, in Normandy, the Seventh Army proposed the commitment of this division in the area of Rennes in December 1943,' remembered Pemsel. 'OKW, however, wanted to commit it to the defence of the important town of Brest, along with a static division and one additional reserve division (the 3rd Parachute Division being the second reserve division).'[29] Schimpf was assigned as the commander of the division at the beginning of January 1944 and immediately assumed command. In February the division was sent to Normandy. 'The Division was in every respect subordinated to the II Parachute Corps, which at that time was located in Melun,' he remembered. 'The troops arrived gradually in separate transports at strength of about 500 each. They consisted of young, still insufficiently trained men, all of whom had volunteered for parachute service and were on the average 21 to 22 years old. Their fighting spirit

---

26. Kurowski, 'Richard Schimpf', *Knight's Cross Holders of the Fallschirmjäger*, p. 199; Hans-Martin Stimpel, *Die deutsche Fallschirmtruppe 1942-1945. Einsätze auf Kriegsschauplätzen im Osten und Westen* (Hamburg: Verlag E.S. Mittler & Sohn, 2001), pp. 144–146; Jeremy Dixon, 'Richard Schimpf', *Luftwaffe Generals. The Knight's Cross Holders* (Schiffer Publishing, 2008), p. 190–192.

27. Generalleutnant Richard Schimpf, *MS # B-541 Operations of the 3 FS Div during the Invasion in France Jun-Aug 1944* (U.S. Army Historical Division, 22 April 1947), p. 26.

28. von der Heydte, *B-839 A German Parachute Regiment in Normandy*, p. 1.

29. Schimpf, *B-541 3rd Parachute Division*, pp. 3, 26.

and morale were accordingly excellent, and a uniform standard of fighter was secured.'[30]

The 3rd Parachute Division was considered the best of the German parachute infantry formations at the time. According to Generals Meindl and Schimpf, there were many reasons for this. First, the division's all volunteer ranks averaged twenty-two years in age. All were true Fallschirmjäger, having completed one of the Luftwaffe's jump schools in either Germany or France, a qualification later replacements lacked. Indeed, according to Schimpf, almost 90 per cent of his soldiers had completed the parachute jumping course.[31] Parachute school candidates were not only extremely well trained but were also subjected to tremendous physical and mental stress and taught to think on their feet. They were tough soldiers imbued with an offensive spirit of independent combat action and convinced they were truly an elite band of brothers. To some extent, they were better than the average German Landser simply because they believed they were.

A second factor that made the 3rd Parachute Division such a superior formation was the fact that it's regimental and battalion commanders were hand-picked and, according to Meindl, were of 'top notch' quality.[32] Additionally, many of the division's paratroopers were veterans of Crete and Monte Cassino. Indeed, some 30 to 40 per cent of its soldiers were described as 'old and experienced' paratroopers. The division's unit commanders, who were described as 'young' and 'vigorous', infused a spirit of leadership in the troops. According to one interrogation report, 'Espirit de corps within the Division was very high because of a combination of these two factors.'[33] Schimpf confirms that the cadre, subordinate commanders and small unit commanders were 'experienced' and 'battle-tested'. 'This gave a good basis with regard to personnel and training of the division,' he recorded, 'if only enough time could have been made available for the proper training of the young replacement troops, who were most eagerly interested in their work.'[34]

---

30. Ibid, p. 3.
31. Generalleutnant Richard Schimpf, *B-020a Normandy Campaign (6 June–24 July 1944)* (U.S. Army Historical Division), p. 2.
32. Eugen Meindl and Richard Schimpf, *ETHINT 78. 3rd Parachute Division in Normandy. An Interview with Eugen Meindl and Richard Schimpf* (U.S. Army Historical Division, 17 January 1946), p. 1.
33. Meindl, *ETHINT 78*, p. 1; Schimpf, *3rd FS Division in Normandy*, p. 1.
34. Schimpf, *B-541 3rd Parachute Division*, p. 3.

During the last days of January 1944, the 3rd Parachute Division was suddenly ordered to move to Brittany. There its organisation and training were to be completed. The transfer into the area around Monts d'Arrée was executed by rail transport. Situated in the centre of Finistère, the Monts d'Arrée are the highest and oldest hills in Brittany. The terrain would have been familiar to the German veterans of Italy. Not exactly mountains in size, they nevertheless provide striking scenery, unique in the region, and perfect walking territory. Consisting of high open moorland (landes) and peat marshes (tourbières), the Monts d'Arrée run roughly east/west, forming the heart of the Armourican area. According to Schimpf, the move delayed the organisation of the division and caused considerably less favourable supply conditions. However, Schimpf soon found the new assembly area far superior to their previous location due to its ideal training conditions.[35] The division trained extensively until June 1944 in sparsely populated areas of the Brittany peninsula, paying particular attention to combat in the hedgerows and in close quarters, small unit defence and attack, and live-fire training with all weapons, particularly the Panzerfaust, a hand-held, anti-tank rocket launcher that Allied troops would grow to respect and fear.[36] 'The thinly populated area, hardly used for farming, offered everywhere the best training possibilities, even for shooting with live ammunition,' observed Schimpf. 'Besides, there were no unwholesome diversionary influences in the line of amusements, such as were usually found in France.'[37] These were exactly the skills and weapons that would be required if an Allied landing in France was to be contained. It's no surprise that Max Pemsel, himself a combat veteran and member of another elite branch of the German Army, the German Mountain Infantry Corps, considered the 3rd Parachute Division the equivalent of two regular infantry units. 'The weakness of the Division lay in its artillery equipment,' he added, qualifying his praise of the unit. 'As the Division had only one artillery battalion at its disposal, it had to be reinforced by Heeres [German Army] artillery.'[38]

Shortly after transferring to its new assembly area, the 3rd Parachute Division received its first combat mission – preventing an Allied airborne landing by annihilating the enemy parachute troops before they were able to establish an airhead and become 'tactically effective'. The focus

---

35. Ibid, p. 4.
36. Meindl, *ETHINT 78*, p. 1; Schimpf, *B-541 3rd Parachute Division*, p. 1.
37. Schimpf, *B-541 3rd Parachute Division*, p. 4.
38. Ibid, p. 26.

was the open ground around the heights of Monts d'Arrée, which OB West considered quite favourable for parachute landings. As a result, the division was deployed in a ring around the potential or probable enemy airborne objectives. 'Considering the relative ease with which Brittany could be defended and the importance of the port of Brest,' remembered General Schimpf, 'such an operation was held possible as the first stage of an invasion.'[39] For such a contingency, the 3rd Parachute Division was assigned to the XXV Infantry Corps. However, the unit's previous subordination to II Parachute Corps remained unaltered. As a result, plans were made to quickly reach any possible terrain favourable for enemy airborne operations and to cover that terrain with fire. Accordingly, some formations, especially the artillery and anti-aircraft units, were quartered in temporary billets on the dominant heights of Monts d'Arrée and a permanent air signal service was established. According to Schimpf, this mission did not overburden his troops and only slightly delayed their training, which remained the main mission of the division.[40]

'The training to make them qualified soldiers made good progress, because of the enthusiasm shown by the young troops, the qualified and experienced officers and the favourable training conditions,' remembered Schimpf. 'Therefore, by the beginning of the invasion this training had been brought up to such a high level that the troops were qualified to hold out and meet the extraordinary requirements of the invasion battle, which lasted for months, without a rest.'[41] The 3rd Parachute Division commander went on to record that instruction consisted first in training the individual soldier for guerilla warfare, considering terrain and weapons. Later it was extended to training for combat at the company and battalion level. 'By instructing the subordinate commanders in the art of map manoeuvre, their ability to make tactical decisions and the techniques of command were strengthened,' recorded Schimpf. In order to prepare the division for commitment in accordance with its specialisation and to awaken and develop esprit de corps among the troops, jump training was carried out rotating the division's troops to the Luftwaffe's parachute training schools in Lyon and Wittstock. By the beginning of the invasion, the bulk of the division had already passed through these courses of instruction, which lasted from three to four weeks.[42]

---

39. Schimpf, *B-020a Normandy Campaign in Normandy*, p. 1.
40. Schimpf, *B-541 3rd Parachute Division*, pp. 4–5.
41. Ibid, p. 5.
42. Ibid, pp. 5–6.

The 3rd Parachute Division was made up of three parachute regiments and supporting formations. Two of Schimpf's regimental commanders were proven exceptional front line leaders. Major Karl Heinz Becker commanded the 5th Parachute Regiment. The thirty-year-old Becker was a veteran of the airborne invasion of Holland and the Eastern Front, where he had been wounded in January 1943. Becker was a Knight's Cross recipient and would later be awarded the German Cross in Gold.[43] Oberstleutnant Sieback commanded 8th Parachute Regiment. Major Kurt Stephani led the 9th Parachute Regiment. The forty-year-old Stephani was also a veteran of the Eastern Front and another future recipient of the Knight's Cross and the German Cross in Gold.[44]

Each of the parachute infantry regiments consisted of three parachute infantry battalions, a mortar company, an anti-tank company, and an engineer company. Divisional combat service and service support units included the 3rd Parachute Artillery Regiment; the 3rd Parachute Engineer Battalion; 3rd Parachute Anti-Tank Battalion; and the Division Trains (supply services).[45] The division was armed with ample heavy weapons. The nine parachute infantry battalions alone were equipped with a total of 332 machine guns and 122 mortars. The three regimental engineer battalions added another fourteen machine guns and eighteen flame-throwers. The 3rd Parachute Engineer Battalion contributed still another thirty-three machine guns and twenty-two flame-throwers to the mix. The parachute anti-tank battalion had three companies, each with three 75mm anti-tank guns, one medium anti-tank gun and four light anti-tank guns. The anti-aircraft battalion, however, had no guns and probably didn't receive any either prior to or during the division's commitment to Normandy as the 2nd Parachute Anti-Aircraft battalion of the 2nd Parachute Division was placed under the operational control of the 3rd Parachute Division during the fighting.[46] Looking at the personnel factor, the division was up to wartime strength except for small parts. However, despite its many strengths, especially in comparison with other Wehrmacht formations in France, its commander was still not satisfied.

43. Kurowski, 'Karl Heinz Becker', *Knight's Cross Holders of the Fallschirmjäger*, p. 17.
44. Kurowski, 'Kurt Stephani', *Knight's Cross Holders of the Fallschirmjäger*, p. 229
45. Schimpf, *B-020a Normandy Campaign*, p. 1; Harrison, *Cross Channel Attack*, p. 238.
46. Zetterling, '3. Fallschirmjäger Division', *Normandy 1944*, pp. 216–217.

'The equipment was only partly up to the T/E [Table of Equipment and Organisation],' remembered Schimpf. 'Machine guns, mortars and anti-tank weapons were lacking and in transportation we were still 50 to 60 per cent short of vehicles. The state of training and the striking power of the troops was good. Their fighting spirit could even be called very good. Eighty-seven per cent of the division had also completed the parachute training course.'[47] However, he lamented, 'The distribution of equipment unfortunately did not proceed as quickly as would have been desirable, considering the comparatively rapid arrival of troop replacements,'[48]

Although it was supposed to be fully motorised, the 3rd Parachute Division suffered from a shortage of motor vehicles. This was a problem endemic to the Wehrmacht in 1944, not only in France, but in Russia and Italy as well. German industry in the Second World War never came close to supplying the armed forces of the Third Reich with the vehicles required to wage modern war. Indeed, the Wehrmacht required as many horses as it did motor vehicles to move men, supplies, and equipment. And Hitler's armed forces never captured or seized enough vehicles to make up the difference. Historian Niklas Zetterling goes so far as to state that the chronic shortages of vehicles and fuel were a much greater hindrance to the rapid movement of Wehrmacht units to Normandy following the invasion than Allied air attacks. He notes, for example, that the quartermaster of the German Seventh Army in Normandy had fewer than 250 trucks available, with a total lift of 500 tons to move fuel, ammunition, and rations as well as to assist non-motorised formations moving to the Normandy front. This was clearly insufficient to sustain a multiple division army. And even when motor vehicles were present, a chronic shortage of fuel prevented units from training.[49] On the eve of the Allied invasion of France, even the elite 3rd Parachute Division was only 40 to 45 per cent motorized, according to a report dated 22 May 1944. The division could only motorise one battalion of each parachute regiment at any given time. The remainder of the division was about one-third motorised.[50]

---

47. Schimpf, *B-020a Normandy Campaign*, p. 2.
48. Schimpf, *B-541 3rd Parachute Division*, p. 3.
49. Zetterling, *Normandy 1944*, pp. 46–47. Zetterling understates the impact of Allied airpower on the inability of Wehrmacht formations to reach the front lines in a timely manner. In post-war interrogations and interviews senior German commanders repeatedly emphasized that Allied airpower crippled their ability to move units to the Normandy front during the day.
50. Zetterling, '3. Fallschirmjäger-Division', *Normandy 1944*, p. 216.

Estimates vary on the strength of the German 3rd Parachute Division on the eve of the Allied invasion. Schimpf, however, whose estimate should be taken as authoritative, notes that by 6 June 1944, the day of the Allied invasion of northern France, the 3rd Parachute Division, with a few exceptions, was manned at 100 per cent of its authorised personnel, and this is confirmed by General Meindl. The strength of the division stood at 15,075 men on 1 March 1944. Twelve weeks later, on 22 May 1944, shortly before the Allied invasion of Normandy, it stood at 17,420 personnel, or in excess of 100 per cent.[51] This made the 3rd Parachute Division the largest infantry division at Normandy. Only three other divisions were larger, and all were part of Hitler's elite SS: 12th SS-Panzer Division 'Hitlerjugend' (20,516 personnel), 1st SS-Panzer Division Liebstandarte 'Adolf Hitler' (19,618), and 2nd SS-Panzer Division 'Das Reich' (18,108).[52] General Meindl records that 70 per cent of the personnel were veteran paratroopers. The 3rd Parachute Division was well equipped and rated as fully qualified for all combat operations by 6 June 1944.[53] II Parachute Corps commander rated the division as 'Ready for combat action, as long as it did not require special preparations,' but added that the unit had only 70 per cent of its authorised weapons and was still missing MG 42 machine guns and anti-tank armaments. Schimpf rated the ammunition situation as 'Satisfactory', noting that there were three to six basic loads (or sufficient ammunition for three to six days of fighting) for the weapons on hand. Meindl's pre-eminent division commander continued to complain about the lack of mobility for what should have been a fully motorised division, calling it 'insufficient'. He assessed the spare parts situation as 'very poor', adding that there was no uniformity in the types of motor vehicles possessed by the division. Moreover, the amount of fuel available for the few vehicles available was 'insufficient'.[54]

Nonetheless, compared with the remainder of German divisions in France in the early summer of 1944, 3rd Parachute Division was a veritable powerhouse. It was well manned, trained, and equipped and one of the few formations in France capable of offensive operations. Even by Allied standards Schimpf's division was considered a force to be reckoned with. According to the British Joint Intelligence Staff (JIS), Schimpf had a third

---

51. Ibid.
52. Zetterling, 'Table 4.1 Strength of German Divisions in OB West Area at the Beginning of June', *Normandy 1944*, pp. 28–29.
53. Meindl, *B-240 II Parachute Corps*, p. 2.
54. Schimpf, *B-541 3rd Parachute Division*, pp. 5–6.

more paratroopers in his division than expected in a normal German Fallschirmjäger formation of its type. The JIS estimated that 3rd Parachute Division had twice the strength of the average infantry division in France. 'In reality, only one field infantry division stood in France, 3 Paratroop,' writes Normandy historian John Ferris. 'The rest were just slightly better LE [Lower Establishment – defensive units ranging from poor to decent in quality] formations, and many of the latter were far worse than even that title would indicate.'[55]

5th Parachute Division

Among the ranks of the 3rd Parachute Division were the cadre and filler personnel for a second airborne formation that was being formed at the time and would be engaged heavily in Normandy, the 5th Parachute Division. To train this new formation, instructors and weapons were taken from the 3rd Parachute Division, undermining Generalleutnant Schimpf's efforts to man and train his own unit. The 5th Parachute Division was formed in March 1944 and sent to Brittany in May. The division was commanded by Generalleutnant Gustav Wilke. Born in Deutsch-Eylau, West Prussia, on 6 March 1898, Wilke had entered the German Imperial Army in 1916, serving as an officer candidate in the 4th Grenadier Regiment and ending the war as a second lieutenant before leaving service in 1920. During the post-war period he served in various grenadier, infantry, and even artillery regiments. On 1 October 1935 Wilke transferred to the Luftwaffe, where he served in a series of increasingly noteworthy positions. During the campaigns of 1940 he was awarded the Knight's Cross of the Iron Cross and he continued to rise through the officer ranks, commanding Luftwaffe Infantry Regiment Wilke in 1942 as a colonel on the Eastern Front and then the newly formed 1st Luftwaffe Field Division in 1943, which he led into battle in the Lake Ilmen area of Russia. Promoted to generalmajor, he was appointed commander of the 2nd Parachute Division shortly after it was transferred to the Eastern Front. The division was almost wiped out over the next several months in the heavy fighting that ensued and by January 1944 was down to 3,200 paratroopers. Nonetheless, it continued to hold its 13-mile long sector. In April 1944, Wilke was given command of the

---

55. John Ferris, 'Intelligence and OVERLORD. A snapshot of 6 June 1944', in John Buckley, ed., *The Normandy Campaign. Sixty Years On* (London: Routledge, 2006), p. 334.

5th Parachute Division.[56] Like most of his Fallschirmjäger contemporaries, Gustav Wilke was an extremely knowledgeable and combat-hardened veteran.

The 5th Parachute Division's organisation included three parachute infantry regiments. The 13th Parachute Regiment was commanded by forty-five-year-old Major Wolf Werner Graf von der Schulenburg, a Knight's Cross recipient and First World War veteran. Schulenburg had participated in the airborne invasions of Holland and Crete, served two tours on the Eastern Front with the 1st Parachute Division's Parachute Regiment 1, and fought with the same division at Monte Cassino in Italy.[57] Major Herbert Noster led the 14th Parachute Regiment. A former policeman, Noster was a veteran of the General Göring Regiment, which later became the 1st Parachute Regiment. He fought with the 2nd Parachute Regiment in the airborne invasion of Holland 1940 and was taken prisoner during the battle for Ypernburg airfield, which initially went very badly for the Germans. Noster was one of many paratroopers, including officers, captured by the Dutch Army and transported to Great Britain. Promoted to major in absentia, he was released from British captivity in November 1943, due to his heavy war wounds, in a POW exchange between Great Britain and Germany.[58] The 15th Parachute Regiment was led by thirty-seven-year-old Major Kurt Gröschke. Gröschke was a recipient of the German Cross in Gold and a future recipient of the Knight's Cross.[59] The regimental commanders in the 5th Parachute Division were as strong as in any formation in the German Seventh Army, including the 3rd Parachute Division.

Each of the three parachute infantry regiments consisted of three battalions, with each made up of three companies and a heavy weapons

56. Hildebrand, 'Gustav Wilke', *Die Generale der deutschen Luftwaffe 1935–1945*, Band III, pp. 520–521; Dixon, 'Gustav Wilke,' *Luftwaffe Generals. The Knight's Cross Holders 1939–1945*, pp. 220–222; French L. MacLean, 'Gustav Wilke,' *Luftwaffe Efficiency & Promotion Reports for the Knight's Cross Winners* (Schiffer Military History, 2007), Vol. 1, p. 241.

57. Kurowski, 'Wolf Werner Graf von der Schulenburg', *Knight's Cross Holders of the Fallschirmjager*, p. 213.

58. Henry L. deZeng IV and Douglas G. Stankey, 'Herbert Noster', *Luftwaffe Officer Career Summaries Section: Section L-R* (April 2017), p. 224. See www. ww2.dk/LwOffz%20L-R%202017.pdf, accessed 8 May 2018.

59. See Kurowski, 'Kurt Gröschke', *Knight's Cross Holders of the Fallschirmjager*, p. 73.

company (81mm mortars and Panzerschreck or Panzerfausts). In addition, each regiment possessed two heavy weapons companies, one with 120mm mortars or light artillery pieces (75mm mountain or light guns) and another with anti-tank guns (75mm AT guns and Panzerschreck or Panzerfausts). For support, the division had the 5th Parachute Artillery Regiment (with three artillery battalions); 5th Parachute Anti-Aircraft Battalion (with one battery of 88mm guns); 5th Parachute Anti-Tank Battalion (with three batteries of 75mm guns); 5th Parachute Engineer Battalion (with four companies); and 5th Parachute Signals Battalion.[60] The 5th Parachute Engineer Battalion was commanded by twenty-five-year-old Major Gerhart Mertens, a recipient of the German Cross in Gold and future recipient of the Knight's Cross and Wound Badge in Gold.[61] There was no shortage of exceptional leaders in Wilke's division.

The 5th Parachute Division had an authorised strength of 17,455 men but reported a ration strength of 12,836 men on 22 May 1944. This made the division the only German formation of its size in Normandy to have the strength of what the British termed a 'second-quality' infantry division (12,000 soldiers). In comparison, four other infantry divisions in Normandy were much weaker than what the Germans termed 'defensive infantry divisions' (10,000 men).[62] The soldiers of the 5th Parachute Division were a mixed lot, with many apparently poorly trained and equipped. 'Actually, you could divide the men into two groups,' observed Obergefreiter Karl Max Wietzorek, a member of the division. 'The first lot had been stationed in France for a year and did not believe in an invasion, only in the Thousand-Year Reich and their beloved Führer, Adolf Hitler. The second group consisted of all the men who had come from the Russian front; mostly sick soldiers, in shoddy patched uniforms, not interested in any more fighting.' Wietzorek was one of the latter. While he had been in hospital recovering from wounds, his unit had been annihilated at

---

60. Generalleutnant Gustav Wilke, *MS # B-820 5th Parachute Division (6 June–24 July 1944)* (United States Army Historical Division, undated), pp. 2, 6; Zetterling, '5. Fallschirmjager-Division', *Normandy 1944*, p. 220; Willi Kammann, *Der Weg der 2. Fallschirmjägerdivision* (München: Schild Verlag, 1998), p. 84; War Department, *TM-E 30-451 Handbook on German Military Forces*, pp. 107–131.
61. Kurowski, 'Gerhart Mertens', *Knight's Cross Holders of the Fallschirmjäger*, p. 151.
62. John Ferris, 'Intelligence and OVERLORD. A snapshot of 6 June 1944', in Buckley, ed., *Normandy Campaign*, p. 320.

Zhitomir on the Kiev road and in February 1944 he was sent back to the Channel coast near St-Malo. 'I was a parachute corporal, wearer of the black wound badge, wearer of the Iron Cross second class, wearer of the parachute badge,' he recounted, 'in other words, a "fully-licensed" parachute soldier, completely entitled to my ration of six cigarettes a week, plus some inferior food, just like my comrades.'[63]

In addition to the questionable quality of his troops, Wilke noted that many of his units were seriously short of equipment, especially artillery and anti-tank guns. And like most Wehrmacht formations in France, the 5th Parachute Division was short of motor vehicles, possessing only 30 per cent of the number authorised.[64] 'The 5th Parachute Division was of little combat value,' assessed Major Friedrich August Freiher von der Heydte, somewhat harshly. Perhaps his unforgiving evaluation was simply a case of an 'old' veteran paratrooper taking the measure of a new generation of Fallschirmjäger that simply couldn't measure up to the giants that came before them. Von der Heydte, a veteran first-generation Fallschirmjager, was the commander of 2nd Parachute Division's 6th Parachute Regiment in Normandy. Evaluating the 5th Parachute Division on the eve of the Allied invasion, he wrote: 'Less than 10 per cent of the men had jump training [and] at most 20 per cent of officers had infantry training and combat experience'. 'Armament and equipment [were] incomplete; only 50 per cent of authorised number of machine guns; one regiment without helmets, no heavy anti-tank weapons; not motorised.'[65] The highly opinionated von der Heydte rated the officers of the division as 'extremely poor', noting that they consisted mainly of Luftwaffe ground personnel without any infantry experience or tactical knowledge. And he recorded that the 5th Parachute Division's commander, Generalleutnant Gustav Wilke, 'was regarded by all the parachute troops as an *ignoramus*.' Later, a battalion commander of the 6th Parachute Regiment ordered to take command of a regiment of the 5th Parachute Division would report to the First Parachute Army that command and control of the division 'were absolutely shocking'.[66] Finally, the division had had only 60 per cent of

63. Alexander McKee, *Caen. Anvil of Victory* (London: Souvenir Press, 1984), pp. 22–23.
64. Wilke, *B-820 5th Parachute Division*, pp. 2, 6; Zetterling, '5. Fallschirmjager-Division', *Normandy 1944*, p. 220; Kammann, *Der Weg der 2. Fallschirmjägerdivision*, p. 84.
65. von der Heydte, *B-839 A German Parachute Regiment in Normandy*, p. 26.
66. Ibid, pp. 33–34.

its authorised manpower, 25 per cent of its light weapons, 23 per cent of its heavy weapons, and only 9 per cent of its motor vehicles.[67] The 5th Parachute Division was the last Fallschirmjager division to receive jump training.

'The Seventh Army was aware of the extremely low combat efficiency of 5th Parachute Division,' recorded Generalleutnant Max Pemsel, the Army Chief of Staff.[68] As a result of its low readiness, the German Seventh Army planned on committing the parachute infantry regiments of the 5th Parachute Division piecemeal to the fighting in Normandy once the invasion began and then only for a short period of time in order to ensure that each formation fed into the battle was as trained and combat ready as possible. The intense and prolonged nature of the battle, however, along with heavy losses and the shortage of replacements would doom Wilke's Fallschirmjäger to remain on the front lines, where they would suffer calamitous attrition.

At the time of the Allied invasion, the 5th Parachute Division sector was located between St-Michel and St-Brieuc. The division command post was located 4km south-south-east of the Dinan, with the 13th Parachute Regiment located at Plancoet, 6km to the north-west; the 14th Parachute Regiment located at Amballe, 19km to the east-south-west; and the 15th Parachute Regiment located 13km to the north-east of Dinan. The division staff, supply and administrative units were located at Evran to the south-south-east. 'The mission assigned was to prevent enemy groups from landing,' recorded General Wilke. 'To repulse by attack any group that had perhaps landed; to hold the positions to the last man.'[69] Under II Parachute Corps, one of the Luftwaffe's best and most capable combat ready formations in June 1944, the 3rd Parachute Division, would be paired with one of its newest and least capable, the 5th Parachute Division. This was a situation all too familiar to German commanders in France on the eve of the Allied invasion.

2nd Parachute Division

Elements of two other German parachute divisions, the 2nd and 6th, would also fight in Normandy. The 2nd Parachute Division in France was commanded by General der Fallschirmtruppe Hermann Bernhard

---

67. Zetterling, '5. Fallschirmjager-Division', *Normandy 1944*, p. 221.

68. von der Heydte, *B-839 A German Parachute Regiment in Normandy*, p. 34.

69. Wilke, *B-820 5th Parachute Division*, pp. 2–3.

Ramcke, a living legend, even among Hitler's elite paratroopers. He had distinguished himself during the First World War as a member of the Marine Assault Battalion and was commissioned an officer. After the end of the First World War he transferred to the Army, fought with the Freikorps, and was accepted into the Reichswehr, the armed forces of the German Weimar Republic, where he commanded an infantry company and then a battalion. In July 1940 he transferred to the Luftwaffe's 7th Flieger Division (which would later become the 1st Parachute Division). Ramcke earned his parachutist–rifleman badge and joined the ranks of the Fallschirmjäger at the age of fifty-one. Following the battle of Crete, he was awarded the Knight's Cross. In the summer of 1942, he oversaw the formation of the Italian elite Folgore Parachute Division. He went on to command the Ramcke Parachute Brigade in North Africa, which distinguished itself in combat against the British, earning him the Oak Leaves to his Knight's Cross. In February 1943, Ramcke was named the commanding officer of 2nd Parachute Division. The following month he and his paratroopers were sent to the Eastern Front. The 6th Parachute Regiment, which was left in Germany to serve as the cadre for the 3rd Parachute Division in Normandy, was reconstituted under the direct command of the First Parachute Army but remained a formal part of the 2nd Parachute Division.[70] Ramcke led the division in intense fighting against the Russians on the Eastern Front and took command again in expectation of the Allied invasion.[71] Three other officers had commanded the division in the interim; Generalmajor Walter Barenthin, Generalleutnant Gustav Wilke and Oberst Hans Kroh. An extremely tough and demanding commander and adversary, Bernhard Ramcke would squeeze the very best performance from the men of his division.

The 2nd Parachute Division, which had been badly mauled on the Eastern Front, was moved in May 1944 to Köln-Wahn for a period of rest and rebuilding. It comprised the 2nd Parachute Regiment, commanded by Oberst Hans Kroh; 6th Parachute Regiment, commanded by Major Friedrich August Freiherr von der Heydte; and 7th Parachute Regiment, commanded by Oberstleutnant Erich Pietzonka. Each parachute infantry regiment consisted of three battalions each. The division also consisted of the 2nd Personnel Replacement Battalion; 2nd Replacement Training Battalion; 2nd Parachute Artillery Regiment (with three artillery battalions

---

70. von der Heydte, *B-839 A German Parachute Regiment in Normandy*, pp. 1–2.
71. Kurowski, 'Bernhard Hermann Ramcke', *Knight's Cross Holders of the Fallschirmjäger*, p. 175.

of three batteries each); 2nd Anti-Aircraft Battalion; 2nd Parachute Anti-Tank Battalion; 2nd Parachute Mortar Battalion; 2nd Parachute Machine gun Battalion; 2nd Parachute Engineer Battalion; 2nd Parachute Signals Battalion; and 2nd Parachute Medical Battalion.[72] Of these units, the 6th Parachute Regiment and 2nd Anti-Aircraft Battalion would be detached from the division and assigned to various higher formations during the battle for Normandy. The division would not begin arriving in Brittany until 19 June and would not complete its concentration until the end of the month. During this period, it would remain part of the German Seventh Army reserve in the Quimper–Landerneau area still building its strength. It was far from combat ready, suffering from a number of deficiencies. Although authorised 306 officers and 10,813 NCO and enlisted personnel, it could muster only 161 officers and 6,470 personnel. As for heavy armament, it could only muster four anti-tank guns (of the sixty authorised), twenty-eight mortars (of the 108 authorised), 497 machine guns (of the 739 authorised) and 171 motorcycles, passenger cars, and trucks (of the 1,875 authorised).[73] During the Normandy Campaign, the division, (minus the 6th Parachute Regiment) would find itself defending the port of Brest in western France under the XXV Army Corps and Army Group D.[74]

6th Parachute Regiment

Only the 6th Parachute Regiment of the division was considered combat ready and fought at Normandy. A cavalryman in the Reichswehr, Major Friedrich August Freiherr von der Heydte left the Army in 1926 to study law, earning his Doctorate in 1932. He re-entered the Army in 1935, serving as the commander of an anti-tank detachment of the 246th Infantry Division during the French campaign. In a 15 November 1939 Efficiency and Promotion report, his rater described him as: 'a very impassioned officer characterised by flexibility, verve and a pronounced mental attitude for operations. Relishes independent decision making and responsibility. Open, decorous in opinions, reliable. To summarise, a personality of probably high warrior-like quality.' A British military intelligence

---

72. Kammenn, '2. Fallschirmjägerdivision 1944 Einsatz in Frankreich (Invasion),' *Der Weg der 2. Fallschirmjägerdivision*.
73. Zetterling, '2. Fallschirmjäger Division', *Normandy 1944*, pp. 214–215; Kammann, *Der Weg der 2. Fallschirmjägerdivision*, pp. 82–88.
74. Ibid.

assessment noted: 'Von der Heydte was an enthusiastic Nazi until he was disillusioned in 1933/34, when he became strongly anti-Nazi.'[75]

Von der Heydte joined Hitler's paratroopers in August 1940, earning his parachutist–rifleman's badge. He commanded the 1st Parachute Battalion, 3rd Parachute Regiment during the battle of Crete, where his paratroopers tied down a numerically superior Allied force, going on to serve with the same unit in Russia. According to another Efficiency and Promotion report, he 'Distinguished himself through prudent leadership of his battalion and ruthless personal action.'[76] He then fought in North Africa as the leader of Kampfgruppe von der Heydte, part of the Ramcke Brigade. In February 1943, he became Chief of Staff of 2nd Parachute Division, but was seriously injured in an aircraft accident requiring more than four months of hospitalisation and convalescence. During his time with the division, Generaloberst Kurt Student, commanding the XI Flieger Corps, submitted a request for an accelerated promotion for Major von der Heydte. Student wrote: 'During the formation of the [2nd Parachute] division, he put his far-reaching knowledge and thorough experience of parachuting to good use for the division and used it to such a great extent that he was able to support the successful establishment and training of the division under the most difficult of circumstances. Major von der Heydte is, without reservation, qualified for promotion to the next higher service grade. His preferential promotion is most warmly recommended by me.'[77] This is high praise indeed, coming from the father of the German Fallschirmtruppe. Major von der Heydte wore the Knight's Cross, awarded in July 1941, and the German Cross in Gold, awarded in March 1942. He assumed command of his newly formed regiment on 1 February 1944.[78]

The 6th Parachute Regiment was reconstituted in early January 1944 at the troop training grounds in Wahn. Training and equipping of the regiment was completed by 1 April. On 1 May the regiment received orders from the Luftwaffe Operations Staff, bypassing the headquarters of the First Parachute Army, to move to the area of Army Group B in

---

75. Sönke Neitzel, ed., 'Oberst Dr. Friedrich August Freiherr von der Heydte', *Taping Hitler's Generals. Transcripts of Secret Conversations 1942–1945* (Frontline Books, 2007), p. 298.
76. McLean, 'Friedrich-August von der Heydte Fallschirmjäger', *Luftwaffe Efficiency & Promotion Reports*, p. 170.
77. Ibid., p. 171.
78. Kurowski, 'Friedrich August Freiherr von der Heydte', *Knight's Cross Holders of the Fallschirmjäger*, p. 95.

France, bringing with it all its air-landing equipment. The regiment was assigned to General Marcks' LXXXIV Corps at St-Lô. 'Corps headquarters and the prearranged command post were located at the northern edge of St-Lô on the road to Carentan,' remembered von der Heydte. 'Corps was in charge of the coastal defence of the entire Cotentin peninsula and the area on both sides of the Vire Estuary ... this covered a coastal strip of about five hundred kilometres.'[79] The regiment's orders were to assume responsibility for defensive measures against enemy parachute and air-landing assaults in the southern part of the Cotentin peninsula. The road distance from the western to the eastern border of the area was almost 35km and from the northern to the southern border almost 20km. 'Corps advised the regimental commander that the defensive measures, planned and directed by Army Group Rommel required that troops were to be scattered throughout the area and that small strong points were to be established from which the surrounding country could be controlled,' recorded von der Heydte.

> Allied parachute units, no matter where they landed, would encounter a handful of well-placed, combat-ready German soldiers. In view of the advantages which such an arrangement offered, the dispersion of the regiment and the difficulty or even impossibility of assembling its units for rapid deployment had to be risked. The regimental commander was under the impression that the commanding general of the LXXXIV Corps was not in complete agreement with this order from Army Group Rommel.[80]

Major von der Heydte recounted that during a visit to the regimental headquarters, Field Marshal Rommel, who had known the regimental commander since the North African campaign, summarised his views concerning the 'proper' strategy. 'The coast,' advised Rommel, 'should be our main line of resistance for the following reasons: the enemy must be destroyed before he even sets foot on land. Once he has succeeded in establishing himself in a beachhead it will be very difficult for us to drive him out again; the invasion will have already been halfway successful.' Von der Heydte writes that Rommel's views were at odds with those of the commander of the Seventh Army. 'In view of the thin line of coastal defence, we will scarcely be able to prevent the enemy from establishing

---

79. von der Heydte, *B-839 A German Parachute Regiment in Normandy*, p. 4.
80. Ibid, p. 5.

a beachhead,' Dollman had told von der Heydte. 'It must be our task then to bring up all our forces as rapidly as possible to this beachhead in order to crush the enemy during the first days while it is still weak and before the enemy has had a chance to extend and improve his positions.' The commander of the 6th Parachute Regiment in Normandy added: 'General Marcks appeared to be of the same opinion.' And he points out that while there was general disagreement among German commanders in France on the most likely locations for the Allied landings, the LXXXIV Corps commander expected them to take place north of the Vire estuary on the eastern coast of the Cotentin peninsula in the Coutances area. 'At the top level,' recorded von der Heydte, 'it was evidently expected that the landings would be concentrated north of the Seine estuary, approximately in the Boulogne area.' This was the German Fifteenth Army area opposite Dover, England.[81]

If they disagreed on the most likely location of the Allied assault, most German commanders recognised the tremendous likelihood of large-scale American and British airborne and air-landing operations. 'It was the general opinion that paratroopers would prefer wide open spaces,' wrote Major von der Heydte. 'When Generaloberst Student, the commanding general of the German Parachute Army, objected to this on the grounds that modern paratroopers were also prepared to jump into wooded areas and villages, his objection was dismissed on the grounds that he was boasting.'[82]

The 6th Parachute Regiment was composed of three battalions, each consisting of three companies, a heavy weapons company (equipped with heavy machine guns and heavy mortars), 13th Mortar Company, 14th Anti-Tank Company, a parachute engineer platoon and a bicycle reconnaissance platoon. The latter were later expanded to form 15th Parachute-Engineer Company and 16th Reconnaissance Companies. In the summer of 1944, the 17th Anti-Aircraft Defence Company, 18th Motor Transport Company, 19th Supply and Maintenance Company and 20th Replacement and Training Companies were added to the regiment. At the same time, the 13th Mortar Company was added to the 17th Anti-Air Defence Company to form the 4th Heavy Weapons Battalion. Each battalion had one signal communications platoon and one supply platoon in addition to the formations already mentioned. The supply platoon was responsible for the establishment of a battalion ammunition distribution

---

81. Ibid, pp. 5–6.
82. Ibid, p. 6.

point and the transportation of ammunition from this point to the front lines by way of transportation units. The regimental staff also had at its disposal a signal communications platoon as well as a motorcycle messenger platoon and a parachute services platoon. The parachute services platoon was responsible for packing the parachutes of the regiment and ensuring they were kept in serviceable condition. The total wartime strength of the regiment was slightly more than 4,500 officers, sergeants and enlisted men.[83]

'The personnel replacements of the regiment at the beginning of 1944 were of high quality,' remembered Major von der Heydte. 'One-third of the officers and about one- fifth of the non-commissioned officers were battle-tried paratroopers, some of whom had fought in Crete, in Russia, and in North Africa.' Oberleutnant Marin Pöppel was one of those officers. A veteran of the German invasions of Poland, Holland, Norway and Crete, he fought as an elite infantryman on the Eastern Front from 1941 to 1943, followed by additional combat tours in Sicily and Italy. Pöppel had been involuntarily drafted into the 6th Parachute Regiment and placed in command of 12th Company and all the heavy weapons of the III Parachute Battalion. An ardent supporter of Hitler and his Nazi Party earlier in the war, he had joined the Fallschirmtruppe as an enlisted soldier and was later commissioned an officer. Wounded in Russia and Italy, his belief in the Führer and the Third Reich had begun to wane as the fortunes of Nazi Germany declined. 'Commanding officers and prospective officers were drawn from paratroopers of the Parachute Training Battalion,' Pöppel wrote in his post-war memoirs. 'Old names appeared, such as Hauptmann Trebes (III Parachute Battalion commander), Hauptmann Bartelmes and that old campaigner Oberleutnant Wagner (9th Company commander), holder of the Wound Badge in Gold. All three were recipients of the Knight's Cross.'[84]

The enlisted personnel of the 6th Parachute Regiment consisted entirely of young volunteers averaging seventeen and a half years in age, making them considerably younger than the typical German soldier in Normandy in 1944, who was thirty-one years old. Indeed, this was even younger than the average soldier of Himmler's elite Waffen SS. 'Four months of training sufficed to weld the regiment into a unified whole adequately prepared for ground combat as well as airborne operations,'

83. Ibid, pp. 2.
84. Martin Pöppel, *Heaven and Hell. The War Diary of a German Paratrooper* (Spellmount Limited, 1988), p. 172.

recalled the regimental commander. Major von der Heydte was known to be opposed to the training methods used at the Luftwaffe's parachute schools in Germany. He requested and was given permission to provide his own jump training to his men and was provided with a squadron of Ju 52s as well as a flight of Me 111s. Using the training grounds at Wahn, he ensured that every member of his regiment completed nine parachute jumps, including three night jumps. About 10 per cent of the men were eliminated at his jump school.[85]

With its high proportion of automatic and heavy weapons, the parachute infantry regiment of 1944 was the ideal formation for defensive operations. On paper the 6th Parachute Regiment would have been armed with a myriad of automatic and heavy weapons, providing it with tremendous firepower and making it the ideal formation for defensive operations. This would have included 750 submachine guns, 224 light machine guns, twenty-four heavy machine guns, forty-eight 81mm and 120mm mortars, fifty-four bazookas, six 75mm light artillery pieces and three 75mm anti-tank guns.[86] Each rifle squad was provided with two machine guns, in contrast to the single machine gun in a German Army infantry squad. Likewise, the firepower of the parachute regiment's heavy weapons companies, with twelve heavy machine guns and six heavy mortars each, was somewhat greater than that of the German Army heavy weapons companies. This increase in firepower of the Luftwaffe parachute infantry regiment in 1944 was no doubt intended to compensate for both the lower quality of soldier and the smaller size of the infantry and parachute regiments that made up the Wehrmacht in 1944.[87]

Not all parachute infantry regiments were created equally. The 6th Parachute's 13th Company was at first equipped with twelve so-called chemical projectors. These were 105mm mortars with a range of 3,500m. However, German industry had discontinued the production of these weapons and obtaining replacements became problematic. As a result, they were later replaced with medium and heavy mortars.[88] The 14th Parachute Anti-Tank Company was made up of one 75mm

---

85. von der Heydte, *B-839 A German Parachute Regiment in Normandy*, pp. 2–3.

86. War Department, *TM-E 30-451 Handbook on German Military Forces*, pp. 130–131.

87. von der Heydte, *B-839 A German Parachute Regiment in Normandy*, p. 3; War Department, *Special Series No. 7. Enemy Airborne Forces*, Section III.

88. von der Heydte, *B-839 A German Parachute Regiment in Normandy*, p. 3.

anti-tank platoon with four guns and three Panzerschreck platoons with six weapons each. The Panzerschreck, or 'Tank Terror', was the popular name for the Raketenpanzerbüchse (abbreviated to RPzB), an 88mm reusable anti-tank rocket launcher (or bazooka). Another popular nickname was Ofenrohr or 'Stove Pipe'. Wehrmacht and Waffen SS soldiers in Normandy also had available the 44mm, one-shot, disposable Panzerfaust. Portable, easy to operate, and deadly at close range, it filled a very real battlefield need for soldiers confronted by enemy armour.[89]

Later, the 6th Parachute Regiment's anti-tank company was also equipped with the Raketenwerfer 43 'Püppchen' or 'Dolly' heavy, anti-tank rocket launcher, a carriage-mounted recoilless rifle with a breechblock that fired the same 88mm rocket used by the Ofenrohr. Because the Püppchen's carriage was not strong enough to stand up to being towed at high speed, and since horse-draft sacrificed valuable time and involved the problem of replacing animal casualties, the Püppchen was generally transported on trucks and used only in positional warfare.[90] Like their Fallschirmjäger brethren, all personnel in 6th Parachute Regiment were also trained in the use of magnetic anti-tank panzerwurfminen, or 'hollow charge anti-tank grenades' as well as the Panzerfaust or 'tank fist', recoilless anti-tank grenade launchers. These were large calibre anti-tank weapons packing a tremendous punch and allowing the trained German soldier or paratrooper to knock out even the heaviest of Allied tanks, albeit at relatively close range, with a high probability of a hit at between 30 and 200 yards, depending on the weapons. It took steady nerves and a well-trained hand to engage a tank at such close range. But in the hedgerows of Normandy, the Panzerfaust, Panzerschreck and Püppchen would prove themselves deadly, if not always reliable, weapons capable of stopping Allied armour in its tracks.[91] The Wehrmacht in Normandy, however, was short of its most effective short-range anti-tank weapons, with some 16,000

---

89. War Department, 'Germany's Rocket and Recoilless Weapons', *Intelligence Bulletin* (Military Intelligence Service, March 1945) Vol. III, No. 7; Gordon L. Rottman, *Panzerfaust and Panzerschreck* (Oxford: Osprey Publishing, 2014), pp. 13, 21.

90. Ibid.

91. War Department, 'German Anti-Tank Weapons', *Intelligence Bulletin*, November 1944 (Washington: Military Intelligence Service, November 1944), Vol. III. No. 3, pp. 74–79.

Panzerfaust (instead of the 120,000 called for) and only 879 Panzerschreck on hand at the time of the invasion.[92]

Boasting about his regiment in a post-war interview, von der Heydte noted that his 15th Company, by way of an experiment, was also provided with several einstoss-flamenwerfers (paratrooper's flame-throwers). According to the regimental commander, these were highly effective weapons. He also noted that his 17th Company, following its activation in the summer of 1944, was equipped with twelve 20mm antiaircraft cannon and four 20mm triple-barrelled guns. These were not only for air defence, but also for direct fire missions against enemy infantry and even light vehicles. As for the regiment's communications systems, it was assessed as 'considerably better than that of an infantry regiment.'[93] Addressing the regiment's motor transport, von der Heydte called it 'inadequate'. On the average, each company had only two trucks. At the time of the Allied invasion, the regiment had seventy-two trucks with a total capacity of slightly more than 100 tons. The inventory included more than fifty different types, including German, French, Italian, and British. Still, the 6th Parachute Regiment was fortunate to have even this number in a corps and army suffering from a severe chronic shortage of vehicles.[94]

Major von der Heydte and many others in OB West considered the 6th Parachute Regiment to be one of the best formations in all of OB West, perhaps *the* most elite. It received a high priority in manning, training, equipping, and arming. As a result, von der Heydte was immensely proud of his paratroopers and his regiment, although pride in their elite soldiers seemed to be a trait of all Fallschirmjäger commanders. This stood in stark comparison to his opinion of the German Army in France in general. The combat-hardened veteran of the Eastern Front wrote:

> The troops available for a defence against an Allied landing were not comparable to those committed in Russia. Their morale was low; the majority of the enlisted men and non-commissioned officers lacked combat experience, and the officers were in the main those who, because of lack of qualification or on account of wounds or illness, were no longer fit for service on the Eastern Front.

---

92. Mark Reardon, *Defending Fortress Europe. The War Diary of the German 7th Army in Normandy 6 June to 26 July 1944* (The Aberjona Press, 2012), p. 311.
93. von der Heydte, *B-839 A German Parachute Regiment in Normandy*, pp. 3–4.
94. Ibid, p. 4.

Indeed, the commander of the 6th Parachute Regiment went on to note that the senior commanders of the Wehrmacht in Germany 'did not appear to have any great confidence in the troops in the west'. Even General Marcks made 'disheartening' comments, following training manoeuvres in the Cherbourg area, when he described the situation as follows: 'Emplacements without guns, ammunition depots without ammunition, minefields without mines, and a large number of men in uniform with hardly a soldier among them.' His remarks would have done little to raise moral or endear Marcks to his soldiers. Finally, von der Heydte assessed the armaments situation in Normandy as 'deplorable', pointing out that 'weapons from all over the world and from all periods of the twentieth century seemed to have been accumulated in order to convey the impression of a mighty force'.[95]

For operations in Normandy Major von der Heydte and his Fallschirmjäger would be under the direct command of Generaloberst Kurt Student's First Parachute Army.[96] Assigned as a reserve formation for the LXXXIV Corps, it would be under the tactical control of the corps, the logistical control of the 91st Air-Landing Division, and the administrative control of II Parachute Corps.[97] During the Allied D-Day landings on 6 June 1944, the regiment would find itself in the Carentan area of the Cotentin peninsula, near the U.S. 101st Airborne Division's drop zones. There it would engage in a series of fierce battles with American paratroopers in the defence of St-Côme-du-Mont, Carentan and St-Lô, making it the first of Hitler's paratroopers to offer battle to the invaders and one of the few to fight the Screaming Eagles of the 101st Airborne Division in a series of separate and bitter encounters that would leave scores of Fallschirmjäger and paratroopers dead and wounded.

6th Parachute Division

Elements of yet another new Luftwaffe parachute division, the still-forming 6th Parachute Division, commanded by Generalleutnant Rüdiger von Heyking, would also be committed to the fighting in Normandy. Born in 1894 in Rastenburg, East Prussia, von Heyking entered military service

---

95. Ibid, pp. 7–8.
96. Harrison, *Cross Channel Attack*, p. 238. 23n.
97. Volker Griesser, *The Lions of Carentan. Fallschirmjager Regiment 6, 1943–1945* (Casemate Books, 2011), p. 79; von der Heydte, *B-839 A German Parachute Regiment in Normandy*, p. 9.

in March 1914 and served as an infantry regiment company commander in 1917. The following year he was posted as an observer in a German aviation bombardment wing. Captured during the war, he was held in a French prisoner of war camp until May 1920. During the inter-war period he had served as the Commander of the Berlin garrison and then on the staff of the 4th Flieger Division. By 1940 he was commanding the 21st Aviation Replacement Regiment and then rose quickly through the ranks to command an aviation bombing wing and the Aviation Demonstration Regiment. In 1943 he commanded the 6th Luftwaffe Field Division, which served with Army Group Centre on the Eastern Front. 'Generalmajor v. Heyking has led the Division since 26.11.42. He is a strong, vigorous personality, commander-type,' wrote his rater in his Efficiency and Promotion Report for the period. 'From the first day on he has held the reins of his Division very tightly. Well-liked by his subordinates. Enjoys being at the front, always well forward, quick to adapt to new situations. Master of the principles of military tactics and is able to explain them in training. Proven National Socialist.'[98]

In 1944 von Heyking found himself as part of the Luftwaffe High Command Führer Reserve. In May 1944, he took command of the 6th Parachute Division.[99] He recorded after the war:

> I was to get all men and material as quickly as possible from the Homeland and I was instructed to reconnoiter personally an area for the Division's initial organisation. The Army High Command assigned to me a Training Staff, which was commanded by Colonel Hartung, with its headquarters at Pont a Mousson. This is where I sent all commanders and sub-commanders for a training course. It was my intention to give training classes ranging from three to four weeks for the cadres of the regiments and battalions to be activated later. These cadres would then be joined with young volunteers coming from the Homeland. Most of the officers and small unit commanders consisted largely of combat experienced personnel and of paratroopers who had

---

98. Neitzel, ed., 'Generalleutnant Rüdiger von Heyking', *Tapping Hitler's Generals*, pp. 298–299; Hildebrand, 'Rüdiger von Heyking,' *Die Generale der deutschen Luftwaffe 1939–1945*, vol. 2, pp. 83–84.
99. Neitzel, ed., 'Generalleutnant Rüdiger von Heyking', *Tapping Hitler's Generals*, pp. 298–299; Hildebrand, 'Rüdiger von Heyking', *Die Generale der deutschen Luftwaffe 1939–1945*, vol. 2, pp. 83–84.

been wounded and discharged from hospitals. The total division strength was, according to the latest Table of Organisation, to be increased to about 20,000 men.

The activation of the 6th Parachute Division's artillery and its training took place separately at Luneville. However, the Allied invasion in France interfered with the training and only one class, lasting three weeks, was completed before further training was cancelled.[100]

Von Heyking selected a sector on the Loire, between Bourges and Nevers, for the division's activation and formation. The division headquarters were established at La Charité. 'This was the very same area where 5th Parachute Division, under Generalmajor Wilke, was activated a short while before,' recalled von Heyking.[101] The 6th Parachute Division, which was to have been subordinated to the German Fifteenth Army guarding the Pas de Calais once it was formed, was to have consisted of three parachute infantry regiments, a parachute artillery regiment, a parachute anti-tank battalion, a parachute engineer battalion, and a parachute motor transport battalion. However, when formation was competed it was composed of the 16th Parachute Regiment and Fallschirmjager Lehr Regiment (Parachute Demonstration Regiment), which formed the core of the 18th Parachute Regiment. Theoretically, each regiment was organised with three parachute infantry battalions of four parachute infantry companies, along with a mortar company and an anti-tank company. The 16th Parachute Regiment was commanded by Oberstleutnant Gerhart Schirmer. A former policeman and pilot, the thirty-one-year-old Schirmer had joined the Fallschirmtruppe in 1939. He had participated in the parachute operation at the Corinth Canal in Greece as commander of the 6th Company, 2nd Parachute Regiment, and later took command of the regiment's II Battalion after its commander was injured. Schirmer and his men captured seventy-two British officers, 1,200 British soldiers, and 9,000 Greek soldiers, including the commander-in-chief of the Greek Army on the Peloponnese. Hauptmann Schirmer later landed in Crete during Operation Mercury as commander of the strategic reserve, capturing Hill 296, for which he was awarded the Knight's Cross. Later, in Tunisia, Schirmer led the 5th Parachute Regiment's III Battalion

---

100. General Rüdiger von Heyking, MS # A-956 Combat Operations of the 6th Parachute Division in Northern France in 1944 (U.S. Army Historical Division, 17 June 1950), pp. 2–3.

101. Ibid, p. 3.

in heavy defensive fighting, assuming command of the regiment after its commander, Oberstleutnant Walter Koch, was put out of action. On 1 January 1944 the thirty-one-year-old Schirmer took command of the 16th Parachute Regiment.[102]

The 18th Parachute Regiment was commanded by forty-one-year-old Oberstleutnant Helmut von Hoffmann, a former German Army cavalry officer, pilot, and Luftwaffe General Staff officer. Fluent in Spanish, he may have served in Spain as part of the Condor Legion. Hoffman spent much of his career prior to 1944 serving on various staffs with only one tour as the commander of a Luftwaffe squadron at the beginning of the war in 1940. He did not enter the ranks of Student's Fallschirmtruppe until March 1944, when he joined the staff of the XI Flieger Corps. Shortly thereafter he was appointed the commander of the 18th Parachute Regiment. Considering the rapid expansion of Hitler's paratroopers, the versatility of the Wehrmacht's officer corps, and the needs of the Luftwaffe, Hoffman was one of a growing number of outsiders who would find themselves commanding Fallschirmjäger formations. One of von Heyking's two regimental commanders was a battle-hardened, experienced and highly decorated leader, with combat tours in Greece, Crete, and North Africa. The other was an 'outsider' and experienced staff officer who had never commanded German ground forces, let alone elite paratroopers.[103]

In addition to his two parachute infantry battalions, von Heyking also commanded the I Battalion, 6th Parachute Artillery Regiment (with three four-gun batteries of 105mm light howitzers); 21st Heavy Rocket Launcher Battalion (with four batteries of 300mm rocket launchers); 6th Parachute Engineer Battalion (still in the process of forming); 6th Parachute Signal Battalion (with two companies forming); 1st Supply Company (which was motorised); and 1st Motor Transport Company (capable of moving 100 tons).[104] According to historian Niklas Zetterling, the Parachute Demonstration Regiment, I Battalion of the artillery regiment, and the

---

102. Kurowski, 'Gerhart Schirmer', *Knight's Cross Holders of the Fallschirmjäger*, p. 203. Kurowski incorrectly states that Schirmer and the 16th Parachute Regiment departed for the Eastern Front in January 1944 after he took command. They did not depart for Russia until 1 August 1944; See deZeng IV and Stankey, 'Gerhart Schirmer', *Luftwaffe Officer Career Summaries, Section S-Z*, p. 47.

103. deZeng IV and Stankey, 'Helmut von Hoffmann', *Luftwaffe Officer Career Summaries, Section G-K*, p. 214.

104. Zetterling, '6. Fallschirmjäger-Division', *Normandy 1944*, p. 223.

heavy rocket launcher battalion were all at 100 per cent of their authorised strength. The engineer and anti-tank battalions were at 66 and 65 per cent respectively, while a personnel replacement battalion was at 42 per cent. The strength of 6th Parachute Division was approximately 10,000 personnel at the beginning of June 1944.[105]

Summary

Some 160,000 Luftwaffe and Army personnel were serving on the staffs and in the ranks of the First Parachute Army, II Parachute Corps, and the 2nd, 3rd, 5th, 6th Parachute Divisions in Normandy and Brittany on the eve of the Allied invasion.[106] Approximately 50,000 were Fallschirmjäger, young and old, novices and veterans, assigned to the combat parachute divisions and regiments that would bear the brunt of the fighting. This was almost twice the number of paratroopers that the Americans and British would commit to the battle in France. However, while the Allied paratroopers would be rotated out of Normandy within weeks, their Fallschirmjäger counterparts were condemned to the brutal fighting without respite for the duration of the campaign. Most would not escape death or captivity.

Eugen Meindl and Hitler's paratroopers in France had done all they could to prepare for the monumental battle that they knew would decide the fate of the Third Reich. Because so much was expected of them, they had been provided with the manpower and weapons commensurate with

---

105. Zetterling, '5. Fallschirmjager-Division', *Normandy 1944*, pp. 223–224; *War Department, Handbook on German Military Forces (March 1945)*, pp. 108, 131. The Parachute Demonstration Regiment was authorised approximately 3,200 personnel, the I Battalion of the artillery regiment approximately 500 personnel, and the heavy rocket launcher battalion approximately 500 personnel. The parachute engineer and parachute anti-tank battalions were authorised 484 and 620 personnel respectively. A personnel replacement battalion would have probably been authorised around 1,000 personnel but would have also been understrength. Personnel in the other support elements of the division would have made up the remainder.

106. Farrar-Hockley, Student, p. 134; Schacht, *P-154 1. Fallschirmarmee Mai bis August 1944*; Meindl, *B-401 II Parachute Corps*, p. 1; Zetterling, 'II. Fallschirm-Korps', 'Fallschirmjäger-Regiment 6', '2. Fallschirmjäger-Division', '3. Fallschirmjäger-Division', '5. Fallschirmjäger-Division', '6. Fallschirmjäger-Division', *Normandy 1944*, pp. 150, 164–224.

their mission of high-intensity defensive fighting in a scenario where air, armour and even artillery support would be problematic. Each parachute infantry regiment, battalion, and even company was expected to be a self-contained defensive strong point with the mission of stopping the Allied landing on the beaches or delaying their breakout from the beachheads pending the arrival of heavier German panzer and panzergrenadier formations that would smash the American lodgement. For the most part, Meindl's Fallschirmjäger would fully repay the investment made in them in France.

Some dreaded the waiting. 'We felt in our bones instinctively that something terrible was to come,' recalled Fallschirmjäger Karl Max Wietzorek.[107] Others kept too busy to worry. 'On 5 June a map exercise is carried out involving all the Battalion's officers and platoon leaders, in which the possibilities of an airborne landing by the enemy are played through,' remembered Oberleutnant Martin Pöppel. 'We dispersed amid laughter and no one has any idea how near we are to the real situation. Only a few hours later all our preparations are put to the test.'[108] The Allies had landed in France.

---

107. Richard Hargreaves, *The Germans in Normandy* (Stackpole Books, 2006), p. 17.
108. Martin Poppel, *Heaven and Hell. The War Diary of a Paratrooper* (Sarpedon Publishing 1996), 174.

Chapter 2

Meindl's Paratroopers on D-Day

On the eve of the Allied invasion of France, Hitler continued to reposition his Fallschirmjäger, second guessing OKW and using his intuition to place Meindl and his paratroopers in terrain where the Führer thought they could do the greatest good. In the middle of March, Rommel ordered the 3rd Parachute Division to the centre of the Brittany peninsula with the mission of repelling Allied airborne landings in the region. OB West considered the Noire Mountains and the hills of Brittany, which were weakly occupied by the Germans, ideal for Allied airborne operations. 'According to the parachutists, the terrain with its many hedgerows and folds was well suited for airborne landings ... since the landing troops could find cover at once and would be difficult to reach with defending fire,' recorded Admiral Ruge of Rommel's staff.[1] The Germans were no doubt concerned that large numbers of Allied paratroopers might join and reinforce the already troublesome Maquis, rural guerrilla bands of French Resistance fighters, in the region. At the end of April the 3rd Parachute Division was followed by the II Parachute Corps' staff and troops. The following month the 2nd and 5th Parachute Divisions were directed to Brittany by Hitler, who feared a landing there. Rommel, however, requested them to be moved near Rennes, from where they could operate in the direction of St-Malo as well as Lorient.[2]

On 4 April 1944, General der Panzertruppen Geyr von Schweppenburg, Commander OB West Strategic Reserve, ordered Meindl to Paris to participate in a series of war games. Rommel had ordered Schweppenburg and the chiefs of staff of all corps and armies, along with the chiefs of staff and operations officers (responsible for planning) of all mobile formations,

---

1. Friedrich Ruge, *Rommel in Normandy. Reminiscences by Freidrich Ruge* (London: Presidio Press, 1979), 159.
2. Ibid, p. 152.

to take part. The Kriegsmarine and Luftwaffe had also been invited to attend. 'For the problem of the exercise I chose an Allied airborne landing with a simultaneous invasion,' recorded Meindl. 'The location was the Brittany peninsula. Commitment of the strategic air force, in my opinion (which carried no weight), would have to be effected before and during an invasion.'[3] During the exercise, the commander of the II Parachute Corps openly disagreed with Hitler and the German High Command's intention to transfer substantial Luftwaffe assets to Normandy only after the beginning of the invasion. Furthermore, he expressed doubts that the Luftwaffe, his parent command, was up to the challenge.

His remarks were not well received. 'My statement had a bombshell effect,' he remembered, 'and the repercussions reached the highest levels of the Wehrmacht ... I had to repeat the war games (which was actually a lecture with ordinary tables and a battle simulation) in Heischberg (Silesia) at the Division Commanders and General Staff Officers course.'[4] As further 'punishment', Meindl was ordered to give a lecture on 6 June 1944 at Rennes for the benefit of the commanders and the operations officers of the divisions stationed along the French coast. Finally, Field Marshal Rommel ordered the commander of the II Parachute Corps to write, overnight, an instructional booklet that could be understood by the ordinary soldier with the title: 'What Every Soldier Should Know About Airborne Landings'. Meindl later remembered: 'I can, in no way, be classified as a writer and I disliked taking up my pen. I think that no Corps in the entire Wehrmacht did less writing than the II Parachute Corps.'[5]

According to Meindl, his booklet was not read or understood by the Wehrmacht leadership. 'They were neither active paratroopers nor airborne soldiers and had never attended any large-scale exercises to get some idea of the subject,' he lamented. 'My warnings were ignored by the High Command as being too pessimistic. Unfortunately, my superiors in the Luftwaffe held the same point of view as the High Command ... They were incapable of thinking in terms of modern warfare. As far back as 1942 I wrote that if we continued to neglect the development of airborne operations, our opponents would develop this modern weapon on a large scale and put it to good use.' If the leadership of the German armed forces did not fully realise the airborne capabilities of the Allies, the same cannot be said of Meindl's soldiers and officers, with whom he worked hard to

---

3.   Meindl, *B-401 II Parachute Corps*, p. 9.
4.   Ibid, p. 9.
5.   Ibid, pp. 9–10.

train and educate: 'My officers and troops understood what I meant. That is why the beginning of the invasion in its full strength did not surprise us, with one exception – the artificial harbours for unloading the largest ships on an open coast line. In my war games, this important prerequisite for a successful landing had been obtained by the capture of a large harbour with airborne troops.'[6]

Meindl believed that for an invasion to succeed, Allied paratroopers had to seize a major harbour on the coast of France and that the anticipated Allied invasion was pending. 'The systemic destruction of our rear communications by the (Allied) strategic air forces from May to June 1944 was the surest indicator that the invasion was imminent,' he recalled. 'When and where the invasion would come was still unknown, but the increasing strength of the bomber formations indicated that it would be launched with incalculable weight. Despite the fact that neither we nor Rommel expected a landing in Brittany, Corps staff and Corps troops were moved to Brittany at the end of April 1944 and the 5th Parachute Division, which was not completely formed, followed in mid-May.'[7]

Meindl devoted the greater part of May to training focused primarily on the defence. II Parachute combat troops moved into open terrain, lived in tents and fighting positions and carried out training with live ammunition. 'All peacetime frills in my corps were forbidden,' he recalled. As a result, the 3rd Parachute Division reached a very high level of readiness by the end of May. The 2nd and 5th Parachute Divisions, attached to the II Parachute Corps at the end of May, were still in the process of being formed. Furthermore, while Meindl rated the quality of the troops in these two divisions as high, the officers and non-commissioned officers were of a lower quality. 'Most of them were paratroopers on paper only,' he remembered. Additionally, resupply of Meindl's Fallschirmjäger by rail became increasingly difficult due to the destruction of railways, bridges and stations by Allied air forces.[8]

The 6th Parachute Regiment also continued to prepare for the invasion, which many felt was imminent. 'The Regiment with all its units, is established in its field positions, which we have worked tirelessly to complete,' wrote Oberleutnant Martin Poppel, whose 12th Company Headquarters was set up in a Normandy farmhouse:

---

6. Ibid, p. 10.
7. Ibid, p. 10–11.
8. Ibid, p. 11.

Alarm exercises by day and by night increases our combat readiness. The whole terrain has been surveyed for heavy weapons, almost every eventuality has been considered ... More arduous labour to extend the positions, put up camouflage nets and set up sniper's [sic] posts. Then the Regiment can wait calmly for the expected attack from the enemy.[9]

Nineteen-year old Fallschirmjäger Karl Max Wietzorek, a veteran of the Eastern Front, awaited the imminent invasion with trepidation: 'We felt in our bones instinctively that something terrible was to come.'[10]

Rommel visited the II Parachute Corps headquarters at St-Quentin twice to confer with its commander. On one visit he was accompanied by several senior officers and division commanders, including Seventh Army Commander Generaloberst Friedrich Dollmann, LXXIV Corps Commander General der Infanterie Erich Straube and XXV Corps Commander General der Artillerie Wilhelm Fahrenbacher. According to Meindl, there were general complaints about the 'intolerable' shortage of ammunition in the coastal divisions and the 'inability' to train artillery and infantry troops who were involved in the 'continual' construction of fortifications. The German II Parachute Corps and the 3rd and 5th Parachute Divisions were the beneficiaries of policies aimed at ensuring they were ready for battle. Hitler's paratroopers in Normandy benefited not only from superior leadership, better soldiers, and better armaments than most of their counterparts in the Wehrmacht, they were also able to devote more time to training. 'The only units specially exempted from work on the fortifications were the two parachute divisions,' records the official U.S. Army history of the campaign. 'Reich Marshal Göring ordered that the parachute divisions not be used for construction except in providing local security for themselves against airborne attack.'[11]

Meindl was also extremely critical of the quality of officers and non-commissioned officers in France:

As a result of their long occupation of France, Belgium or Holland, the staffs and officers of these so-called static divisions

---

9. Martin Pöppel, *Heaven and Hell. The Diary of a German Paratrooper* (Spellmount Limited: 1988), p. 174.
10. Hargreaves, *The Germans in Normandy*, p. 17.
11. Harrison, *Cross Channel Attack*, p. 252.

had become unaccustomed to front line conditions. They no longer understood the meaning of war, were spoiled, and were unaccustomed to live ammunition. Added to this was the fact that units were spread out over a large area, so that only individual and small unit training could be carried out.

In comparison, the paratroopers and soldiers of the II Parachute Corps were living in the field and training as complete units. 'Duty was hard, but instructive, particularly for the (new) recruits. The morale was excellent,' recalled Meindl proudly, 'in contrast to that of the quasi-soldiers in the Communications Zone, who were always quartered in towns and villages. I knew I could rely on the Corps in any circumstances and hoped that I would also have the 2nd and 5th Parachute Divisions at this stage in one or two months.' Unfortunately for General Meindl and his men, the Allied invasion interfered, and the II Parachute Corps hastened to the invasion front with only the 3rd Parachute Division.[12]

Rommel no doubt shared with Meindl and all those present his views on the expected invasion. He had few doubts that the Allies would succeed in establishing a lodgement on the European Continent and had earlier told Generalleutnant Fritz Bayerlein, commander of the elite SS Panzer Lehr Division and a comrade from his North Africa days: 'The enemy will probably succeed in creating bridgeheads at several different points and in achieving a major penetration of our coastal defences. Once this has happened, it will only be by the rapid intervention of our operational reserves that he will be thrown back into the sea. This requires that these forces should be held very close behind the coastal defences.'[13] Rommel also shared with Meindl and his paratroopers his views regarding the Allied use of airborne forces: 'We have to expect that the enemy will use the most advanced methods against us – for example an airborne landing at night – and yet we can still win. Like a cunning hunter we will have to lay in wait for the wild birds descending from the air,' he stressed. 'Make the officers versatile for fighting against airborne and panzer troops,' he directed. 'A regimental commander will have to be with his troops in the field. Envision swarms of locusts falling from the moonlit sky.'[14]

---

12. Meindl, *B-401 II Parachute Corps*, pp. 11–12.
13. B. H. Liddel Hart, *The Rommel Papers* (New York: De Capo Press, 1953), p. 454.
14. Ruge, *Rommel in Normandy*, p. 137.

On an 18 May visit to Meindl and the men of the II Parachute Corps, Rommel told the officers of the 5th Parachute Division: 'We officers must be able to cope with all difficulties. There will always be ways and means. We will have to be optimistic at all times. Even when things don't go right the first time, there will always be a way out. The main thing is to perfect training and to use every means to strengthen the defence.'[15] Ironically (and fortunately for the Allies), Hitler's field marshal best qualified to react rapidly and energetically to the Allied landings in Normandy would not be with his troops when the invasion began. He would be visiting his wife in Germany for her fiftieth birthday.

Rommel was not the only one to miss the beginning of the Allied invasion. A host of Wehrmacht commanders were absent from their units when the American and British landings began. Major von der Heydte recorded that lower headquarters 'were astonished' when they learned that all division commanders and one regimental commander from each division, the corps artillery commanders, and the commanders of the corps headquarters reserves were ordered to report to Rennes on 6 June 1944 at 0830 hours in order to spend the entire day in an army group exercise. 'It was rumoured that this map exercise had been ordered by the Wehrmacht High Command,' recalled the 6th Parachute Regiment commander, 'although the possibility existed that it was an idea of Rommel, who, in North Africa, liked to issue his orders in the form of a map exercise.' The majority of the officers who had been ordered to report, left for Rennes on the evening of 5 June and spent the night there. 'Consequently, about 50 per cent of the division commanders and possibly 25 per cent of the regimental commanders were not with their troops during the night of 5 June 1944.'[16]

Operation Overlord began just after midnight on 6 June 1944, when 23,400 paratroopers of the American 82nd and 101st and the British 6th Airborne Divisions landed on the flanks of five invasion beaches in Normandy between 0130 and 0230 in the morning. Captain Barney Ryan, of the 101st Airborne Division, later described landing near St-Côme-du-Mont and the flooded fields surrounding it, where his unit would fight long and hard in the days to come. 'The anti-aircraft and small-arms fire was horrendous, and our plane began taking violent evasive action,' he wrote. 'The ground was ablaze with enemy fire. Trace bullets seemed to be coming in all directions and I instinctively pulled my legs up to make a

---

15. Ibid, p. 164.
16. Heydte, *B-839 A German Parachute Regiment in Normandy*, p. 8.

small target.'[17] At 0630 in the morning the paratroopers were followed by the first of the assault landing forces totalling six divisions and numbering 130,000 men. The landings were supported by more than 6,050 ships (including 4,266 landing craft and barges) and 6,340 combat aircraft, including 3,380 bombers.[18] To prevent the Germans from reaching the beachheads, the Allied air forces flew more than 200,000 sorties between 1 April and 5 June, dropping almost 200,000 tons of bombs on rail and road communications, Luftwaffe airfields and military installations, industrial targets, and coastal batteries and radar positions. Although nearly 2,000 Allied aircraft were lost in this period, the bombers had wreaked havoc with the German lines of communications and supply routes.[19]

The American, British, and Canadian divisions that landed on D-Day were the lead elements of Lieutenant General Omar Bradley's First U.S. Army (V, VII, VIII and XIX Corps and 82nd and 101st Airborne Divisions); Lieutenant General Sir Miles Christopher Dempsey's Second British Army (1, 8, 12 and 30 Corps); Lieutenant General H. D. G. Crerar First Canadian Army (2nd Corps); and Lieutenant General F. A. M. Browning's British airborne troops (1 and 6 Airborne Divisions). Facing the brunt of the invasion forces on the German Seventh Army sector was General der Artillerie Erich Marcks' LXXXIV Corps. Marcks, who had lost a leg in Russia during Operation Barbarossa and was considered one of the most capable commanders of the German General Staff, was one of Hitler's fighting generals. His LXXXIV Corps, consisting of six divisions, was the highest German command headquarters directly affected by the action on and around the invasion beaches. Marcks commanded all or elements of six divisions.[20]

Because his 6th Parachute Regiment belonged to the Luftwaffe, Major von der Heydte's headquarters was linked to the German Air Force

17. Ian Gardner and Roger Day, *Tonight We Die as Men. The Untold Story of the Third Battalion 506 Parachute Infantry Regiment from Toccoa to D-Day* (Osprey Publishing, 2011), Chapter 5. 'God, let me live 'til morning', Kindle.

18. HQ British Army of the Rhine, *Notes on the Operations of 21 Army Group 6 June 1944–5 May 1945* (1 September 1945), pp. 4, 6.

19. Major L. F. Ellis, *History of the Second World War. United Kingdom Military Series. Victory in the West, Volume I. The Battle of Normandy* (London: HMSO, 1962), pp. 67, 72, 109.

20. HQ First U.S. Army, 'After Action Report. 6 June 1944–1 August 1944', RG 407, Box 1823, File 101-.03 A/A Report, NARA, College Park, Maryland, p. 3.

aircraft warning network in Cherbourg. The regimental commander was thus notified on the evening of 5 June at 2300 hours of the approach of Allied transports and fleets by the aircraft warning network. He remembers:

> At 2300, the regiment was alerted. A few minutes after the alert order had been transmitted to all elements of Parachute Regiment 6, a severe air bombardment began to the north and north-west of the regimental sector, about twenty kilometers from the regimental command post located in Périers. Shortly after midnight, the 1st Battalion, located in Raids, reported the landing of Allied paratroopers and about 0300 hours it reported the capture of the first prisoners, Americans, who reported that they belonged to the U.S. 101st Airborne Division.

According to von der Heydte, his III Parachute Battalion later brought in 'a few score' of the U.S. paratroopers. Oberleutnant Martin Pöppel noted:

> Soon they are standing in front of us, these big fellows from the United States, giants of men with beefy faces. Their equipment is only of moderate quality in general, but the medical equipment is impressive. Each soldier is carrying morphine and tetanus injections. Of course, their rations also include cigarettes, chocolate, biscuits, coffee and gum. The most comical are the long daggers which each of them carries strapped to his foot or at his belt, just like we have our flick blades in the right-hand pocket above the knee.[21]

The Screaming Eagles (named after their patch) of the 101st Airborne Division would become the 6th Parachute Regiment's nemesis in Normandy.

One of those who helped capture scattered groups of U.S. paratroopers was Gegreiter Herbert Peitsch, a mortarman in the 6th Parachute Regiment's 7th Company. A veteran of the Eastern Front, where he had been decorated with the Iron Cross, Peitsch had joined the regiment in January 1944 just after it had been transferred to Normandy. He had been present when General Student visited the regiment on 5 June, the evening

---

21. Pöppel, *Heaven and Hell*, p. 176.

before the invasion. Peitsch and his mortar section are credited with knocking out several air-landed vehicles, probably American jeeps, with mortar fire on D-Day. As a result, the II Battalion commander, Hauptmann Rolf Mager, a veteran of Crete, Russia, and Italy, recommended him for the Knight's Cross. Peitsch was described as 'a tower of strength in the fighting'.[22]

Major von der Heydte's Fallschirmjäger battled the American paratroopers all around them in the early morning darkness. Another one of those who clashed with the Screaming Eagles was Oberfeldwebel Alexander Uhlig. A first-generation Fallschirmjäger, Uhlig had earned his parachutist–rifleman certificate in 1938 with the General Göring Regiment and saw action in Poland and Norway. He had joined the 6th Parachute Regiment as it was being formed in March 1943, becoming a platoon leader in the regiment's 8th Company. After the commander of the 16th Company had been killed on D-Day, Uhlig assumed command, eliminating an American penetration with thirty-five men. Using Panzerfaust anti-tank weapons to fire on buildings occupied by U.S. paratroopers, Uhlig and his men captured 'several hundred prisoners', earning the twenty-five-year-old the Knight's Cross.[23]

American Alex Haag, from a German-speaking family in Wisconsin, recounted being captured by von der Heydte's men:

> My knowledge of German came back in a hurry when I heard the Krauts issuing orders. We were surrounded by men of the German 6th Parachute Regiment and they used all oral means of communications. I had a pretty good idea of what was going on although when their company commander gave the order to close in and finish us off, I wished I have never heard or understood a word of German. They closed in on us and set up two machine guns, one on each end of the hedgerow. After a few minutes of tremendous small arms and machine gun fire, a lieutenant hollered, 'Give up!'

---

22. Kurowski, 'Rolf Mager' and 'Herbert Peitsch', *Knight's Cross Holders of the Fallschirmjäger*, pp. 141, 169.
23. Kurowski, 'Alexander Uhlig', *Knight's Cross Holders of the Fallschirmjäger*, p. 255. According to Gardner and Day, the Germans took several hundred U.S. prisoners, including eighty paratroopers on D-Day alone, in the first two days of the invasion. See Gardner and Day, *Tonight We Die as Men*, Chapter 7.

Haag had started with six men, when the Fallschirmjäger had moved in on them. 'By this time, we were no match as our ammo was low and quite a few of us were wounded, and I think there were three dead,' he recalled. He surrendered and was taken to a chapel, where he found several his battalion officers, along with two medical officers being held by the men of the 6th Parachute Regiment.[24]

At least one Fallschirmjäger from the 5th Parachute Division managed to make his way to the fighting at the beginning of the invasion. Leutnant Ulrich Radermann, a survivor of Crete and Russia, was on 'anti-invasion' duty at Rennes, the headquarters of the 5th Parachute Division, when the Allies landed. Ulrich had been recovering in France, which he described as 'paradise' after two years in the hell hole that had become the Eastern Front. He reported to his commander, Generalleutnant Gustav Wilke, who ordered him 'to find out what the situation was'. 'We knew only that enemy airborne troops had landed,' recorded Ulrich later. 'We had received no orders and it was all very unsatisfactory. Communications were proving difficult owing to air attack and a certain amount of Resistance sabotage.' Ulrich selected a reliable NCO and the two headed north toward the sound of the guns on a motorcycle with sidecar. 'When we reached the 84th Corps HQ we found panic and complete lack of decision-making,' he remembers. 'I did not know what to make of it, and when I tried to telephone my own HQ at Rennes … it proved impossible to get through. It was still quite early, about nine o'clock, when we set off north.' Ulrich and his sergeant traveled rapidly and soon encountered German patrols, which warned them of American paratroopers in the area. The two Fallschirmjäger were ambushed soon afterward and captured. 'We found ourselves prisoners of some Americans who had blackened faces and looked very fierce,' he recalled. Ulrich escaped when most of the U.S. soldiers departed on patrol, leaving only two of their number to guard their prisoners. He was forced to abandon his injured sergeant, who told him it was his duty to try to escape. Ulrich was found by members of the 21st Panzer Division and was finally able to get a message back to his commander at the 5th Parachute Division headquarters in Rennes. 'My sergeant

---

24. George Koskimaki, *D-Day with the Screaming Eagles* (Casemate, 2011), pp. 110–111. Koskimaki jumped into Normandy with the 101st Airborne Division on D-Day and is considered one of the leading historians of the unit in the war.

was not recovered,' he recounted later, 'but remained a POW. I met him again after the war.'[25]

In the meantime, Major von der Heydte's regiment was finding itself in a peculiar predicament. It was subordinated to the LXXXIV Corps for tactical purposes, the II Parachute Corps for administrative purposes, and the 91st Air Landing Division for logistical purposes. Nonetheless, as U.S. paratroopers dropped all around him he was unable to establish contact with any of his three higher headquarters. All German telephone lines in the regimental sector had apparently been cut by French resistance groups. 'Linesmen who were sent out were attacked at several locations,' he wrote. 'Darkness made it impossible to ascertain whether they were fired on by isolated American paratroopers or French partisans.'[26] Pöppel recalled:

> Damn, our map exercise has suddenly turned into the real thing, I hurry to my main observation post with my company HQ personnel. We release the safety-catches on our weapons, but nobody knows exactly where the enemy is yet. According to the reports there have been parachute drops in the whole area ... The night is stormy and wild. From time to time the moon lights up the darkness.[27]

If von der Heydte's Fallschirmjager were less than impressed with their American counterparts, the same can be said of the paratroopers of the 101st Airborne Division regarding the German soldiers they encountered. Colonel Robert Sink, the commander of the 506th Parachute Infantry Regiment (PIR), called his struggle to assemble his men while under fire 'an odd kind of action'. Sink remembered: 'With all their advantages, these Germans could not get their heads up. They fired from whatever cover they happened to be holding and not one man among them moved out to engage the invaders in personal encounter.' The U.S. regimental commander believed this held true all over the Cotentin peninsula, wherever soldiers of the 82nd and 101st Airborne Divisions landed. 'The enemy seemed gripped by mortal terror,' he wrote. 'His men would fire but they would not move out.' Fortunately for the Americans, there was

25. Edmund Blandford, *Two Sides of the Beach. The Invasion and Defence of Europe in 1944* (Castle Books, 2001), p. 30–31.
26. Heydte, *B-839 A German Parachute Regiment in Normandy*, p. 10.
27. Pöppel, *Heaven and Hell*, p. 175.

more sound than fury in the reception that greeted them. The shocked and frightened Landsers and Fallschirmjäger were unable to bring any concentrated fire on the vulnerable paratroopers as they descended or crawled across the open fields looking for their comrades. As a result, Sink's men were able to take the fight to the enemy. The 506th PIR took many German prisoners on D-Day, including a number from the 6th Parachute Regiment. 'Many here quite young; some over age,' observed Sink. 'They did not appear to be first-class troops physically, though their ammunition supply was plentiful, and their equipment was good. The majority were willing to talk.'[28]

At 0600 von der Heydte succeeded in establishing communications with the Seventh Army by way of his French landlady's private telephone and the French post office at St-Lô. General Marcks ordered the 6th Parachute Regiment 'to clear the Carentan area of enemy paratroopers, beginning immediately' and 'to attack from that area the enemy paratroopers who have landed in the region between Carentan and Ste-Mère-Église in the rear of the 709th Grenadier Division and destroy them.' All German troops still holding out in the new regimental combat zone were placed under von der Heydte's command:

> Because the regiment was insufficiently motorised, it was no easy task for the battalion commanders to withdraw their units from the widely separated strong points and to assemble them in the Meautis area, west of Carentan. South of the Carentan–Périers road, the III Battalion was still engaged in combat with scattered groups of enemy paratroopers who fought stubbornly; the battalion to the south-east and east covered the assembly of the regiment. I and II Battalions reached the assembly areas in the early afternoon without making contact with the enemy.[29]

According to Max Pemsel, the fact that the 6th Parachute Regiment did not reach its assigned assembly area until the afternoon proves that the extensive dispersal of the regiment for immediate protection against enemy air landings, as ordered by Field Marshal Rommel, was 'not prudent'. 'In 1944 in Normandy we committed the same error which

---

28. Centre of Military History, *Regimental Study No. 3. 506 Parachute Infantry Regiment in Normandy Drop* (Historical Manuscripts Collection 2, File No. 8–3.1 BB3 (Washington, Fort McNair), pp. 8, 35.
29. Heydte, *B-839 A German Parachute Regiment in Normandy*, p. 11.

the British made at Crete in the spring of 1941 and which was the main reason for their loss of the island,' observed Pemsel.[30] Pemsel failed to address Allied air supremacy over Normandy, which made daylight movements of Wehrmacht troops and equipment problematic, along with the scarcity of motor vehicles as key factors, which prevented the timely movement of the 6th Parachute Regiment and other German Seventh Army troops to the front lines.

Major von der Heydte made his way to Carentan ahead of his regiment. He found the town free of Allied troops and almost free of German ones as well. Between 1000 and 1100 hours, again without encountering any enemy troops, von der Heydte reached St-Côme-du-Mont, where a German battalion had dug in. The town lies on the French National Route 13, the main communications artery linking the Cherbourg peninsula and Carentan. Here von der Heydte awaited further orders. In the meantime, he climbed the church tower for a better look. 'An overwhelming picture presented itself to the regimental commander,' he wrote. 'Before him lay the coast and the sea. The horizon was strewn with hundreds of ships, and countless landing boats and barges were moving back and forth between the ships and the shore, landing troops and tanks. It was almost a peaceful picture.' The panorama reminded the Fallschirmjäger officer of a beautiful day on the Wannsee, a lakeside suburb in south-western Berlin. 'The noise of the battle could not be heard and from the church tower of St-Côme-du-Mont there was no sign of German defensive activities. Only a shot rang out here and there whenever the sentries of the German battalions came in contact with Allied paratroopers.'[31]

Major von der Heydte was perhaps unaware that heavy anti-aircraft fire from the German flak guns at Carentan and St-Côme-du-Mont had given the American transports, ferrying thousands of soldiers of the 101st Airborne Division into France, a rough welcome much earlier in the morning, forcing them to take evasive action in all directions and scattering their paratroopers everywhere. 'This ground fire leaped up at the parachutists as they responded to the jump signal,' recorded Samuel Lyman Atwood (S.L.A) Marshall, the famed U.S. Army Historical Officer and later chief historian of the European Theatre of Operations. The 1,000 soldiers of III Battalion, 1058th Regiment, 91st Air Landing Division, charged with defending St-Côme-du-Mont, had acquitted themselves

---

30. Ibid, p. 11.
31. Ibid, p. 11.

well, deluging the Americans with concentrated machine gun and mortar fire once they reached the ground.[32]

The Germans were engaging paratroopers of Colonel Howard Johnson's 501st PIR, along with elements of the 3rd Battalion, 506th PIR. The men of the 101st Airborne Division had landed in the proximity of the town on D-Day with the mission of seizing the locks at La Barquette, blowing the bridges on the St-Côme-du-Mont–Carentan road, capturing St-Côme-du-Mont if possible, and destroying the railway bridge to the west. Of these objectives, the lock at La Barquette was the most important. The Screaming Eagles had seized the locks quickly and Johnson's men dug in on the other side, awaiting the inevitable Wehrmacht counter-attack. The Americans, however, continued to be exposed to blistering artillery, mortar and small arms fires from St-Côme-du-Mont. They reacted by calling for naval fire support from the U.S.S. *Quincy*. The heavy cruiser was a godsend for the lightly armed paratroopers. Its nine 8in (200mm) and twelve 5in (125mm) guns quickly silenced all German opposition. By midday Colonel Johnson had brought up the rest of his force, consolidating and expanding his defensive position.[33] Fierce resistance in and around St-Côme-du-Mont had prevented an American advance on the bridges over the Douve River. The III Battalion, 1058th Infantry Regiment, held St-Côme-du-Mont and the surrounding high ground in force and strongly resisted every move in their direction. The 6th Parachute Regiment held Carentan and the road and rail bridges. According to the official U.S. Army history of D-Day, opposition from the two German formations was 'much more determined than anywhere else in the coastal sector'.[34]

Heydte established his command post in a defile just south of St-Côme-du-Mont, then ordered his battalions to join him via the Douve Canal. He then directed the II Battalion to advance on Ste-Mère-Église and attack and 'annihilate' any enemy encountered there. The I Battalion was to move to the high ground near St-Marie-du-Mont and protect the 6th Parachute Regiment from any enemy thrusts from the sea. The III Battalion was to return to Carentan to provide the regiment with a defence in depth. Finally, the III Battalion, 1058th Infantry Regiment, which had been attached to von der Heydte, was to remain with the regimental

---

32. Centre of Military History, *Regimental Study No. 3. 506 Parachute Infantry Regiment in Normandy Drop*, p. 16; Harrison, *Cross Channel Attack*, p. 288; Gardner and Day, *Tonight We Die As Men*, Chapter 5.
33. Harrison, *Cross Channel Attack*, pp. 288–289.
34. Ibid, p. 288.

commander in St-Côme-du-Mont. The I and II Parachute Battalions moved at about 1900 hours and by midnight reached their designated areas without encountering any enemy.[35]

Unbeknown to Major von der Heydte, the 6th Parachute Regiment at St-Côme-du-Mont had concentrated amidst a hornets' nest, surrounded by four American parachute and glider infantry regiments of the 101st Airborne Division. Less than 1,000 yards to the south of the Fallschimjäger, and blocking the way to Carentan, was Colonel Sink's 506th PIR. Some 3,500 yards to the north-west were the men of Colonel George V. H. Moseley's 502nd PIR around La Croix Pan. To the north-east 3,500 yards away were the paratroopers of Colonel Howard Johnson's 501st PIR near Vierville. And to the east, another 4,000 yards away, were the glidermen of Colonel George S. Wear's 327th Glider Infantry Regiment (GIR), which had arrived in Normandy by ship.[36] Theoretically, each of the three parachute regiments should have numbered 2,029 men, or about half the strength of the 6th Parachute Regiment. The GIR would have brought another 1,678 men into the fight.[37] Altogether the division, which had a total strength of 14,200 men with all attachments, dropped 6,670 paratroopers into Normandy.[38]

However, every unit assembled on the ground well below its normal strength due to the inclement weather, widely scattered drops, jump injuries and combat casualties. By the end of D-Day only 2,500 Screaming Eagles were under centralised command.[39] The 101st Airborne Division's mission was to secure the line of the lower Douve River, first by seizing the strategic lock on the Canal de Vire et Taute at La Barquette and then by blowing the river bridges. In that way, it would stand ready to assist the advance of American forces out of Utah beach and to the west or to

---

35. Heydte, *B-839 A German Parachute Regiment in Normandy*, p. 12; Harrison, *Cross Channel Attack*, p. 298.
36. For 101st unit locations see Centre of Military History, *Regimental Study No. 1. The Carentan Causeway Fight* (Historical Manuscripts Collection 2, File No. 8–3.1 BB1 (Washington: Fort McNair), p. 7; For 101st commanders see War Department, '101st Airborne Division', *Order of Battle of the United States Army World War II. Divisions* (Paris: Office of the Theatre Historian, 20 December 1945), pp. 381–391.
37. Gordon L. Rottman, *US World War II Parachute Infantry Regiments* (Osprey Publishing, 1990), p. 12.
38. Koskimaki, *D-Day with the Screaming Eagles*, pp. 69, 91.
39. Harrison, *Cross Channel Attack*, p. 288.

fend off any German counter-attacks from the east.[40] Von der Heydte and his regiment stood between the American paratroopers and the success of that mission.

As the 6th Parachute Regiment was moving to engage the paratroopers of the 101st Airborne Division, General Meindl was ordered to move the II Parachute Corps to the front with the 3rd Parachute Division and another German Army division 'to engage enemy paratrooper units which had landed near Coutances and to drive them back to the sea'. For tactical purposes the corps was subordinated to General Marcks' LXXXIV Corps.[41] The 2nd and 5th Parachute Divisions, which had not yet finished forming, remained in the rear for further organisation but, according to Meindl, 'their training suffered considerably from the effects of the invasion'. The 5th Parachute would not be transferred to the LXXXIV Infantry Corps in Normandy until July 1944, while the 2nd Parachute Division remained in the vicinity of Brest under the command of Generalleutnant Ramcke.[42]

Generalleutnant Richard Schimpf had learned about the Allied invasion when he received a telephone call from the II Parachute Corps Operations Office:

> I was told that according to information received from the Seventh Army, enemy parachute troops had landed near Coutances, that the beginning of the invasion so long expected was to be assumed, and that airborne and amphibious operations from the sea could also be expected at other places. An increased state of alert (Alarmstufe II) was ordered for the division ... I transmitted the alert order to the units directly subordinated to the division and pointed out the necessity of increasing the vigilance of the area around Mons d'Arrée. However, I prohibited a premature full alert, which would only have disturbed the troops in getting their rest and would have unnecessarily consumed their strength.[43]

---

40. Centre of Military History, *Regimental Study No. 2. The Fight at the Lock* (*Historical Manuscripts Collection 2, File No. 8–3.1 BB2* (Washington: Fort McNair), p. 1.
41. Meindl, *B-401 II Parachute Corps*, p. 13.
42. Ibid, p. 1.
43. Schimpf, *B-541 3rd Parachute Division*, pp. 6–7.

One-third of the 3rd Parachute Division was motorised; the other two-thirds followed on foot. 'I carried out a reconnaissance in the direction of Coutances and established the fact that an error had been made in reporting airborne troops in this area,' Meindl remembered after the war.

> Thereafter I went to St-Lô and reported to General Marcks. I was informed of the situation and received orders to advance as fast as possible with all available elements to the sector north-east of St-Lô and to check the enemy thrust toward St-Lô. After my arrival the 352nd Infantry Division, a static Army division already engaged in action, and the approaching 17th SS Panzergrenadier Division 'Götz von Berlichingen', under Graf von Ostendorff, were to be subordinated to me in addition to the 3rd Parachute Division.[44]

Generalleutnant Max Pemsel, the Seventh Army Chief of Staff, recorded:

> The Allied attack from the sea began at 0715 hours, i.e. when the tide was low, which made most of the underwater obstacles ineffective. The commitment of the enemy airborne troops – now estimated the strength of three divisions ... and the extensive use of fire preparations from air and sea proved effective. Tanks and other mobile forces were enabled to push forward through the beaches in the lineal coast or to bypass islands of resistance which were still intact.[45]

By the end of the day the Allies had succeeded in breaching Hitler's vaunted Atlantic Wall and landing nine divisions and more than 133,000 personnel by sea. The advanced contingent of the First U.S. Army in Normandy consisted of three infantry divisions, numbering 57,000 men, and two airborne divisions with another 15,500 men. As important as the manpower were the 395 U.S. M4 Sherman medium tanks that made it onto the beaches by the end of the first day. This equated to more than two full-strength German '1944 Panzer Divisions', or almost four of the

---

44. Meindl, *B-401 II Parachute Corps*, p. 13.
45. Generalleutnant Max Pemsel, *MS # B-763 The Seventh Army in the Battle in Normandy* (U.S. Army Historical Division, March 1948), p. 3.

understrength panzer divisions the Wehrmacht deployed in France in June 1944.[46]

The landings had been supported by more than 14,000 air sorties of all types. Casualties totalled 10,000 men, including approximately 6,000 Americans, with half of the U.S. casualties on Omaha beach.[47] By midnight, the assault forces of the U.S. VII Corps' 4th Infantry Division had seized a strip of land nearly 4,000 yards wide and 10,000 yards deep in some places, while those of V Corps' 1st and 29th Infantry Divisions conquered a band of terrain approximately 10,000 yards wide, straddling the coastal road, and averaging 2,000 yards deep, with the deepest point measuring 3,000 yards. According to a First U.S. Army report for Normandy: 'It was evident that the airborne divisions had accomplished highly successful results.'[48] The night of D-Day passed without serious interference by the Germans.

By the morning of 7 June, glider reinforcements of the 101st Airborne Division and soldiers from the U.S. 4th Infantry had cut off both I and II Battalions of the 6th Parachute Regiment, unbeknown to Major von der Heydte. The regimental commander ordered both battalions to maintain contact with each other and to pull back and form a defence crescent of St-Côme-du-Mont. Only the II Battalion acknowledged receipt of the order and reported that it was not in touch with the I Battalion. Most of von der Heydte's paratroopers were now fully engaged in battle. During the morning, the 1st Battalion of the U.S. 506th PIR advanced on Vierville north-east on the road to St-Côme-du-Mont and attacked the town supported by a platoon of Sherman tanks from the 746th Tank Battalion that had reached the paratroopers. The 746th was an independent armour unit attached to the U.S. 4th Infantry Division. The Americans had previously identified several hundred German troops milling in the open south of Vierville and decided to take the town. Paratroopers and tanks attacked together from the north and south. 'Under pressure from two sides the Germans surrendered,' reported Major Salve Matheson, a

---

46. For personnel and tank U.S. figures see Steven Zaloga, *The Devil's Garden. Rommel's Desperate Defence of Omaha Beach on D-Day* (Stackpole Books, 2013), pp. 13, 240; For German tank figures see War Department, *Company Officer's Handbook of the German Army (31 March 1944)* (Military Intelligence Division, 31 March 1944), p. 91.

47. Ellis, *Victory in the West* I, pp. 222–223.

48. Headquarters First United States Army, 'After Action Report. 6 June 1944–1 August 1944', pp. 6, 7.

regimental staff officer for the 506th PIR. 'About 150 surrendered ... The majority of those taken were from the 6th Parachute Regiment. These troops were well equipped and clothed but gave a story of marching and countermarching and not knowing what was going on.' One item of equipment captured by the U.S. paratroopers was a wheeled 75mm LG (Leichtgeschütz) 40 Fallschirmjager recoilless rifle. 'This was the first and only weapon of this kind encountered by the regiment though its value was not realised,' reported Matheson.[49] Major Dick Winters of Company E, 506th PIR called the battle at Vierville 'a lively engagement' during which his battalion destroyed two companies of enemy paratroopers, killing 150 and capturing another 140. 'The majority of the prisoners belonged to the 6th Parachute Regiment,' he remembered. 'Their regimental headquarters had deployed them to their present area about two weeks prior to D-Day. Many were extremely young; some were over-age. They did not physically appear to be first-class troops, though their ammunition supply was plentiful, and their equipment was good. The majority of the prisoners seemed willing to talk. This lack of discipline changed as we began our drive toward Carentan.'[50]

In its initial major encounter with the Screaming Eagles of the 101st Airborne Division, Major von der Heydte had lost not only an entire company of Fallschirmjäger, but also an advance outpost on the road leading to St-Côme-du-Mont and Carentan. Worse was yet to come.

The 6th Parachute Regiment was facing a crisis. The I Battalion was cut off from St-Marie-du-Mont and unable to establish communications with the II Battalion near Ste-Mère-Église. 'Unhappy with the results so far, the battalion formed an all-around defence in an open field for the night,' continued Sherer. 'As darkness came, the I Battalion then lost the support of the 4th Battery of the 191 Artillery Regiment [of the 91st Air Landing Division]: a fire ambush of American naval artillery on the battery position led to the loss of twenty-seven men, and caused the battery officers to issue an order to abandon the position.'[51] That fire was coming from the

---

49. Major Salve H. Matheson, 'The Operations of the 506th Parachute Infantry in the Normandy Invasion, 5–8 June 1944', in Jonathan Gawne, ed., *Lessons Learned in Combat: Normandy Paratroopers* (Ballacourage Books, 2014), Chapter 10. 'Personal Experiences of a 506th Regimental Staff Officer', Kindle.

50. Major Dick Winters, *Beyond Brand of Brothers. The Memoirs of Major Dick Winters* (New York: Berkley Publishing Group, 2006), p. 98.

51. Griesser, *The Lions of Carentan*, p. 95.

Quincy, which supported the paratroopers of Colonel Johnson's 501st PIR earlier in the day.[52] Major von der Heydte's III Battalion also came under American artillery fire, which killed Hauptmann Helmut Wagner, a first-generation Fallschirmjäger. Wagner, who had been awarded the Knight's Cross for his bravery during the German invasion of Crete as a platoon leader in the 6th Company, I Battalion, 1st Parachute Regiment, commanded the 6th Parachute Regiment's 9th Company at Normandy. He was killed when his dugout near St-Côme-du-Mont received a direct hit. According to one biography: 'Wagner wasn't one to make much of himself, preferring instead to let his actions speak for him.'[53]

More gliders, bringing in supplies for the men of the 101st Airborne Division, continued to land all around them. These were part of the glider resupply missions scheduled for D-Day and D+1 that brought in thousands of badly needed parachute and glider infantry reinforcements, along with dozens of artillery pieces and anti-tank guns, and tons of ammunition, rations, and medical supplies. One early morning mission provided the U.S. division with enough fresh equipment to support them for several days.[54] Hauptmann Emil Preikschat, the battalion commander, soon learned that American paratroopers were also being reinforced at St-Marie-du-Mont and attacking the town, driving out the soldiers of the 91st Air Landing Division. On the morning of 7 June Preikschat decided to pull the battalion back to St-Côme-du-Mont and to hold there. The situation, already precarious, turned to disaster when during the crossing of the marshy area around Vierville the German paratroopers ran into entrenched paratroopers of the 3rd Battalion, 506th PIR and 1st Battalion, 501st PIR. An intense and bitter firefight ensued that pitted an entire battalion of Fallschirmjäger against an understrength battalion of American paratroopers. It became known as the Battle of Hell's Corner.

Colonel Johnson, with approximately two companies, was dug in near the La Barquette Lock, a key American objective. Johnson had lost paratroopers to 'particularly vicious' German artillery and sniper fire the

---

52. Centre of Military History, *Regimental Study No. 2. The Fight at the Lock*, pp. 33–34
53. Kurowski, 'Helmut Wagner', *Knight's Cross Holders of the Fallschirmjäger*, p. 261.
54. U.S.A.F. Historical Study 97. 'Glider and Resupply Operations', in Gawne, *Lessons Learned in Combat: Normandy Paratroopers*, Chapter 15. 'CHICAGO and DETROIT – The Initial Glider Mission', Kindle; Gardner and Day, *Tonight We Die as Men*, Chapter 8.

previous night. Moreover, his force had already fought one battle with approaching Wehrmacht soldiers the previous day, killing and capturing about twenty as they had stumbled into his position. The paratroopers had enough ammunition for only a single day's combat but were supported by eight Browning .30 calibre light machine guns and four 60mm mortars. There was also one 81mm mortar, but it was considered of dubious value as it consisted of the tube only and without the base plate the men couldn't keep it operating in the mud.[55] Most of the elite U.S. parachute infantrymen were armed with either the .30 calibre M1 Garand rifle, the standard weapon of the U.S. infantryman, along with 156 rounds of ammunition, or the .30 calibre M1A1 Carbine with the folding wire stock, developed specifically for the airborne forces. While most Wehrmacht soldiers were still armed with the bolt-action Kar-98 rifle, the semi-automatic Garand, with its five-round self-loading clip, was in general issue throught the U.S. Army. Some of the paratroopers carried either the .45 calibre M1A1 Thompson sub-machine gun or the cheaper .45 calibre M3A1 'Grease-gun' for additional firepower. Many were also armed with the .45 calibre M1911A1 pistol, along with three clips of ammo. Several were also probably equipped with the 2.36in (59mm) M1 Rocket Launcher or 'Bazooka' to deal with tanks, buildings and bunkers. Every member of the 101st Airborne Division also jumped into combat with a No. 75 'Hawkins' anti-tank mine and a No. 82 'Gammon' anti-tank grenade, along with four fragmentation grenades.[56] Like their Luftwaffe opponents, each of Johnson's paratroopers was a walking arsenal.

At about 1500 hours, Preikschat and his Fallschirmjäger approached the Americans from the north, unaware of their presence. 'Their formation was greatly scattered, and they came on irregularly as they were advancing through the swamps,' observed Johnson. 'The uniforms blended with the colours of the swamp and there were no other identifying means or marks.' The American colonel decided they were Germans and at battalion strength. 'They seemed to be on a straight march to the river and they acted quite openly, as if they were under no special apprehension that

---

55. Centre of Military History, *Regimental Study No. 2. The Fight at the Lock*, pp. 37–38.
56. Rottman, *US World War II Parachute Infantry Regiments*, p. 56; David Miller, *Fighting Men of World War II. Allied Forces Uniforms, Equipment & Weapons* (Chartwell Books, 2011), pp. 68–95; Leroy Thompson, *The M1 Garand* (Osprey Publishing, 2012), pp. 4, 48.

there were enemy forces in the vicinity.'[57] Johnson instructed his men to wait until a single machine gun on his position's right flank opened fire. That would be the signal 'for everyone to cut loose'. Every man that could be spared from elsewhere was moved up to the north-east corner of the 501st's position and six of the eight light machine guns were shifted to that part of the perimeter. The mortars were already well set in deep pits in the centre of Johnson's position. It took about thirty minutes to complete these moves.[58]

Preikschat and his men continued to advance, closing the distance between the two forces. As they did so, they were engaged by a two-man patrol from Johnson's command. Soon after Lieutenant Fred A. Owens and Private Leo F. Runge began firing on the advancing Fallschirmjäger, however, their machine gun jammed. The two paratroopers beat a hasty retreat as the Werhmacht soldiers continued their movement. The short engagement, however, won sufficient time for Johnson to finish redeploying his soldiers and their heavy weapons. 'The German wave came on slowly, seeming to ripple along as its individuals moved labouriously through the maze of swamps, hummucks, canals and occasional hedgerows,' recorded the American regimental commander. 'Though they seemed to be zigzagging back and forth to take advantage of the stretches of dry ground, on the whole they remained fairly well bunched.' Johnson was amazed that the Germans had not put out any advance security. By 1600 hours the Fallschirmjäger had approached to within 350 yards of the American position. 'That was the interval that Johnson wanted,' recorded S.L.A. Marshall, who interviewed the regimental commander shortly after the battle. 'He was measuring the delicate balance within a clearly defined tactical problem. The Germans should be brought close enough that the first volleys could sweep them with a killing fire. But they should not be permitted so close that by charging they could overwhelm his force by sheer weight of numbers.'[59]

The U.S. Army's Browning .30 calibre medium machine gun in the war was in no way the equal of its Wehrmacht counterpart, the dreaded MG-42, the standard German medium machine gun, which could deliver a buzzsaw of 1,200 bullets a minute. In comparison, the American weapon

---

57. Centre of Military History, *Regimental Study No. 2. The Fight at the Lock*, p. 49.
58. Ibid, pp. 50–51.
59. S. L. A. Marshall, *Night Drop. The American Airborne Invasion of Normandy* (Boston: Little, Brown and Company, 1962), p. 313.

was capable of firing only 600 rounds per minute.[60] But in prepared defensive positions and at 350 yards the six Brownings would have been able to unleash devastatingly accurate fire on the approaching Fallschirmjäger. At Johnson's signal the first machine gun opened fire, followed almost instantly by the remainder of the regiment. 'Those who were watching saw many of the enemy fall. But they could not tell how many had been hit and which ones were diving for cover,' remembered Johnson.[61] 'Within a few seconds, not one German was to be seen,' wrote Marshall. 'The hedges, canal banks and hummocks had swallowed them.'[62]

The Germans reacted immediately, a sign of well-trained troops, by taking cover and sending up a rocket, which was the signal for supporting mortar and artillery fire from St-Côme-du-Mont and Carentan upon the American position.[63] 'The enemy mortars at St-Côme-du-Mont and the 88s in Carentan resumed their pounding of the ground around the lock,' recorded Marshall.[64] The fact that the Germans were able to receive supporting artillery and mortars so quickly indicates that it had been coordinated in advance and that the men of the I Battalion may have been headed to the lock at La Barquette, which the 6th Parachute Regiment had been trying to reach since the beginning of the invasion.

The surprised and scattered Fallschimjäger tried to cut their way through the Americans. 'The flooded areas, which had been created to hinder the Allied airborne landings, thwarted them in this plan, as the enemy now used the swamps to their advantage,' writes German historian and paratrooper Volker Griesser, observing that the Fallschirmjäger had to move and fight in mud up to their chests. 'The result,' he records, 'was further close combat with the American paratroopers, which cost the remains of the I Battalion.'[65] No matter what they tried, Preikschat's men

60. Miller, 'Browning Automatic Rifle M1918A2', 'Browning Model 1919A4', *Fighting Men of World War II. Allied Forces*, pp. 80–81; David Miller, 'MG42', *Fighting Men of World War II. Axis Forces: Uniforms, Equipment & Weapons* (Chartwell Books, 2011), p. 145.
61. Centre of Military History, *Regimental Study No. 2. The Fight at the Lock*, pp. 50–51.
62. Marshall, *Night Drop*, p. 313.
63. Centre of Military History, *Regimental Study No. 2. The Fight at the Lock*, pp. 50–51; Mark Bando, *Vanguard of the Crusade: The 101st Airborne Division in World War II* (Casemate Publishing, 2012), p. 91.
64. Marshall, *Night Drop*, p. 313.
65. Griesser, *The Lions of Carentan*, p. 96.

could not get through the Americans. 'As German soldiers waded toward us, they came so close as we fired that their features were clearly visible,' remembered machine gunner Marvin van Buskirk of C Company, 1st Battalion, 506th PIR, who was on the flank of the Fallschirmjäger's advance with his pal Howard Miller. 'Many were killed and many surrendered.'[66] American paratrooper Bob Webb wrote of the battle: 'The Germans kept coming and we kept killing them. It was like shooting fish in a barrel. A couple of times they played tricks on us by waving a white flag. When they reached our position, they'd pull out a machine gun pistol and open fire. We didn't take any more of that nonsense and just kept shooting.'[67] Preikschat's paratroopers were shot down in scores as they tried to fight their way through the ambush or escape by wading through the marshes. Intense fire poured in from all around, even from above. 'The Americans had posted sharpshooters in the trees,' remembered Obergefreiter Karl-Heinz Mayer, a machine gunner of the 3rd Company. 'Even when one of them was hit, he did not fall down, because these boys had belted themselves in.' Hit in the face by an American sniper, Mayer crawled into a gutter. 'The war was over for me,' he recounted.[68]

On the evening of 7 June, Preikschat's I Battalion, including the wounded Mayer, surrendered to Colonel Howard Johnson and his men after a problematic and extended parlay session. Among those captured were Gefreiter Toschka, from the 3rd Company, and Gefreiter Abledinger, from the 4th Company, who told their U.S. interrogators that American paratroopers had jumped behind them and taken them prisoner. Neither had attended any formal German Luftwaffe jump school. Both had received all their jump training, including seven jumps, at Wahn. Toschka and Abledinger professed themselves to be 'anti-Nazi'.[69] 'The battalion commander came in near the last,' remembered Johnson. 'He was a lieutenant colonel and a typical Nazi.' Some 150 Germans had been killed or badly wounded and another 300 were taken prisoner. The battalion commander and all four of his company commanders had either been killed or captured. A few Fallschirmjäger escaped towards Carentan. Johnson's losses during the afternoon firefight were ten killed and thirty

---

66. Mark Bando, *101st Airborne. The Screaming Eagles at Normandy* (MBI Publishing Company, 2001), p. 53.
67. Gardner and Day, *Tonight We Die as Men*, Chapter 8.
68. Griesser, *The Lions of Carentan*, p. 97.
69. C.S.D.I.C, 'S.I.R. 350 KP/4120 (M/A) Gerf. Abledinger, KP/4506 (M/A) Gefr. Toschka', RG 165, NARA II.

wounded.[70] The worst for the Fallschirmjäger, however, was not yet over. As the Americans were forming up their prisoners along the road to the south of Johnson's Command Post, the German 88mm artillery piece, which had been plaguing the paratroopers since their arrival at La Barquette, resumed firing from Carentan. One of its rounds landed squarely on the German captives, killing Captain Reynolds, the American regimental adjutant, and twenty of the prisoners. Many others were wounded. 'The survivors,' recorded Johnson, 'whimpered and cried and begged him to send up a white rocket.' The American regimental commander refused. 'We don't dare do that; we don't know what it means,' he told his men, adding: 'If any man tries to break away from this column, shoot him.'[71]

All through the following night, German casualties continued to drag themselves out of the swamp and into the American perimeter. U.S. patrols were sent out from Hell's Corner to search for others. Lieutenant Rich Reinhold of the regimental intelligence section was shot by a wounded Fallschirmjäger as he was searching for injured survivors after the German surrender. Preikschat's I Battalion had neither the medical supplies nor the personnel to take care of the multitude of wounded prisoners, so the task fell to the American paratroopers. 'The aid station soon ran out of bandages,' records Johnson. 'The men tore up undershirts, sheets and whatever they could lay their hands on. The sulpha and blood plasma supply ran low and was conserved for the more desperate cases.'[72] Paratrooper Bill Galbraith was shocked by the scene at the aid station:

> With the Germans in their grey uniforms it looked like a scene from *Gone with the Wind*,' he wrote. 'There were about 200 prisoners waiting to be collected; most were from the 6th Parachute Regiment. Some had been shot up pretty bad. We were told that the day before, as they were being marched up the road, the 88 across the river opened up and blew them into rag dolls. There was no medication available and you had to feel a little sympathy for them – it was a painful sight.[73]

---

70. Centre of Military History, *Regimental Study No. 2. The Fight at the Lock*, p. 56; Bando, *101st Airborne. The Screaming Eagles at Normandy*, p. 53.
71. Centre of Military History, *Regimental Study No. 2. The Fight at the Lock*, p. 56; Bando, *Vanguard of the Crusade*, p. 91.
72. Centre of Military History, *Regimental Study No. 2. The Fight at the Lock*, p. 57.
73. Gardner and Day, *Tonight We Die as Men*, Chapter 9.

The Screaming Eagles remained at Hell's Corner, where they were resupplied, through the next day.

'With enemy units ahead of them, with a whole Regiment of elite enemy troops behind them, and with marshland to south, all that the Battalion could do was to take up a position of all-around defence and defend themselves to the last man,' wrote Oberleutnant Martin Pöppel.[74] Pöppel and von der Heydte were unaware that the I Battalion had outnumbered the Americans by two-to-one and that in their hurry to get to St-Côme-du-Mont the Fallschirmjäger had failed to conduct proper reconnaissance or to observe strict march security, bunching up and falling blindly into a large-scale ambush even after being fired upon by two of Johnson's paratroopers. They were the second German force to do so that day, indicating that Johnson's men were well dug in and camouflaged in the relatively flat terrain. 'The I Battalion, as the regimental commander learned later, had already been annihilated on 7 June and the battalion commander had surrendered,' reflected von der Heydte bitterly. 'Only twenty-five men succeeded in making their way to the regiment on 9 June through the marshy terrain along the Douve.'[75] The commander of the II Parachute Battalion also tried in vain to establish contact with the regiment. Failing to do so, he decided to fall back to Carentan by breaking through the U.S. defensive positions in his rear.[76] In its second major encounter with the 101st Airborne Division, the 6th Parachute Regiment had walked blindly into an ambush, been taken by surprise, and lost an entire battalion of more than 500 elite paratroopers, leaving von der Heydte in a state of shock. The Battle of Hell's Corner was the first time in the war that American forces annihilated a full battalion of German Fallschirmjager in a single battle.

While Preikschat and his battalion were fighting for their lives, Eugen Meindl was ordering the transfer of the 3rd Parachute Division, led by its motorised elements, to Avranches. The mission assigned to Schimpf and his paratroopers was 'the construction of a defensive front taking into account that the enemy was to be thrown back into

---

74. Pöppel, *Heaven and Hell*, p. 180.
75. Harrison, *Cross Channel Attack*, p. 298; von der Heydte, *B-839 A German Parachute Regiment in Normandy*, p. 14. Harrison writes that Heydte's battalion surrendered to a man, while von der Heydte makes it clear that was annihilated.
76. Heydte, *B-839 A German Parachute Regiment in Normandy*, p. 14.

the Channel later during a counter-attack.'[77] According to General Schimpf, General Meindl called him on 7 June 1944 toward 1100 hours and ordered the following by telephone. 'I do not give the exact wording but the general sense,' recorded the commander of the 3rd Parachute Division:

> Now the beginning of the invasion is certain. Aside from the parachute troops already landed on the Cotentin Peninsula and at the mouth of the Orne River, landings on a larger scale from the sea are now also taking place. II Parachute Corps has the mission to throw back the enemy from the St-Lô sector and east of it to the north, together with the 3rd Parachute Division (which, immediately, is to be also tactically subordinated to the Corps), the 352nd Infantry Division and the 17th SS Panzergrenadier Division, which is to be brought forward and to win back possession of the coast. The 3rd Parachute Division is to be transferred immediately to the Avranches area in all its strength, utilising all available motor vehicles. The rest of the Division is to march on foot. The next orders will be issued in Avranches, where a messenger point (meldestalle) is being established.[78]

'The intent was to transfer the division as rapidly as possible in order to make contact with the enemy and prevent the expansion of his bridgehead, formed during the invasion,' remembered Schimpf. 'We were subsequently to deal a powerful counterblow with replacements hurriedly brought up, before the enemy had strengthened still further his hold on the continent. It was not yet possible to establish an estimate of the numerical size of the enemy forces. The aim of the enemy could only be the expansion of the bridgehead in order to get hold of a base sufficiently large for further operations.'[79]

'In pursuance of orders, full alert was given immediately, and the troops were prepared for their imminent departure by a warning order,' recorded the 3rd Parachute Division commander. 'Up to that moment, in spite of continuous remonstrations at higher headquarters (administrative centres), the process of rendering the Division mobile (fully motorised)

---

77. Schimpf, *B-020a Normandy Campaign*, p. 2.
78. Schimpf, *B-541 Operations of the 3rd Parachute Division During the Invasion of France*, pp. 7–8.
79. Schimpf, *B-020a Normandy Campaign*, pp. 2–3.

had not advanced sufficiently so that, from the very first, the effects of the situation were extremely detrimental.' On careful consideration, Schimpf decided that, at best, only a single battalion from each parachute regiment could be rendered mobile and that only about a third to half of the rest of his Division troops (engineer, artillery and anti-tank units) could be motorised. Only the Flak (anti-aircraft) Battalion, organised in Germany and transferred as an integral unit, and the parachute signal battalion were sufficiently supplied with motor vehicles, so that the bulk of their forces were mobile. Furthermore, he assumed that the motorised groups would be thrown into battle as soon as they arrived. 'Therefore, in order to later on avoid mixing up units or difficulties during relief it seemed advantageous to transfer one battalion of each regiment ahead and to take over command myself until the area could be divided into regimental sectors,' recorded the division commander. 'I therefore decided to put on the march a motorised advanced party consisting of one battalion from each of the parachute infantry regiments, two engineer companies, two batteries of the 3rd Parachute Artillery Battalion, one company of the panzerjäger (anti-tank) battalion, the entire FLAK battalion and the signal battalion in such a manner that they would be able to cover the largest possible distance by using to advantage the night of 7/8 June.'[80]

On 7 June at 1700 hours, Schimpf sent his division operations officer, a special missions staff officer (ordonnanzoffizier), and the division signal's officer ahead to receive orders and to establish an advance message centre in Avranches:

> I personally supervised the departure of the motorised group and the preparation of two future groups to be formed for marching on foot. On 8 June at 0600 hours I followed the motorised group, which I overtook in the region east of St-Méen. To our satisfaction, but also to our astonishment, no enemy air reconnaissance was carried out during the day and, above all, no fighter-bomber activity covered the road of advance, so that the march could take its own course without interference or losses.[81]

At about 1600 hours Schimpf arrived at the south exit of Avranches, where he met those officers he had sent ahead. They informed him that the Allies had captured Bayeux and had probed their way

---

80. Schimpf, *B-541 3rd Parachute Division*, p. 8.
81. Ibid, p. 8.

through the forest of Cerisy. New orders would be issued at 1800 hours by the commanding general at les Cheris (10km south-east of Avranches). 'After having ordered the 4th Special Mission Staff Officer to reconnoiter and establish a provisional Division Command Post in St-Georges (north-east of Avranches), I drove to the II Parachute Corps Headquarters,' continued Schimpf. 'There I received the order to push forward to the north edge of the Forest of Cerisy, after the arrival of the motorised group. Furthermore, I was to hold this forest against the enemy attacking from the north and especially from Bayeux until the bulk of my Division was brought forward. After returning to my Division Headquarters at St-Georges, I prepared my order with appropriate details of execution for the Commander of the motorised advance troops, Major Becker.[82]

On the morning of 9 June, the commander of the 3rd Parachute Division drove to St-Lô and reported to Generalleutnant Marcks, asking for details concerning the tactical situation. He recorded:

The arrival of the motorised group directly north of St-Georges was reported to me after my return. This group received orders for the afternoon of 10 June to push forward via Dorigny–Rouxeville–Bérigny to the north edge of the Forest of Cerisy. I myself reconnoitered a Division Command Post north of Torigni, which I finally established in a farmhouse in the little forest west of La-Chapelle-du-Fest (3km north of Torigni). In the evening I transferred my staff there. After arrival of the motorised group in the region north of Torigni, all motor transport vehicles were sent to meet the two marching groups on foot in order to facilitate and accelerate their transport.[83]

In the meantime, Schimpf's battalions, which were to follow on foot, were alerted and organised into two serials, with Oberstleutnant Ernst Liebach in command. General Schimpf ordered these non-motorised elements of the division to reach the combat area 'as quickly as possible' while at the same time 'maintaining unit integrity'. He wanted the flexibility of being able to commit them directly into battle as organised formations if the tactical situation so dictated. As the paratroopers of the 3rd Parachute

---

82. Ibid, pp. 9–10.
83. Ibid.

Division had to remain concealed from enemy air reconnaissance and attacks, night marches became the norm.[84]

Schimpf remembered:

The advance began on 7 June 1944 at 1900 hours with two march serials (A and B) under the control of the commanders of the 8th and 9th Parachute Infantry Regiments. The majority of the three to six days' ammunition had to be left behind for lack of transport space. The troops carried one day's ammunition with them in addition to their field packs and small arms ammunition in pouches. Therefore, when arriving at the first march destination (Carhaix) a general exhaustion was noticeable among the troops, who were unaccustomed to marching. Furthermore, their new paratrooper boots caused a considerable amount of footsoreness. An immediate relief was provided by hiring carts such as are customarily used in the country. (It was impossible to procure motor vehicles and fuel.)[85]

According to Schimpf, each battalion required forty-five carts to transport their weapons and equipment, along with foot-weary soldiers. The limited march capacity of the heavy work horses from northern France necessitated the use of relays and every other day new vehicles were hired. The increased length of the march column, with its attendant difficulty of camouflage, forced the march commander to avoid main roads and all cities and towns, and to use side roads. Difficulties in orientation, which were partly due to the lack of maps, were resolved by the increased use of guides. Mobility was also further improved by the use of confiscated bicycles. These rendered a large part of the march groups, including liaison groups, advance parties and guides, mobile. 'The short nights required a rigorous pace to reach the march average of 40km per day,' recorded Schimpf:

In the darkness, the draft horses of the carts had to be led by the bridles and often the troops had to help turn the wheels. These night marches demanded from the troops a high standard of discipline and perseverance. They welded the units together before combat began and showed the calibre of troops to be

---

84. Ibid, p. 10.
85. Ibid, pp. 11–12.

good … From their cantonment area around Hede, the troops who were resting during the day were able to observe for the first time the approaching flight of a tight bomber formation with fighter escort and also a bombing raid on Rennes. The enemy superiority, existing beyond any doubt, made a great impression upon the troops and increased the camouflage discipline of each individual.[86]

Schimpf later stressed that the 'feared hindering of the march by the French resistance movement' never materialised. 'Some isolated instances of interference during the first three days are not worth mentioning,' he added. 'The attitude of the French people was reserved but correct.'[87]

While the II Parachute Corps and 3rd Parachute Division were moving northward, U.S. reinforcements were pouring into Normandy. The Americans had followed their initial assault force with more than 30,000 personnel and 3,000 vehicles at Omaha Beach, with a second wave of 26,000 soldiers and 4,000 vehicles due by the end of 7 June. Another 30,000 Americans and 3,500 vehicles had landed at Utah Beach.[88] In comparison, the German Seventh Army had been able to muster only 4,800 reinforcements, twenty artillery pieces 'with little ammunition,' six tanks, and no combat aircraft.[89] 'Hour after hour, day after day, the enemy landed new forces without encountering interference,' recorded Seventh Army Chief of Staff Max Pemsel. 'On the German side there were not even the means to replace the losses suffered by the combat troops.'[90]

In the first two days of fighting, German officers who had battled the U.S. Forces perceived several traits of the American soldier in Normandy. One was the tendency of U.S. soldiers to talk in the 'clear' (without the use of codes) on their radios. According to Oberstleutnant Fritz Ziegelmann of the 352nd Infantry Division, radio intercepts helped 'to confirm or correct our own reports and … to recognise his intentions.' As for the fighting abilities of the American soldier: 'In the villages, the infantry fought stubbornly and skilfully. In open terrain the impetus of the attack … soon

---

86. Ibid, pp. 11–12.
87. Ibid, p. 12.
88. HQ First United States Army, 'After Action Report. 6 June 1944–1 August 1944', pp. 4, 6.
89. Oberstleutnant Fritz Ziegelmann, MS # B-433 352nd Infantry Division (7 June 1944) (U.S. Army Historical Division, undated), p. 6.
90. Pemsel, B-763 The Seventh Army in the Battle in Normandy, p. 10.

came to an end when the infantry met with strong German resistance. The infantry fighting was replaced by fighting with heavy weapons, with material.' Ziegelmann was referring to the tendency of advancing U.S. soldiers to go to ground once they came under fire and to rely on airpower and artillery, rather than their own rifle, machine gun and mortar fire, to destroy or dislodge their opponents.

These shortcomings, however, did not prevent the Americans from inflicting 1,200 casualties on defending troops of the 352nd Infantry Division, including 200 killed, 500 wounded, and 500 missing, and another as many as 800 casualties (including an entire Fallschirmjager company and Fallschirmjager battalion) on the 6th Parachute Regiment by 7 June.[91] This was an impressive tally by attacking troops against soldiers in a prepared defence and especially against German paratroopers.[92]

'Our infantry fought with unexcelled courage and endurance,' recorded Ziegelmann, who would fight for the remainder of the Normandy campaign with the II Parachute Corps. 'The effectiveness of enemy weapons and the numerical superiority of the enemy resulted, however, on 7 June in a flagging fighting strength … The unity of the front began to break up. The questions "Where is the German Air Force?" and "When is retaliation going to begin?" were often heard.'[93] It was a question on the lips of every German Landser and Fallschirmjäger fighting in Normandy.

---

91. Ziegelmann, *B-433 352nd Infantry Division (7 June 1944)*, pp. 10–11.
92. Ibid.
93. Ibid.

Chapter 3

6th Parachute Regiment at St-Côme-du-Mont

Having been taken by surprise on 6 June, the Wehrmacht in France reorganised for battle. OB West divided the front into two sectors. Seventh Army was given responsibility for the western sector, extending from Cotentin to Bayeux. Panzer Group West was placed in charge of the eastern sector, running from Bayeux to the Dives River. This delineation of the fighting front placed the German Seventh Army's infantry divisions opposite the First U.S. Army, while Panzer Group West's panzer divisions mainly fought opposite General Dempsey's British Second Army. The Seventh Army would fight the Americans with two corps: LXXXIV in the west at the base of the Cotentin peninsula and II Parachute (attached for operations only) in the east in the vicinity of St-Lô. LXXXIV Corps would initially oppose the U.S. VII Corps, and later the VIII Corps as well, with the 91st Air Landing, 243rd and 709th Infantry Divisions. II Parachute Corps and 3rd Parachute Division, along with the 17th SS Panzer and 77th Infantry Divisions, would face off against the U.S. V Corps.[1] To highlight the importance Hitler placed on first containing

---

1. Seventh Army controlled four corps in France during the Normandy campaign: II Parachute, XXV, LXXIV and LXXXIV. See Generalmajor Freiherr Treusch Buttlar-Brandenfells, *MS # B-672 OB West* (U.S. Army Historical Division, 5 December 1947), p. 61; See also Major Percy Ernst Schramm, *MS # B-034 OKW War Diary (1 April–16 December 1944)* (U.S. Army Historical Division, 31 December 1947), p. 32. Schramm mistakenly lists the 37th Infantry Division, rather than the 77th Infantry Division, as being under II Parachute Corps command. There was no 37th Infantry Division at Normandy and it was the 77th that served under Meindl.

the British at Caen, then eliminating them altogether, Panzer Group West would command four powerful corps, including (from west to east) the XLVII Panzer, the II SS Panzer, the I SS Panzer and the LXXXIV Corps. The Americans would benefit from the fact that the vast majority of the Wehrmacht's elite Army and SS panzer divisions, along with almost all of its assault gun, heavy Werfer, artillery, and independent anti-tank battalions and brigades, would fight as part of Panzer Group West against the British and Commonwealth forces to the east.[2]

Meindl and the II Parachute Corps would find themselves fighting with one of the newest and weakest Wehrmacht formations in France under their command. The 77th Infantry Division was a formation so new that it didn't appear on the U.S. War Department's February 1944 Order of Battle for the German Army.[3] It had been formed in January 1944 and had a manpower strength of 9,095 officers and men, plus another 1,410 Hiwis at the beginning of the invasion. On D-Day the division was located near St-Malo and the following day it was ordered to Normandy as soon as it could be relieved by the 5th Parachute Division. Motorised parts of the 77th Infantry Division reached a position east of Granville on 8 June and, two days later, other elements would reach Valognes, where they would be committed on both sides of the Merderet with most of the division in the area north of Coutances.[4]

The first two days of the invasion had not gone well for Major von der Heydte and his 6th Parachute Regiment. An entire company had been taken by surprise and killed or captured at Vierville on D-Day and another entire battalion had been annihilated at Hell's Corner on D+1. In two short days the regiment had been stripped of almost half its parachute infantry companies, the core of its fighting strength. Von der Heydte's Fallschirmjäger prepared to once again battle paratroopers of the 101st Airborne Division as they advanced on St-Côme-du-Mont. The Americans recognised that some German formations were fighting a delaying action in and around the town to cover the Carentan causeway bridges, so that other Wehrmacht troops would have a chance to cross

---

2. See Zetterling, *Normandy 1944*.
3. War Department, *Order of Battle of the Germany Army February 1944* (Washington D.C: Military Intelligence Division, February 1944). 76th Infantry Division and 78th Infantry Division are listed on pp. 193–194 but no 77th Infantry Division. The next War Department Order of Battle update would not be published until 1945.
4. Zetterling, '77. Infanterie-Division', *Normandy 1944*, p. 230.

them as they retreated. In fact, many Wehrmacht units were doing so in disorder. The U.S. paratroopers had captured 'numerous' stray German soldiers near St-Côme-du-Mont, who revealed the general outline of their defences around the town. 'The bulk of these were from the 6th Parachute Regiment,' reported Major Salve Matheson of the 506th PIR.[5] S.L.A. Marshall recorded:

> These were no doubt men of the two defeated formations trying to make their way back to their lines. They were in good company. By D Plus 2 Day, the chief enemy factions seemed to be responding only to one impulse, to get away, if they could, beyond the Carentan marshes. While every hour had brought greater cohesion in the American force, the rate of disintegration in the enemy was even more rapid. It is indicated that these contrasting effects were due less to heavy German losses in the early hours than to shock resulting from surprise.

Marshall concluded: 'The enemy appears to have become the victim of an acute terror which numbed his movements,' adding: 'Some of the enemy elements appear to have been bolting in planless escape.'[6] St-Côme-du-Mont was defended by what remained of the II and III Battalions of the 6th Parachute Regiment and III Battalion, 1058th Regiment.

Early on the morning of 8 June the Americans attacked the town with three battalion elements from the 501st and 506th PIRs on line and a battalion element from the 401st GIR following the assaulting forces on the right. The 506th Parachute Infantry had approximately 650 men in its ranks by this time and had already lost 600 men killed, wounded and captured.[7] The 501st Parachute Infantry and 401st Glider Infantry together probably added another 1,300 men for a total attacking force of close to 2,000 paratroopers and glider infantry. The plan called for one parachute battalion to attack the town frontally from the north, while the

---

5. Major Salve H. Matheson, Chapter 10. 'The Operations of the 506th Parachute Infantry in the Normandy Invasion, 5–8 June 1944,' in Gawne, *Lessons Learned in Combat: Normandy Paratroopers*, Kindle.
6. CMH, *Regiment Study Number 3. 506th Parachute Infantry Regiment in Normandy*, p. 53.
7. Matheson, 'The Operations of the 506th Parachute Infantry in the Normandy Invasion, 5–8 June 1944', in Gawne, *Lessons Learned in Combat: Normandy Paratroopers*, Chapter 10. Kindle.

other two battalions enveloped it from the north-east, cutting the road to Carentan. The glidermen, in the second wave, were to then proceed to the main road beyond the town, get to the Carentan causeway, and blow the bridges. The attacking troops were ill prepared. Most reached the Line of Departure at almost the last minute and in a state of near exhaustion from continuous movement and combat over the previous two days. At 0445, just as first light was breaking, U.S. preparatory artillery fire, high-explosive shells mixed with white phosphorus, was unleashed on the town and the surrounding area. The guns had registered on fifteen targets in St-Côme-du-Mont and the surrounding area the previous night. 'To the watching infantry (most of whom were seeing their first barrage) it looked powerful and accurate enough to crush resistance,' wrote Marshall.[8]

Major von der Heydte described the artillery barrage as 'heavy', writing that it lasted thirty minutes and caused casualties among his men.[9] The defenders responded by putting up a heavy smokescreen of their own to the north of the town, leading the Americans to believe that they were withdrawing their outpost forces between the town and the advancing U.S. soldiers. Initially, German defensive fire was light. At around 0600 the first groups of American paratroopers and glidermen rose and began to move forward along the hedgerows and ditches. At Les Droueries, a small cluster of buildings located less than 1,000m to the north-east from the centre of St-Côme-du-Mont, the assault forces ran into the first body of Fallschirmjäger and Landsers, who appeared to be pulling out. 'The shelling had begun to rout the Germans out of their positions and when they saw infantry coming on, they tried to pull away completely,' wrote S.L.A. Marshall. The Screaming Eagles continued to advance, shooting at targets as they popped out from behind the hedgerows. 'The killing distance was anything from 50 yards down to a few feet,' recorded Marshall. Some thirty-five enemy soldiers were killed going through Les Droueries. The Americans overran most of the prepared enemy positions north-east of St-Côme-du-Mont. 'The German paratroopers who had come in the night before had extended the position by moving into a line of foxholes west of Les Droueries. They pulled out when the American advance started,' wrote Marshall. 'Instead of using the position as a pivot for manoeuvre, the enemy mobile troops tried to back away. In doing

---

8.   Marshall, *Night Drop*, pp. 324–325.
9.   von der Heydte, *B-839 A German Parachute Regiment in Normandy*, p. 14.

so they were destroyed in detail.'[10] Major von der Heydte personally witnessed the disintegration of the German line as first individual soldiers and then entire groups began withdrawing westward from St-Côme-du-Mont. The retreating soldiers belonged to the 1058th Infantry Regiment.[11]

Enemy artillery fire, however, soon stopped the 101st Airborne Division's attack in its tracks. The emboldened German defenders began to fight back fiercely in small groups from the hedgerows. Furthermore, the various U.S. battalions had become entangled with each other, draining all momentum from the American advance. As they were sorting themselves out, Hauptmann Horst Trebes' III Battalion counter-attacked from both sides of the St-Côme-du-Mont road. A paratrooper since 1938, Trebes was a veteran of Poland, Holland Crete, and Russia and a recipient of the Iron Cross First Class.[12] 'The action began with the crackle of rifles and Schmeissers fired from a distance with bullets flying erratically overhead,' recorded Marshall. 'The noise became steadily louder, the aim better, as the Germans worked their way forward along the hedgerows and ditches.' The battle now swung back and forth as the Fallschirmjäger counter-attacked six times in an effort to drive the Screaming Eagles off the St-Côme-du-Mont – Carentan road. 'Each attack was a little better organised than the one which preceded it. Each time the volume of fire built up more threateningly,' documented Marshall. 'Each time, the Germans closed to within one hedgerow of the ... forward line.' The Americans fought back, driving their attackers off time after time. At 1430 the Fallschirmjäger made their strongest attack yet, delivering the heaviest fire of the day against the American right flank. 'The fire became too hot. The right flank dissolved and fell back one hedgerow,' wrote Marshall. The cavalry now came to the rescue in the form of three American M-5 Stuart light tanks. They moved in frontally against the Germans, raking the hedgerows with their six .30 calibre machine guns as they advanced. The American paratroopers fell in behind the Stuarts, following them forward. Obergefreiter Fischer destroyed one vehicle with a Panzerfaust as it reached the battalion command post. The Fallschirmjäger, however, were forced to fall back in the face of the coordinated armour and infantry assault, leaving their dead and wounded

---

10. CMH, *Regiment Study Number 3. 506th Parachute Infantry Regiment in Normandy*, pp. 54–60.
11. Heydte, *B-839 A German Parachute Regiment in Normandy*, p. 14; Harrison, *Cross Channel Attack*, p. 357.
12. Kurowski, 'Horst Trebes', *Knight's Cross Holders of the Fallschirmjäger*, p. 249.

behind. But they were not yet defeated. They counter-attacked once more before the battle was over, killing a U.S. tank commander and three American officers, while leaving behind twenty more dead paratroopers.[13] German hopes of retaking ground east of the Douve River died with the 6th Parachute Regiment's failed attack.

With St-Côme-du-Mont lost, the 6th Parachute Regiment began to fall back to Carentan. To the regimental commander's dismay, engineers of the 91st Air-Landing Division prematurely destroyed the northern bridge over the Douve River to Carentan at 1400 hours, leaving the II and III Battalions of Parachute Regiment 6 stranded on the wrong side of the river. 'It was not easy for the regimental elements committed at St-Côme-du-Mont to withdraw across the Douve,' wrote von der Heydte. 'The majority of the men had to swim in order to reach the embankment of the Cherbourg–Carentan railway line. The Americans apparently did not realise until later that this withdrawal was taking place.'[14] While crossing flooded fields and marshes to reach safety, the II Battalion lost most of its heavy weapons.[15] The Fallschirmjäger, however, reached the city, where they occupied defensive positions without further interference from the Americans.

In all, the Screaming Eagles of the 101st Airborne Division suffered more than 300 casualties taking St-Côme-du-Mont, a large part of the attacking force. By 1630 the second major battle in two days between the Fallschirmjäger of the 6th Parachute Regiment and the Screaming Eagles ended with another American victory. But the cost had been heavy, with the U.S. paratroopers learning that their German counterparts were top notch soldiers to be reckoned with. Just as U.S. troops were moving into St-Côme-du-Mont, Field Marshal Rommel was meeting with his subordinates in the area. They agreed with him that the main factor in the Cotentin peninsula was that the American forces attacking to the west of Isigny had not yet established contact with the Carentan bridgehead. The 6th Parachute Regiment, which Rommel and his generals agreed had been fighting 'far better than expected', were ordered 'to defend Carentan to the last man.'[16] Major von der Heydte and his men had not seen the last of their nemesis – the Screaming Eagles of the 101st Airborne Division.

---

13. CMH, *Regiment Study Number 3. 506th Parachute Infantry Regiment in Normandy*, pp. 61–67.

14. Heydte, *B-839 A German Parachute Regiment in Normandy*, p. 15.

15. Griesser, *The Lions of Carentan*, p. 105.

16. CMH, *Regiment Study Number 3. 506th Parachute Infantry Regiment in Normandy*, pp. 68–70.

As the third day of intense ground fighting in France was ending, the Americans continued to expand their bridgeheads, pressing forward against stiffening resistance, while pouring more men, vehicles and supplies into Normandy. On 7 and 8 June, the 2nd Infantry Division, part of Major General Leonard Gerow's V Corps, landed at Omaha Beach, while the lead elements of the 90th Infantry Division arrived at Utah Beach to join Major General Lawton J. Collins' VII Corps. V Corps had the mission of driving south and capturing St-Lô by D+9. VII Corps was tasked with cutting across the Cotentin peninsula and securing the beachhead against an attack from the south, then driving north to take the port of Cherbourg by D+8. Aided by follow-on forces, the corps would then turn south, join up with V Corps and jointly drive to Avranches by D+20, establishing a line that ran from Avranches to Vire and Falaise and then north to include the road network east of Caen. The British were to take Vire and Falaise by D+20.

On the morning of 9 June U.S. Army Air Forces began using an airfield at St-Laurent-sur-Mer completed by USAAF engineer units the night before. It became the first operational American airfield in France and the first of 241 airfields the Americans would build in France, Belgium, Holland, Luxembourg, and Germany over the next fourteen months.[17] These airfields allowed the Allies to station fighters and fighter-bombers on the Continent and to apply their overwhelming air supremacy deeper into France. American P-47 Thunderbolts and P-51 Mustangs, along with British Spitfires and Typhoons, would hound the German Seventh Army and Hitler's Fallschirmjäger unmercifully during the 1944 Battle of France.

That same afternoon, Field Marshal Rommel met at the German Seventh Army headquarters with General Dollman and his staff. According to Max Pemsel, Rommel declared that the Americans must be denied the Cherbourg fortress and harbour and that the joining of the Allied beachheads must be prevented at all costs. 'He did not, as [Seventh] Army did, fear that the enemy would stage new air landings to speed up operations against Cherbourg,' recorded Pemsel, adding: 'The German Armed Forces High Command (OKW) expected another large-scale enemy landing along the Channel coast near the Fifteenth Army ... The Field Marshal closed on an optimistic note, expressing his belief that the counter-attack would succeed after all forces now in the

---

17. Wesley Frank Craven and James Lea Cate, *The Army Air Forces in World War II. Vol. 3, Europe: Argument to V-E Day (Office of Air Force History, 1983)*, pp. 562–563.

process of being brought up had arrived.'[18] As Rommel was meeting with the Seventh Army, Lieutenant General Omar Bradley was coming ashore at Omaha beach to join his First U.S. Army headquarters near Pointe Du Hoc. With him came the lead elements of the 2nd Armour Division. These new arrivals allowed the Americans to increase pressure on the Germans all along the First U.S Army sector. 'It was obvious that unless strong forces were brought up even the defensive battle could not be continued successfully,' warned Max Pemsel. 'The Army left no doubt about this in its report to Army Group.'[19]

By 10 June, the Americans had succeeded in merging their bridgeheads into a single lodgement 60km long and 10 to 12km deep, with Bayeux in Allied hands and Caen in German possession. 'The landing had succeeded, and the two beachheads were now connected,' reported the First U.S. Army. In the American sectors, soldiers of the U.S. VII Corps had forced Wehrmacht forces back across the Douve River. The Germans quickly regrouped in Carentan, a key road junction and key American objective. At the same time, the U.S. 29th Infantry Division attacked Isigny and completed the link-up between the two American beaches, then pushed south across the Isigny–Bayeux road to the high ground overlooking the Aure River. The situation for the German Seventh Army was bad and worsening. 'Enemy tanks were reported advancing from Isigny to St-Lô,' remembered Max Pemsel. 'The Vire bridges were in danger. The Commanding General of LXXXIV Corps therefore suggested to the (Seventh) Army that a defensive front be constructed behind the Vire River. Despite the lack of available reserves, (Seventh) Army did not consent, in the hope that II Parachute Corps, rapidly approaching from Brittany, would arrive in time.'[20]

On the day the beachheads were linked, the First U.S. Army forces in Normandy consisted of the V and VII Corps and eight powerful divisions arrayed along a 25-mile front. These included all or elements of the 1st, 2nd, 4th, 29th, and 90th Infantry Divisions; the 82nd and 101st Airborne Divisions; and the 2nd Armoured Division. The backbone of the American army at Normandy was its infantry divisions, which would bear the brunt of the fighting and dying in the bocage. Each was organised into three infantry regiments (with three battalions each) and an artillery regiment

18. Pemsel, *B-763 The Seventh Army in the Battle in Normandy*, p. 11.

19. Ibid, p. 10.

20. HQ First U.S. Army, *After Action Report 6 June 1944–1 August 1944, p. 11; Pemsel, B-763 The Seventh Army in the Battle in Normandy*, p. 10.

(with four artillery battalions), and support elements (engineer, medical, signal, ordnance, quartermaster, and reconnaissance). U.S. infantry divisions had a strength of 14,253 men, the majority in its twenty-seven rifle companies. Firepower consisted of twelve 155mm and fifty-four 105mm howitzers, fifty-four 81mm and ninety 60mm mortars, and 236 heavy (.50 cal.) and 157 light (.30 cal.) machine guns.[21] In comparison, the German 1944 type infantry division had a paper strength of approximately 12,800 personnel and was armed with eighteen 155mm and thirty-six 105mm howitzers, twenty-eight 120mm and forty-eight 81mm mortars and 566 heavy machine guns. The German division had over five times more submachine guns than its American counterpart (1,503 vs. 295).[22] On paper the Wehrmacht formations possessed fewer personnel, but more heavy artillery, anti-tank weapons (including the Panzerfaust) and proportionally greater firepower than its American equivalent. The drawback, of course, was that artillery and machine gun ammunition requirements were heavier and Allied air interdictions made it increasingly difficult for the Germans to move either their forces or supplies forward. The American infantry divisions and regiments possessed more infantrymen, allowing them to sustain greater casualties and remain in combat longer. They were also considerably more mobile than their Wehrmacht counterparts, enabling them to shift forces and move supplies to the fighting front faster. More importantly, U.S. infantry was backed by ever-growing numbers of artillery pieces available at the corps and army level, and even from the Allied navies, along with thousands of fighters, fighter-bombers, and bombers overhead eager to engage the Wehrmacht's ground forces. The latter, however, were reliant, for the most part, on clear weather.

The Germans proved unable, in the first days of the Normandy campaign, to either prevent the expansion of the Allied lodgement or the arrival of follow on forces. A planned counter-attack for 7 June by the I SS Panzer Corps' 12th SS Panzer Hitlerjugend and Panzer Lehr Divisions did not take place until two days later, due to heavy and continuous Allied air attacks.[23] To win some of the credit if the attack succeeded and no doubt to regain some of his lost prestige with the Führer, Hermann Göring proposed that his Fallschimjäger support a planned German

---

21. Shelby L. Stanton, *World War II Order of Battle* (New York: Galahad Books, 1984), pp. 8–10.
22. Harrison, *Cross-Channel Attack*, Appendix F 'Comparative Fire Power of the U.S. and German 1944 Type Infantry Divisions'.
23. Pemsel, *B-763 The Seventh Army in the Battle in Normandy*, p. 12.

counter-attack towards Bayeux with an airborne operation. 'The idea of committing strong parachute forces, especially in the planned counter-attack at Bayeux, originated with Reichsmarschall Göring,' remembered Generaloberst Alfred Jodl, the Chief of the Operations Staff of the OKW and the Deputy to Field Marshall Keitel, Chief of the Werhmacht High Command. 'I spoke against it and the Führer agreed with me.' According to Jodl:

> We did not have trained paratroopers. We would have had to pull out several regiments of the 2nd, 3rd, and 5th Parachute Divisions and train them in jumping at short notice. And these divisions were being used in ground combat and could not be spared at the moment when every last man was needed to implement the breakout of the bridgehead. I doubted that the necessary transport aircraft could be brought up and, even if they were, they would certainly fail in their mission of flying over the enemy front where even our fighter planes dared not venture. A night jump would have required a week's training and we didn't have the time.

Responding to his interrogators after the war as to why no paratroopers were brought in from the divisions in Italy, Jodl answered: 'The parachute divisions in Italy had no jump training either. It would have taken 14 days to 3 weeks to bring them up. We didn't have the time.'[24]

Jodl was being disingenuous with Hitler. Major von der Heydte's 6th Parachute Regiment and most of Schimpf's 3rd Parachute Division were jump qualified and could have jumped into Bayeux if so ordered and if the aircraft had been made available. It was the reason that von der Heydte had been ordered to move to Normandy with all his regiment's parachutes and jump equipment. But Jodl was correct in pointing out that the lack of German transport aircraft and, more importantly, Allied air supremacy over the beaches were major challenges that prevented the Luftwaffe from conducting this operation. Moreover, Hitler's paratroopers were needed on the ground to resist the growing American pressure all along the front and prevent a breakout from the beaches. When it was finally launched, the I SS Panzer Corps assault on the Allied left flank was defeated by the

---

24. Navy Department Library, *Oral History World War II Invasion of Normandy (1944)*, 'Generaloberst Alfred Jodl, German Army' at www.history.navy. mil/library/online/normandy_jodl.htm

British, forcing Panzer Group West on the defensive.[25] 'Events proved Rommel to be right,' wrote Generalleutnant Hans Speidel, Rommel's Chief of Staff at Army Group B:

> The enemy air supremacy and the flexible conduct of his air forces made it impossible to bring up panzer divisions from the interior of France to the coast in time and impossible to put them into action as a unit. The panzer divisions were broken up before they could reach the Normandy front. Had there been more panzer forces close to the front and could they have been used in the first three critical days after the initial landing, the circumstance would have been considerably different.[26]

Vizeadmiral Friedrich Ruge, Rommel's senior naval adviser recorded:

> After the counter-attack had fizzled out by 9 June, it was apparent that the enemy could hold firmly to his beachhead and unmolested, out of reach of German artillery, could continuously land reinforcements of men and material. The beachhead also had sufficient depth for the construction of fighter landing strips; in short, the beachhead was completely suited to serve as a starting point for a major land offensive. In addition, it extended far enough into the south-eastern half of the Cotentin Peninsula to promise an early capture of Cherbourg, the major port that, in the long run, the Allies needed despite an artificial harbour which, utilising prefabricated parts, they had swiftly erected at Arromanches.

Ruge went on to note: 'With the successful landings and creation of a beachhead suitable for the preparation of a large breakout operation, the enemy had reached his first and second objectives. It now became the main task of Army Group B to prevent the breakout, should the attempt to crush the beachhead fail.'[27] General der Infanterie Gunther Blumentritt was even more pessimistic: 'In a few days we had realised

---

25. Pemsel, *B-763 The Seventh Army in the Battle in Normandy*, p. 12.
26. Lieutenant General Hans Speidel, *Invasion 1944. The Normandy Campaign from the German Point of View* (New York: Paperback Library, 1968), p. 60.
27. Ruge, *Rommel in Normandy*, p. 174.

that our forces and means were not strong enough to reverse the situation.'[28]

As the 3rd Parachute Division was marching toward the fighting, the II Parachute Corps had been attached to General Marcks' LXXXIV Infantry Corps, arriving in its assigned area of operations 10 to 20km east of Avranches. In the meantime, motorised elements of the 3rd Parachute Division reached the area north-west of Brécey, located some 40km north-east of Avranches. Upon arriving near Coutances, General Meindl discovered that reports of Allied airborne landings in the region were erroneous. 'Thereafter I went to St-Lô and reported to General Marcks,' recalled Meindl. 'I was informed of the situation and received orders to advance as fast as possible, with all available elements, to the sector north-east of St-Lô and to check the enemy thrust toward St-Lô.'[29] The LXXXIV Infantry and II Parachute Corps had been caught flatfooted by the Allies, with the bulk of the latter's combat formations, including the 3rd Parachute Division, a considerable distance from St-Lô. In order to accomplish its mission, elements of Generalleutnant Dietrich Kraiss's 352nd Infantry Division, a regular Army division already engaged in intense combat, along with Generalmajor der Waffen-SS Werner Ostendorff's 17th SS Goetz von Berlichingen Panzergrenadier Division, were subordinated to the II Parachute Corps. Both formations would fight long and well with General Meindl and his II Parachute Corps, and they are worth examining in greater detail.

The 352nd Infantry Division had been activated by the German Seventh Army at St-Lô in November 1943 from a cadre of the 321st Infantry Division of Army Group Centre in Russia. By October 1943 the 321st Infantry had been decimated by the Red Army in its counteroffensive following the failure of Operation Zitadelle at Kursk. The 352nd Infantry was one of ten new Type 1944 infantry divisions created in the winter of 1943, utilising cadres from divisions disbanded on the Eastern Front. Due to heavy troop losses in Russia by the fall of 1943, the Third Reich had almost exhausted its manpower base and was badly in need of fresh divisions for Russia, the Balkans, and even Europe. The solution was to reduce the size of the standard division and to compensate for this reduction with an increase in firepower. As a result, the Infantry Division

---

28. General der Infanterie Guenther Blumentritt, *MS # B-283 Evaluation of German Command and Troops* (U.S. Army Historical Division, 25 March 1966), p. 66.
29. Meindl, *B-401 II Parachute Corps*, p. 13.

Type 1944 was created. This new formation consisted of three regiments (2,008 men each) of two battalions each. The previous division model had consisted of three infantry regiments (of 3,240 men each) of three battalions each for a total manpower strength of approximately 17,200 officers and enlisted men. In comparison, the manpower strength of the new division type was approximately 12,000 men, of which only 6,800 were combat troops, including 1,500 Hiwis. The ten new divisions were to be fleshed out with recruits born in 1926 and conscripted in November 1943. They were to be combat ready by May 1944. Initially it was planned that these divisions would then be sent to the Eastern Front.[30] From the first, however, the raising, equipping, and training of ten new infantry divisions, albeit of reduced size, proved too much for the German Army's overstrained supply services.

By the end of January 1944, the 352nd Infantry Division had only four combat-ready infantry battalions and four artillery batteries, and the unit did not establish its fourteen companies until February. Once organised they were trained as anti-tank companies for the Eastern Front. 'The replacements were mostly teenagers and were physically unfit for all but limited military duty,' recorded Oberstleutnant Ziegelmann, the division's new chief of staff. Ironically, Ziegelmann had previously served as the Chief Quartermaster (responsible for all classes of supply) for the German Army High Command. He was intimately familiar with all aspects of procurement issues. Although the actual deployment date and location for the division remained uncertain, the unit's officers and men generally assumed that they would be sent to the Eastern Front sometime after 1 March 1944. As a result, training focused on combat operations against the Red Army. Equipping of the new formation fell on Ziegelmann, who assessed that on 1 May 1944 half the officers were inexperienced and a third of the sergeants' billets were unfilled due to a lack of competent personnel.[31]

By 6 June 1944, the 352nd Infantry Division had a strength of 12,734 men, making it the second largest standard infantry division in Normandy.[32] It was composed of the 914th, 915th and 916th Infantry Regiments, the

---

30. Oberstleutnant Fritz Zieglemann, *MS # B-432 History of the 352 Infantry Division* (U.S. Army Historical Division, undated).
31. Ibid.
32. Zetterling, 'Table 4.1 Strength of German Divisions in OB West Area at the Beginning of June', *Normandy 1944*, p. 28. Only the 353rd Infantry Division, with 13,300 men, was larger than the 352nd.

352nd Artillery Regiment, the 352nd Anti-Tank Battalion, the 352nd Engineer Battalion and the 352nd Fusilier Battalion, a reconnaissance formation. The last was equipped with sixty light machine guns, three heavy machine guns and twelve 80mm mortars, the same armament provided to each of the infantry battalions. The infantry gun companies in the 914th and 915 Infantry Regiments were equipped with two 150mm and six 75mm howitzers, while that of the 916th Infantry Regiment was equipped with only two 150mm and two 75mm howitzers. The anti-tank companies in each of the infantry regiments were equipped with three 75mm anti-tank guns. The first nine batteries of the artillery regiment each had four 105mm howitzers, while the last three were equipped with four 150mm howitzers. None of the batteries were motorised and there was only a single basic load of artillery ammunition available, enough for a single day's fighting. Still, this required the division to move 300 tons of ammunition. Most of the 352nd Infantry Division's recruits were between eighteen and nineteen years old, young men from farming communities in Germany.[33]

The division suffered from a lack of training and ammunition. Prior to March 1944 its soldiers were given only three opportunities to fire their weapons and had thrown only two hand grenades. Due to the shortage of fuel, training of vehicle drivers lagged. Although the tempo of training improved after March it was hampered by the amount of time the unit's soldiers spent working on the Atlantic Wall. On average, a German soldier spent nine hours on such work each day, while training for only three hours.[34] In addition to training to repel the imminent Allied invasion, the division was also tasked, in accordance with Field Marshal Rommel's orders, with improving the beach defences along their part of the coast, building and maintaining defensive positions from the coast inland all the way down to St-Lô, and providing security for the entire region. Kraiss and his men were responsible for all construction and security in a sector 30km long and 25km deep – an impossible task for 13,000 men.[35] Rommel was

33. George Nafziger, '352nd Infantry Division', *The German Order of Battle. Infantry in World War II* (Greenhill Books, 2000), p. 309. Zetterling, '352. Infanterie-Division', *Normandy 1944*, pp. 277–278; Vince Milano and Bruce Conner, *Normandiefront: D-Day to Saint-Lô Through German Eyes* (The History Press, 2012), p. 49.

34. Zetterling, '352. Infanterie-Division', *Normandy 1944*, pp. 277–278; Milano and Conner, *Normandiefront*, p. 14.

35. Milano and Conner, *Normandiefront*, p. 20.

no less hesitant to issue unrealistic orders to his units than Adolf Hitler. Finally, to make matters worse, once trained, elements of the division, along with their equipment, weapons and ammunition, were sent to the Eastern Front, which remained the Wehrmacht's priority. Replacement personnel, weapons and ammunition were slow to arrive in France.

Although First U.S. Army intelligence reports had indicated that the 352nd Infantry Division was near St-Lô on the eve of the invasion, it had deployed elements of the 916th Infantry Regiment, reinforced with one battalion from the 716th Infantry Division, behind the American landing beaches at Omaha beach prior to the Allied landings. The 352nd Infantry Division's 914th Infantry Regiment was deployed around Isigny, while the 915th Infantry Regiment was located in reserve south-east of Bayeux.[36] From their fighting positions near the beaches, General Kraiss's Grenadiers poured a storm of accurate and devastating artillery, mortar, and machine gun fire into the lead elements of the V Corps' 1st and 29th Infantry Divisions, inflicting such heavy casualties that it prompted General Bradley to consider cancelling the assault there altogether and moving the remainder of the invasion force to Utah beach. Only the last-minute transfer of units of the division to the east, where the British appeared a greater threat than the apparently defeated Americans, saved U.S. invasion forces at Omaha beach from further slaughter and possible annihilation. As a result, the Americans called the 352nd Infantry Division, whom they would encounter while fighting Eugen Meindl's II Parachute Corps for the next several weeks, 'highly disciplined'.[37]

The 352nd's performance on the first day of the invasion showed what the German defenders were capable of, despite their many deficiencies, if properly led, trained, equipped, and supplied. The 916th Infantry Regiment, however, had paid the price for holding its ground against overwhelming odds. By 7 June it had suffered heavy losses and, according to its chief of staff, was 'severely weakened physically and morally'.[38] According to Ziegelmann, by the evening of 8 June the division could no longer be considered 'a complete infantry division' due to its heavy losses. The 352nd had lost some 2,000 men, along with more than two batteries of artillery. 'In the final analysis, it was due to the courage and the still prevailing endurance of the German infantry soldier that on 8 June it had been possible

36. Zetterling, '352. Infanterie Division', *Normandy 1944*, p. 278.
37. Centre of Military History, *The U.S. Army Campaigns of World War II. Normandy* (Washington, D.C; 1994), pp. 28–29.
38. Ziegelmann, *B-433 352nd Infantry Division (7 June 1944)*, p. 7.

to prevent a breakthrough,' recorded Ziegelman, 'especially to the south, despite the manyfold superiority of the enemy in every respect.' By 9 June the division was fighting with 2,700 men and twenty-six light and heavy artillery pieces.[39] Nonetheless, it held a sector 45km wide against 'weak' attacks from an American force that its chief of staff estimated at 5,000 infantry supported by at least forty-eight pieces of artillery, forty tanks and thirty-six Allied fighter-bombers overhead continuously.[40]

Ziegelmann and his officers noticed an increased confidence in the U.S. soldiers facing them, especially the men of the 29th Infantry Division and their supporting armour battalion. Still, he observed: 'We had the feeling that the enemy divisions had not learned to work together properly as yet and that liaison between them was poor. Had the thrust of the 29th Infantry Division been continued further in an easterly direction, it would have resulted in the entire front of the 352nd Infantry Division – which was thin in any case – being rolled up!'[41] By 10 June the division's leadership was doubtful that they could prevent an American breakthrough in the direction of St-Lô, noting: 'It was far too sorely in need of rest and reinforcements.' That day General Kraiss's grenadiers received 'honourable mention' as 'the premier division' in the German High Command's daily communiqué.[42]

The 17th SS Panzergrenadier Division Götz von Berlichingen had begun forming in November 1943 with detachments from the 10th SS Panzer Division and was not yet fully combat ready when the invasion occurred. The unit was composed of the 17th SS Panzer Battalion (with three assault gun companies), the 37th and 38th SS Motorised Infantry Regiments (each with three infantry battalions, a self-propelled infantry gun company, an anti-aircraft battery, a reconnaissance company, and an engineer company), the 17th SS Artillery Regiment (with three artillery battalions of three batteries each), the 17th SS Armoured Reconnaissance Battalion (with five companies) the 17th SS Self-Propelled Anti-Tank battalion (with three companies), the 17th SS Anti-Aircraft Battalion (motorised) (with three 88mm and one 37mm batteries) and the 17th SS

---

39. Ziegelmann, *B-434 352nd Infantry Division. The Fighting on 8 June 1944*, pp. 9–10.
40. Ziegelmann, *B-435 352nd Infantry Division. An Account of the Fighting on 9 June 1944*, p. 9.
41. Ibid, p. 7.
42. Ziegelmann, *B-436 352nd Infantry Division. The Fighting on 10 June 1944*, p. 10.

Engineer Battalion (motorised). Although impressive in manpower, with more than 17,300 men, even this elite formation suffered from a severe shortage of 233 officers and 1,541 non-commissioned officers, although it did have a surplus of 741 enlisted personnel, the equivalent of an extra battalion. The shortage of trained leaders was a major deficiency for this elite SS formation. Other weaknesses included a lack of motor vehicles, along with a shortage of machine guns, 75mm artillery pieces, and Panzerfaust anti-tank weapons, a problem that affected most divisions in Normandy. Due to its late formation the unit was not combat ready when the Allies landed in Normandy. On 1 June it reported that one-third of the men had twenty-two weeks of training and the remainder had twenty-five weeks.[43]

Lack of transport meant that the division could not be moved immediately to Normandy following the Allied invasion. The most that could be accomplished on 6 June was route reconnaissance of all roads to Normandy by elements of the division. The following day the first units began to move. The 17th SS Armoured Reconnaissance Battalion reached Balleroy, halfway between St-Lô and Bayeux, by 8 June, despite being subjected to intense attacks by Allied fighter-bombers. These attacks caused only slight losses. Four of the division's six infantry battalions also began the march to Normandy on 7 June. The fact that they were not fully motorised suggests that, like the 3rd Parachute Division, they used a combination of available motor vehicles and foot marches to reach their destinations. The remaining two battalions used bicycles. The 2nd Company, 17th SS Flak Battalion (with its 88mm anti-aircraft guns, ideal in the anti-tank role) also began moving north on 7 June, while the division's self-propelled assault guns were loaded on trains. The armoured fighting vehicles were unloaded on 9 June between Montreuil and Fleche and moved toward Mayenne. On 10 June the 17th SS Armoured Reconnaissance Battalion went into action, reinforcing the weakly held 352nd Infantry Division sector, while the advanced elements of the 37th SS Panzergrenadier Regiment reached La Chapelle (south-east of St-Lô).[44] Despite the immense Allied air superiority, the division was still able to move to Normandy and get into battle with relatively few

43. Zetterling, '17. SS Panzer-Grenadier-Division 'Gotz von Berlichingen', *Normandy 1944*, p. 363; Nafziger, '17th SS Panzergrenadier Division "Gotz von Berlichingen"', *The German Order of Battle. Waffen SS and Other Units in World War II* (De Capo Press, 2000), pp. 115–117.
44. Zetterling, '17. SS Panzer-Grenadier-Division "Götz von Berlichingen"', *Normandy 1944*, pp. 365–366.

losses. Its arrival on the battlefield allowed the 352nd Infantry Division to hold the line pending the arrival of the II Parachute Corp's Fallschirmjäger formations.

In the meantime, the advanced elements of the 3rd Parachute Division were finally reaching the battlefield. Meindl remembered:

> When we arrived on 8–9 June, the reconnaissance battalion of the 17th SS Panzergrenadier Division was already engaged just north and north-east of Foret de Cerisy. The 352nd Infantry Division was still in the vicinity of St-Clair with its west flank on the Vire. As I considered St-Lô to be the most important objective for the enemy, I moved the arriving elements of the 3rd Parachute Division between the 17th Panzergrenadier Division's reconnaissance battalion and the 352nd Infantry Division. The 3rd Parachute Division was to constitute the backbone of my defence. It was very important to us to bring up the 3rd Parachute Division and also the remainder of the 17th SS Panzergrenadier Division as quickly as possible, for every day gained was precious. I intended to attack whatever enemy units had landed with these two divisions as soon as they arrived.[45]

General Schimpf recorded:

> When the advanced group under the command of Major Becker had reached the region of Berigny on both sides of the St-Lô–Bayeux roads on 10 June and probed into the Cerisy Forest, they only encountered weak enemy security detachments there, I was of the opinion that possessing the forest was of decisive importance for the future conduct of the battle, especially for the planned attack. Therefore, I decided to thrust forward on the next afternoon to the forest of Cerisy, together with the reconnaissance battalion of the 17th SS Panzergrenadier division, which had already arrived on my right ... On the left, contact with the 352nd Infantry Division was maintained solely by liaison patrols.[46]

Schimpf's intent was to attack along both sides of the St-Lô–Bayeux road through the forest. First, however, he awaited the arrival of the remainder

---

45. Meindl, B-401 II Parachute Corps, pp. 13–14.
46. Schimpf, *B-020a Normandy Campaign*, p. 4, p. 14.

of his 3rd Parachute Division. His attack, however, was stillborn. 'After having informed the Command General of the II Parachute Corps of my intention, I was forbidden to thrust into the Forest of Cerisy because a considerable portion of the 352nd Infantry Division sector had been assigned to me, due to the heavy losses this division had suffered during the first few days of the invasion.'[47] The 352nd had, by this time, suffered 2,000 casualties.[48] 'As a result my front became a mere line of combat outposts,' recalled Schimpf. 'The bulk of the division was still on the march from Brittany. I set the point of main effort north of Bérigny, where the greatest danger of an enemy attack lay. If the Americans, at that time, had launched an energetic attack from the Forest of Cerisy, St-Lô would have fallen then already and would not have been held for another whole month.'[49]

A key road junction where seven roads came together, U.S. possession of St-Lô would rupture the thin German line and allow the Americans to move their forces in almost any direction. Schimpf wrote:

> The elements of the Division already available (totaling the strength of a reinforced regiment) occupied the sector of St-Germain-d'Elle–Bérigny–Couvains. Due to the lack of artillery, the bulk of the flak battalion had to be committed as an anti-tank battle group, in some cases directly on the front line. The situation was extremely critical, also because contact with the neighbouring divisions was very loose, maintained by liaison reconnaissance patrols. The attempt to tighten the contact on the right by advancing the right wing of the division further toward the north-east did not succeed on account of a heavy enemy counter-attack against and out of La Vacquerie.[50]

A successful attack by Meindl and his command from the Cerisy Forest northward would have allowed the II Parachute Corps to drive a wedge between the two American corps and to reach the beachheads some 8 miles away. Such an attack would have been disastrous for U.S. forces. Route 172, running north-east from St-Lô to Bayeux, provided an ideal axis of advance for an attack by Wehrmacht forces to split the American

---

47. Schimpf, *B-541 3rd Parachute Division*, p. 14.
48. Zetterling, '352. Infanterie-Division', *Normandy 1944*, p. 278.
49. Schimpf, *B-541 3rd Parachute Division*, p. 14.
50. Ibid.

and the British beaches. The forest itself, running for approximately 5 miles along the road from Isigny to north of Balleroy, was key terrain for the Germans, providing ideal cover and concealment for their forces as they massed for the expected attack. The attack, however, would have to wait as the II Parachute Corps was needed elsewhere to stem a more threatening American advance. The cancellation was fortuitous for the 3rd Parachute Division. The Americans had anticipated just such a move and positioned the 1st Infantry and 2nd Armoured Divisions on the flanks of the forest. Furthermore, neither Meindl nor his men had yet been at the receiving end of the large-calibre guns of the Allied fleets or the swarms of fighter-bombers that circled menacingly overhead. This made the likelihood a successful offensive against the American and British beachheads, especially without robust support from the Luftwaffe, extremely doubtful. While Meindl was focusing on the Cerisy Forest, the Americans were preparing to attack Carentan.

General Kurt Student inspecting his Fallschirmjäger early in the war.
Student was the creator of Germany's Fallschirmjäger and Commander
of the First Parachute Army in Normandy. Hitler's paratroopers were
the Third Reich's spear and shield during the Second World War. In the
early years of the conflict they were in the vanguard of Nazi Germany's
offensive strategy. After Germany's 'disastrous victory' at Crete, where
they suffered devastating losses, they were used in a ground defensive
role, earning a reputation as skilled, tenacious and fanatical defenders
committed to preventing the Allies from ever reaching the Third Reich.
(Author's Collection)

**Fallschirmjäger in paratrooper
helmet and smock.** Some 160,000
Luftwaffe and German Army
personnel were serving on the
staffs and in the ranks of the First
Parachute Army, II Parachute
Corps, and the 2nd, 3rd, 5th
and 6th Parachute Divisions in
Normandy. Approximately 50,000
were Fallschrimjager, young and
old, novices and veterans, assigned
to the combat parachute divisions
and regiments that would bear the
brunt of the fighting. (Author's
Collection)

Luftwaffe Parachutists Badge (Fallschrimschützenabzeichen). This badge, with a gilt eagle diving across a silvered acorn and oakleaf wreath, was awarded to each recruit after six successful jumps. Those entitled to wear it, jealously preserved it, especially when the later, so-called 'Fallschirmjäger' units, comprised largely of personnel who had never made a single jump, were being formed. (Author's Collection)

Field Marshal Erwin Rommel, Commander of German Army Group B, responsible for the defence of northern France, visited Eugen Meindl's II Parachute Corps HQ several times during the Normandy campaign. Fortunately for the Allies, Hitler's field marshal best qualified to react rapidly and energetically to the Normandy invasion was not with his troops when the invasion began. He was visiting his wife in Germany on her fiftieth birthday. (Author's Collection)

Generalleutnant Hermann Bernhard Ramcke, Commander of the 2nd Parachute Division at Brest. By the end of July 1944, the 2nd Parachute Division was understrength and lacking many major weapons systems. The division would fight the Americans short four of its nine parachute infantry battalions and most of its heavy weapons as well as bereft of many of its combat-seasoned paratroopers. However, the walls and artillery of Fortress Brest would make up for some of these deficiencies. (Author's Collection)

General Hermann Ramcke with General Kurt Student, First Parachute Army. A fanatical, diehard Nazi, hardcore anti-Semite, and blatant racist, Ramcke was nonetheless a legendary Fallschirmjäger and considered one of the bravest German soldiers of the war. The parachute division commander was often at the forefront of the fighting in Brest. (Author's Collection)

Studio photo of a German paratrooper in full jump kit with jump smock, black leather gauntlets, MP-40 submachine gun, and Zeiss binoculars. Not visible are his MP-40 magazine pouches, leather map case, canvas-covered water bottle and drinking cup, external knee pads, Luger holster with pistol, and side-lacing jump boots. (Author's Collection)

Aerial reconnaissance photos of a picturesque French town in Normandy untouched by combat. The Normandy campaign left many French cities, towns, and villages in ruins. (U.S. Army)

Aerial View of Normandy on 12 June 1944. Note the myriad of hedgerows. Unlike the Fallschirmjäger, who had trained to take full advantage of the unique French terrain in Normandy, the United States Army was unprepared for combat in the hedgerows and had to adapt quickly. (U.S. Air Force)

General Eugen Meindl with Field Marshal Erwin Rommel in Normandy. A veteran of the Wehrmacht's campaigns in Scandinavia, Russia, and Crete, Meindl cared deeply for his soldiers, trained them hard, and squeezed the very best performance from the commanders and paratroopers of the II Parachute Corps. (Author's Collection)

Major Friedrich August Freiherr von der Heydte, Commander of the 6th Parachute Regiment in Normandy. Considered the best German parachute regiment in France, the 'Lions of Carentan' were the first of Hitler's paratroopers to battle American forces landing in Normandy. The unit's repeated clashes with the U.S. Army's 101st 'Screaming Eagles' Airborne Division left its commander traumatised and the regiment debilitated. (Author's Collection)

Generalleutnant Richard Schimpf, Commander of the 3rd Parachute Division in Normandy. A veritable powerhouse, Schimpf's division was the largest and most elite German infantry formation in Normandy. It was well trained and equipped, and one of the few Wehrmacht units rated as capable of offensive operations. According to a First U.S. Army intelligence report:'The ranks of the 3rd Fallschirmjäger Division looked upon their commander… as a god.'(Author's Collection)

Generalleutnant Gustav Wilke, Commander of the 5th Parachute Division in Normandy. Although one of the Luftwaffe's newest and least capable formations, the 5th Parachute Division would acquit itself well at Hill 122 and Monte Castre. Its accomplishments and sacrifices, however, have never been truly recognised. (Author's Collection)

Generalleutnant Rudiger von Heyking, Commander of the 6th Parachute Division in France 1944. This ill-fated formation, which was still in the process of forming (and sending a regiment to the Eastern Front) when the Allies landed in France, managed to send a single kampfgruppe to bolster German defences against General George Patton's U.S. Third Army. It was quickly overrun and annihilated.(Author's Collection)

Fallschirmjäger of the 6th Parachute Regiment move ammunition on a trolley through the bocage. Trolleys for moving ammunition, food, and other supplies were ideal for the rough terrain of Normandy. (Courtesy Volker Griesser)

U.S. Army L-5 light aircraft, March 1944. The eyes of American commanders, these aircraft were used to spot and call in artillery on Wehrmacht ground troops. Highly manoeuvrable, they could loiter for hours above the battlefield. (U.S. Army Signal Corps)

Panzer IVs, the workhorses of the Panzerwaffe, provided stellar support to Hitler's paratroopers in Normandy. The elite Fallschrimjager were often paired with equally elite SS panzer formations. (Author's Collection)

North American P-51 Mustang over France. American fighter-bombers, which dominated the skies over Normandy, were the terror of Wehrmacht ground troops, attacking anything that moved on the ground, even individual vehicles and soldiers. (U.S. Air Force)

GIs en route to Normandy. To the Germans, each day seemed to bring another American infantry division to Normandy. In all, thirteen U.S. infantry divisions fought in the Normandy campaign. Between D-Day and 21 August, the Allies landed 2,052,299 men in northern France. (U.S. Army Signal Corps)

Me 109 and Fw 190. The Luftwaffe's iconic fighters were mostly absent from the Normandy campaign. Those brave enough to make an appearance were quickly overwhelmed by swarms of Allied fighters. (Author's Collection)

American infantrymen found the bocage bewildering. They suffered heavy losses to the well-emplaced and camouflaged Germans before mastering the challenges of hedgerow fighting. (U.S. Army)

A weary paratrooper of the 6th Parachute Regiment in Normandy. Hitler's paratroopers in France fought without respite and often short of ammunition and food. (Courtesy Volker Griesser)

Major von der Heydte with the Commander of the 17th SS Panzergrenadier Division General Ostendorff. The 17th SS was another new Wehrmacht formation. It had been formed the previous spring and had little combat experience. Major Von der Heydte's Fallschirmjäger were not impressed with their SS colleagues. The feeling was mutual. Ostendorff blamed von der Heydte for the German loss of Carentan. (Courtesy Mark Reardon)

Fallschirmjäger of the 6th Parachute Regiment with a captured U.S. Army jeep and trailer. Chronically short of food, weapons, and transport, German paratroopers put captured Allied equipment to good use. (Courtesy Volker Griesser)

An M-4 Sherman tank drives off an LST. Every day saw the arrival of more American tanks and artillery to support the U.S. infantry divisions fighting in Normandy. Five U.S. armoured divisions participated in the Normandy campaign. In all, the Americans employed more than 4,200 tanks during the campaign. (U.S. Army)

A StuG III with its crew. Low silhouette, heavily armoured and armed assault guns such as these provided the Fallschirmjäger with lethal direct fire support against American tanks. (Author's Collection)

German paratrooper wearing the Knight's Cross and Iron Cross First Class. This paratrooper is wearing the splinter-camouflaged jump smock. The number of Knight's Crosses awarded to Hitler's Fallschrimjager is testimony to their skill and tenacity in resisting the American invasion of France. (Author's Collection)

American paratroopers fought Hitler's Fallschirmjäger to a standstill. The U.S. 82nd and 101st Airborne Divisions led the U.S, invasion of the Cotentin Peninsula. The American paratroopers were rated by their Fallschirmjäger opponents as the best American troops they battled. (Author's Collection)

Fallschirmjäger of the 6th Parachute Regiment move into position during the fighting for Carentan. Frequent changes of position and camouflage were the German key to survival on the Normandy battlefield. The Wehrmacht quickly discovered that the U.S. Army was well-trained in combat in urban terrain. At Carentan, American infantry, armour, and artillery, fighting as a team, quickly overwhelmed the Fallschirmjäger and SS troops.(Courtesy Steven Zaloga)

An American M7 'Priest' 105mm Howitzer Motor Carriage advances through Carentan. Developed to support armour operations, the M7 used the M4 Sherman tank chassis. The M7 received its nickname from the pulpit-style cupola fixture.(U.S. Army)

Chapter 4

6th Parachute Regiment at Carentan

The battle of Carentan was one of the most important clashes of the Normandy campaign. A city with a population of 4,000 in 1944, it is located along the Douve River, 10 miles from where it enters the Atlantic. Carentan was connected to the Douve by a short stretch of canal. The buildings in the town were all old and strongly built of stone, including the church tower from which Major von der Heydte could see the sea and the invasion beaches. An excellent road and railway network ran through the area. Several paved roads intersected the city, including the main road to Cherbourg in the north. The entire area, except for the city and to the south-west, was swampy and crisscrossed by drainage ditches, streams and canals. Nowhere did the terrain rise above 30m.[1] German possession of the vital crossroads allowed the Seventh Army to move reinforcements unhindered up to the battle front from Coutances and Périers to the south-west, and to attack either Ste-Mère-Église, located 8 miles to the north-west, or Isigny, 7 miles to the north-east. The Americans had to seize this key road junction to facilitate the link-up of the Omaha and Utah beaches.

The battle of Carentan would once again pit Fallschirmjäger against Screaming Eagles. 'Up to the morning of 8 June 1944, at least the regiment's non-commissioned officers and other enlisted men still hoped that it would be possible to drive back into the sea the Americans who had landed and to mop up the bridgehead north of the Vire estuary,' wrote Major von der

---

1. Captain Ronald C. Speirs, Chapter 12. 'The Operations of the 2nd Platoon, Company D, 506th Parachute Infantry (101st Airborne Division) in the Vicinity of Carentan, France, 11–13 June 1944', in Gawne, *Lessons Learned in Combat: Normandy Paratroopers*, Kindle.

Heydte. 'After the withdrawal behind the Oure even the private soldier knew that the first battle of the invasion had been lost by the Germans. The morning of 8 June marked the beginning of the second catastrophic act of the drama in Normandy for the 6th Parachute Regiment: the battle for Carentan.'[2] The Americans had the measure of their Fallschirmjäger opponents and knew the fight for the city would be a tough one: 'They attacked strongly when ordered and were armed with a high percentage of automatic weapons,' reported one 101st Airborne Division platoon leader. 'They wore special camouflage suits and paratrooper helmets. Their morale seemed good.' The U.S. paratroopers believed that one major reason that the morale of the 6th Parachute Regiment was so high was that 'fighting the Americans was preferable to fighting both the Russians and the cold weather.'[3]

Field Marshal Rommel considered the defence of Carentan vital not only to prevent the junction of the two American beachheads, but also to forestall any attempts by First U.S. Army to cut across the Cotentin peninsula by a drive south-west across the Vire River toward Lessay and Périers to the south-west of Carentan. As a result, he had ordered the 6th Parachute Regiment, already in the city, reinforced with two Ost battalions and the remnants of the defenders of Isigny. Rommel committed General Meindl's II Parachute Corps, en route from Brittany, to further counter the American threat. Under Meindl, General Ostendorff and his 17th SS-Panzergrenadier Division were assigned the primary mission of blocking an Allied thrust from Carentan. Meindl ordered Ostendorff to occupy positions south-west of Carentan and be prepared to counter-attack south of the city. These plans, however, were frustrated by the difficulty of moving the II Parachute Corps forward to the battlefront. On 8 June, the movement of Meindl's troops was delayed by Allied air attacks and sabotage by the French Resistance. Ostendorff's division was forced by continuous and heavy air attacks on the railways to make most of its march northward by road. A shortage of fuel further delayed the move. As a result, the advanced elements of Ostendorff's panzergrenadiers did not reach their assigned areas south-west of Carentan until 11 June.[4]

The first phase of the battle of Carentan, the Battle of St-Côme-du-Mont, had already been fought, with elements of four parachute infantry and

2. von der Heydte, *B-839 A German Parachute Regiment in Normandy*, p. 15.
3. Speirs, Chapter 12. 'Personal Experience of a 506th Rifle Platoon Leader', in Gawne, *Lessons Learned in Combat: Normandy Paratroopers*, Kindle.
4. Harrison, *Cross Channel Attack*, p. 360.

glider regiments of the 101st Airborne Division, supported by light tanks, taking the town on 8 June and driving the remaining German defenders of the 91st Air-Landing Division and 6th Parachute Regiment across the Douve River and into Carentan. By 2200 hours that night the 101st Airborne Division had completed all the missions initially assigned to it in Operation Overlord and was preparing for its attack on Carentan. The Screaming Eagles assembled three regiments along the Douve River with a fourth in reserve near Vierville. The 502nd PIR was on the German left flank from the junction of the Douve and Merderet Rivers to Houesville. The 506th PIR was in the centre astride the St-Côme-du-Mont–Carentan road. The 327th GIR was on the right flank at La Barquette and Le Port. The 501st PIR was in reserve. The scheme of the attack had been worked out in England.[5]

The weakened 6th Parachute Regiment defended Carentan at the two most likely points of the American main effort – the III Battalion guarded the road from St-Côme-du-Mont in the north-west and II Battalion the road from Le Port, in the north-eastern edge of the city. The Fallschirmjäger were supported by a battalion of the 709th Infantry Division, along with the two Ost battalions (consisting of Russians), elements of the 1058th Infantry Regiment, and fragments of various units that had withdrawn from the Isigny area. Considering these formations unreliable, Major von der Heydte posted the bulk of them on the eastern edge of Carentan, a move he would later regret. He and his Fallschirmjäger would bear the brunt of the American attack.[6] In light of the importance of the city to the Germans, Wehrmacht forces were amazingly ill prepared for a prolonged fight. According to von der Heydte, the defenders of Carentan suffered from three major disadvantages. The first was the lack of artillery, except for a single battery of 88mm guns. The second was 'the slow but steady giving way' of the units on either side of the 6th Parachute Regiment, forcing the Fallschirmjäger to cover an expanding defensive sector. The third was the shortage of ammunition, especially for the infantry heavy weapons, which were the foundation of the defence. 'Originally, the regiment had been instructed to obtain its ammunition from an ammunition distributing point where no ammunition had as yet been stored,' recorded the 6th Parachute Regiment's commander. 'Then it was

---

5.   Ibid, p. 357.
6.   von der Heydte, *B-839 A German Parachute Regiment in Normandy*, pp. 15–16; Harrison, *Cross Channel Attack*, p. 357 identifies elements of the 1058th Infantry Regiment at Carentan.

assigned one which, it turned out, had been destroyed in an enemy air raid; and finally, it had to depend on an ammunition point which, because the bridges leading to it had become impassable, could be reached only by taking long detours.'[7] Despite these deficiencies, von der Heydte and his men had been ordered to hold Carentan.

The attackers faced equally daunting challenges in taking the city. They would have to advance along the elevated road between St-Côme-du-Mont and Carentan that crossed a wide stretch of marsh just before entering the city. For more than half a mile the route was a coverless defile. However, a reconnaissance of the four bridges leading to Carentan along a single road found only one bridge heavily defended and another demolished. Why the Germans had failed to destroy all four bridges was a mystery to the commanders of the 101st Airborne Division. Senior Wehrmacht officers probably anticipated that they would need the crossing intact for a major counter-attack against the American bridgehead. The status of the bridges and an aerial reconnaissance of Carentan led most of the commanders of the Screaming Eagles to believe that the city was lightly defended. A 101st Airborne Division G-2 intelligence assessment, estimating that there was only a battalion of German troops in the city, buttressed this belief.[8] Having tangled twice with the Fallschirmjäger of 6th Parachute Regiment, the Screaming Eagles didn't underestimate their opponents. 'The troops of the Fallschirmjäger-Regiment 6 and 17. SS-Panzergrenadier-Division were highly trained and highly disciplined,' remembered Sergeant Ed Shanes of Easy Company, 'unlike some of the enemy soldiers previously encountered by the 101st Airborne Division.'[9]

The Screaming Eagles planned on making a two-pronged attack across the causeway and through the town of Brévands in the north-east to envelop the city. The final plan called for the 327th Glider Infantry to make the main effort, crossing the Douve near Brévands to clear the area between Carentan and Isigny and join the V Corps near the crossing over the Vire River. Since the key to possession of this area was Carentan, the 327th planned to use the bulk of its force to attack the city from the east. At the same time, the 502nd Parachute Infantry would cross the causeway over the Douve River north-west of Carentan, bypass the city on the west,

7. von der Heydte, *B-839 A German Parachute Regiment in Normandy*, pp. 16–17.
8. CMH, *Regimental Study No. 1. The Carentan Causeway Fight*, pp. 1–3, 6.
9. Ian Gardner, *Airborne. The Combat Story of Ed Shames of Easy Company* (Osprey Publishing, 2015), Chapter 4. 'The River Runs Red', Kindle.

and seize Hill 30. To secure Carentan after its capture, the 101st Airborne Division had the additional mission of occupying the high ground along the railway west of the city as far as the Prairies Marécageuses.[10]

The 327th Glider Infantry started crossing the mouth of the Douve at 0145 on 9 June, but suffered heavy losses from friendly mortar fire, slowing its attack. However, all three battalions of the regiment were across by the following day. The glider infantrymen met units of V Corps east of Carentan in the form of the 29th Infantry Division's 29th Reconnaissance Troop and Company K of the 175th Infantry Regiment. At 0145 the next morning the 3rd Battalion, 502nd Parachute Infantry, began their advance toward Carentan, moving along the tarmac road running from La Croix Pan to Carentan. The route was an elevated road, 6 to 9ft above the surface of a salt water marsh, extending on either side of the road for some distance. The reeds and marsh grasses that covered the water surface were not thick enough to provide more than scant cover for anyone moving along the causeway. Nor was there sufficient dirt on the embankment to dig in. The complete exposure of the causeway threatened any approach by attacking troops. The men were subjected to such blistering German artillery, mortar, and machine gun fire from the front and right flank as they moved across the causeway that they were unable to advance. With the assault bogged down, the attack was cancelled and the men were recalled.[11] It was the middle of the afternoon of 10 June before the battalion tried again. 'The men moved in a low crouch or crawled, and it took three hours for the point to cross the first three bridges,' records the U.S. Army's official history. 'Then the enemy opened fire from a farmhouse and hedgerows, methodically searching the ditches with machine guns.' Only a few men were able to squeeze by a gate at the fourth bridge before the assault bogged down once again. The defenders poured fire on the advancing paratroopers from 37mm anti-tank and 75mm artillery pieces firing from their front and flank. These were joined by 50mm mortars and machine guns. The Americans retaliated with their own 81mm mortars, which had been moved up to support the attack just short of the fourth bridge. After midnight, however, German resistance slackened, and three parachute infantry companies were able to filter men through the bottleneck and across the last bridge, where they could deploy on either side of the road.[12]

---

10. Harrison, *Cross Channel Attack*, p. 357.
11. CMH, *Regimental Study No. 1. The Carentan Causeway Fight*, pp. 9–13.
12. Harrison, *Cross Channel Attack*, p. 359. See map in CMH, *Regimental Study No. 1. The Carentan Causeway Fight*, p. 17 for deployment of German weapons.

German opposition was centred on a large farmhouse to the west of the elevated causeway on ground that rose sharply from the marshes. On the morning of 11 June, the paratroopers of the 3rd Battalion, 502nd Infantry, stormed the building at bayonet point under the cover of smoke and concentrated machine gun fire, following an intense artillery barrage. The Screaming Eagles found enemy defensive positions and machine gun emplacements in the hedgerows. These were overrun, and the Wehrmacht soldiers killed with grenades and bayonets.[13] 'Dead Germans lay thick over the ground and in the foxholes,' recorded Marshall. 'The only live ones in sight were mortally stricken. Survivors of the machine gun crews had quit their stoutly fortified bunkers along an earth mound just beyond the farmhouse and pulled back through the orchard toward the railway; only a few got trapped before they could leg it.'[14] German machine gun fire from the nearby hedgerows and 88mm artillery fire from Carentan began to rake the road and nearby ditches, forcing the Americans to take cover and draining the momentum from the assault. 'The volume of German fire rose steadily, and the paratroopers felt again the pressure of an invisible enemy who revealed himself only through the swelling sound as his mechanisms [rifle and machine gun fire] pushed nearer,' wrote Marshall. 'All that saved the Americans was that the enemy did not have sufficient artillery.'[15] The men of the 502nd PIR, too exhausted to renew their advance, set up a defensive line and held on during determined Wehrmacht counter-attacks on 11 June.

Once again it was left to Hauptmann Horst Trebes's III Battalion to show the Screaming Eagles what the Fallschirmjäger of the 6th Parachute Regiment were made of. Trebes's battalion certainly merited the nickname 'The Lions of Carentan'. Just as at St-Côme-du-Mont, they moved stealthily along the hedgerows, then threw themselves at their opponents in a series of fierce and well-coordinated counter-attacks. Marshall noted:

> The enemy came right on down the hedgerows, moving in parallel lines toward these two companies on the American left, At the same time, other enemy riflemen came crawling along the ditch on the outside of the road. These lines of advance were continued throughout the afternoon. Each attack had the same pattern. Toward the close of the action the Germans had trouble

---

13. Harrison, *Cross Channel Attack*, p. 359.
14. Marshall, *Night Drop*, p. 368.
15. CMH, *Regimental Study No. 1. The Carentan Causeway Fight*, pp. 86–88.

coming forward as they were obstructed by the bodies of their own dead, the machine guns covering the enemy riflemen within 25 feet of their own muzzles.[16]

Firing in short bursts of six to seven rounds, the crew of one American machine gun kept their weapon in action for six hours. 'It took a lot of ammunition,' remembered one paratrooper, who counted ten dead Germans within 25 yards of his gun when the action closed.[17] By the end of the battle the machine gun crew had burned through twenty boxes and some 5,000 rounds of ammunition.[18] American attempts to call in artillery support were foiled by the Germans, who jammed the radios of the Screaming Eagles. Both Fallschirmjäger and paratroopers suffered heavy casualties in a series of short, but intense, firefights that lasted throughout the long afternoon. Finally, the Americans were able to contact their headquarters. Shortly afterward, three U.S. artillery battalions began to fire dangerously close, killing many Germans, but also some of the Americans. 'We lost good men, but we had to have that fire,' remembered one Screaming Eagle bitterly afterward. The 'very intense' artillery barrage turned the tide of the battle, hurling back the determined Fallschirmjäger and allowing the U.S. soldiers to hold their ground. Afterward American patrols found fields and orchards full of dead Germans.[19]

In the meantime, the 327th Glider Infantry pressed in on Carentan from the north-east. Their initial objective was to seize the road and railway bridges over the Vire–Taute Canal and seal the city from the east. The regiment advanced rapidly until at 1800 hours it was stopped within 500 yards of its objective by 88mm artillery fire from the east bank. The glider men reorganised and resumed the advance with two battalions abreast on either side of the Carentan–Isigny road. They fought until midnight through the last 500 yards and succeeded in finally clearing the enemy from the east bank and digging in along the hedgerows beside the canal. Rather than attempt to rush the bridge, the commander of the 327th Glider Infantry decided on moving a portion of his force across on a partially demolished footbridge. During the morning of 11 June, three companies crossed under enemy mortar fire, but were unable to advance more than

---

16. Ibid.
17. Ibid.
18. Marshall, *Night Drop*, p. 405. Each box of machine gun ammunition contained 250 cloth-linked rounds.
19. CMH, *Regimental Study No. 1. The Carentan Causeway Fight*, pp.97–98.

100 yards before they were stopped by enemy fire from the outskirts of Carentan.[20]

By the evening of 11 June the First U.S. Army decided to commit another regiment to the offensive on the city to re-energise the attack and to coordinate the two wings of the assault by bringing the entire force under the command of Brigadier General Anthony McAuliffe, the division artillery commander. The new plan called for the 506th Parachute Infantry to take over the attack on the west toward Hill 30 from the 502nd. The 327th Glider Infantry would continue to hold east of Carentan while attacking with a reinforced battalion from the north-east. The 501st Parachute Infantry would be taken from their defensive positions north of the Douve and committed through the Brévands bridgehead. It would drive east of the 327th Glider Infantry in a wider envelopment of Carentan designed to link up with the 506th Parachute Infantry south of the city at Hill 30.[21]

While the Americans were reorganising for what they hoped would be the final push on Carentan, the Fallschirmjäger in the city were running desperately short of ammunition. By 11 June the ammunition situation for the 6th Parachute Regiment was so critical that Major von der Heydte contacted the First Parachute Army headquarters in Nancy directly and requested resupply via Ju 52 transport planes or Heinkel 111 bombers rigged with external canisters. 'All the rifle ammunition … was collected and used for machine guns with the result that the riflemen were reduced to fighting with nothing but hand weapons,' remembered the regimental commander.[22] OB West considered the need so critical that a mission was flown during the night of 11–12 June and 18 tons of infantry ammunition and 88mm shells were dropped to the regiment on a field south of Raids, some 7 miles south-west of Carentan. This was the first air supply mission attempted by the Wehrmacht in Normandy.[23] Von der Heydte lauded his higher headquarters. 'During the night of 11 June, supply by air was actually carried out by the [First] Parachute Army in an exemplary fashion. The ammunition was dropped south of Raids on a field, which had been marked off by lights about 14km behind the front lines.'[24]

---

20. Harrison, *Cross Channel Attack*, pp. 360–361.
21. Ibid, p. 361.
22. von der Heydte, *B-839 A German Parachute Regiment in Normandy*, p. 17.
23. Harrison, *Cross Channel Attack*, p. 360.
24. von der Heydte, *B-839 A German Parachute Regiment in Normandy*, p. 17.

The 6th Parachute Regiment was not the only formation struggling to survive in Normandy. On 11 June OB West reported that Wehrmacht operations had become 'extremely aggravated' or 'could partially not be carried out at all' due to:

1. The enemy's superiority in the air (up to 27,000 sorties a day);
2. The effect of the enemy's naval artillery;
3. The equipment of the enemy;
4. The employment of parachutists and glider troops

The OB West report concluded: 'The troops of all arms are fighting doggedly and with extreme tenacity despite the employment of enormous quantities of material by the enemy.'[25]

Major von der Heydte and the 6th Parachute Regiment were feeling the effects of these Allied strengths. That night Carentan burned under intense concentrations of naval, artillery, mortar and tank destroyer gun fire. Two battalions of the 506th Parachute Infantry attacked at 0200 on 12 June and advanced rapidly against light resistance. Three hours later the 2nd Battalion, 506th Parachute Infantry, attacked the city. Despite interdictory artillery and machine gun fire, the battalion entered Carentan within a few hours. At about the same time the 327th Glider Infantry on the north-west side attacked out of the woods at Bassin a Flot and drove rapidly into the centre of town. The two units linked up at 0730. Only stragglers remained to contest possession of the battered city. While the concentric attacks squeezed into the city, the wider envelopment made equally rapid progress as the 510st Parachute Infantry swept down east of Carentan, making contact with the 506th Parachute Infantry half an hour after they entered it.[26]

The 6th Parachute Regiment, however, had pulled out of Carentan before dark on 11 June without being observed. 'Contrary to expectations, he succeeded in evacuating Carentan in broad daylight without interference by the enemy, who seemed to be reorganising his forces,' recorded Major von der Heydte, writing about himself. 'There is no doubt that during this evacuation of Carentan, as during the crossing of the Douve on 8 June, a determined pursuit by the Americans would have led to the annihilation of the regiment.'[27] The 6th Parachute Regiment and its subordinate elements, occupied a new defensive position south-west of

---

25. Schramm, B-034 OKW War Diary. The West, p. 36.
26. Harrison, Cross Channel Attack, pp. 363–364.
27. Heydte, B-839 A German Parachute Regiment in Normandy, p. 17.

Carentan. Hill 30, at the south-western edge of the city, constituted the most important point of the new position.'[28] The regiment lost much of its remaining heavy weapons, large-calibre ammunition, and equipment, as well as a field kitchen, 'containing a meal – still warm', when paratroopers from the 506th Parachute Infantry captured fifty horse-drawn wagons on the road out of Carentan.[29]

After the war, von der Heydte would justify his evacuation of Carentan by arguing that the move had been approved by his higher headquarters. He wrote:

> The regimental commander had advised the LXXXIV Corps of his decision to surrender Carentan, and corps had approved this step, The regimental commander was therefore all the more astonished when, on the afternoon of 11 June, just after the main body of the regiment had evacuated its former position, the commander of the 17th SS Panzergrenadier Division suddenly appeared and informed him that the division would arrive in the Carentan area the same night in order to take over the defence of Carentan. If the commander of the 6th Parachute Regiment had known only a few hours sooner that this division, whose foremost elements had already reached the Périers area early on the morning of 11 June, would be brought up, he would certainly never have made the decision to surrender Carentan. The LXXXIV Corps too had apparently not been informed in time of the arrival of this division, for there is no doubt that the corps, which maintained constant radio communication with the regiment, would have immediately transmitted this information, which after all had considerable bearing on the regiment's decisions; besides, the corps would never have approved the regiment's decision to evacuate Carentan. Consequently, it can only be assumed that the army, army group, or the Wehrmacht High Command, in this case going over the head of the corps, had ordered a division into the Carentan sector.'[30]

---

28. Ibid, p. 17.
29. Matheson, Chapter 10. 'The Operations of the 506th Parachute Infantry in the Normandy Invasion, 5 – 8 June 1944', in Gawne, *Lessons Learned in Combat: Normandy Paratroopers*, Kindle.
30. von der Heydte, *B-839 A German Parachute Regiment in Normandy*, pp. 17–18.

Seventh Army Chief of Staff, then-Oberst Max Pemsel, was scathing in his criticism of Major von der Heydte for yielding the city: 'The premature surrender of Carentan on the afternoon of 11 June, which the commander of the 6th Parachute Regiment decided on his own responsibility, was an incomprehensible and ill-advised step on his part, since he had been informed of the commitment of the 17th SS Panzergrenadier Division at Carentan in advance and not afterward, as claimed by the author,' recorded Pemsel. 'According to the records of the Seventh Army, they informed the LXXXIV Corps by telephone as early as 1300 on 10 June and then again on 11 June at 1145 that 'the 17th SS Panzergrenadier Division was assembled for the attack on Carentan.' According to statements made by the Chief of Staff of the LXXXIV Corps, he apprised the commander of the 6th Parachute Regiment in person of the commitment of this division not later than 10 June. Pemsel continued: 'Neither the army nor the corps were in accord with this independent decision of the commander of the 6th Parachute Regiment, because one of the most essential tasks of the Seventh Army of necessity should have consisted in preventing, as long as possible, the Americans from establishing contact between their forces on the Cotentin peninsula and their forces stationed east of the Vire and with the British.' And he went on: 'Afterwards, an attempt was made to justify the premature surrender of Carentan, which was a vital junction point, by pointing to the shortage of ammunition. It was, at this time, impossible to unequivocally fix the responsibility for this action. As a result of the previous severe and disastrous battles, the commander of the 6th Parachute Regiment had suffered a temporary physical and mental breakdown. This also explains his "misguided order" which, following the surrender of Carentan, he issued in connection with the occupation of the decisively important Hill 30 south-west of Carentan.' Pemsel tempered his criticism by remarking: 'Only the fact that his command of the regiment had so far been outstanding and that he made a speedy recovery prevented the commander of the 6th Parachute Regiment from being punished or relieved of his command.'[31]

Major von der Heydte's fate, however, was not in the hands of either Max Pemsel or the Seventh Army, but in those of individuals with considerably more seniority: Generaloberst Kurt Student, the commander of Hitler's Fallschirmtruppe, and General der Fallschirmtruppe Eugen Meindl, the II Parachute Corps commander. Historian Volker Griesser writes that the attacks on von der Heydte over the loss of Carentan

---

31. Ibid, p. 18.

ceased 'only after Generals Student and Meindl, independent of each other, declared that they would have acted in the exact same way in such a hopeless situation'.[32] Moreover, the 11 June German High Command communique stated that under the leadership of Major von der Heydte, the Fallschirmjäger of the 6th Parachute Regiment had 'distinguished themselves in heavy battles in the enemy beachhead, and in the destruction of the enemy paratroopers and air landing troops landing in the area'.[33] 'To my pleasure, the Colonel tells me that the Regiment has been mentioned in the Wehrmacht Report and sends his congratulations to our Regimental Commander,' relates Oberleutnant Martin Poppel, after reporting to the field headquarters of the LXXXIV Corps. 'He says that the whole Corps is extremely impressed by the performance of the Regiment,' he continues, adding 'They haven't understood how badly we are led.'[34]

Pöppel's memoir of the war is unusual for that of a Fallschirmjâger officer in that he is critical of von der Heydte's leadership during the fight for Carentan and records his regimental commander's erratic behaviour during the battle. 'I reckon that the Staff has been drinking and has nothing better to do than to deprive its company commanders of their sleep,' he writes at one point, after being dressed down over the field telephone for not being in his observation tree. 'Crazy questions from the Old Man,' he writes at another, after ordering harassing fire on the Americans with his large guns rather than his machine guns. 'As a result of telling the truth I get a dreadful dressing down ... It's enough to make you puke – the Old Man has gone crazy.'[35] In the end, von der Heydte relieved Pöppel of his command of the 12th Company and appointed his own adjutant in his place. 'The scum up there always stick together,' writes the young Fallschirmjäger lieutenant in anger, 'the Adjutant naturally sticks by his Command and won't accept responsibility for his order.'[36]

From a strictly military point of view, Major von der Heydte's actions are justified. The commander of the 6th Parachute Regiment no doubt wanted to ensure that he had constant eyes on the Americans, who had already defeated him twice and who were massing for an attack on Carentan. Second, he no doubt wanted to conserve his very limited

---

32. Griesser, *The Lions of Carentan*, p. 118.
33. Ibid, p. 118.
34. Pöppel, *Heaven and Hell*, p. 205
35. Ibid, p. 202.
36. Ibid, pp. 202–203.

artillery ammunition and keep the location of his previous artillery pieces hidden from the enemy until the last minute. Already a veteran of the fighting in Normandy, Major von der Heydte was well aware that American airpower and artillery would batter his guns and other heavy weapons to pieces once they were discovered. He needed to keep them hidden until the last possible moment. No doubt this was the reason for his orders to his company commander to reoccupy his observation point and to use machine gun fire to harass the enemy paratroopers. As for relieving Pöppel, von der Heydte, trying to command an entire regiment plus attached units in extremely difficult circumstances, simply did not have the time to spend on repeatedly correcting the errors of a single lieutenant. The appointment of his adjutant as the new commander also makes sense, as that officer had spent enough time with his commander to know exactly what he wanted. Although Pöppel's comments must, accordingly, be taken with a grain of salt, they nonetheless provide some credence to Pemsel's allegations that the commander of the 6th Parachute Regiment had suffered 'a temporary physical and mental breakdown' as a result of 'the previous severe and disastrous battles'. Perhaps von der Heydte had not fully recovered from the aircraft accident more than a year earlier that had left him seriously injured and required more than four months of hospitalisation and convalescence. Perhaps under the constant strain of combat and lack of sleep, he had suffered a relapse. Or perhaps he was still in shock over the loss of half of his precious parachute regiment to the Americans. Either way, his behaviour and leadership at Normandy following the Allied invasion caused his superiors and subordinates alike to rightfully question his mental state.

Having ceded control of Carentan, a city critical to Seventh Army's defensive plans, Major von der Heydte compounded his mistake by not posting Fallschirmjäger on Hill 30, a piece of key terrain located at the south-west outskirts of the town. Instead he assigned its defence to his Ost battalions, manned with Russians and Poles, along with the leftovers of other Seventh Army units assigned to him. The Americans, recognising the importance of the terrain, quickly rolled over these formations and occupied the hill. After the war, von der Heydte attempted to justify his decision by arguing that he had intended to rehabilitate his Fallschirmjäger as well as two battalions attached to the 6th Parachute Regiment immediately behind the new position on 12 June and not to commit them again to battle until that night. 'On the basis of his previous, although very limited, experience with the Americans, he did not expect them to attack until 13 June,' wrote the regimental commander.[37] At this point in the Normandy campaign, however, von der Heydte had more experience battling the Americans and especially the 101st Airborne Division, than any other German officer in the LXXXIV Corps and probably in the entire Seventh Army. His regiment's series of costly missteps since the Allied invasion at Vierville, St-Côme-du-Mont and Carentan had unhinged the German Seventh Army's entire defensive scheme by permitting the Americans to initiate operations to cut off the Cotentin peninsula sooner than would have been the case had all three locations been held for longer.

Although von der Heydte certainly shares a great deal of the blame for the fall of Carentan, the ultimate responsibility for the loss of the key road junction lay with the German High Command, Army Group B, and Field Marshal Rommel. All overestimated the capabilities of their own very limited forces in the city and underestimated the fighting abilities of their American foes, their rates of advance, and the supporting fire they had available to them. This was a trait common to most Wehrmacht commanders in Normandy during the first weeks of the invasion. Field Marshal Rommel had failed to reinforce Carentan in a timely manner with sufficient forces, armament and ammunition, leaving the 6th Parachute Regiment to fight alone against a multi-division American concentric attack backed by massive amounts of U.S. naval and field artillery and air support. Had von der Heydte not pulled his Fallschirmjäger back when he did, his entire regiment would have been crushed. It is clear in reading his post-war monograph that the German parachute commander had no intention of sacrificing himself or his men for a defensive scheme that he knew to be faulty.

As Carentan was falling to the Americans, the rest of the 17th SS-Panzergrenadier Division was arriving in the St-Lô area. According to Meindl, combat elements of the 3rd Parachute Division also arrived in the area 'surprisingly fast' due to a combination of forced marches and vehicle shuttle movements. 'I intended to attack on 15 or 16 June 1944,' he recalled. However, the German Seventh Army did not agree with the II Parachute Corps' commander's intentions, as the American beachhead was expanding successfully toward Cherbourg. '(Seventh) Army was concerned about Cherbourg, but in my opinion, this city was of secondary importance,' complained Meindl. As a result, the II Parachute Corps commander was forced to commit the 17th SS-Panzergrenadier Division west of the Vire River between Vire and Carentan, another key

---

37. von der Heydte, *B-839 A German Parachute Regiment in Normandy*, p. 20.

road junction. The plan of attack fell apart as the 3rd Parachute Division remained his only formation capable of offensive operations. Instead, the division occupied a sector from the Cerisy Forest to the vicinity of St-Jean-de-Daye, 5 miles north of St-Lô.[38] Generalleutnant Max Pemsel provides additional insight on the cancellation of the II Parachute Corps' planned attack. 'The attack aimed at capturing the Forest of Cerisy, as proposed by the division commander (General Schimpf) might have been successful, but it had to be carried out with insufficient forces,' recorded Pemsel. 'The danger of completely exhausting the division during the attack was great, as the division was poorly trained for attacks. Therefore, Seventh Army prohibited the attack.'[39] General Dollman had no intention of sacrificing the highly regarded defensive capabilities of Schimpf's elite division in a questionable attack with insufficient forces. Its failure could have easily decimated the Fallschirmjäger and left a gaping hole in his lines. Pemsel recorded:

> The strength of the 3rd Parachute Division rested in the defence because the division was well trained for it. The paratroopers felt at home in this bush terrain and as individual fighters felt themselves superior to the enemy's material. In the defence the Division was fortunate to be able to extract reserves up to battalion strength. The Army had no anxiety about the sector held by the 3rd Parachute Division, despite its width. The division justified the confidence placed in it.[40]

In fact, Meindl's attack had been overcome by events. Having lost Carentan, Rommel was now determined to get it back. The 17th SS-Panzergrenadier Division, with the 6th Parachute Regiment under its command, was ordered to retake the city and its vital crossroads. Major von der Heydte's men were not impressed with their SS colleagues. 'The 17th SS was one of the new divisions that had been put together in the spring and basically had no combat experience,' remembered Obergrefreiter Gerd Schwetling, of II Battalion's 6th Company. 'Maybe that's what caused their snobbery. They hadn't had any interactions with Fallschirmjäger yet.'[41] A 12 June attack was delayed by Allied air

---

38. Meindl, *B-401 II Parachute Corps*, pp. 14–15.
39. Schimpf, *B-541 3rd Parachute Division*, p. 27.
40. Ibid, p. 27.
41. Griesser, *The Lions of Carentan*, p. 118.

attacks. 'Everywhere there's an atmosphere of feverish excitement and expectancy,' remembered Oberleutnant Martin Pöppel. 'Will our troops manage to drive the enemy back?' he asks, uncertainly. 'The whole thing seems to be a highly doubtful business, and it seems very unlikely that we'll be able to force home our attack.'[42] If the Fallschirmjäger were doubtful, the panzergrenadiers of the 17th SS Division were not: 'The SS think they can do it easily, they've arrived with enormous idealism – but they'll get the surprise of their lives against this enemy, which is not short of skill itself.'

Ostendorff's panzergrenadiers and von der Heydte's Fallschirmjäger launched their assault early the next morning following a fifteen-minute artillery barrage beginning at 0545. At 0600 the artillery stopped firing and the attackers surged forward. 'At the stroke of 06.00 hours our artillery fire creates a fire-screen above the positions to be attacked,' recorded Pöppel. 'Simultaneously the tanks advance, accompanied by the infantry. The enemy line has already been reached, with hardly any shots fired from there.'[43] The 17th SS Panzergrenadier Division attacked to the north-east with the 37th SS-Panzergrenadier Regiment on the west side of the Périers–Carentan road to recapture Carentan. In the event of good progress, the 38th Panzergrenadier Regiment was to continue the attack to St-Côme-du-Mont and establish a defensive bridgehead there. The 6th Parachute Regiment, reinforced by two platoons of SS panzergrenadiers, was responsible for securing the right flank of the attack, and taking and holding the Carentan train station. The assault was supported by the four artillery battalions of the 17th SS-Panzer artillery regiment and its 150mm and 105mm guns, along with two SS assault gun batteries from the 17th SS-Panzer Battalion.[44] Additional firepower was provided by the II Battalion of the 191st Artillery Regiment (91st Air-Landing Division) and two heavy howitzer batteries of the 352nd Infantry Division. The 352nd Infantry Division anchored the 17th SS-Panzergrenadier Division's right flank, while the 91st Air-Landing Division secured the left.[45] The 13 June German attack on Carentan was a much larger affair than is generally recognised, even in the U.S. Army's official Second World War history. The

---

42. Pöppel, *Heaven and Hell*, p. 206.

43. Ibid, p. 207.

44. Ibid, pp. 205–206.

45. M. Wind and H. Günther, eds., *Kriegstagbuch 30 Oktober 1943 bis 6 Mai 1945, 17. SS Panzer-Grenadier-Division 'Götz von Berlichingen'* (München: Schild Verlag, 1993). This book has no pagination.

Wehrmacht was throwing everything it had available in Normandy into the attack.

This powerful force hit the American 506th and 501st Parachute Infantry Regiments, which had just kicked off their own attack, at about 0630, driving them back during the morning to within 500 yards of Carentan. Major Dick Winters of the 506th PIR remembered that 'all hell broke loose as we prepared our final attack to drive the enemy from the outskirts of Carentan. Both sides opened up with artillery, mortars, machine guns, and rifle fire – everything we had, and I am sure everything they had. There was a hail of firepower going in both directions. Under that intense fire, our sister company broke and ran.'[46] The Germans advanced hurling grenades and firing machine guns. 'At that moment a squad of enemy soldiers burst out of the trees to our direct front,' remembered Lieutenant Ronald C. Speirs of Company D, 506th PIR. 'They were paratroopers, recognised by their distinctive helmets and uniforms. They were about 25 yards away and firing as they came. The platoon from behind the wall cut them down with aimed rifle fire and killed them all before any reached the wall.'[47] Despite the successful defence, Speirs decided to withdraw his platoon of paratroopers out from under a storm of German hand grenades. 'Severe fighting raged from hedge to hedge, at close quarters and hand to hand,' recalled Major von der Heydte. 'The paratrooper forces nevertheless succeeded in gaining several hundred meters of terrain north of the railway embankment, while the SS panzergrenadier units were stopped cold in unfamiliar terrain where observation was obstructed.'[48] The Americans brought down intense concentrations of mortar fire on the hedgerows directly in front of their positions. One 81mm mortar reportedly fired 1,000 rounds at ranges between 300 and 500m. When they had expended all their ammunition, the mortarmen rushed into the front lines to fight with their rifles, filling the gaps left by the dead and wounded. The Germans answered with accurate 88mm fire at long ranges that succeeded in knocking out all of one U.S. airborne battalion's 57-mm anti-tank guns and rocket launchers. At least four of the 88mm

---

46. Winters, *Beyond Band of Brothers*, p. 107.
47. Speirs, Chapter 12. 'The Operations of the 2nd Platoon, Company D, 506th Parachute Infantry (101st Airborne Division) in the Vicinity of Carentan, France, 11–13 June 1944', in Gawne, *Lessons Learned in Combat: Normandy Paratroopers*, Kindle.
48. von der Heydte, *B-839 A German Parachute Regiment in Normandy*, p.21.

rounds were duds, which saved an entire section of U.S. soldiers from annihilation. The outcome of the battle hung in the balance.[49]

In a desperate attempt to halt the attack, the 101st Airborne Division moved the 502nd Parachute Infantry into the city to reinforce the defenders and hold Carentan. At 1030 hours an armoured task force from the U.S. 2nd Armoured Division composed of the 2nd Battalion, 66th Armoured Regiment and 3rd Battalion, 41st Armoured Infantry Regiment, arrived to support the Screaming Eagles. In the early afternoon the U.S. tankers, armoured infantrymen, and paratroopers counter-attacked, supported by the eighteen 105mm guns of an armoured field artillery battalion.[50] 'What a wonderful sight it was to see those tanks pouring it on the Germans with their heavy .50-calibre machine guns and then plowing straight into the enemy hedgerows with all those fresh infantry soldiers marching alongside the tanks as though they were on a maneuver back in the States,' recalled Major Winters.[51] Fallschirmjäger paratrooper and panzergrenadier fought armoured infantryman in a series of fierce encounters. At 0915 hours the German right flank, which had advanced 500m, reported that it had encountered strong resistance and was unable to advance without tank support. At 0950 the I Battalion, 37th SS Regiment, reported that the attack was at a standstill in front of Carentan: 'Enemy attack from Carentan with tanks.' By 1045 the SS panzergrenadiers and Fallschirmjäger were falling back 'under massive enemy pressure.'[52] 'Then everything happens with lightning speed,' recalls Martin Pöppel. The Command of the SS troops has realised that our own position cannot be held and orders a rapid withdrawal to the initial position. The troops are pouring back but can still be intercepted and made to reinforce the line of defence. Then the Americans rush forward, but at least they've given us enough time to gather.'[53] Following their counter-attack, the Americans took up defensive positions from Baupte, west of the city, to the Carentan–Périers road.[54] Carentan would remain in American hands. 'On the 12th Carentan

---

49. Speirs, Chapter 12. 'The Operations of the 2nd Platoon, Company D, 506th Parachute Infantry (101st Airborne Division) in the Vicinity of Carentan, France, 11–13 June 1944', in Gawne, *Lessons Learned in Combat: Normandy Paratroopers*, Kindle.
50. Harrison, *Cross Channel Attack*, p. 365.
51. Winters, *Beyond Band of Brothers*, pp. 107–108.
52. Pöppel, *Heaven and Hell*, p. 207.
53. Ibid, pp. 207–208.
54. Harrison, *Cross Channel Attack*, p. 365.

fell,' reported General Eisenhower to the Combined Chiefs of Staff. 'The Germans made desperate but fruitless efforts to recover the town and reestablish the wedge between our forces. Our initial lodgement area was now consolidated, and we held an unbroken stretch of the French coast from Quineville to the east bank of the Orne.'[55]

LXXXIV Corps Chief of Staff Oberstleutnant Freidrich von Criegern was furious at the loss of the city and the failure of the Luftwaffe to support the offensive. The German Air Force had promised to soften up the American positions around Carentan the night before and to support the advance of the Waffen SS and Fallschirmjäger the morning of the attack. That support had failed to materialise. 'What was decisive was not merely the lack of support, rather the effects of the absence of the promised support on the fighting will of the troops who were not yet battle-hardened,' he complained.[56] Once again, Rommel and the German High Command had let down their soldiers. They had failed to ensure that the promised Luftwaffe support appeared. Without the German Air Force, the attack on Carentan stood little chance of regaining the city. Major von der Heydte recorded:

> The casualties among the SS forces were unusually high. The fighting spirit of the inexperienced troops was weakened; and an ever-increasing number of individual SS soldiers as well as whole groups straggled to the rear so that the commander of the 6th Parachute Regiment had to instruct his adjutant to check the fleeing SS forces and assemble them in the vicinity of his regimental command post. In some instances, the adjutant was compelled to enforce this order at the point of a gun.[57]

The 17th SS-Panzergrenadier Division suffered 456 casualties (including seventy-nine killed, 316 wounded, and sixty-one missing), along with the loss of thirteen assault guns.[58] Oberstrumführer Reinhardt, the commander of 1st Battalion, 37th SS-Panzergrenadier Regiment, taken prisoner after the battle of Carentan by soldiers of the 4th Infantry Division near Sainteny,

---

55. General Dwight D. Eisenhower, *Report by the Supreme Commander to the Combined Chiefs of Staff on the Operations in Europe of the Allied Expeditionary Force* (Washington, D.C.: Centre of Military History, 1994), p. 26.
56. Hargreaves, *The Germans in Normandy*, pp. 78–79.
57. von der Heydte, *B-839 A German Parachute Regiment in Normandy*, p. 21.
58. Zetterling, '17. SS-Panzer-Grenadier-Division', *Normandy 1944*, p. 366.

told his American interrogators that his battalion had been promised 'very heavy support'. The actual attack was carried out 'without any of these supports, with considerable casualties in the battalion and a great loss of confidence among the men, who had been told of the promises and were disgusted at their non-fulfillment.' According to Reinhardt, 60 per cent of his battalion was lost and the only officers surviving, including his adjutant and the company commanders of the 1st and 4th Companies, were prisoners of war. By the evening of 14 June, his battalion strength had been reduced to 200 men.[59]

'So, the counter has failed, just as we thought it must,' wrote Oberleutnant Martin Pöppel, dejectedly. 'No breakthrough to St-Côme-du-Mont. Our casualties are very high, particularly in the SS battalion and on our left flank.' Pöppel's company suffered moderately heavy losses, including ten killed, twenty-six wounded, and six missing, or approximately one quarter of the unit's authorised strength of 170 men. In all, the 6th Parachute Regiment lost another company's worth of paratroopers killed, wounded and missing during the battle. 'Yet again, it's generally the best men who have been lost,' continued Pöppel sadly. 'And we've had to leave the badly wounded men in the hands of the enemy since we couldn't take them with us during the retreat.'[60] The Fallschirmjäger pulled back and spent the rest of the day digging in and awaiting the inevitable American counter-attacks.

'Over the course of the war, 2nd Battalion, 506th PIR, participated in many battles, but without a doubt the toughest fighting of the war was the German counter-attack at Carentan on June 13, 1944,' remembered Major Dick Winters. 'On this day the regiment was pushed back and almost overrun by the enemy.'[61] The American paratroopers were relieved by U.S. infantrymen and moved out of the lines to clean up, eat hot meals, have their wounds tended to, and rest in hotels in the rear. For the next five days they would sleep in real beds between clean sheets. Major von der Heydte and his Fallschirmjäger remained on the front lines.

Carentan should have been a major centre of German resistance against the advancing First U.S. Army, much like Caen was in the Anglo–Canadian Second Army sector in the east. The Wehrmacht's defence of Caen condemned the British and Canadians to three gruelling months

---

59. C.S.D.I.C., Report SIR 651, RG 165, NARA II.
60. Pöppel, *Heaven and Hell*, p. 208; War Department's, *Handbook on German Military Forces*, p. 132.
61. Winters, *Beyond Band of Brothers*, p. 108.

of debilitating high-intensity combat. That battle tied down fourteen Allied infantry and armour divisions and eight brigades and cost more than 50,000 casualties before it was finally over. Later in the Normandy campaign, St-Lô would become a much smaller-scale Caen for the Americans. Already in the first week following the Allied invasion, the Wehrmacht's reaction of too little and too late had resulted in the premature loss of Carentan. This was a catastrophe for the Germans and a windfall of incredible magnitude for the Allies. Just as Rommel feared, it opened the path for operations against the entire Brittany peninsula to the west and against St-Lô to the south. In hindsight, the First U.S. Army's seizure of the critical communications node probably shortened the Normandy campaign by weeks if not months. Hitler understood this only too well. The loss of the city infuriated him, even more so because he had ordered radio Berlin to announce its recapture by the Wehrmacht earlier that day. The Führer issued an order demanding that everyone in strong points, points of resistance and other defensive positions surrounded by enemy units must defend his position to the last man and last bullet in order to allow time for preparation for the counter-attack and the reconquest of the coast. The Führer Order ended with: 'No orders to retreat will be issued.' According to historian Stephan Badsey: 'Hitler's orders on 12 June set the attritional agenda for the rest of the Battle of Normandy ...'[62]

Unfortunately for Major von der Heydte, his battle of Carentan was not yet over. While still supervising the withdrawal of his Fallschirmjäger, the commander of the 6th Parachute Regiment was escorted to the command post of the 17th SS Panzergrenadier Division, where he came face-to-face with a furious General Ostendorff. 'There he was reproached by the division commander for his arbitrary actions and his "cowardice in the face of the enemy", as indicated by his order to withdraw,' recalled von der Heydte. 'The division commander informed him that he was under arrest and that very night had him questioned by an SS military judge.' Fortunately, von der Heydte was rescued the next day once again by General Meindl in his new capacity as the temporary commander of the LXXXIV Corps. Meindl approved the conduct of the commander of the 6th Parachute Regiment during the attack on Carentan. The next day Ostendorff released von der

---

62. Leonard Rapport and Arthur Norwood, Jr., *Rendezvous with Destiny. History of the 101st Airborne Division* (Konecky & Konecky, 1948), p. 233; Badsey, 'Culture, controversy, Caen and Cherbourg. The first week of the battle', in Buckley, *The Normandy Campaign 1944*, p. 111.

Heydte and allowed him to return to his regiment.[63] With the conclusion of the battle for Carentan, the 6th Parachute Regiment broke contact with the American 101st Airborne Division, its first opponent during the invasion battles. Fallschirmjäger and Screaming Eagle would not meet again until Operation Market Garden, the Allied airborne and ground invasion of Holland in September 1944.

After the war, Major von der Heydte was frequently asked his opinion of his American counterparts. His response is worth noting in its entirety:

> The calibre of the American paratroopers who fought against the regiment was outstanding; they were excellently trained in combat techniques and their armament and equipment were first class. The regiment experienced similar stubborn fighting only against the Russian NKVD divisions, the British 52nd (Highland) Division, and the Canadian 1st Infantry Division. However, as in the German parachute forces, the tactical ability of the American command, from the lower echelons up to and including division level, did not always appear to be on a par with the excellent combat efficiency of the units. During the first days of the invasion, the Americans could have saved a great deal of time and avoided many casualties if their troops had made their jumps and landing directly into the target to capture individual objectives of tactical importance, such as the Douve bridges north of Carentan. In Normandy, as later on at Arnhem, the Americans seemed to have employed the same tactics of jumping and landing some distance away from the target and then attacking the tactically important individual objectives on the ground, a method which did not always lead to immediate victory. In 1944, the Americans seemed to be unfamiliar with the procedure of capturing villages or small towns from the air by jumping into them. I am not in a position to offer any opinion concerning the tactical aspects of night jumping, because I have no data indicating the speed with which these units were able to assemble nor the percentage of those who made false landings. The Americans proved to be far superior to the Germans in the employment of troop-carrying gliders at night. It was odd that the Americans did not use Sturzlastensegler (dive gliders) even where their commitment would have been advantageous.

---

63. von der Heydte, *B-839 A German Parachute Regiment in Normandy*, p. 23.

In the opinion of the German parachute troops, 'the American 101st Airborne Division, and particularly the 506th Regiment (commanded by Colonel Robert F. Sink), far surpassed the other American airborne units because its commander and staff were on a par with the outstanding efficiency of the troops themselves.'[64]

Major von der Heydte's criticisms notwithstanding, the Screaming Eagles had captured all their D-Day objectives by the end of 6 June 1944, ensuring, with the 82nd Airborne Division, the security of the American beaches and paving the way for the capture of Carentan, the isolation of the Cotentin peninsula and the fall of Cherbourg. The paratroopers of the 101st Airborne Division had fought and defeated the Fallschirmjäger of the 6th Parachute Regiment on three separate occasions, killing or capturing four parachute companies of von der Heydte's I Battalion in a single battle lasting several hours and eliminating another three parachute companies in two separate battles. The Americans had clearly improved on what the Luftwaffe had begun with its Fallschirmtruppe.

The Screaming Eagles were equally impressed with Major von der Heydte and his self-styled 'Lions of Carentan'.[65] The battle for the city was their last major engagement in Normandy before moving into defensive positions near Cherbourg and then heading to England by LSTs. According to one veteran of the unit, the division had suffered 4,670 casualties, or more than 70 per cent of it total strength.[66] Most of the dead, wounded and missing were the result of the division's battles with Hitler's paratroopers on D-Day and at Vierville, St-Côme-du-Mont and Carentan.

The day that Carentan fell, Rommel reported that the Allied air forces had 'complete control' of the air over the battle area 'up to 100km. behind the front' and that 'almost all transport on roads, byroads, and on open country is prevented by day by strong fighter-bomber and bomber formations'. 'Troops and staffs are forced to hide in terrain which provides cover during the day,' he observed 'in order to escape these continual attacks from the air.' Commenting on the effects of Allied naval artillery, he wrote: 'The effect is so strong that operations with infantry or panzer formations in the area commanded by this quick-firing artillery is not possible.' And writing on the technology of the Allied armies, he continued: 'The material

---

64. Ibid, p. 24.
65. Taken from Volker Greisser's title for his history of the 6th Parachute Regiment, *The Lions of Carentan*.
66. Robert Bowden, *Fighting with the Screaming Eagles. With the 101st Airborne From Normandy to Bastogne* (Casemate, 2010), p. 77.

equipment of the Anglo–Americans with numerous new weapons and war materials is far superior to the equipment of our divisions.' Rommel went on to add: 'Furthermore, their superiority in artillery and extremely large supplies of ammunition are increasingly apparent.' Finally, with regard to American and British airborne formations, Hitler's youngest field marshal reported: 'Parachute and airborne troops are used in such large numbers and so effectively, that the troops attacked have a difficult task in defending themselves. If enemy airborne forces land in territory unoccupied by us, they immediately make themselves ready for defence and can be defeated only with difficulty by infantry attacks with artillery support.' He concluded: 'Since the enemy can cripple our mobile formations with his Air Force by day, while he operates with fast-moving forces and airborne troops, our position is becoming extremely difficult.'[67]

The 6th Parachute Regiment now joined Meindl's II Parachute Corps, which consisted of the 17th SS-Panzergrenadier Division, a 'considerably weakened' 352nd Infantry Division, and General Schimpf's 3rd Parachute Division, holding a line from north of St-Lô in the west to Caumont in the east. Meindl had also been placed in command of the LXXXIV Corps following the death of General Marcks. 'General Marcks met a heroic death at the hands of enemy fighter-bombers on his way to the front,' recorded Meindl. 'General Marcks' death was a great loss. He knew the Normandy front as no one else did.'[68] Marcks was killed on the morning of 12 June while on a daily round of troop unit inspections. 'It is due solely to his leadership that the enemy's breakthrough to Cherbourg was stopped and that the situation in the northern front of the Cotentin peninsula was brought under control,' reported the Seventh Army War Diary. 'Seventh Army has seen to it that General Marcks' name will be mentioned in the Wehrmacht Daily Bulletin.'[69] General Meindl was placed in command pending the arrival of General der Artillerie Wilhelm Fahrmbacher and his orientation on the situation in Normandy. The II Parachute Corps had now grown to include the 3rd Parachute and 77th Infantry Divisions, along with the 353d Infantry Division and Kampfgruppe of the 265th, 266th, and 275th Infantry Divisions, which were en route to Normandy.[70]

67. James A. Wood, ed., *Army of the West. The Weekly Reports of German Army Group B from Normandy to the West Wall* (Stackpole Books, 2007), pp. 60–61.
68. Meindl, *B-401 II Parachute Corps*, pp. 14–15.
69. Reardon, *Defending Fortress Europe*, p. 62.
70. Ibid, pp. 62–63.

Marcks was the second German Army general to perish at Normandy. Generalleutnant Wilhelm Falley, Commander 91st Air-Landing Division, was the first general officer of the Wehrmacht to die in battle in Normandy. He was killed by American paratroopers of the 82nd Airborne Division near Ste-Mère-Église on 6 June returning from the war games in Rennes.[71] Marcks was one of eleven Wehrmacht corps commanders to be killed in action in 1944 on the Western Front.[72] He would be followed within a week by Generalleutnant Heinz Helmich, Commander of the 243rd Infantry Division (killed on 17 June in a fighter-bomber attack) and Generalleutnant Rudolph Stegmann, Commander of the 77th Infantry Division (killed on 19 June in ground combat).[73] They in turn would be joined by the commanders of the 326th, 352nd, 708th, and 242nd Infantry Divisions before the 1944 Normandy campaign was concluded.[74] The combat deaths of one German corps and six division commanders in the Normandy campaign, (four of them within the first two weeks), highlights an important tenet of the Wehrmacht's battlefield doctrine: all leaders, even general officers, were expected to lead from the front and to die if necessary. It was what Hitler expected of all his generals. And it was what the Führer expected of his Landsers and Fallschirmjäger fighting to contain the Americans in Normandy.

---

71. 'Report on Information obtained from PW CS/5(M) Uffz Baumann, Stab 91 Inf Div, captured near Pont L'Abbe Jun 44'; French L. MacLean, *Quiet Flows the Rhine. German General Officer Casualties in World War II* (Fedorowicz, 1994), p. 130; Dermot Bradley, et. al., 'Wilhelm Falley', *Deutschlands Generale und Admirale. Teil IV Die Generale des Heeres 1921–1945. Die militärischen Werdegänge der Generale, sowie der Ärzte, Veterinäre, Intendanten, Richter und Ministerialbeamten im Generalsrang*, Band III (Osnabruck: Biblio Verlag, 1995), p. 415.

72. MacLean, *Quiet Flows the Rhine*, p. 170.

73. Ibid, p. 130.

74. See MacLean, *Quiet Flows the Rhine*, pp. 130–131; Bradley, et. al., 'Edgar Arndt,' *Die Generale des Heeres 1921–1945*, Band I, pp. 86–87. MacLean, *Quiet Flows the Rhine*, p. 170.

Chapter 5

3rd Parachute Division at Hill 192

B y the middle of June 1944, the II Parachute Corps was defending a line running about 3 miles north and north-east of St-Lô from St-Germain-d'Elle in the east to the Vire River in the west. The 3rd Parachute Division was positioned on the right, east of the St-Lô–Bérigny road. A kampfgruppe of the 353rd Infantry Division defended the centre, north-east of the town. Remnants of the battered 352nd Infantry Division held the left, to the north.[1] The German High Command realised the importance of St-Lô with its four major roads leading south-west, south, and south-east. Its capture would facilitate an Allied breakout from Normandy. It was thus essential to the entire Wehrmacht position in France that St-Lô remained in German hands. The Seventh Army's position, however, was far from encouraging. 'It was obvious that the available forces, including those in [the] process of being brought up, were by no means sufficient for successful defence in the long run,' recorded General Seventh Army Chief of Staff, Generalleutnant Max Pemsel.'[2] Field Marshal Rommel and Army Group B believed the greatest Allied threat was to Caen, that Normandy could be abandoned to prevent a British thrust on Paris, and that all reinforcements possible should be sent to the Caen sector. Seventh Army commander Paul Hausser and staff believed the threat to western Normandy to be more acute, demanding the 353rd Infantry Division be sent, to replace the 'completely exhausted' 352nd Infantry Division, along with a reinforced regiment of the 3rd Parachute Division to reinforce the St-Lô sector and stem growing American pressure

---

1. Donald L. Gilmore, ed., 'Toward St. Lo', *U.S. Army Atlas of the European Theatre in World War II* (New York: Barnes & Noble, 2004), p. 34.
2. Pemsel, *B-763. The Seventh Army in the Battle in Normandy*, p. 26.

in that critical area. Army Group B had compromised and sent a regiment from the 3rd Parachute Division.[3]

The U.S. First Army's order of battle in Normandy consisted of the three U.S. Corps: V Corps (1st and 2nd Infantry Divisions and the 2nd Armoured Division); VII Corps (4th, 9th, 79th, 90th Infantry Divisions, 82nd Airborne and 101st Airborne Divisions); XIX Corps (29th and 30th Infantry Divisions). Having captured Carentan and pushed south from the American beachheads, the army's next mission was to capture the deep water port of Cherbourg. For months it would be the only large port in Allied hands. The basic Neptune Plan assigned the capture of Cherbourg to the VII Corps.[4] VII Corps opened its assault on the Cherbourg peninsula on 14 June.

At about the same time that the US VII Corps launched its offensive, German Seventh Army units were informed of Hitler's plan to place an 'iron ring' around the Allied beachheads, which was to hold out until the arrival of fresh troops and material made it possible to attack the American and British lodgement and wipe it out. 'Never before, either in Russia or in North Africa, had the troops of Parachute Regiment 6 witnessed on the German side such an accumulation of material and troops for purely defensive purposes,' marveled Major von der Heydte, whose regiment had withdrawn to the line running from Vaudrimesnil to a point south-west of Méautis to Reffuveille to Prairie de Gorges with the 17th SS Panzergrenadier Division following the battle of Carentan. 'In the sector on both sides of the Carentan–Périers road, commanders and troops did their utmost to form this iron ring,' he wrote.[5] The American focus on the Cotentin peninsula and Cherbourg provided elements of the German Seventh Army with a respite, which they put to good use. 'The troops committed in the forward line, at least those in the sector of Parachute Regiment 6, utilised the three-week lull in the fighting to dig in and to establish a consecutive system of positions, with a double line of trenches at the focal defence points,' remembers Major von der Heydte.[6] According to von der Heydte, the lull was interrupted only by small-scale

---

3. Ibid, pp. 27–28.
4. Elbridge Colby, *The First Army in Europe 1943–1945* (The Battery Press, 1969), pp. 29–32.
5. von der Heydte, *B-839 A German Parachute Regiment in Normandy*, p. 25.
6. Ibid.

reconnaissance, patrol operations and light artillery action on the part of both the Americans and Germans. The 17th SS-Panzergrenadier Division had in the meantime brought up its second regiment, which had not participated in the battle for Carentan, and committed it on the right flank of the sector to the east of the Carentan–Périers road around St-Georges-de-Bohon. Seventh Army knew that Périers would be the next objective.[7]

The 2nd Infantry Division, which would be facing Hitler's paratroopers at Hill 192, had landed in Normandy on 7 June 1944 as part of V Corps and taken over the central sector of the beachhead area. Considered one of the American Army's 'good' units, it had fought its way southward from the beaches and in four days of non-stop combat had defeated the Germans in a series of towns and the Cerisy Forest, before reaching St-Georges-d'Elle, 25km from the beaches. The 'Indian Head' division consisted of the 9th, 23rd, and 38th Infantry Regiments, each supported by an artillery battalion. The soldiers of the 2nd Infantry Division first encountered Fallschirmjäger of the 3rd Parachute Division on 12 June at St-Georges-d'Elle. 'They now faced elite troops, haughty and of high morale, meticulously trained and primed for fighting, indoctrinated with the Nazi creed to the point of fanaticism,' recorded the division history. 'Lead elements of the 3rd Parachute Division had just begun arriving when they were encountered by the 23rd Infantry. Prisoners taken indicated that they came from Rennes, Brittany.'[8] The two sides battled over the town, which changed hands many times, for the next month.

After ten days of fierce fighting among the hedgerows against elements of three German divisions, the V Corps slowly advanced until the forward line, curving to the east and south-east, was located just north of Hill 192 by 16 June. Elements of the 2nd Division battled to take Hill 192 against the German 3rd Parachute Division, which was firmly entrenched on the hill. After four failed battalion-sized attacks between 12 and 16 June, and a multi-battalion assault on 18–19 June, resulting in 1,200 casualties, the 2nd Infantry Division was firmly entrenched near the north base of Hill 192.[9] For the last attack, the Americans massed twenty battalions of artillery along a 3,000-yard front, literally blasting their way through the Germans.[10]

---

7. Ibid.
8. Walter M. Robertson, *Combat History of the 2nd Infantry Division in World War II* (The Battery Press, 1980), p. 26.
9. Martin Blumenson, *Breakout and Pursuit*, p. 150.
10. Colonel Henry G. Spencer, *Nineteen Days in June 1944 (Henry Grady Spencer, 2014)*, Chapter 10. 'Objective: Hill 192, June 18–19, 1944', Kindle.

Yet even more than 200 artillery pieces were not enough for U.S. forces to hold the hill against the inevitable counter-attacks. Only limited objective attacks were made by V Corps during the remainder of June.

The terrain north of Hill 192 was typical of the Normandy beachhead area. The fields were crisscrossed with hedgerows that marked the boundaries of cultivated areas. Although the distance between hedgerows varied, the average distance near Hill 192 was about 75 yards. From Omaha Beach to Hill 192 the ground was flat and made up of small orchards and farmland. The Cerisy Forest, west of Balleroy, provided the only large sized concealment area. This was captured by V Corps before the Germans could utilise it. Two small rivers, the Aure and the Elle, ran from east to west through the beachhead area, while the large Vire River ran north from St-Lô to Isigny.[11] German defences in the 2nd Infantry Division sector ran from the base of Hill 192 westward toward St-Lô, 3 miles away, and then to the sea.

Although it had been pounded so heavily by American artillery that it appeared on aerial photos as a 'moth-eaten white blanket,' Hill 192 was a strong position.[12] Located 16 miles south of Omaha beach, 2 miles south-west of St-Georges-d'Elle, and 2 miles east of St-Lô on the St-Lô–Bayeux road, the hill was the dominating natural terrain feature in the beachhead area. The hill was not a commanding peak, but rather a long, sugarloaf hill, about 1,000 yards wide, 1,200 yards long and only 50m higher than the surrounding ground. American artillery had destroyed a tower in the trees on its summit, which the Germans had rebuilt. From it they could see Omaha beach and the intervening terrain, 16 miles to the north. Hill 192 was completely covered on the north side with hedgerows about 3–4ft high with a thickness of about 2–3ft at the base. They were built of closely packed earth and rock, and were usually sodded and topped with a hedge, whose roots further strengthened the wall. Of various sizes and shapes, the hedgerows surrounded fields and lined sunken roads. About a third of the fields were orchards, the rest under cultivation. Small groups of farm buildings dotted the area. Most of the south side of Hill 192 was completely covered by thick woods that contained very few trails. Thus,

---

11. Lieutenant Colonel Frank T. Mildren, 'The Attack of Hill 192 by the 1st Bn, 38th Infantry (2nd Division), July 11, 1944, (Normandy Campaign)' (Fort Leavenworth, Kansas: School of Combined Arms, 1946–1947), p. 4.

12. Martin Blumenson, *United States Army in World War II. The European Theatre of Operations. Breakout and Pursuit* (Washington, D.C: Centre of Military History, 1989), p. 151.

each field was a battleground in itself and each hedgerow was an obstacle, affording observation and fields of fire only to the next hedgerow. On Hill 192, the Germans had excellent observation of not only the 2nd Infantry Division sector, but also the 29th and 1st Infantry Divisions to the west and east, respectively. From the hill, the Fallschirmjäger directed artillery fire over the entire area of V Corps' zone, with roving guns firing from multiple firing points.[13] 'The enemy's observation points were 'looking down our throats' and would continue to do so until Hill 192 could be reduced,' recorded the 2nd Infantry Division history. 'Vicious fighting took place among the hedgerows, while the Germans waited to spray the fields with fire or propped up dummies in their foxholes and attacked with knives.'[14]

Facing the Americans was General-Lieutenant Richard Schimpf's 3rd Parachute Division. Upon notification of the Allied invasion at Normandy and orders to move to the front, Schimpf had dispatched an advance guard, Kampfgruppe Alpers, named after Major Friedrich Alpers, Knight's Cross recipient and commander of the 1st Parachute Infantry Battalion, 9th Parachute Infantry Regiment. Kampgruppe Alpers consisted of one battalion each from the 8th and 9th Parachute Infantry Regiments, two companies from the 3rd Parachute Engineer Battalion, two batteries from the 3rd Parachute Artillery Regiment, and one company of the 3rd Parachute Anti-Tank Battalion, along with detachments from the 3rd Parachute Flak and 3rd Parachute Signals Battalion. Alpers and his men departed on the night of 6/7 June and reached Avranches by the morning of 7 June. Elements of the 9th Parachute Infantry Regiment reached St-Germain-d'Elle on the same day, while the 8th Parachute Infantry Regiment took up positions north and north-west of this village on the same day. General Marcks, the Seventh Army commander, told Schimpf to begin planning an attack along the St-Lô–Bayeux road in support of the I SS Panzer Corps

---

13. Captain Henry L. Calder, 'The Operations of the 2nd Battalion, 23rd Infantry (2nd Infantry Division) in the Attack on Hill 192, West of Berigny, France 12–16 June 1944 (Normandy Campaign)' (Fort Benning, Georgia: Advanced Infantry Officers Course, 1949–50), p. 2; Mildren, 'The attack of Hill 192 by the 1st Bn, 38th Infantry (2nd Division), Jul 11, 1944', pp. 4–5; Lieutenant Colonel D. C. Little, '105mm Howitzer Battalion in Attack of a Position, Hill 192, Normandy, 11 Jul 44', (Fort Leavenworth, Kansas: Command and Staff College, 1946–47), p. 12; Henry G. Spencer, *Nineteen Days in June* 1944, p. 185.
14. Robertson, *Combat History of the 2nd Infantry Division in World War II*, p. 29.

attack on the British lodgement. However, the attack was cancelled after Panzergruppe West headquarters was bombed by the British. By 10 June, the German situation in Normandy was so critical that both Field Marshals Rommel and von Rundstedt cancelled all offensive operations, with the result that the 3rd Parachute Division took up defensive positions. The 9th Parachute Infantry Regiment established itself 4km north of Bérigny near St-Georges-d'Elle. The 5th Parachute Infantry Regiment went into the line to the east of it. The 3rd Parachute Artillery Regiment positioned its guns to cover the line from St-Germain-d'Elle to Bérigny and Couvains.[15]

General Schimpf, the commander of the Wehrmacht's largest and most elite infantry division in Normandy, was proud of his men and their long and difficult march from the extreme west of the Brittany peninsula to the front line in Normandy. 'In making the 350km long march in eight to ten nights ..., the young paratroopers passed their first performance test and trial by fire with flying colours,' he recorded after the war. 'The development of the situation unfortunately did not permit the granting of even a single day of leave for the troops, who badly needed rest.'[16] Schimpf and his men found Allied control of the skies over Normandy extremely difficult to deal with, but not insurmountable. 'Due to the enemy's air superiority all tactical and supply movements had to take place only along secondary roads, which frequently caused delays,' remembered Schimpf. 'The signal communications with army headquarters were being maintained by telephone and telegraph service. Thanks to the excellent service of my signal corps, who at that time made superhuman efforts, I was never very long out of communications with my units.'[17] 'With allowance for the enemy air activity it was astonishing that the supply service still functioned to a moderate degree. Despite the scant number of tons of supply on hand, the growing stretches of road to be covered due to the failure of the railways, and finally the limitations of supply activities at night it was possible after all to move up the supplies for the division in a barely tolerable manner. Only very few replacements were arriving during this period.'[18]

---

15. Fritz Roppelt, *Der Vergangenheit auf der Spur: 3 Fallschirmjager Division. 1943–1945* (Roppelt, 1993), p. 109.
16. Richard Schimpf, *B-541 Operations of the 3 FS Div during the Invasion of France June–Aug 1944*, p. 13.
17. Schimpf, *B-020a Normandy Campaign*, p. 6.
18. Ibid.

Oberst Max-Josef Pemsel, Seventh Army Chief of Staff, lauded Schimpf and his men, who had arrived at the front in the nick of time: 'It was remarkable that the Division suffered hardly any losses in men and material to enemy air force activities on its ten-day march from the extreme west of the Brittany peninsula to the front line in Normandy. The reasons were good organisation of the marches and insufficient enemy observation from the air and by agents in the area.'[19] Combat operations escalated on 11 June, when the Americans launched a major attack, preceded by heavy artillery barrages, aimed at capturing St-Lô. 'The attacks, strongly supported by tanks, resulted in local penetrations near St-Georges-d'Elle and St-Quentin,' remembered Schimpf. 'However, it was possible to seal them off.' During the battle, an encircled battalion of the 5th Parachute Regiment had managed to fight its way back to German lines carrying all its wounded.[20] The paratroopers were fed into a defensive line. By the night of 17 June, units of the 3rd Parachute Division were concentrated in their assembly area near Caumont–St-Lô, where they were assigned a 24km sector and the mission to hold. The Germans were faced by three American divisions. 'I was surprised that the enemy, despite his numerical superiority, let it go so far,' noted Schimpf, relieved. 'His combat reconnaissance must have failed him.'[21] Max Pemsel notes that German Seventh Army had no anxiety about the division's wide sector and was confident in the unit's ability to carry out its mission as the fighting power of the 3rd Parachute Division had been assessed as equal to two German Army standard divisions.[22] Pemsel fails to mention that this was because the 3rd Parachute Division, with 10,000 Fallschirmjäger in its ranks, was by far the strongest of any division-size formation in the German Seventh Army in Normandy. On 1 July, its closest contender, the 17th SS Panzergrenadier Division, had 8,600 men in its ranks. The less than stellar 353rd Infantry Division had 8,000. And even the elite 2nd SS Panzer Division had only 5,000 men.[23] Furthermore, the division was superbly

19. Schimpf, *B-541 Operations of the 3 FS Div during the Invasion of France June–Aug 1944*, pp. 26–27.
20. Ibid., p. 17.
21. Schimpf, *B-020a Normandy Campaign*, p. 4.
22. Max Pemsel, 'Commentary on the report by Generalleutnant Schimpf, Richard', in Schimpf, *B-541 Operations of the 3 FS Div during the Invasion of France June–Aug 1944*, pp. 26–27.
23. Steven J. Zaloga, *St. Lô 1944: The Battle of the Hedgerows* (Osprey Publishing, 2017), Chapter. 'Opposing Armies: The German 7. Armee', Kindle.

trained and armed, and ready for combat. 'The strength of the Parachute Division rested in defence,' recorded Pemsel, 'because the Division was well trained for it. The paratroopers felt at home in this bush terrain and as an individual fighter, felt himself superior to the enemy's material.'[24]

The 3rd Parachute Division defended with the 8th Parachute Regiment on the right, 5th Parachute Regiment in the centre, and 9th Parachute Regiment on the left. The 3rd Parachute Engineer Battalion and, sometimes, one battalion of each parachute infantry regiment located to the rear of their regimental sectors, constituted the reserve. Due to the shortage of reserves, no large-scale counter-attacks could be executed in the parachute division sector. German tactics called for sealing off enemy penetrations and immediately launching local counter-attacks. During the first weeks of combat, the division had a single artillery battalion, located behind the centre of the division sector, in support. A heavy anti-aircraft battery was employed by the 8th Parachute Regiment for engaging ground targets. A second German Army artillery battalion arrived to support the division at the beginning of July. According to Schimpf, no support was available from the Luftwaffe.[25] However, the U.S. 2nd Infantry Division history notes that it was occasionally strafed by Luftwaffe planes, some of which were shot down.[26]

Over the next several weeks, Schimpf and his Fallschirmjäger were constantly in battle against 'powerful reconnaissance and pinning down operations' conducted by single American battalions. 'The defence against these continuous attacks, which were executed like combat patrols, was excellent training, which familiarised the German troops with the enemy's manner of fighting,' recorded Schimpf:

> The fact that a considerable number of tanks were put out of action, mostly by close-combat weapons, did away with the tank terror complex. On the other hand, the constant state of alert and the increased difficulty of each movement on the combat field brought about by excellently directed enemy artillery and mortar fire, meant a heavy physical burden for the troops.

---

24. Max Pemsel, 'Commentary on the report by Generalleutnant Schimpf, Richard', in Schimpf, *B-541 Operations of the 3 FS Div during the Invasion of France June–Aug 1944*, pp. 26–27.
25. Schimpf, *B-541 Operations of the 3 FS Div during the Invasion of France June–Aug 1944*, 14–15, 18–19.
26. Robertson, *Combat History of the 2nd Infantry Division in World War II*, p. 30.

Schimpf described the American tactics as 'more schematic' and 'inflexible' than the Germans and surprise attacks as 'extremely rare', providing the defending Fallschirmjäger with the opportunity to take appropriate countermeasures in a timely manner. American objectives were extremely limited and, according to Schimpf, U.S. commanders failed to exploit success by continuing their thrusts in depth, which would have been quite possible and would have resulted in serious consequences for the Germans due to their weak defences. 'Therefore, it was nearly always possible to establish new defensive front lines,' he concluded. According to Schimpf, U.S. combat aircraft seldom appeared over the 3rd Parachute Division front, choosing instead to harass the supply echelons and focus on road traffic, all but shutting down movement during daylight hours. 'The almost complete lack of German fighter formations and inadequate number of anti-aircraft forces made this easy for the American air force,' he lamented. 'Losses in men and material were high during this six weeks of defensive fighting that had to be endured without a break, during which the losses were replaced only inadequately.'[27] Later, Schimpf would attribute the success of his 3rd Parachute Division's apparently impossible defensive mission during the first weeks of the Normandy invasion in the face of overwhelming odds to three factors: U.S. forces extreme timidity in battle; the excellent morale of his paratroopers and their high level of training; and the combat leadership of the NCOs, whose battle experience proved capable. 'The tactics used changed steadily, insofar as they were not conditioned by the terrain. Thereby we often succeeded in deceiving the enemy,' recalled Schimpf. 'I still remember distinctly how strongly I was impressed by the inventive spirit of my men during my frequent visits to the front lines.'[28]

The Americans believed that Hill 192 and the territory on either side was held by the 3rd Parachute Division's 9th Parachute Infantry Regiment. In fact, elements of two parachute infantry regiments defended that ground: 3rd Battalion, 9th Infantry Parachute held the crest of the hill facing the U.S. 2nd Infantry Division's 38th Infantry Regiment; 1st Battalion, 5th Parachute Infantry Regiment defended the eastern side of the hill, facing the 2nd Infantry Division's 23rd Infantry Regiment.[29] The

27. Schimpf, *B-541 Operations of the 3 FS Div during the Invasion of France June–Aug 1944*, pp. 24–25.
28. Schimpf, *B-020a Normandy Campaign*, pp. 5–6.
29. Zaloga, *St. Lô 1944: The Battle of the Hedgerows*, Chapter 'The Campaign: Hill 192', Kindle edition.

Fallschirmjäger maintained a tight counter-reconnaissance screen, made maximum use of sunken roads and hedges, and employed roadblocks, wire entanglements and minefields. The Americans expected the Germans to defend with 'determination' and 'vigour', and to employ local counter-attacks to hold their positions, although there seemed to be few, if any, German tanks in the area. Furthermore, U.S. intelligence officers estimated that the II Parachute Corps did not possess an impressive amount of artillery. In fact, the II Parachute Corps possessed only a single battalion at the beginning of July with about 330 rounds per gun. However, three additional battalions were in the process of being deployed from Italy to Normandy to support the Fallschirmjäger corps. The Americans were certain that the Germans had pre-registered the artillery they did have to cover the approaches to Hill 192 with 'precision' fire.[30] 'These new defenders all wore mottled camouflage suits and seemed to be all armed with automatic weapons,' remembered American Lieutenant Colonel D.C. Little, an artillery battalion commander, who participated in the battle. 'They were clever, tenacious foes. They fired their "burp" guns from trees, hedgerow corners, and buildings.'[31] Furthermore, snipers were everywhere, even in the trees, which grew as high as 20ft above the hedgerows.[32]

Between 17 June and 11 July, while the Americans awaited the order to resume the attack, Schimpf's paratroopers converted each hedgerow on the northern slope of Hill 192 into a maze of dugouts and firing positions, an intricate system of mutually supporting positions. According to Little:

> Tunnels were dug at ground level through the hedgerows to afford apertures at the base of the hedgerows. Pits dug through the tops of the hedgerows were zigzagged for greater protection. Machine guns and towed and self-propelled anti-tank guns fired from prepared positions throughout the defended area. Movement laterally and to the front was covered by the hedgerows themselves and the many orchards and tree-lined

30. Zaloga, *St. Lô 1944: The Battle of the Hedgerows*, 'Opposing Armies: The German 7. Armee', Kindle edition. 'Blumenson, *Breakout and Pursuit*, p. 151.
31. Little, '105mm Howitzer Battalion in Attack of a Position, Hill 192, Normandy, 11 Jul 44,' p. 13.
32. Robertson, *Combat History of the 2nd Infantry Division in World War II*, p. 31.

trails throughout. Mortars were emplaced in countless positions and covered every American position and avenue of advance.[33]

Good camouflage and well-concealed positions made the firing points, gun and mortar, and anti-tank positions almost impossible to see from the American side. Some dugouts were as deep as 12ft with underground passageways leading to concealed, firing positions within the hedgerows. The firing slits from these positions were covered by vines growing out of the hedgerows. Machine guns were located under hedgerows at junctions to cover all possible approaches. During the ten days preceding the battle, the Fallschirmjäger managed to badly shoot up almost every American patrol sent out trying to find gaps in their positions. 'The Germans ... employed deadly and vicious anti-personnel mines against patrols,' recorded the 2nd Division history. 'Mortars and automatic weapons, even self-propelled 88s, blazed away at patrol parties on the slightest provocation, playing hide and seek with the Division's artillery.'[34] The same thing happened to patrols from other U.S. units attempting to penetrate their flanks. This was not only due to the paratroopers' counter-patrolling skills, but also, according to several U.S. commanders, to a lack of tactical competence in scouting and patrolling among American infantry divisions.[35] 'The Germans' greatest asset was the calibre of the troops themselves,' recalled Little:

They were always in the next hedgerow. Our patrols sent out at night were shot up badly or gobbled up entirely. If we withdrew a hedgerow or two to bring down fire on their positions, they followed us back and were again in the next hedgerow. I watched as a group of paratroopers was being questioned after the hill had been captured. One ragged bearded survivor expressed the esprit of the 3rd Parachute Division when he was asked what he thought of the Americans now. Looking fixedly at his questioner he answered without hesitation 'Germany will win!'[36]

---

33. Little, '105mm Howitzer Battalion in Attack of a Position, Hill 192, Normandy, 11 Jul 44,' p. 13.
34. Robertson, *Combat History of the 2nd Infantry Division in World War II*, p. 30.
35. Mildren, 'The attack of Hill 192 by the 1st Bn, 38th Infantry (2nd Division), Jul 11, 1944,' p. 5.
36. Little, '105mm Howitzer Battalion in Attack of a Position, Hill 192, Normandy, 11 Jul 44', p. 16.

Replacements for the 3rd Parachute Division arrived sporadically and too few in number. On 1 July, sixty Fallschirmjager arrived by truck from Gardelegen and Nurnberg. They were divided up among the companies of the 9th Parachute Regiment, which was in desperate need of reinforcements following heavy losses during the last week of June. Only the night before, fourteen paratroopers had been killed around St-André-de-l'Épine during an American attack that had been repulsed. Among the replacements were several lightly wounded paratroopers, who now re-joined their respective companies.[37]

The Fallschirmjager had learned to respect the soldiers facing them. Some even feared them. 'It was Hill 192, near Bérigny,' recounted Fallschirmjäger Erwin Schmieger of the 9th Parachute Regiment's 3rd Parachute Infantry Company during a post-war interview. Schmieger had joined the Wehrmacht in March 1943 at the age of eighteen. He had enlisted as a paratrooper in the Luftwaffe on 5 May 1944 as a machine gunner. 'For a fortnight we were told to guard the front line along the edge of the wood, each of us in a hole in the ground 50m apart, as the rest of the company headed down the road to St-Lô at night. Opposite us were madmen with Indian heads ...' Schmieger tapped his left shoulder, indicating the place where the Americans of the 2nd Infantry 'Indian Head' Division had their unit insignia sewn.

> There were no rules ... Everyone had their knives drawn ... we were soldiers! Suddenly, in the night, there was a noise. It was a friend who thought he had seen someone go down. A few minutes later we heard a cry that went straight through me; they had slaughtered him! I could hear him crawling toward me through the leaves and I spent the entire night in my foxhole trembling with fear. I had other fears, but nothing like that. I'd only just turned nineteen. When we took roll call in the morning, there were only half of us left.[38]

The U.S. V Corps plan called for the 2nd Infantry Division to attack Hill 192, with the 23rd Infantry assaulting on the left, the 2nd Battalion 38th Infantry assaulting on the right, and the 1st Battalion 38th Infantry attacking frontally on a 600-yard front. Seizure of Hill 192 would provide

---

37. Georges Bernage, *Objective Saint-Lô. 7 June 1944–18 July 1944* (Pen & Sword Military, 2017), pp. 177–178.
38. Bernage, *Objective Saint-Lô*, p. 121.

the Americans with control of the hill and the St-Lô–Bérigny road. The 1st Battalion planned on committing eight tanks from the 741st Tank Battalion to its attack on the right-front of its sector. The attack was supported by artillery from the 3rd Armour Division, two battalions of artillery from the 1st Infantry Division, V Corps Artillery, two Tank Destroyer battalions and two companies of 4.2in mortars, along with the 741st Tank Battalion.[39] 'Air support included armed reconnaissance with planned and on-call missions. The 2nd Division plan of attack called for demonstrations on the fronts adjacent to Hill 192 to divert the attention of the defenders and get them to commit their reserves and supporting weapons prematurely. After hearing of the fire support available for his frontal attack, 1st Battalion commander Lieutenant Colonel F. T. Mildren wrote: 'I figured the battalion could almost walk up the hill without too much effort. I was due for quite a surprise and found I greatly underestimated the ability of the German 3rd Parachute Division.'[40] Major Spencer was informed by his commander that all he had to do was to follow the artillery barrage up the hill. High explosives would do the rest.[41]

At 0500 hours on 11 July the artillery battalions began their preparatory fires, joined by the armoured artillery battalions, 4.2in mortars, and the infantry battalion's own 60 and 81mm mortars. The artillery barrage lasted for an hour, increasing in intensity, as the Americans pounded the German paratroopers and hedgerows with growing numbers of tanks, mortars and artillery pieces. The eight 105mm artillery battalions supporting the attack fired more than 25,000 rounds, an average of 300 rounds per artillery piece, and more than 45,000 tons of high explosive. Except for three days during the Battle of the Bulge, this was the heaviest expenditure of ammunition in the history of the 2nd Infantry Division's 38th Field Artillery Battalion. Tanks and bazookas knocked out German assault guns concealed in a destroyed village, while U.S. infantrymen, who had crept within grenade distance, destroyed enemy machine gun and anti-tank gun emplacements.[42]

Gefreiter Helmut Kaslacka, of the 9th Parachute Regiment, was one of the Fallschirmjäger defending Hill 192. Kaslacka had made

---

39. Mildren, 'The attack of Hill 192 by the 1st Bn, 38th Infantry (2nd Division), Jul 11, 1944', p. 7.
40. Ibid.
41. Spencer, *Nineteen Days in June 1944*, Chapter 10. 'Objective: Hill 192', Kindle.
42. Blumenson, *Breakout and Pursuit*, p. 152.

his ten qualifying parachute jumps at the Luftwaffe's airborne school at Wittstock. Arriving in France, he was assigned to the 3rd Parachute Division in Brittany, near Brest. 'When the invasion started we move out approximately 30–40km daily, but only at night,' he recorded in a 24 July 1944 letter to a friend. 'During the day American fighter bombers controlled the area. Then we were put into [the] line East of St. Lô, approximately 5km away from the town.'[43] The strength of Kaslacka's company was 170 paratroopers when the American artillery opened fire on Hill 192:

> Then 11 July arrived and the most terrible and gruesome day of my life. At 0300 our company sector got such a dense hail of artillery and mortar fire, that we thought the world was coming to an end. In addition to that, the rumbling of motors and rattling could be heard in the enemy lines – tanks. It scared the pants off us. We could expect a very juicy attack. If we thought that the artillery fire had reached its climax, we were disillusioned at 0530. At that time a tremendous firing started which continued to 0615. Then tanks arrived. The movement of tanks, however, is somewhat difficult here in Normandy. As we at home have our fields fenced in by wire and wooden fences, so the fields over here are lined with hedgerows. They are about five feet high and have the same thickness. These hedgerows are winding crisscross through the terrain. We dig in behind these walls and the Americans do the same. It is a regular hedgerow war.[44]

At 0600 hours the 2nd Infantry Divisions infantry–engineer–tank teams jumped off for the attack. Each team consisted of a twelve-man infantry squad, a four-man engineer demolition team, and an M-4 Sherman tank with a special rack over the motor compartment that carried thirty satchel charges of TNT. Each satchel charge contained 20lb of explosives. When a tank was called forward by the infantry platoon leader, the engineer team would place charges against the hedgerow and blow a hole big enough for the tank to get through.[45] The infantry–engineer–tank teams followed 50

---

43. 'A German Soldiers Last Letter', in Robertson, *Combat History of the 2nd Infantry Division in World War II*, p. 34.
44. Ibid.
45. Charles D. Curley, *How a Ninety Day Wonder Survived the War. The Story of a Rifle Platoon Leader in the Second Indianhead Division During World War II* (Ashcraft Enterprises, 1991), p. 82.

yards behind a rolling artillery barrage intended to form a protective shield against the hill's defenders. 'The artillery bombardment so shattered the hill that foxholes dug later in the slopes caved in,' recorded the division history. [46] The Americans instantly ran into the heaviest concentration of German artillery and mortar fire the veteran GIs had ever encountered. 'Our casualties were heavy in Company A on the left,' remembered Lieutenant Colonel Mildren. 'Nevertheless, we managed to overrun their initial positions, which happened to be a covering shell.' The Americans gained little ground against the German main defensive position. 'In spite of all the fire cover we could place in this sector, all movements by our units were met by intense and accurate small arms fire, that came from positions within the hedgerows,' recorded Mildren. 'We could not locate those positions and could not see any Germans.'[47]

Every attempt at a manoeuvre by the Americans was met by intense machine gun and rifle fire, as well as constant artillery and mortar fire. Due to the cleverly concealed Fallschirmjäger positions, the 2nd Infantry Division soldiers could not direct artillery or tank fire on any known emplacements; 'Consequently we were merely shooting "in the dark",' lamented the battalion commander.[48] Two Sherman tanks were hit by Panzerfausts. The explosion resulting from the detonation of the satchel charges carried on the tanks by the engineers completely blew off the turrets. 'Very little was found of the crew,' remembered one American officer. Another tank hit a mine. The Germans had laid large numbers of anti-personnel and anti-tank mines in the field between hedgerows. A fourth Sherman was destroyed by artillery, leaving only one tank with the assaulting company. Additional tank support was not forthcoming as the tankers were hesitant to risk more vehicles, laden with explosives. Several hours elapsed before the Americans removed all the explosives from their tanks and got them back into action.[49]

By 0900, the lead attacking companies had suffered 60 per cent casualties. However, other elements of the U.S. battalion overran several German positions. Fifteen Fallschirmjäger surrendered, running to the rear with their hands in the air as the American infantry advanced. Paratroopers who refused to capitulate were killed at point-blank range or

---

46. Robertson, *Combat History of the 2nd Infantry Division in World War II*, p. 33.
47. Mildren, 'The attack of Hill 192 by the 1st Bn, 38th Infantry (2nd Division), Jul 11, 1944', p. 8.
48. Ibid., p. 8.
49. Ibid.

buried alive in their strong points by Sherman dozer tanks.[50] Air support for the attack was postponed due to a heavy fog. When the skies cleared, American planes attempted to bomb and strafe the defenders. Some of the aircraft missed their targets, bombing their own troops instead, knocking out an aid station and communications and throwing the infantrymen into confusion that delayed further attacks. However, after reorganising themselves, the Americans pressed their attack from multiple directions and were surprised to find themselves making steady progress. Having suffered heavy casualties and on the verge of being outflanked, the remaining Fallschirmjager were to withdraw and fight a delaying action.[51] Kaslacka's letter continued:

> Well, on that 11 July the tanks were rolling toward us. They shot with their guns through the hedgerows as though cake dough. Sharpshooters gave us a lot of trouble. You must know however, that the Americans are using H.E. ammunition, which tears terrible wounds. Around 1000 the order came to withdraw, as the position could not be held. I had one wounded in my MG position. When I wanted to get him in position with the help of someone else, a shell landed 2 yards away from us. The wounded fellow got another piece of shrapnel in his side, and the other fellow also was wounded. I however did not get one single piece of shrapnel. Anyway, on that day I escaped death just by a few seconds a hundred times. A piece of shrapnel penetrated through the leather strap of my MG and was thus diverted from my chest. In this way I could name many instances.[52]

By 1400 hours two U.S. companies had reached the top of Hill 192. They then commenced the difficult move through the heavy woods to the far side of the hill. Meanwhile, a battalion of the 23rd Infantry Battalion had outflanked the enemy position, placing tank fire on houses concealing German strong points and using rifle-grenades on crew-served weapons in the hedgerows. The Fallschirmjäger withdrew rapidly. Although

---

50. Martin Blumenson, *Breakout and Pursuit*, p. 152; Curley, *How a Ninety Day Wonder Survived the War*, p. 88.
51. Mildren, 'The attack of Hill 192 by the 1st Bn, 38th Infantry (2nd Division), Jul 11, 1944,' p. 9.
52. Robertson, *Combat History of the 2nd Infantry Division in World War II*, pp. 34–35.

the Americans were encountering only artillery and mortar fire, it took the rest of the afternoon to move down the hill and cut the St-Lô–Bérigny road. There, American artillery killed a large concentration of paratroopers, while Sherman tanks from the 741st Tank Battalion knocked out two German self-propelled guns supporting them. The slow advance was due to the condition of the woods, which had been devastated by American artillery and mortar fire and the presence of numerous anti-personnel mines laid in the few sunken roads that were available for a covered approach. By late afternoon, the 2nd Infantry Division soldiers had consolidated their positions and started to dig. 'We did not receive an enemy counter-attack – the Germans being content to fire mortar and artillery concentrations on our newly won positions,' remembered Lieutenant Colonel Mildren. 'As a matter of fact, during daylight hours we could not move around on the forward slope of Hill 192, because we were easily seen by the enemy, and each of our visible movements was followed by a mortar barrage from the Germans.'[53] The 2nd Infantry Division's 23rd and 38th Infantry Regiments suffered sixty-one killed and 239 wounded during the last battle for Hill 192.[54]

The German 9th Parachute Regiment suffered even heavier casualties defending Hill 192, including 100 dead, 250 wounded and 200 missing.[55] The dead included two rifle company commanders and two platoon leaders from the 1st Parachute Battalion; seven rifle platoon leaders from the 2nd Parachute Battalion; and a company commander and six platoon leaders from the 3rd Parachute Battalion. 'Less than 200 prisoners were taken, but the enemy dead were many times the number of prisoners,' remembered Little, proud of the role American artillery had played in the battle. 'Many German dead, killed by time-fire [mechanically set airbursts] and bursts on the tops of hedgerows, had to be dug out of holes and hedgerow emplacements.' Kaslacka's letter, later found by the Americans, concluded:

53. Mildren, 'The attack of Hill 192 by the 1st Bn, 38th Infantry (2nd Division), Jul 11, 1944,' p. 10.
54. 'Casualty Appendices to Hill 192 Combat Interviews (13–18 June [sic] 1944),' *2nd Infantry Division Combat Interviews*, RG 407, NARA; According to Blumenson, *Breakout and Pursuit*, p. 153, the Americans suffered 405 prisoners, including sixty-nine killed, 328 wounded, and eight missing; Curley, *How a Ninety Day Wonder Survived the War*, pp. 91, 94.
55. Roppelt, *Der Vergangenheit auf der Spur*, p. 155.

At 1135 I left the platoon sector as last man. Carried my machine gun through the enemy lines into a slightly more protected defile and crept back again with another fellow to get the wounded … On our way back, we were covered again with terrific artillery fire. We were just lying in an open area. Every moment I expected deadly shrapnel. At that moment I lost my nerves. The others acted just like me. When one hears for hours the whining, whistling, and bursting of shells and the moaning and groaning of the wounded, one does not feel too well … Our company has only 30 men left.[56]

What remained of Kaslacka's company was moved to a quieter sector, where it prepared to meet another American attack. Having participated in hand-to-hand combat on 11, 12, and 13 July, he was recommended for the Luftwaffe Ground Assault Badge for achievement in ground combat.[57]

The Seventh Army Commander, General Hausser, ordered General Meindl and the II Parachute Corps to hold Hill 192 at all costs. But it was too late. The Americans were already too heavily entrenched. U.S. artillery placed harassing fire on the Bérigny road, while the infantry repulsed a series of small and ineffective German counter-attacks over the next several days. By the end of July, the 9th Parachute Regiment had suffered 1,365 casualties, including 285 killed, 727 wounded, and 353 missing; 147 of the missing paratroopers were captured during the battle for Hill 192.[58] The parachute regiment's casualties were so heavy that its commander, Major Kurt Stephani, was said to have wept.[59] Among those killed was Gefreiter Helmut Kaslacka. Between 6 June and 25 July, the 3rd Parachute Division suffered 6,053 casualties, including 123 officers and 5,930 enlisted personnel, of whom 1,224 were killed.[60]

By the time Hill 192 had fallen, a total of thirteen American attacks south-east of St-Georges-d'Elle had been repulsed by Major Karl Heinz Becker's 5th Parachute Infantry Regiment, another of the 3rd Parachute Division's formations fighting for its life. With a series of attacks ranging from company to regimental strength and supported by large numbers of

---

56. Little, '105mm Howitzer Battalion in Attack of a Position, Hill 192, Normandy, 11 Jul 44', p. 24.
57. Robertson, *Combat History of the 2nd Infantry Division in World War II*, p. 35.
58. Roppelt, *Der Vergangenheit auf der Spur*, pp. 619–623, 693.
59. Ibid, p. 150.
60. Ibid, p. 159.

tanks and artillery pieces, the Americans destroyed most of the German forces defending south-west of St-Georges-d'Elles. Like Hill 192, St-André-de-l'Épine was abandoned after Wehrmacht forces suffered, by their own description, 'extremely heavy casualties in men and equipment'. The II Parachute Corps attempted to form a new line of resistance stretching from Bérigny, along the main road to St-Lô as far as La Calvaire–Hill 150–Bellefontaine using its last reserves. Due to the heavy casualties suffered by the 3rd Parachute Division, II Parachute Corps proposed the immediate commitment of the 5th Parachute Division's 14th Parachute Regiment. Seventh Army, however, refused to release the regiment because of the even more critical situation in the LXXXIV Army Corps sector. Near La Meauffe, elements of the 3rd Parachute Division repulsed the main effort of the newly arrived American 35th Infantry Division, which also launched several smaller attacks against the 352nd Infantry Division. A German counter-attack in the VII Corps sector with tanks from the elite Panzer Lehr division against the U.S. 9th Infantry Division sector sought to rectify the situation and relieve the situation in the west. However, the attacks were poorly coordinated with supporting troops and launched in a hasty, haphazard fashion, resulting in their failure.[61]

Near the end of the month, General Meindl believed he had an accurate measure of the U.S. First Army's tactics in Normandy. On 26 June, he issued 'Combat Procedures Against Numerically and Materially Superior Opposing Forces' to the soldiers of his II Parachute Corps. This important document is worth citing in full:

1. Daily reports from the front show that our losses are too high compared to the achievement. These, by the most part, are caused by artillery and mortar fire. These steady losses reduce our combat strength, nor can further replacements be expected. They must be reduced since our reserves are rapidly disappearing. Reinforced shelters, deep fox holes, well camouflaged trenches, taking advantage of our natural cover in each and every prepared position, etc., will reduce our losses considerably. It is every officer's and every non-commissioned officer's responsibility to see that men under adverse conditions take above protection measures.
2. It is a mistake when opposed by materially superior enemy to have the front lines too strongly manned during the day time. The front lines

---

61. 'History of the VII Corps for the Period 1–31 July 44 (Report after action against the enemy)', pp. 10–11, RG 407, NARA.

cannot entrench deeply enough to prevent recognition by the enemy, therefore, they will suffer heavier casualties. They will suffer most from enemy artillery and mortar fire. If the front lines are strongly manned it will not be possible to effect a defence in depth nor to launch an immediate counter-attack. In this type of country, automatic weapons fire will not stop an enemy attack (especially if smoke is employed or the attack is made at night) but: a. By pre-determined field of fire by our heavy weapons (including artillery and mortar fire) covering the potential areas of approach and penetration. b. by thoroughly concealing the strength of [the] MLR [Main Line of Resistance] the enemy is deceived. c. By immediately executing a counter-thrust in the MLR as soon as the enemy has penetrated our lines.

3. I am under the impression that some people tend to regard the foremost outpost as [the] MLR and consequently allow their defence in depth to be insufficiently manned. Before the actual MLR you must have observation posts to prevent a surprise enemy attack even though a preparatory artillery barrage be employed. It is the function of these outposts to bear the initial impact of enemy assault and to prevent his reconnoitering of the MLR. The observation posts, as well as the combat outposts, will be placed in advance parts of our territory. It is a disgrace to the troops in the area before the MLR to allow a single penetration by the enemy. Obstacles, mines, snipers, patrols should make such a penetration impossible. A reconnaissance in force of the MLR should be immediately recognised and counter measures so employed that the effort is destroyed at birth. A few successes will inspire our troops with confidence of having overcome a numerically superior enemy. If possible, the forward outposts should advance leaving behind dummy positions in order to nullify the effectiveness of the enemy artillery fire. If the enemy assault is concentrated in a narrow sector after a heavy preparatory artillery barrage our forces should counter-attack his flank. We must immediately employ the same methods of defence as 1918. From deep zones of defence, from numberless well camouflaged defensive strong points, with well-chosen fields of fire will the successful counter-thrust and counter-attack emerge. Inter-locking fields of fire must cover the entire front. By the courageous counter-attacks of our reserves will the penetration of our enemy be stopped and destroyed.

4. It is the mission of the infantry to separate the enemy infantry from supporting tanks by well-aimed single fire. Well entrenched, well camouflaged and clever exploitation of terrain, they let the tanks approach. Well-coordinated sudden fire at close range is destruction

to the enemy. The anti-tank troops will destroy the tanks by surprise fire from the flanks. The defensive weapons further behind the lines (including artillery) will remain camouflaged and silent. This is essential to counteract a tank penetration.

5. Artillery and mortar batteries in their prepared positions are responsible after artillery preparation. The enemy cannot receive any supporting fire. They must pin down the enemy reserves by concentrated fire and destroy them. Whoever in the heat of the battle waits for a call from infantry for supporting fires sends the fire too late. Because of a scarcity of ammunition, we cannot afford to fire at random. The units must have their own special observer to see the effects of the fire on the target. The observers in forward outposts will be totally concerned with the infantry actions. Therefore, Battalion and Battery commanders will have to employ tactics, observe and direct the fire themselves to get best results in the heat of battle.

6. Channels of communication will be disrupted by fire, therefore we have to rely on radio and messengers. The Battalion and Company messengers should be thoroughly familiar with routes. The same applies to supply columns and evacuation columns for wounded.

7. Goldbricks and stragglers will be most severely dealt with. The efficient non-com or officer will attend to this. A lightly wounded man will not need support to get to the first aid station. Those supporting helpers are goldbricks. Whoever leaves his friends in the heat of this battle with only a light wound while he can still fight is a coward and should be treated as such.[62]

Marked 'Destroy After Reading' and discovered by American forces three weeks after it was written, 'Combat Procedures Against Numerically and Materially Superior Opposing Forces' was a reflection of all that Meindl and his paratroopers had learned fighting the Americans in Normandy for almost three weeks. The II Corps commander recognised that the conflict in France, against a numerically and materially superior enemy, had stagnated into positional warfare and that the Wehrmacht was unlikely to receive any substantial reinforcements for some time to come. The Wehrmacht thus had to make do with what was available and maximise

---

62. Eugen Meindl, 'Combat Procedures Against Numerically and Materially Superior Opposing Forces', dated 26 June 1944 in 'G-2 Periodic Report, 182100 July 1944, 35th Infantry Division', CG VII Corps, RG 407, 207–21 to 207–2.2, Box 3844, NARA

the use of terrain and all weapons available to reduce casualties. 'Combat Procedures Against Numerically and Materially Superior Opposing Forces' was no doubt intended for the leaders and soldiers of the German Army units attached to the parachute corps as well as for Fallschirmjäger replacements. Already debilitating, ground combat in France was about to get much more problematic for U.S. forces.

Chapter 6

5th Parachute Division at Hill 122 and Mont-Castre

Centrally located at the base of the Normandy peninsula is the Prairies Marécageuses de Gorges, a large swamp located between Carentan, in the east, and La Haye-du-Puits, to the west near the coast. The Prairies was a formidable barrier to military operations. The Germans utilised this natural feature, hinging their main defence, the Mahlmann Line, to the western edge of the swamp. The Wehrmacht's main line of resistance extended eastward from high ground south of La Haye du Puits, anchoring the left flank, then across Hill 122, on whose southern slope was located the dense Forêt de Mont-Castre, thence to the western side of the Prairies Marécageuses de Gorges. The Mahlmann Line had been constructed in 1942 and named after Generalleutnant Paul Mahlmann, commander of the 353rd Infantry Division, as part of Wehrmacht wargames, in which German forces defended from an attack in the north. It consisted of dirt fortifications, some with wooden roofs. There were many trenches and deep firing positions in foxholes, as well as observation posts on Hill 122.[1]

Defending this line were a hodgepodge of mostly understrength German units, including the 243rd Infantry Division with the 2nd Battalion,

---

1. Georges Bernage, *3–9 juillet 1944 Objectif La Haye-du-Puits* (Heimdal 2013), pp. 5, 11; Blumenson, *Breakout and Pursuit*, p. 59; Zettering, '77. Infanterie Division' '243. Infanterie Division' '353. Infanterie Division,' Normandy 1944, pp. 229, 242, 281; Captain Paul R. Steckla, 'The Operations of the 3rd Battalion, 358th Infantry, 90th Infantry Division in the Battle of Foret de Mont-Castre, France, 10–12 July 1944 (Normandy Campaign)' (Fort Benning, Georgia: The Infantry School, 1947–1948), p. 6.

942nd Grenadier Regiment and 1st Battalion, 353rd Artillery Regiment of the 353rd Infantry Division in the west; the 5th Parachute Division's 15th Parachute Regiment in the centre; and the 77 Infantry Division with the 1st Battalion, 941st Grenadier Regiment of the 353rd Infantry Division in the east. The 353rd Infantry Division's 941st Grenadier Regiment and 942nd Grenadier Regiments occupied a forward outpost line extending from La Haye-du-Puits to the western edge of the Prairies Marécageuses de Gorges. The 941st Grenadier Regiment, with the 15th Parachute Regiment on its right, anchored the division's right flank, forward of the Forêt du Mont-Castre. Elements of the 77th Infantry Division defended on the north edge of Mont-Castre. Hill 122, core of the Mahlmann Line, remained the commanding terrain feature of the entire Cotentin peninsula. The Germans employed it to good advantage. Visibility was practically unlimited in all directions. From this location they had observed all troop movements since the assault on Utah beach. Observers had little difficulty adjusting artillery fire on targets in the overflowing lodgement area. The ability to manoeuvre was lost to attacking forces until this feature was seized.[2]

With an elevation of 300m, the Forêt de Mont-Castre is located north-west of Lastelle, north-east of Gerville-la-Forêt and south of Lithaire. Mont-Castre was a ridge extending 3 miles in an east–west direction. The western half, near La Haye-du-Puits, was bare, with two stone houses in ruins on the north slope. The eastern half, densely wooded, offered cover and concealment, and dominated the surrounding flatland for miles. No roads mounted to the ridge line, only trails and sunken wagon traces, 'a maze of alleys through the somber tangle of trees and bush', records the official U.S. Army history of the Normandy invasion.[3] By holding the hill mass, the Germans could deny the Americans movement southward. Possession of Mont-Castre was a prerequisite for the U.S. advance toward Périers. And seizing Périers was a precondition for the American breakout out of Normandy. By the beginning of July 1944, the First U.S. Army in Normandy consisted of four U.S. corps: V Corps (1st, 2nd, 29th Infantry Divisions); VII Corps (4th, 9th, 83rd Infantry Divisions); VIII Corps (8th,

---

2.   Bernage, *3–9 juillet 1944 Objectif La Haye-du-Puits*, pp. 5, 11; Zettering, '77. Infanterie Division' '243. Infanterie Division' '353. Infanterie Division', *Normandy 1944*, pp. 229, 242, 281; Steckla, 'The Operations of the 3rd Battalion, 358th Infantry, 90th Infantry Division in the Battle of Foret de Mont-Castre, p. 6.

3.   Martin Blumenson, *Breakout and Pursuit*, p. 64.

79th, 90th Infantry Divisions, 82nd Airborne Division); XIX Corps (29th, 30th, 35 Infantry Divisions). The 3rd Armoured Division at Isigny was the army reserve.[4]

Commanded by Major General Eugene M. Landrum, the 90th Infantry Division landed at Utah beach on 8 June. Since then it had fought at Pont l'Abbe and Gourbesville under the U.S. VII Corps, capturing the latter on 15 June. Four days later, the 90th joined the U.S. VIII Corps. The division had taken heavy casualties during its advance from the Normandy beaches, more than 3,500 men between 8 through 28 June. By the beginning of July, 40 per cent of its personnel were replacements.[5] It had also experienced leadership problems, resulting in the relief of its commanding general, Brigadier General Jay W. MacKelvie, and two regimental commanders. The official history of the U.S. Army in Normandy notes that the 90th Division had lacked 'cohesion and vigor' and its ability to achieve its objectives as the Corps' main effort during its planned attack on Mont-Castre 'was an unknown quantity'.[6] The 90th consisted of the 357th, 358th, and 359th Infantry Regiments, four medium artillery battalions, and the 90th Reconnaissance Troops. As it advanced southward it received a tank battalion (first the 746th and by the time of the battle of Mont-Castre, the 712th), the 607th Tank Destroyer Battalion, and the 537th Anti-Aircraft Artillery Battalion as attachments.[7]

The 'Tough 'Ombres' of the 90th Infantry Division were scheduled to launch their attack on Mont-Castre, a two-regimental affair, at 0500 hours on 3 July. It was part of a U.S. First Army wide offensive designed to win ground and gain the Americans manoeuvre space. Omaha and Utah beaches were still the only means of getting men and material for the build-up into the

---

4. War Department, *American Forces in Action Series. St-Lo (7 July– 19 July 1944)* (Historical Division, 21 August 1946), p. 2.
5. 'Battle Casualties Zone of Combat Continental Europe in Compliance with WAR-41940', 26 May, Attention SPXOM from General Lee to General Eisenhower E33677, Historical Reference Collection, Centre of Military History; Msg CM-IN-14997,' 18 June 1944; Msg CM-IN-19242,' 23 June 1944; Msg CN-IN 592,: 1 July 1944. My thanks to Lieutenant Colonel (Retired) Mark Reardon for compiling and providing me with these reports.
6. Major General J. A. Van Fleet, *Tough Ombres. The Story of the 90th Infantry Division* (Stars and Stripes, 1944), p. 8; Blumenson, *Breakout and Pursuit*, p. 63.
7. Stanton, *World War II Order of Battle*, p. 163.

American zone. Thus, First Army was seriously hampered in concentrating its supplies and moving its troops off the beaches.[8] The 359th Infantry Regiment, on the right, was to advance about 4 miles through the hedgerows to the thickly wooded slopes of Mont-Castre, take Hill 122, and meet the 79th Infantry Division south of La Haye-du-Puits. The 358th Infantry Regiment, on the left, was to force the corridor between Mont-Castre and the Prairies. In possession of the high ground, in contact with the 79th Infantry Division, and holding the corridor east of Mont-Castre, the 90th Infantry Division's 357th Infantry Regiment would then be committed through the corridor to the initial corps' objective. The attack was supported by the heavy weapons of the 357th Infantry Regiment, along with the tanks and tank destroyers of the 712th Tank Battalion and the 607th Tank Destroyer Battalion. In addition to the division's four organic artillery battalions, the attack was supported by a battalion of the corps artillery and the four artillery battalions of 4th Infantry Division. The 9th Infantry Division, with another four artillery battalions, had also been alerted to furnish fires on request.[9] Hill 122 was to be the 90th Division's main objective.

'Our big problem had two names,' remembered one American officer who participated in the battle for Hill 122 and Forêt de Mont-Castre. This was a small mountain 122m above sea level. It was about 3km long and 2km wide, and there was a second small mountain about the same size just south of it.' The officer went on:

> From the top of Hill 122 the Germans could observe the Atlantic Ocean on both the east and west sides of the peninsula and many miles to the north. The slopes were very steep, and it was almost impossible to walk up them without grabbing onto something. In addition, there was heavy brush on all sides of the hill. Our line of departure for the attack was about 6 kilometers from Hill 122, and we knew we would be under observation from there during most of the time we were attacking.[10]

Facing the 90th Infantry Division was a battalion of parachute infantry from Major Kurt Gröschke's 15th Parachute Infantry Regiment and a

8. War Department, St-Lo, p. 2.
9. Blumenson, *Breakout and Pursuit*, p. 64; Stanton, '90th Infantry Division,' *World War II Order of Battle*, p. 163.
10. John Colby, *War from the Ground Up. The 90th Division in WWII* (Eakin Publications, 1991), p. 98.

company from Major Gerhart Mertens' 5th Parachute Engineer Battalion. Both formations were part of Generalleutnant Gustav Wilke's 5th Parachute Division. According to Major von der Heydte, commander of the elite 6th Parachute Regiment: 'The 5th Parachute Division was of little combat value. Less than 10 per cent of its men had jump training, at most 20 per cent of the officers had infantry training and combat experience. Armament and equipment [was] incomplete; only 50 per cent of the authorised number of machine guns; one regiment without helmets, no heavy anti-tank weapons; not motorised.'[11] Subsequent events at Mont-Castre suggest that one must take von der Heydte's judgement with a large grain of salt.

According to 5th Parachute Division soldiers, the unit's senior leadership was problematic. General Wilke was described as an 'Eastern Prussian Junker type' who enjoyed the social life and showed little interest in military matters. His Chief of Operations, Major Reimers, a former Luftwaffe Flak officer, was thought to be 'haughty' and possessing 'no tactical knowledge'. A '100 per cent Nazi', he was disliked by his subordinates. Hauptman Kanthagg, the Chief Supply Officer, and his deputy, Hauptman Saegebarth, had both been promoted from the ranks and were described as '100 per cent Nazis'. The Chief Intelligence Officer, Hauptman Schirmer, was described as a 'coward' who treated prisoners badly. The paratroopers thought even less of the rest of the divisional staff, most of whom were former Nazi officials without any combat experience.[12] Fortunately for the division, and the Germans in Normandy, the best officers were serving as commanders in the parachute regiments, battalions, and companies.

Gröschke and Mertens were stellar commanders, even by the high standards of the German Fallschirmjäger. Groschke was a veteran of Poland, Holland, the Luftwaffe's airborne invasion of Crete, the Eastern Front and Italy. In Italy, his parachute infantry battalion had single-handedly stopped an attack by an Indian regiment on the Sango River. Later, as temporary commander of the elite 1st Fallschirmjäger Regiment, his forces prevented the Allies from breaking through to the Cassino–Rome Road. Gröschke was a recipient of the Knight's Cross and the German Cross in Gold. Mertens was a veteran of the Balkans, Crete and a two-time

---

11. Zetterling, '5. Fallschirmjäger Division', *Normandy 1944*, pp. 220–221; Wilke, *B-820 5th Parachute Division (6 June–24 July 1944)*
12. C.S.D.I.C., S.I.R 834 KP/43677 O/Fw Leyendecker, 'German Paratroop Formations', 6 August 1944, RG 165, NARA

veteran of the Eastern Front. In Russia he had led his men out of a Russian encirclement and, though twice wounded, fought at several critical points. He was a recipient of the German Cross in Gold, the Iron Cross First Class, and the Wound Badge.[13] Merten's paratroopers described him as a 'highly efficient, capable, and fanatical' officer'.[14] Others added that he was 'stiff' and a '100 per cent Nazi'.[15]

Gröschke's 3rd Battalion commander, Major Heinz Meyer, was yet another extraordinary Fallschirmjäger. A veteran of the German airborne invasions of Holland, Norway, and Crete, and of Italy and Russia, he was a recipient of the German Cross in Gold and the Knight's Cross, earning the latter in Italy after his battalion destroyed more than half a dozen American tanks with anti-tank mines and short-range weapons.[16] The 15th Parachute Regiment at Normandy included two future Knight's Cross awardees: Oberleutnant Karl Berger, the 3rd Battalion Adjutant, and Oberfeldwebel Karl Koch, assault platoon leader in the 3rd Battalion.[17] Thus, even this late in the war and despite statements to the contrary by other German commanders and staff members denigrating the unit, the 15th Parachute Regiment at Mont-Castre was well led and contained a host of stellar commanders and NCOs capable of squeezing the best performance from their paratroopers.

Since the Allied landings on D-Day, the 15th Parachute Regiment, the first formation from the 5th Parachute Division dispatched to the front (along with the 5th Parachute Artillery Regiment), had been attached to the Kampfgruppe König, the German 77th Infantry Division, and, later, the 353rd Infantry Division, fighting west of Carentan and at La Haye-du-Puits. The regiment had 95 per cent of its authorised weapons and equipment, but only 30 per cent of its motor vehicles. This suggests that Wilke had received additional arms and equipment since May and

---

13. Kurowski, 'Kurt Gröschke' and 'Gerhart Mertens', *Knight's Cross Holders of the Fallschirmjäger*, pp. 73, 151.
14. 'Tactical Interrogation Report No. 30, Annex No. 1 to G-2 Periodic Report No. 30, 27 July 1944', RG 407 VII Corps, 207.21 to 207–2.2, 17 June 1944, Box 3844, NARA.
15. C.S.D.I.C., S.I.R 834 KP/43677 O/Fw Leyendecker, 'German Paratroop Formations', 6 August 1944, RG 165, NARA
16. Kurowski, 'Heinz Keyer', *Knight's Cross Holders of the Fallschirmjäger*, p. 153.
17. Kurowski, 'Karl Berger' and 'Karl Koch', *Knight's Cross Holders of the Fallschirmjäger*, pp. 21, 115.

had cross-levelled across the entire division (taking from one formation to give to another) to frontload the 15th Parachute Infantry Regiment in terms of men and equipment, while awaiting further shipments of weapons and gear for his remaining paratroopers. The Fallschirmjäger's journey to the front had been arduous. By 12 June, when it departed for Normandy, General Wilke estimated that 80 per cent of the division's wire communications had been destroyed by artillery and bombs and that all the radio equipment had been smashed. Contact between units had to be maintained by messengers on motorcycles or in staff cars.[18]

One of the 5th Parachute Division soldiers defending Mont-Castre was eighteen-year old Heinz Bonkowski, of the 15th Parachute Regiment's III Battalion, 15th Parachute Company, commanded by Hauptmann Freundörfer. Bonkowski had experienced the war first-hand when he was only fifteen years old; in the summer of 1941, the first Allied bombs fell on his home town near Dortmund. The bombs wrecked buildings and killed neighbours. Bonkowski would forever remember the ambulances and the terrified population. He would also remember the four-engine bomber shot down over the city and the single parachute gliding to the ground. During their march to the Normandy front, Bonkowski's column was attacked by Allied aircraft, panicking the horses and wounding several soldiers, some mortally. 'If you come any closer I'll shoot you,' a wounded nineteen-year-old from Recklinghausen, whose legs had been blown off, had screamed at Bonkowski as he approached. 'I will not live as a cripple!' he shouted. The experience had shaken the younger Dortmunder. 'Chaos still enveloped the scene as soldiers, officers, medics, horses, and wounded men cluttered the road,' he remembered. After days of non-stop marching, the exhausted men of the 15th Parachute Regiment and their horse-drawn wagons, filled with ammunition, explosives, and mines, arrived on the Cotentin peninsula, where they prepared to meet the Americans. The soldiers of the 15th Parachute Company (most, like Bronkowski, were Fallschirmjager in name only, having never been sent for jump training) learned to constantly scan the skies for enemy observation aircraft and to remain absolutely still when they appeared. Failure to do so normally resulted in a barrage of U.S. artillery and mortar rounds that reduced their numbers.[19]

---

18. Wilke, *B-820 5th Parachute Division*, p. 3–4, 6.
19. Arve Robert Pisani, *Bocage. The Battle for Normandy* (Aperture Press, 2018), pp. 244–246.

At Mont-Castre Bonkowski's regiment was supported by assault guns from Sturmgeschütz Abteilung 902. The brigade had been formed as 'Lehr-Abteilung' from the Sturmgeschütz school at Tours in western France. It arrived in Normandy on 11 June with thirty operational StuG IIIs and was attached to the II Parachute Corps.[20] These were only a small fraction of the 248 StuG assault guns assembled by the Germans on the new Western Front in June 1944.[21] The combination of veteran, first-generation Fallschirmjäger commanders and their parachute infantry and engineers, supported by low-silhouette German assault guns capable of operating almost invisibly in the hedgerows of Normandy, spelled trouble for the Americans.

By the beginning of July, the German strategic situation in Normandy was precarious. According to the commander of the II Parachute Corps:

> At the end of June 44, we had come to the point where we could no longer consider a continuous defence. The elastic band had stretched as far as it could go; it was now ready to snap anywhere along the entire front. There were no more strong reserves which could have sealed off, let alone repel, an enemy penetration. It was only through the keen thinking of my subordinates that the right points were patched up at the right time. I informed higher headquarters of the situation without mincing words, in order that I would receive reinforcements, at least in artillery or mortar ammunition. The answer I received was that other units were in worse position than I and that my paratroopers were the anchor of the whole front.[22]

Meindl went on to add that, up to this point in the battle, it had been the II Parachute Corps alone that had withstood all attacks on the Seventh

---

20. Steckla, 'The Operations of the 3rd Battalion, 358th Infantry, 90th Infantry Division in the Battle of Foret de Mont-Castre, France, 10–12 July 1944 (Normandy Campaign)' (Fort Benning, Georgia: The Infantry School, 1947–1948), p. 6; 'Sturmgeschütz-Abteilung 902,' http://stugiii.com/stugunits/heerunits.html; Zetterling, 'Sturmgeschütz-Abteilung 902', *Normandy 1944*, p. 209.

21. Thomas Anderson, *The History of the Panzerwaffe, Volume 2: 1942–1945* (Oxford: Osprey Publishing, 2017), Chapter 7. 'D-Day: Defeat in the West', Kindle.

22. Meindl, *B-401 II Parachute Corps*, p. 32.

Army front. 'We were not lacking in the knowledge of how to do things, but we lacked the reserves, men, ammunition, weapons, and above all the Luftwaffe and one or two days of real rest so that the officers and men could get some sleep. Instead of that, there was just one phrase, "Hold Fast". In that way we were heading for disaster.'[23] The Allies had no intention of providing the German Seventh Army or the men of the II Parachute Corps with a respite.

At 0530 hours on 3 July, the U.S. attack on Mont-Castre kicked off as scheduled, under a driving, drenching rain. Persistent rains had hampered U.S. efforts in Normandy in June and July. The early summer of 1944 was the wettest since 1900. Extended rains had turned the marshlands west of Carentan into a deep quagmire, complicating cross-country movement. 'Rains also added immeasurably to the daily miseries endured by the foot soldier,' writes historian Michael Doubler. 'Low visibility and cloud ceilings often grounded all aircraft, denying the ground forces the support of fighter-bombers and aerial observers that was so desperately needed.' During 19–23 June, a major channel storm had ravaged the invasion beachheads, severely restricting the movement of supplies onto the mainland. As a result, shortages in key commodities hampered U.S. operations during the battles in the bocage.[24]

Initially, the 90th Infantry Division made rapid progress. Two hours later, however, resistance had stiffened. By the end of the day, American troops had driven the defenders from some positions, advancing less than a mile, while suffering more than 600 casualties. 'The 90th Division's performance had been less than stellar,' recorded U.S. Army historian Martin Blumenson, perhaps being overly critical. 'Tankers and infantrymen did not work closely together; commanders had difficulty keeping their troops moving forward; jumpy riflemen fired at the slightest movement or sound.'[25] The attack had only dented the outpost line of resistance. It had failed to penetrate to the main defences. 'The Germans haven't much left,' wrote one observer, 'but they sure as hell know how to use it.'[26]

---

23. Ibid, p. 33.
24. Captain Michael Doubler, *Busting the Bocage: American Combined Arms Operations in France 6 June–31 July 1944* (Pickle Partners Publishing, 2013), Chapter 1. 'The Operational Setting', Kindle.
25. Blumenson, *Breakout and Pursuit*, p. 65.
26. 2nd Lieutenant Stanley W. Seeley, 'After Action Report 712th Tank Battalion, 3 July 1944, July 1944–March 1945' (Headquarters 712th Tank Battalion: 20 August 1944), p. 107; Blumenson, *Breakout and Pursuit*, p. 65.

In the 358th Infantry Regiment sector, the American infantry pulled back, while the artillery drenched Mont-Castre with high-explosive and white phosphorus. 'I have fought on all fronts, but I have never seen such artillery. It was withering,' remembered one German private, who had served earlier on the Eastern Front against the Red Army and was later captured by the Allies. 'For accuracy and strength, it far surpassed anything I have ever experienced.'[27] U.S. riflemen advanced once again. The appearance of a German StuG assault gun and two half-tracks, probably from Sturmgeschütz Brigade 902, caused panic. The Americans retreated. Two tanks of the supporting 712th Tank Battalion were knocked out by enemy artillery and assault guns. One German StuG was destroyed by the American tankers. The Germans, as capable as the Americans of creating their own version of artillery hell, even with their limited resources, poured 'a good volume' of artillery into the attackers, which delayed further attacks that day. 'The Regiment had heavy losses as the German artillery observers had a field day,' remembered John H. Cochran, Jr. of the 359th Infantry Regiment. 'We encountered many land mines, and when they slowed us down, in came the artillery.'[28] Harassing fire continued through the night, complicating the 90th Infantry Division's reorganisation and resupply.[29] The first U.S. attack on Mont-Castre had failed. 'The fighting in the thick undergrowth of the forest will never be forgotten by those of us who went through it,' remembered another American veteran of the fighting. 'How any of us survived the intense, concentrated artillery fire will never be understood.'[30] The German Seventh Army commander, General Paul Hausser, was satisfied with the conduct of his troops. His principle concern was his supply of artillery ammunition.[31]

The 90th Infantry Division resumed its attacks on 4 July after a ten-minute artillery barrage. Heinz Bonkowski crouched in his fighting position, listening to the explosions all around him. 'The ground vibrated and beat against his chest with each burst,' recorded one historian, who

---

27. 'Effects of Allied Artillery and Air Bombardment, 271st Infantry Division, July 1944', Intelligence Summary 52, 20 August 1944, from First US Army, G-2, Periodic Report No. 74, cited in Donald Graves, *Blood and Steel. The Wehrmacht Archive: Normandy 1944* (London: Frontline Books, 2013), Chapter 14. 'Effects of Allied Artillery and Air Bombardment', Kindle.
28. Colby, *War from the Ground Up*, p. 106.
29. Blumenson, *Breakout and Pursuit*, pp. 65–66.
30. Colby, *War from the Group Up*, p. 108.
31. Blumenson, *Breakout and Pursuit*, p. 64.

interviewed the young German paratrooper. 'The smoke choked his nose and throat and his eyes burned, until he felt he couldn't endure it any longer. Shockwaves tore through the forest and glowing shrapnel struck the tree trunks with loud hisses. It seems impossible to Heinz that anyone could survive this inferno.'[32] But the Germans not only survived, they retaliated immediately with their own artillery. Counter-battery fire was so intense that the Americans expected a counter-attack, causing the regimental commanders to delay their attacks. However, no counter-attack materialised. When the American artillery shifted away from their positions, Bonkowski and his comrades put their individual weapons and machine guns into action. Bonkowski fired short salvos from his StG 44 assault rifle, reloading quickly each time a magazine was empty. The G.I.s from the 90th Infantry Division were so close that he could see them between the trees, almost within hand grenade range. He dropped one with a burst of machine gun fire, unsure if the American was dead or wounded.[33]

'The Boche gave no respite,' recorded the 90th Infantry Division history, 'assisted by his excellent observations which pinpointed our disposition as of dusk, he continued a hell of artillery, mortar and harassing machine gun fire which increased the problems of resupply and readjustment of local supports and reserves.'[34] The Americans started moving forward once more. German armoured vehicles appeared again. 'The infantry withdrew in haste and some confusion,' notes the official U.S. history of the battle. Attempts throughout most of the day to resume the offensive failed. Then at dusk, the 359th Infantry Regiment rallied and advanced for almost 2 miles.[35] 'The Americans were superior in personnel and material,' remembered General Wilke. 'Moreover, the German troops were not relieved by reserves or by changes within a regiment, they were not given time to sleep and rest in so-called "reserve positions" or "rest positions".'[36]

As the Americans approached his well-concealed position, Bonkowski could hear German cries for medics and commands in English. Running out of ammunition, he tossed two grenades at the attackers. Struck in the

---

32. Pisani, *Bocage*, p. 253.

33. Ibid., p. 254.

34. 'After Action Report, July 1944, 90th Infantry Division', *90th Infantry Division History & Research*, www.90thidpg.us/Research/90thDivision/History/AAR/july44.html

35. Blumenson, *Breakout and Pursuit*, p. 66.

36. Wilke, *B-820 5th Parachute Division*, p. 4.

helmet by a flying object, he slipped into unconsciousness, collapsing to the bottom of his trench. When he awoke, he found himself looking into the barrel of a U.S. M-1 Garand held by a red-headed American soldier. For Heinze Bonkowski, and many of his Fallschirmjäger comrades at Mont-Castre, the war was over.[37]

The slackening in German opposition was attributed to three factors. The first was heavy American attacks to the west of the 3rd Parachute Division. By noon the German LXXXIV Corps, to the west (left) of the II Parachute Corps, was fighting for its life. The second was the heavy losses sustained from the devastating American artillery attacks. 'The increasing enemy artillery and mortar fire caused 90 per cent of our casualties,' remembered General Meindl. 'As the attacks were nearly always made in the same sector, the only way to provide the regiments with a certain amount of relief was to keep changing their sector.'[38] Finally, heavy Wehrmacht casualties all along the Normandy front and the lack of reserves necessitated regrouping on a shorter front.[39] By the beginning of July, the Germans had suffered 65,000 casualties (as compared to 61,000 for the Allies, including 35,300 Americans). German losses were heavier than expected, while those of their opponents were lighter and less dramatic than predicted. And while OKW had dispatched only 10,000 replacements to Normandy to make up its losses in July, the Allies had another 250,000 men and nearly 58,000 vehicles backlogged in England still waiting to be landed in France.[40]

According to Eugen Meindl, the overall quality of replacements arriving in Normandy from Germany was low. 'The replacements from Germany after 1943 were poor and the ones that came after 1944 were completely untrained and did not bring weapons with them. The young people were undernourished, and even though they had the strong will to fight, they could not cope with the hardships of life at the front.'[41] Meindl went on, however, to laud the quality of replacements being sent to the

---

37. Pisani, *Bocage*, p. 256.
38. Meindl, *B-401 II Parachute Corps*, p. 34.
39. Blumenson, *Breakout and Pursuit*, p. 66.
40. Robert M. Citino, *The Wehrmacht's Last Stand. The German Campaigns of 1944–1945* (University of Kansas Press, 2017), pp. 250, 252; Horst Boog, et. al, *Germany and the Second World War. Volume VII. The Strategic Air War in Europe and the War in the West and East Asia, 1943–1944/45* (Clarendon Press, 2015), p. 597.
41. Meindl, *B-401 II Parachute Corps*, p. 17.

II Parachute Corps, suggesting that the Luftwaffe's Fallschirmjäger force was receiving a high priority on replacements. 'Approximately 90 per cent of the replacements,' he noted, 'had a capital fighting spirit and, contrary to officers and non-commissioned officer replacements, learned quickly.'[42]

U.S. infantrymen fighting for their lives in Normandy in July 1944 knew little of the problems faced by Hitler's Fallschirmjäger. German artillery fire, infiltrating paratroopers and the hedgerows were such impediments to the 90th Infantry Division's offensive that the commander postponed further attacks on 4 July. In one U.S. infantry regiment, 90 per cent of its 125 casualties were caused by enemy mortar and artillery shells. 'Tired and soaking wet from the rain, the riflemen were reluctant to advance in the face of enemy fire that might not have been delivered in great volume,' recorded Blumenson, 'but that was nonetheless terribly accurate.'[43] On the second day of the attack, the 90th Infantry Division exceeded the 600 casualties it had suffered on the first day. The Americans had lost about a battalion of infantry a day in casualties attacking Mont-Castre. The 'Tough 'Ombres" had run into elite soldiers every bit as hard-hitting as themselves. 'Mont-Castre, dominating the countryside, loomed increasingly important,' noted the official U.S. Army history. 'Without it, the division had no observation; with it the Boche had too much.'[44]

Believing the Germans were weakening, General Landrum committed his 357th Infantry Regiment, the 90th Infantry Division's reserve, hoping that fresh troops could outflank Mont-Castre. The regiment went into battle the next day, enjoying only moderate success. The 359th Infantry Regiment, however, made substantial gains supported by effective artillery strikes and air support, the latter of which attacked enemy supply and reinforcement routes. The regiment fought to the north and north-east slopes of Mont-Castre in a series of small unit actions, with German paratroopers resisting aggressively and launching local counter-attacks whenever possible. The failure of the 357th Infantry on the left and the 359th Infantry on the slopes of Mont-Castre compelled General Landrum to commit a battalion of the 358th Infantry to reinforce his troops. This was the beginning of a gradual shift of the division strength to the right. Under constant air and artillery strikes and in danger of being enveloped, the Germans fell back. By nightfall, four American infantry battalions were

---

42. Ibid., p. 31.
43. Blumenson, *Breakout and Pursuit*, p. 67.
44. Ibid.

perched precariously on Mont-Castre, as well as the highest point on the ridge, Hill 122.[45]

On the morning of 6 July, the remaining two battalions of the 358th Infantry were committed to the battle. The Fallschirmjäger counter-attacked throughout the day, supported by three tanks and artillery, which pounded the Americans all through the day and night. The counter-attacks continued under the cover of darkness. Shortly before midnight the paratroopers launched a violent counter-attack against the 357th Infantry Regiment, badly mauling two U.S. infantry companies and pushing them back. The two companies were reorganised as one unit and fought as such for the next several days. Two other infantry companies, holding the flanks, were cut off by German infiltration. Mortar and artillery fire was hourly increasing in intensity.[46] 'Only the commitment of the 2nd SS-Panzer Division combat group and Fallschirmjäger Regiment 15 prevented appreciable success on the part of the enemy,' recorded Generalleutnant Max Pemsel, Seventh Army Chief of Staff.[47]

On the morning of 7 July, U.S. forces, reinforced by tanks, were still holding their ground. However, more rain, deep mud, the difficulty of defining the enemy front, and German artillery hindered attempts to further consolidate their position or to advance.[48] An attack by the paratroopers of the 15th Parachute Regiment drove the 357th Infantry Regiment out of the town of Beau-Coudray. According to American veterans of the fighting, the better part of two U.S infantry companies were killed, wounded, or captured in hand-to-hand fighting. In all, the Germans counter-attacked more than a dozen times.[49] The entire front was alive throughout the night of 7 July. Small groups of Germans attacked and harassed the Americans. Shortly after midnight, a battalion of paratroopers scaled the wooded southern slopes of Mont-Castre and launched a 'noisy fanatical assault' against the 358th Infantry Regiment, retaking the high ground and driving one U.S. battalion back onto the reverse, northern slope. This was Major Heinz Meyer's III Battalion, with Lieutenant Karl Berger, the adjutant, taking part

---

45. Ibid., p. 68.
46. 'After Action Report, July 1944, 90th Infantry Division', *90th Infantry Division History & Research*, www.90thidpg.us/Research/90thDivision/History/AAR/july44.html
47. Pemsel, *MS # B-763 The Seventh Army in the Battle of Normandy*, p. 65.
48. Blumenson, *Breakout and Pursuit*, p. 69.
49. Colby, *War from the Group Up*, p. 103.

in the battle.[50] German paratroopers also infiltrated down into the valley. Others attacked the 359th Infantry Regiment from the east and south. German mortar and artillery fell all along the 90th Division front. Early the next morning, the Americans issued instructions that all units were to mop up rear areas, consolidate and improve positions and continue to exert pressure on the Germans by patrols and small arms and artillery fire. A resumption of the general attack the following day was to be postponed.[51]

The 1st Battalion, 357th Infantry Regiment, alone fought off fifteen separate counter-attacks, firing 6,000 81mm mortar rounds.[52] U.S. infantry companies were under heavy pressure and very low on ammunition. One company command post was attacked by German tanks and the entire command group killed or captured. The Americans planned their own counter-attack with infantry supported by tanks. However, heavy fire delayed the organisation of the attack and it was subsequently postponed until dawn. During the day, captured documents substantiated by air reconnaissance reports and ground observation revealed the presence of the elite 2nd SS Panzer Division 'Das Reich' in the Corps zone. Captured German officers reported that it would attack on 8 July to recapture the Mont-Castre forest. The direction of the attack would strike the U.S. 8th Infantry Division, scheduled to relieve the 90th Infantry Division in the forest on 8 July, squarely in the flank. As a result, the 8th Infantry Division was shifted westward and the 90th Infantry Division left with the mission of taking Mont-Castre. The U.S. 79th Infantry Division, on the extreme right, had advanced almost abreast of the 90th Division, bypassing La Haye-Du-Puits. The U.S. 83rd Infantry Division, on the left, had made only limited progress in three days of fighting. The 90th Infantry Division history stated that across the entire front of the U.S. VII and VIII Corps, German resistance was as strong as on the first day of the offensive.[53]

The attack of the 2nd SS Panzer Division planned for 8 July was defeated. 'Extraordinarily strong artillery fire, ranging far into the rear area, as well as constant fighter-bomber attacks delayed portions of 2nd

---

50. Kurowski, 'Karl Berger', *Knight's Cross Holders of the Fallschirmjäger*, p. 21.
51. 'After Action Report, July 1944, 90th Infantry Division', *90th Infantry Division History & Research*, www.90thidpg.us/Research/90thDivision/ History/AAR/july44.html
52. Colby, *War from the Group Up*, p. 103.
53. 'After Action Report, July 1944, 90th Infantry Division', *90th Infantry Division History & Research*, www.90thidpg.us/Research/90thDivision/ History/AAR/july44.html

SS-Panzer Division, so that it was not launched until evening,' recorded the Seventh Army Chief of Staff. 'Advancing via Mobecq, the German forces succeeded in recapturing the western part of the Foret de Mont-Castre.'[54] 'Das Reich' had been transferred to the LXXXIV Corps and was committed piecemeal, as formations were transferred from east to west, as four different kampfgruppe: one to support the German defence of La Haye-du-Puits, two to support the 17th SS Division's counter-attack north-west of St Lô, and a fourth to support the II Parachute Corps as a mobile 'counter-attack' reserve.[55] The latter was supporting the 15th Fallschirmjäger Regiment at Mont-Castre.

The 90th Infantry Division attack scheduled for 8 July was cancelled. The 'Tough 'Ombres' spent the day consolidating their gains. The Americans, already sensitive to the threat of infiltration, became even more so after the survivors of two infantry companies that had been cut off made their way back to U.S. lines and informed their superiors that both companies had been wiped out. That day, German pressure slackened. 'It was later determined that the paratrooper force, having accomplished its mission of restoring the line, had been replaced by a less elite combat group,' recorded the 90th Infantry Division After Action Report for July 1944. That night three companies of German paratroopers were 'serenaded' by U.S VIII Corps Artillery.[56]

The Americans continued to strengthen their positions on 9 July. 'In the first five days of the fighting the 90th had [suffered] over 2,000 casualties,' remembered one veteran of the fighting. 'But we still had not broken the Mahlmann Line.'[57] German night attacks against the 358th and 359th Infantry Regiments were repulsed. Attempts to infiltrate U.S. positions continued throughout the night. The pause in American offensive operations afforded a brief respite to Major Gröschke's paratroopers. 'Conditions for the German troops became increasingly worse as the American supply of personnel, weapons and ammunition improved daily,' recorded General Wilke. 'Their cooperation and close contact between the

---

54. Pemsel, *B-763 The Seventh Army in the Battle of Normandy and the Fighting Up to Avranches*, p. 65.

55. James Lucas, *Das Reich. The Military Role of the 2nd SS Division* (London: Cassell, 1991), p. 135.

56. 'After Action Report, July 1944, 90th Infantry Division', *90th Infantry Division History & Research*, www.90thidpg.us/Research/90thDivision/History/AAR/july44.html

57. Colby, *War from the Group Up*, p. 116.

Allied air forces and the army, it must be admitted, was excellent. Such cooperation is only possible with a superior air force. It was this superior air power of the Allies that eventually brought about the final turn of events and decided the outcome of the war.'[58]

By 10 July, the day the 90th Division resumed its offensive, losses for General Wilke's 5th Parachute Division totalled 70 per cent killed and wounded. 'Two battalions of the 14th Parachute Regiment lost 50 per cent of their personnel and material on 23 and 24 June when each battalion was hit by about 450 bombs,' recorded Wilke.[59] The 15th Parachute Regiment, together with elements of the 77th Infantry Division, now defended the Mont-Castre Forest and Hill 122 along a 10km line with only 1,840 men.[60] I Battalion held the left; III Battalion defended the centre; II Battalion protected the fight. 3rd SS Panzergrenadier Regiment of the 2nd SS-Panzergrenadier Regiment was positioned at the centre and to the rear of the 15th Parachute Regiment as a mobile reserve.[61] 'Das Reich' was one of the few German panzer divisions sent to the American sector in July, a reflection of how serious the Wehrmacht considered U.S. First Army's attacks. By 10 July, the elite SS formation had suffered more than 1,200 casualties.[62] The German situation was considered so critical that General Paul Hausser was already considering withdrawing to a shorter line. Reinforcements were en route in the form of the 275th Infantry Division and the rest of the 5th Parachute Division.[63] Hausser was concerned that the line would rupture before the reinforcements arrived.

'If Hill 122 had been bad, the fight down the south side through the forest was just as bad, perhaps worse,' records one official 90th Infantry Division history. 'German paratroopers, almost invisible in camouflage clothing, were young, strong, fanatically determined and skilled in individual combat. Directions and contact were difficult to maintain. Undergrowth and murky weather limited visibility to twenty-five

---

58. Wilke, *5th Parachute Division*, p. 4.
59. Ibid., p. 6.
60. General of the SS Paul Hausser, *MS # A-974 Normandy. Seventh Army from 29 June to 24 July 1944* (U.S. Army Historical Division: Koenigstein, 16 August 1950), p. 16.
61. 'Fôret de Mont-Castre, 10 July 1944', map compiled and provided by Lieutenant Colonel (Retired) Mark Reardon to the author.
62. Zetterling, '2. SS-Panzergrenadier-Division "Das Reich"', *Normandy 1944*, pp. 323–324.
63. Hausser, A-974 *Normandy*, p. 16.

yards, more often to only five.'[64] The attack met fierce resistance, with the Germans counter-attacking repeatedly. 'The Boche engaged our infantry with hand grenades and close-range MG fire from trees, spider trap holes and carefully camouflaged dug-in positions in the tangled under growth, inflicting heavy casualties,' recorded the 90th Division AAR for July 1944. A platoon of Sherman tanks broke through the heavy underbrush to support the infantry and evacuate wounded. Two were destroyed by StuG III assault guns. A third was immobilised by the marshes.[65] So desperate were the Germans to halt the American advance that the Luftwaffe was committed in strength, a memorable occasion for the defenders in Normandy. 'On our front we had air support only once,' remembered General Eugen Meindl, commander of the II Parachute Corps. 'This was on 10 July 44, when twenty to thirty planes attacked ground targets north-east of St-Lô. The result was astounding. During the night we had some peace from the usual harassing fire and could take supplies right into the firing line from vehicles. This was a sign of how unaccustomed the enemy was to air attacks at the time. According to our standards, the attack had been a pretty tame affair. I watched it myself; it was scattered and inaccurate.'[66]

The air attack, however, was too little and too late. The Americans persisted, rupturing the German lines and forcing the defenders to withdraw 3,000m southward along the entire division front. 'A retreat was unavoidable, in order to preserve the coherence of the front,' recorded General Hausser. 'We succeeded in preventing a breakthrough and preparing the withdrawal ... The losses were heavy.'[67] Hausser's Seventh Army claimed to have captured 859 prisoners and destroyed 135 tanks and five armoured cars, and shot down nineteen aircraft with infantry weapons between 3 and 13 July.[68]

By 11 July, the Germans had been driven out of Mont-Castre Forest. The 90th Division AAR for July recorded: 'The battle of the Foret De Mont-Castre had been won. Blood, guts and superior equipment had finally broken the Mahlmann line.' The cost to the 90th Division had been high.

---

64. Van Fleet, *Tough Ombres*, p. 13.
65. Van Fleet, *Tough Ombres*, pp. 14–15; 'After Action Report, July 1944, 90th Infantry Division, 90th Infantry Division History & Research', www.90thidpg.us/Research/90thDivision/History/AAR/july44.html
66. Meindl, *II Parachute Corps*, p. 39.
67. Hausser, *Normandy*, pp. 18, 20.
68. Ibid., p. 22.

The Americans estimated that German losses were even heavier. For nine continuous days and nights the 90th Infantry Division had fought without respite against a seasoned and entrenched enemy and, despite being badly battered, had emerged from the fight victorious.[69] Although the Americans had reached the foot of Hill 122 by 5 July, it had taken a further four days to drive the Germans from the hill. On 12 July, U.S. forces finally reached Le Plessis-Lastelle at enormous cost to both armies. The 90th Division had suffered 26 per cent of all the casualties suffered by the Allied armies in all theatres of the war during that week. The 3rd Battalion of the 358th Regiment, which started with nineteen officers and 582 men, lost eleven officers and 343 men in a single day of fighting. By the end of the battle, only eight officers and 220 men remained in the ranks.[70] It took a further five days of fighting to reach the town of Périers, just 8 miles away.

The Germans had also suffered heavily. 'Amongst those units suffering unusually heavy losses was the II Parachute Corps, whose soldiers were committed to a debilitating battle,' remembered General Meindl. 'By 12 July 1944, the 3rd Parachute Division had suffered 4,064 casualties. A two-battalion kampfgruppe of 353rd Infantry Division had suffered losses of 485 men, while a three-battalion kampfgruppe of the 266th Infantry Division had lost 316 men. And a one-battalion kampfgruppe from the 343rd Infantry Division had lost 184. Since the battle strength of the units is sinking noticeably every day as a result of superior equipment of the enemy and their uninterrupted artillery fire,' he warned. 'Even the best of troops are no longer in a condition to drive off for any length of time any attempts at a breakthrough.'[71]

Assessing the fighting qualities of the U.S. soldier, General Wilke noted: 'The American infantryman must be termed very cautious and timid. Generally, they advanced only when they did not encounter any resistance. In case of the slightest resistance, artillery, tanks and air support were requested immediately by radio. The American infantryman only continued the advance when the area had been cleared.'[72] The 5th Parachute Division commander's evaluation of U.S. equipment was more laudatory: 'The American equipment was not only superior to that of any

---

69. 'After Action Report, July 1944, 90th Infantry Division', *90th Infantry Division History & Research*, http://www.90thidpg.us/Research/90thDivision/ History/AAR/july44.html
70. Colby, *War from the Ground Up*, p. 117.
71. Wood, *Army of the West*, p. 140.
72. Wilke, *B-820 5th Parachute Division*, p. 5.

other army, but it was also practical and easy to handle. Their mortars and artillery delivered exact and effective fire, especially when cooperating with the artillery observation planes.'[73] Writing about American air power, he noted:

> In view of their variety of fighter bombers, their efficiency, and the employment of four engine bombers as medium artillery, the American air forces dominated overwhelmingly the combat area. The German Luftwaffe was almost completely absent. From dawn to dusk the Allied fighter bombers, flying by the hundreds over the combat area and also in the rear area, compelled not only the front line troops to take shelter but they destroyed their weapons, disturbed traffic and supply on all roads even those reaching far into the German lines of communications. Every village, farm or house where uniforms were seen was strafed. Every motor vehicle, motorcycle, even cyclists and pedestrians were forced to take shelter.[74]

Wilke concluded:

> It was the Allied fighter bombers and bombardment planes that prevented the reserves from moving up, that smashed the front, its personnel and material, that brought about eventually the victorious decision, not only at the invasion front but on all fronts and last but not least in Germany, because they had paralyzed the country's industry and economy.[75]

By the end of the battle of Mont-Castre, the German Army and Waffen SS in Normandy had suffered more than 100,000 casualties, including 2,300 officers and 9,938 NCOs. The dead included nine general officers, seven general staff officers and 137 company commanders, a testimony to the intensity of the fighting and the propensity of German Army officers to lead from the front.[76] Wehrmacht losses translated into an average loss of 2,500 to 3,000 men a day. Losses in supplies and equipment were described as 'extraordinarily high' and only seventeen replacement tanks

---

73. Ibid.
74. Ibid.
75. Ibid.
76. Wood, *Army of the West*, p. 113.

were brought in to replace the approximately 225 that had been lost. 'The divisions which have been brought in are not used to battle conditions,' noted the weekly Army Group B report for the period, 'with their small contingents of artillery, anti-tank weapons, and other means of engaging tanks in close combat they are not able to offer effective resistance to enemy large-scale attacks for any length of time after being subjected to concentrated artillery fire and heavy air raids for hours on end. It has been proved in the fighting that even the bravest unit is gradually shattered by the well-equipped enemy, and loses men, weapons and territory.'[77]

Losses amongst the II Parachute Corp were equally high. Meindl reported that of 1,000 replacements allotted to the 6th Parachute Regiment, 800 had become casualties in a very short period. The main reason given for this 80 per cent casualty rate was the lack of experience. 'Troops must be first trained by experienced soldiers behind the lines,' recorded Meindl. 'However, the present conditions cannot be altered just yet, as we have no more reserves.'[78] Allied gains and German casualties left Generalfeldmarschall Erwin Rommel pessimistic: 'Our troops are fighting heroically, but even so the end of this unequal battle is in sight.'[79]

The battles for Hill 192 and Hill 122 were predominantly infantry and artillery affairs. In both, the Germans and Americans headed for the high ground, with the former getting there first. Both sides needed the high ground because of the vista it afforded to artillery observers and to deny this advantage to the enemy. In the land of hedgerows, the side with the dominating hill was the proverbial one-eyed man in the land of the blind. The high ground was more important for the Germans because they didn't have as much artillery as the Allies, so they needed to use it as effectively as possible. At Normandy, as in every major battle in history, the high ground acted as a force multiplier. With their air supremacy, the Americans could rely on aerial-borne artillery observers. In a theatre where Allied forces possessed aerial supremacy, aerial forward observers were considered the best means of observing enemy targets. In the U.S. First Army, each of its fourteen infantry and armour divisions had ten light aircraft, L-4 Piper Cubs or the larger L-5 Stinson Sentinels, assigned for observation and liaison missions. Additionally, each of the four corps headquarters had from fifty to seventy such, a total of almost 400 light observation aircraft. Each of these carried a skilled forward observer

---

77. Ibid., pp. 137–138.
78. Ibid., pp. 140.
79. Ibid., p. 139.

equipped with radios linked to the fire-direction centres of supporting artillery units. The FOs called fire on forward enemy positions as well as on valuable targets in the German rear area and adjusted barrages in support of American ground attacks. Historian Michael Doubler writes: 'During the Normandy battles, aerial forward observers conducted the majority of target-fire missions with "universally excellent" results.'[80] The Wehrmacht did not possess such a capability, especially at Normandy, where any German Army or Luftwaffe aircraft that took to the skies was immediately set upon by packs of Allied fighters and almost immediately eliminated.

The biggest difference between the battles of Hill 192 and Mont-Castre was that the 90th Infantry Division already had a month's worth of combat experience before the latter took place. True, the division suffered heavy casualties in that month, losing many experienced soldiers. But it also lost or shed many incompetent and ineffective commanders at all levels. Even so, American commanders had problems coordinating their infantry and tank assaults (with U.S. infantry and Sherman tanks operating on different radio frequencies) and getting their soldiers to keep moving forward under fire toward their objective. Still, the 90th Infantry Division was able to seize Mont-Castre much faster than the 2nd Infantry Division had seized Hill 192. It was also, however, a reflection of the growing American strength in Normandy in terms of men and weapons and, conversely, the weakening German position. The Wehrmacht was losing men and arms in Normandy, especially experienced combat leaders, faster than they could be replaced. It was also expending artillery and mortar ammunition quicker than they could be resupplied, especially with Allied fighters interdicting the Wehrmacht's lines of communications.

Wehrmacht and U.S. forces suffered similar casualties at Hill 192 and Mont-Castre, although they accumulated much more rapidly at the latter battle. At Mont-Castre, both sides sustained approximately 2,000 casualties.[81] German casualties were distributed amongst the 5,600 front line paratroopers and soldiers from the 15th Parachute Regiment and the 15th Parachute Engineer Battalion, as well as elements of the German 33rd, 77th, 91st, and 265th Infantry Divisions, which had been fed into the battle. The myriad of Wehrmacht formations defending Mont-Castre and the surrounding area is reflective of the German High Command's desperation to retain the high ground. The pressure exerted by the U.S.

---

80. Doubler, *Busting the Bocage*, Chapter II. 'The Battle', Kindle.
81. Blumenson, *Breakout and Pursuit*, p. 71.

90th Infantry Division forced the German LXXXIV Corps to commit its last reserves. The German Seventh Army also committed some reserves, while OKW was forced to release control of its only theatre reserve, the 15th Parachute Regiment.[82]

Both the U.S. 358th Infantry Regiment and the German 15th Parachute Infantry Regiment, which led the fighting for each side, suffered the heaviest, with some 900 casualties each. Surprisingly, Sturmgeschütz Abteilung 902 lost only three StuG IIIs by 11 July, with two drivers and five vehicle commanders listed as killed, a testament to the skill of the German panzer troops and the difficulty of spotting and knocking out these vehicles in the bocage.[83] During the battle of Mont-Castre, the Americans captured paratroopers from virtually every company committed in the space of a few days, with 430 Germans captured by 8 July. This was very different from the battle of Hill 192, where U.S. forces had a difficult time taking prisoners from the German 3rd Parachute Division. This didn't mean that the men of the 5th Parachute Division were less effective soldiers than those of the 3rd Parachute Division. Rather, the defenders at Mont-Castre, like Heinz Bonkowski, were put in a position where they had to surrender more frequently due to unrelenting attacks from multiple directions, American air and artillery superiority, lack of replacements and a shortage of ammunition and supplies. Almost 200 paratroopers of the 3rd Parachute Division surrendered at Hill 192 on 11 July 1944, when faced with continuing resistance or death. Despite Nazi and American propaganda to the contrary, the Fallschirmjäger of the 3rd and 5th Infantry Divisions were simply unwilling or unable to fight to the death at both Hill 192 and Mont-Castre. They did the best they could. Those capable of doing so, withdrew to fight another day. Those unable to withdraw, surrendered.

American sources indicate that General Wilke's Fallschirmjäger fought much harder and better than expected by the German High Command or even other elite Fallschirmjäger, like Major von der Heydte, before the battle. Their heroism and sacrifice, however, were obscured in the fiery bocage of Normandy, where valour and boldness were an everyday occurrence in both armies. The men of the 15th Parachute Regiment and the 5th Parachute Engineer Battalion never received the credit due to them for their skilled and tenacious defence of Mont-Castre and Hill 122. Without their sacrifices, the German line would have collapsed much sooner than it did.

---

82. Ibid., p. 72.
83. Zetterling, 'Sturmgeschütz-Abteilung 902', *Normandy 1944*, p. 210.

Chapter 7

3rd Parachute Division at St-Lô

Following the loss of Carentan, the most important battle for the Wehrmacht in France and Hitler's paratroopers in Normandy was the battle for St-Lô. By 12 July, all U.S. 21st Army Group objectives in the Hill 192 area had been seized, with the Americans in firm control of the St-Lô–Périers road from Bérigny to La Calvaire. The following day, General Bradley approved the outline plan for Operation Cobra – the American breakout from Normandy in the St-Lô area.[1] But first, the Allies had to seize the critical crossroads, with its two main routes and five other tarmac roads converging on the town. Bombed since D-Day, St-Lô had been reduced to rubble in June, when U.S. forces attempted unsuccessfully to first capture the town.[2]

General Meindl's II Parachute Corps, holding the sector between the Vire and Drôme Rivers, was responsible for the defence of St-Lô. Three kampfgruppe, one each from the 353rd, 266th, and 352nd Infantry Divisions under the operational control of the 352nd Division, defended on the left (west). Schimpf's 3rd Parachute Division, its headquarters north-west of Torigni-sur-Vire between the St-Lô–Vire road and the Vire River, defended in the east. From D-Day to 12 July, the 3rd Parachute Division had suffered 4,064 casualties. The 5th Parachute Regiment held the right; 9th Parachute Regiment defended the centre; 8th Parachute Regiment anchored the left.[3] The 3rd Parachute Engineer Battalion and one parachute infantry company from each regiment probably served as the divisional reserve,

---

1. Mary Williams, *U.S. Army in World War II. Special Studies. Chronology 1944–1945* (Washington, D.C: Centre of Military History, 1994), p. 229.
2. Blumenson, *Breakout and Pursuit*, p. 146.
3. Colonel Ernst Blauensteiner, 'Appendix 2. II FS Corps Situation Beginning of July 1944', *MS # B-261 II. Normandy 6 June–24 July 1944* (U.S. Army Historical Division, October 1946), The 3rd Parachute Division HQ was in

based on standard practice.[4] In support was the II Parachute Corps' 12th Assault Gun Brigade. It had begun the Normandy battles in June with its full authorisation of 32 StuG III assault guns.[5] However, only about a third of these were still operational by the beginning of July.[6] 'Although the troops in line were spread thin across a wide front, they were veterans,' wrote Army historian Martin Blumenson. 'The corps commander, Meindl, though concerned with what amounted to a manpower shortage for his wide front, felt certain that the defensive skill of his troops and excellent positions would offset to a great extent the rather sparse dispositions. He was confident he could keep the Americans out of St. Lo.'[7] Meindl's command post and his 12th Assault Gun Brigade were located near Fervaches at the centre of his sector behind his paratroopers. 'St-Lô had to be held as long as possible,' remembered the II Parachute Corps' commander.[8]

The 29th Infantry Division, on the north-east approaches to St-Lô, was the main effort of the U.S. XIX Corps' two-division attack on the town. The 29th and 35th Infantry Divisions, holding an 8-mile front only 4 miles from St-Lô, were to attack abreast in narrow zones. The 29th Division, on the left (east), was to take the town. It would be supported by four battalions of 155mm howitzers, a battalion each of 4.5in guns and 8in howitzers, and a battalion of 105mm guns.[9] The division had landed in Normandy on 6 June, one of its infantry regiments storming Omaha beach with the 1st Infantry Division and suffering heavy losses. The now veteran unit was comprised of the 115th, 116th, and 175th Infantry Regiments, four field artillery battalions, the 747th Tank Battalion (attached), and the 821st and 823rd Tank Destroyer Battalions (attached). The division had seen

the same location according to Appendix 3. II FS Corps Situation 22 July 1944. Blauensteiner was General Meindl's trusted Chief of Staff.

4. Blumenson, *Breakout and Pursuit*, p. 148; Zetterling, '3. Fallschirmjäger-Division', *Normandy 1944*, p. 218; Schimpf, *B-541 Operations of the 3 FS Division*, p. 16.
5. Thomas Anderson, *Sturmartillerie: Spearhead of the Infantry* (Oxford: Osprey Publishing, 2016), Chapter 6. 'Stalingrad and Beyond', Kindle.
6. For a good discussion of the 12th Parachute Assault Gun Brigade, see 'Fallschirm-Sturmgeschutz-Brigaden', www.freebooters.org /modules. php?name= Forums&file=viewtopic&t=449, accessed on 12 March 2018.
7. Blumenson, *Breakout and Pursuit*, p. 148.
8. Meindl, *B-401 II Parachute Corps*, p. 37.
9. Blumenson, *Breakout and Pursuit*, p. 153.

considerable combat since D-Day, suffering more than 7,000 casualties by the middle of July 1944.[10] Its strength on 1 July 1944 was 807 officers and 14,296 men, or close to full strength.[11] Although the U.S. 21st Army Group attempted to bring all infantry divisions participating in offensive operations up to full strength, it was unable to do so with the 29th Infantry Division before its attack on St-Lô.[12]

Prior to the final push on the town, the 29th Infantry Division commander, Major General Charles Gebhardt, had created a special training course near Couvains. M4 Sherman tanks and infantry squads practised new tactics to fight in the hedgerows, including the use of new explosive breaching techniques. General Gebhardt had his ordnance company weld iron prongs to his tanks so that they could ram holes in the hedgerow banks to facilitate the placing of demolitions. 'This series of exercises, formulated to season the men for the operation to come, found a platoon of infantrymen, a platoon of tanks, and a demolition team working as one unit and advancing on a limited objective,' noted the 116th Infantry Regiment after action report for July 1944. 'The Infantrymen, Engineers, and Tank Corps worked splendidly in completing their problem … The coordination exercises proved invaluable when our troops took up the main attack early in July.'[13] Another tactical change was to train the infantrymen to cross the hedgerow square through the centre and not along the lateral hedgerows on the sides of the fields, as they'd done in the past. The sides offered the false promise of shelter. The Germans had

---

10. Stanton, '29th Infantry Division', *World War II Order of Battle*, p. 107; 'Battle Casualties Zone of Combat Continental Europe in Compliance with WAR-41940, 26 Ma 1944, Attention: SPXOM, from General Lee to General Eisenhower, E-33677, Historical Reference Collection, CMH; Msg CM-IN-14997m 18 June 1944; Msg CN-IN-19242, 23 June 1944; Msg CM-IN-592, 1 July 1944; Msg CM-IN-13339, 16 July 1944; Msg CM-IN-14180, 17 July 1944.
11. 'After-Action Report July 1944. Phase V – Capture of St. Lo', 29th Infantry Division, *World War II Unit Histories & Officers*, p. 1, www.maryland military history.org/files/AftActRpt-29ID-44–07.pdf, accessed on 11 March 2018.
12. Blumenson, *Breakout and Pursuit*, p. 154.
13. 'After Action Reports, Action Against Enemy, 13 July 1944', 116th Infantry, *World War II Unit Histories & Officers*, p. 2., www. unithistories.com/units_ index/default. asp?file=../units/ 116th%20Inf. Reg%20AAR %20july%20 1944.htm.

learned to position a machine gun in each corner to mow down infantry squads moving along the side hedgerows. These combined arms tactics were summarised as 'One Squad, One Tank, One Field'. By these means, and with heavy artillery support, the 29th Infantry Division commander hoped to make a rapid, sustained advance.[14]

General Gebhardt designated the high ground near the town rather than St-Lô itself (which had been bombed from the air and shelled from the ground) as the 29th Infantry Division's immediate objectives. This included another Hill 122 north of the town, the Martinville ridge to the east (also known as Hill 147), and the heights south-east of St-Lô. 'With these in his possession and with the 2nd [Infantry] Division holding Hill 192, Gebhardt hoped that by threatening to encircle the city he would compel the Germans to evacuate,' assessed Blumenson.[15] 'The next mission of the 116 Regiment was to capture and hold the high ground overlooking the strategically located town of St-Lo,' remembered Sergeant John Slaughter. 'Jerry knew the importance of this communication hub to the final breakout of the Cotentin peninsula. Strongly entrenched, the Germans were dug in on the dominating high ground along a ridge road leading to the hamlet of Martinville, called Martinville Ridge. Among ourselves, we called it "the Ridge of Death".'[16]

Opposite the Americans were Fallschirmjäger from the II Battalion, 9th Parachute Regiment, 3rd Parachute Division, commanded by Hauptmann Reil Rudolf. The regiment was haemorrhaging men, having suffered more than 200 casualties since the beginning of July.[17] The soldiers of the 29th Infantry Division had learned to respect their German counterparts. 'The aggressiveness in which the enemy made its bid against our troops was accentuated by his use of flame-throwers and a type of fire which can be described only as crafty. This fire apparently was employed chiefly as a delaying element and as a means to create panic among our troops,' noted the 116th Infantry Regiment AAR. 'It was discovered that the enemy went

14. Blumenson, *Breakout and Pursuit*, p. 154; Steven Zaloga, *St. Lô 1944. The Battle of the Hedgerows*, 'East of the Vire', (Oxford: Osprey Publishing, 2017), Kindle.

15. Blumenson, *Breakout and Pursuit*, p. 154.

16. John Robert Slaughter, *Omaha Beach & Beyond. The Long March of Sgt. Bob Slaughter* (Zenith Press, 2009), p. 134.

17. Rudi Frühbeißer, *Opfergang deutscher Fallschirmjäger. Normandie – Ardennen* (Eigenverlag 1966), pp 13, 92–96.

so far as to use fire-crackers, suspended from trees on long fuses. This ruse undoubtedly was used to throw our troops off balance while meeting the counter-attacks.'[18] Since landing in Normandy, the U.S. First Army had experienced extremely heavy concentrations of artillery and mortar fire that had caused much damage to its communications. The G.I.s of the 29th Division had encountered their first dug-in German paratroopers at an orchard near Dufayel, between St-Lô and Couvains, in the first week of July. 'The fighting in this engagement was waged at close range, small arms and hand grenades brought into play,' recorded the 116th Infantry AAR.[19] The Germans had anchored their defence of St-Lô on the hills north and north-east of the town.[20]

The American attack on St-Lô was pre-empted by Meindl's paratroopers. On 11 July, just before daybreak, the II Parachute Corps launched a diversionary feint at the Bois de Bretel in support of an attack west of the Vire by the SS-Panzer Lehr Division. A German patrol cut the field telephone wires of the U.S. 115th Infantry Regiment. Enemy artillery and mortars opened fire. 'Two paratrooper companies supported by engineers struck the thinly deployed troops of the 115th, overran the American lines, encircled part of an infantry battalion, and drove a company of 4.2in mortarmen from their positions,' reported Martin Blumenson. 'Without communication and direction from higher headquarters, heavy mortar support, or knowledge of the extent of the German effort, small groups fought isolated engagements in the early morning light. At 0730 hours, judging that they had done their duty by Panzer Lehr, the German assault companies broke contact and withdrew to their former positions.'[21]

The surprise attack was conducted by a company-size assault group with soldiers from two companies comprising Shock Troops Kersting, named after the commander of the 5th Parachute Company, Oberleutnant

---

18. 'Action Against Enemy, Reports After Action', 13 July 1944, *116th Infantry – After Action Report*, p. 1.
19. '116th Infantry – After Action Report,' 13 July 1944, *World War II Unit Histories & Officers*, p. 1, www.unithistories.com/units_index/default. asp?file=../units/116th%20Inf.Reg%20AAR%20july%201944.htm, accessed on 11 March 2018.
20. Blumenson, *Breakout and Pursuit*, p. 148.
21. Blumenson, *Breakout and Pursuit*, pp. 155–156; Frühbeißer, *Opfergang deutscher Fallschirmjäger*, p. 102.

Werner Kersting, who had been killed on 2 July.[22] The paratroopers were supported by the fires of two machine guns, two mortars, and an 88mm anti-aircraft cannon.[23] 'Then a frightful melee, where it was impossible to distinguish friend from foe and one could only recognise terrible cries and curses in German, as shovels and other instruments struck American helmets,' remembered Gefreiter Rudi Frühbeißer of the 1st Company, I Battalion. Frühbeißer had turned eighteen on 22 June and was already a veteran of the 9th Parachute Regiment less than a month later. 'You couldn't fire your weapon without risking hitting your own comrades,' he wrote. 'Ziehlke, from the 3rd Company, fires his flare gun directly into the chest of an American, who runs away like a wild beast as he turned into a burning, screaming torch. Flares bursting at high altitude fall slowly to the ground on small parachutes. The entire area is bathed in a milky white light.'[24] According to American reports, the German assault group was accompanied by flame-throwers. One U.S. rifle company was overwhelmed and cut to pieces. 'Very quickly, small groups began to fight back and continued to do so until dawn, using rifle butts, grenades, and bayonets,' reported the commander of the 115th Infantry, trying to present his regiment in the best possible light. The 1st Battalion suffered 150 casualties during the night attack in the Bois de Bretel.[25] At around 0730 hours, the Fallschirmjager collected their wounded and fell back to their starting positions. They were pursued by American artillery and air strikes, which severed German field telephone wires, cutting off all communications with headquarters.[26] After the battle, an American officer declared that the raid had been 'magnificently planned and executed'.[27] The attack disrupted the 115th Infantry's scheduled offensive, alerting the 29th Division that the Germans were prepared to defend St-Lô tenaciously and in strength.[28] After reorganising, 1st Battalion, 115th Infantry, jumped off six hours late, at 1100, under the protective fire of the 3rd Battalion

---

22. Frühbeißer, *Opfergang deutscher Fallschirmjäger*, p. 101; Bernage, *Objective Saint-Lo. 7 June–18 July 1944* (Pen & Sword Military, 2017), pp. 169, 200, 202.
23. 'Action Against Enemy, Reports After Action', 13 July 1944, *116th Infantry*, p. 1.
24. Frühbeißer, *Opfergang deutscher Fallschirmjäger*, p. 101; Bernage, *Objective Saint-Lô*, pp. 169, 200, 202.
25. Bernage, *Objective Saint-Lô*, pp. 202–203.
26. Frühbeißer, *Opfergang deutscher Fallschirmjäger*, p. 103.
27. Bernage, *Objective Saint-Lô*, p. 203.
28. Blumenson, *Breakout and Pursuit*, p. 155.

with the small villages of La Luzerne and Bellefontaine as its objective. Meeting fierce resistance, it advanced only 500 yards by 2200 hours, before darkness brought an end to its efforts.[29]

In the meantime, two battalions of the 116th Infantry had launched their own methodical tank–infantry attacks, preceded by a heavy artillery barrage. Progress was steady, but slow, against determined resistance. The German outpost line was well-defended and heavily mined. With mortars firing on the Martinville ridge and Sherman tanks knocking out German assault guns, it took the Americans five hours to advance six hedgerows. 'Tanks can be heard,' remembered Frühbeißer. 'Panzerschrecks and Panzerfausts are dug out of the fighting positions and made ready. MGs are prepared to fire again, and everyone is lying in wait.' According to the young Fallschirmjäger, American infantry, throwing phosphorous grenades and accompanied by flame-throwing tanks, broke into the 9th Parachute Regiment's positions. 'Woe to the wounded who cannot walk anymore,' recorded Frühbeißer, as the area became a sea of flames. Using their anti-tank weapons, mines, and even explosive charges, the German paratroopers counter-attacked, knocking out several Shermans.'[30] The Americans, however, pressed the paratroopers, who suddenly gave way and fell back. As soon as the 2nd Infantry Division to the east of the 29th Division had secured the crest of Hill 192, the Germans gave way all along the line. Major Kurt Stephani, 9th Parachute commander, had ordered his paratroopers to break contact with the Americans and establish a new defensive line. The 116th Infantry moved rapidly to the Martinville ridge by noon, then turned westward, and began to move down the ridge toward St-Lô. General Gebhardt pushed the regiment to reach the town itself. However, even after his division reserve, a battalion of the 175th Infantry, was sent to reinforce the advance, the objective proved beyond its grasp. By the end of the day, the U.S. infantry battalion, with tanks in close support, was entrenched on the southern slope of the Martinville ridge, overlooking the Bérigny road, and prepared to move on St-Lô the following day. That evening, German mortars and artillery ripped into the now exposed Americans, depleting their ranks. By the end of the day,

---

29. '115th Infantry Regiment After Action Report', July 1944, p. 1, *World War II Unit Histories & Officers*, www.unithistories.com/units_index/default. asp?file=../units/115th%20Inf.Reg%20AAR%20july%201944.htm, accessed 11 March 2018

30. Frühbeißer, *Opfergang deutscher Fallschirmjäger*, p. 104.

the 29th Division had lost almost 500 men.[31] The 3rd Parachute Division, fighting against the 29th and 2nd Infantry Division, had suffered some 4,064 casualties in three days.[32]

The 9th Parachute Regiment suffered 575 casualties, the majority from artillery and air strikes, including 104 killed, 250 wounded, 197 missing, and twenty-four captured.[33] Most of the missing were obliterated by artillery and air strikes, bulldozed over by Sherman tanks, or captured by American soldiers. Though its losses would have rendered the regiment combat ineffective, it was kept on the line as no replacement formations were available. New fighting positions were dug and covered with boards, heavy beams and layers of earth. Replacements were brought forward; ammunition and food delivered. The line was straightened, facilitating its defence.[34] Major Stephani took his losses hard. 'The regimental commander comes back to the command post ... sits down at the table, puts his head in his hands, and cries silently to himself,' recorded Frühbeißer. 'He is no longer able to bear the great loss his regiment has suffered. Each of the fallen, whether enlisted soldier or officer, takes a piece out of his life. What good is it to him if his regiment has defended and conquered, if he can no longer bring back his death-defying young paratroopers and dashing officers.'[35] According to Frühbeißer, the 'terrible' cries of the wounded in the aid station next to the command post and the regiment's heavy losses plunged the remaining officers into a deep depression.

By the end of 11 July, the German situation on the Cotentin peninsula was deteriorating rapidly. The 3rd Parachute Division had lost Hill 192 to the U.S. 2nd Infantry Division. Furthermore, a 10 July Panzer Lehr counter-attack west of the Vire River against the American 9th and 30th Divisions around the village of Le Dézert had been defeated with the loss of thirty tanks, forcing the elite German division to withdraw back over the Vire Canal to safety. 'A counter-attack by Panzer Lehr Division (Bayerlein) had no decisive effect and the division had to be withdrawn,' assessed Meindl, growing increasingly pessimistic about the Wehrmacht's chances for success in Normandy:

31. Blumenson, *Breakout and Pursuit*, p. 156; Zaloga, *St. Lô 1944*, 'East of the Vire', Kindle.
32. Steven Zaloga, *St. Lô 1944. The Battle of the Hedgerows* (Osprey Publishing, 2018), p. 74.
33. Frühbeißer, *Opfergang deutscher Fallschirmjäger*, p. 101.
34. Ibid., p. 109.
35. Ibid., p. 108.

This panzer attack was launched (in terrain with limited observation) in two wedges along the two roads leading to St. Jean de Daye from the south and south-west. The enemy was too strong in the air and on the ground for the attack to succeed, particularly as the enemy had complete mastery of the air and the terrain flanking the roads was very wet. Normandy called for tank tactics different from those used in Russia, but the tankers did not want to be informed of it, much less believe it. In any case, neither here nor later in the Percy area, did a counter-attack succeed. The successes of 1941–1942 were a thing of the past for panzer forces. Later, in the open terrain of France, the units had either been destroyed (by enemy air forces) or were exhausted. From that time on, the infantryman and paratrooper had little to say in favour of panzers. The tankers did not get out of their tanks long enough to study terrain, and never bothered to think how the impenetrable terrain could be used to their advantage, as we did with our less manoeuvrable assault guns. These we used to great advantage by splitting them into small bands, which worked Indian fashion. Once again, obsolete ideas and a false tradition had stood in the way of success.[36]

The II Parachute Corps commander reported that his entire front had 'burst into flame'. Powerful U.S. artillery barrages, some 13,000 rounds on that day alone, had reduced the 3rd Parachute Division to 35 per cent of its authorised strength by nightfall. The remnants of the 353rd Infantry Division had been reduced from 1,000 to 180 men. Meindl requested a regiment of the 5th Parachute Division, arriving from Brittany, be sent to reinforce his sector. General Hausser refused, deeming that the defeat of Panzer Lehr made the region west of St-Lô more critical. The Seventh Army commander insisted that the Martinville ridge be held at all costs. In response, Meindl remarked that someone was soon going to have to come up with a brilliant plan if they were to counter the American pressure. Meanwhile, the II Parachute Corps established a new line during the night. The positions extended north across the Bérigny road and over the Martinville ridge to tie in with Hill 122 and faced eastward to meet the threat that had developed on the Martinville ridge.[37]

---

36. Meindl, *B-401 II Parachute Corps*, p. 39.
37. Blumenson, *Breakout and Pursuit*, p. 157; Zaloga, *St. Lô 1944*, 'East of the Vire', Kindle.

On 12 July, the 29th Infantry Division pressed the attack, making little headway. German artillery and mortar fire immobilised the 115th and 175th Infantry Regiments, inflicting 500 casualties on the Americans. The 9th Parachute Regiment lost thirty-four Fallschirmjäger, including seven dead, twenty wounded and seven missing. By 13 July, the 29th lacked the strength to seize Hill 122, despite the commitment of dive bombers blasting the ground ahead of the infantry and neutralising the high ground, artillery providing close protection and tanks on point. Bad weather neutralised air support, lack of proper coordination nullified the tanks, and, more importantly, German artillery and mortar fire, once again stopped the Americans in their tracks.[38] Another forty Fallschirmjäger fell in the battle, including six killed, thirty-two wounded and two missing. 'In the 1st Company, near St-Pierre-de-Semilly, Oberjäger Mayer ... falls ... [shell] splinters in his chest and legs. Four men are also wounded,' recorded Rudi Frühbeißer. 'In the 2nd Company, Fallschirmjäger Chulz is hit with an explosive bullet in the stomach and dies pitifully. In the 1st Company, Oberjäger Müller is shot in the lungs,' The heaviest casualties, however, were among the II Battalion.[39] U.S. forces resorted to dropping leaflets on the Fallschirmjäger. 'The Americans must have erred, because the leaflets were [intended] for the 5th Parachute Regiment,' reflected Frühbeißer.

Soldiers of the 5th Parachute Regiment, Hill 192 was your left flank. Hill 192 was a position defended by your comrades of the 9th Parachute Regiment. The Fallschirmjäger of the 9th Parachute Regiment tried to hold the position, but even the best soldier has no chance against the superiority of our artillery and guns, the deadly fire of our grenade launchers. The foxholes they dug over long, tedious nights only provided protection for a short time. But when we, the Americans, attacked, your comrades were lost. The 9th Parachute Regiment was almost destroyed today. You will not fare any better. Did they promise you that your tanks would advance, that your artillery would support you, that your supplies would soon come through? They also promised that to the boys of the 9th Parachute. And how that ended, you now know!

The leaflets warned the men of the parachute regiment that further resistance was suicide. If they wanted to survive and return home after

38. Frühbeißer, *Opfergang deutscher Fallschirmjäger*, p. 110.
39. Ibid., pp. 111–112.

the war they should follow the example of their comrades, who had surrendered.[40] The leaflets caused the paratroopers to reflect on their situation. However, Hitler's paratroopers in Normandy were more likely to fight on and less likely to surrender than their German Army counterparts. Still, the Wehrmacht was taking no chances. Perhaps it was shortly after this, with U.S. forces constantly pressing forward, pounding the defenders with mortars, artillery and air strikes, and verging on a breakthrough, that the Germans started laying mines behind their own troops to prevent their own men from retreating. Corporal Rudolph Entler, of the 5th Parachute Regiment's 11th Company, told his U.S. captors that only the unit commanders knew the locations of these 'S' (bouncing anti-personnel) and 'T' (anti-tank) mines, which had been placed in the narrow passageways through the hedgerows. 'Losses were almost only from artillery,' Entler told the Americans.[41]

On 14 July, recognising that the 29th Division was no longer capable of seizing Hill 122 without a rest, Major General Charles H. Corlett, the XIX Corps commander, committed the 35th Infantry Division, on the right (west) of the 29th Division, to take the hill. The division kicked off its attack on 15 July, forcing General Meindl to reinforce Hill 122 with troops from the 266th Infantry Division, another recently formed and understrength formation, and the 30th Mobile Brigade, a battalion-size formation heavy in machine guns and mortars and well equipped for defensive missions. The brigade, which had been raised as a reserve bicycle regiment a year earlier, had been returned to the II Parachute Corps after being relieved by Panzer Lehr in the sector west of the Vire. In the meantime, well-directed German mortar and artillery fire tore into the exposed soldiers of the 30th Infantry, bringing their attacks to a temporary halt. Supported by artillery and air strikes and braving German counter-attacks, the U.S. infantrymen regrouped, pressed on, and crossed the crest of Hill 122 on 16 July. 'As German artillery and mortar shells continued to fall on the hill, American troops had an astonishingly clear view of St-Lô, barely a mile away,' wrote Martin Blumenson.[42]

---

40. Ibid., p. 111.
41. 'Report 143. Rudolph, Entler, Cpl, 11th Co, 5th Prcht Regt, FPN L50510', Tactical Interrogation Report, IPW Team 60-B, 134th INF, 3 Aug 1944, *134th Infantry Regiment*, www.coulthart.com/134/ipw-index-44-8.htm
42. Blumenson, *Breakout and Pursuit*, pp. 157–159, 161–162; Zetterling, 'Schnelle Brigade 30', *Normandy 1944*, p. 162.

The Germans were expected to continue their fierce resistance of St-Lô. 'Prisoners testified that they had been ordered to hold their positions "to the last man" and under any circumstances,' reported the official U.S. Army history of the battle. The Americans were increasingly encountering elite enemy parachute and engineer troops, although not in sufficient strength to indicate any chance of a large-scale successful counter-attack. Furthermore, the defenders had strengthened their positions with additional self-propelled assault guns, used to fire directly into the hedgerows, and half-track-mounted machine guns, used for quick, close fire-support. More ominously, U.S. First Army reports indicated a considerable movement of enemy forward and west toward the American sector and St-Lô. These included the 272nd and 343rd Infantry Divisions and the 11th Panzer Division. It was imperative that U.S. forces seize the town before German reinforcements could arrive.[43]

The German Seventh Army War Diary spoke of a 'furious struggle', in which American artillery and air added to the troubles of the defence. The 9th Parachute Regiment had distinguished itself, repulsing eight attacks and destroying seven tanks in close combat. A penetration of the Martinville sector was reported to be 'isolated', but the right wing of the II Parachute Corps' 352nd Division had been forced to withdraw from the main line of resistance west of the Isigny road (Hill 122 sector).[44] Having lost the heights overlooking St-Lô, the Germans struggled to replace their losses and contain the Americans.[45] As a result of the heavy fighting, the 3rd Parachute Division was in a perilous condition, with only about a third of its original strength. 'The self-sacrificing battles of the next three days were such a strain on each fighter, and the 9th Fallschirmjäger Regiment suffered such severe losses of men and material, that the regiment had to be relieved,' remembered General Schimpf:

> For lack of other available troops, the relief could only be made by the 8th Fallschirmjäger Regiment, which was less occupied on the right wing of the division. As the Division had no more reserves at its disposal, the relief was only possible by bringing forward a company formed out of the divisional signal battalion. On the one hand, the relief of one company at a time caused a big loss of time and on the other hand, led to the mixing up of the

---

43. War Department, *St-Lo*, p. 102.
44. Ibid., p. 107.
45. Ibid.

units, which greatly reduced their intended effectiveness and led to considerable losses during the continuous attacks at the main front. The relief took place from 15 to 17 July.[46]

It was at around this time, mid-July, that 'the exceptionally high German losses made it necessary to attach the 15th Fallschirmjäger Regiment [5th Parachute Division] as a combat element to the 3d Fallschirmjäger Division', according to General Meindl's trusted Chief of Staff, Colonel Ernst Blauensteiner, who went on to note: 'However, this regiment had already been greatly weakened during the battle for the Foret de Mont-Castre.'[47]

The 29th Infantry Division attacked again with two battalions at 0600 on 16 July, running into strong resistance from German positions along the St-Lô–Isigny road. Mobile 88mm anti-tank guns, mortars, and concentrated machine gun fire halted the advance after a gain of only 300 yards. Units of the 29th Division remained on the defensive for the remainder of the day as German units, well supported by their artillery, moved back onto the Martinville Ridge, penetrating between two U.S. regiments. After an intense artillery barrage, lasting two hours, three tanks and a company of paratroopers, supported once again by flame-throwers, hurled themselves at one isolated U.S. infantry battalion. 'The enemy infantry was never able to get close enough to use the flame throwers, and left the slope strewn with dead as they were driven back,' notes the War Department history. A second attack, supported by tanks, was also repulsed. 'Confusion on the German side, or lack of communications between the enemy artillery and infantry, was evidenced by many German artillery concentrations on positions which the Americans knew were held by the enemy,' recorded the War Department history.[48] The day ended with the Americans and Germans both firmly entrenched on the Martinville Ridge.

The 9th Parachute Regiment suffered fifty-four casualties in the day's fighting, including seventeen dead, thirty-six wounded and one missing.[49] General Meindl recognised even before the next attack that the II Parachute Corps could hold the town 'only a few more days', a conclusion he shared with General Hausser, the Seventh Army commander. 'Hausser agreed gloomily with me,' recorded Meindl, 'but would not alter Hitler's orders.

---

46. Schimpf, *541 Operations of the 3 FS Division*, p. 17.
47. Blauensteiner, *Normandy*, pp. 3–4.
48. War Department, *St-Lo*, pp. 108–109.
49. Frühbeißer, *Opfergang deutscher Fallschirmjäger*, p. 118.

My suggestions would have meant giving up France. I remember the date and substance of this conference as 16 July is my birthday.'[50] That day, the St-Lô–Moon Road was made the boundary between the 3rd Parachute Division and the 352nd Infantry Division.[51]

While the paratroopers of the 3rd Parachute Division were fighting with the II Parachute Corps to prevent the Americans from taking St-Lô, the 5th Parachute Division was fighting with the German LXXXIV Corps to the west of Meindl. The LXXXIV Corps' front extended from Lessay in the west to Hébécrevon in the east, placing (from west to east) the solid 2nd SS-Panzer Division, the depleted 17th SS-Panzergrenadier Division, and the powerful Panzer Lehr Division adjacent to the II Parachute Corps. Three weak German formations, the 243rd, 353rd and 77th Infantry Divisions, guarded the corps' westernmost flank. [52] On 13 July, Generalleutnant Fritz Baylerein, the commander of Panzer Lehr, requested that the 14th Parachute Regiment be sent to reinforce the division. Two days later, the German Seventh Army committed Hauptmann Schmidt's I Battalion from the regiment. It arrived late on the evening on 15 July and helped Panzer Lehr check the American advance west of Pont-Hébert, just to the West of Meindl.[53] The following day, the U.S. 90th Infantry Division encountered Kampfgruppe Mertens, consisting of the 5th Parachute Engineer Battalion (commanded by Major Gerhart Mertens), the 177th Artillery Regiment, and the 177th Anti-Tank Company from the 77th Infantry Division, in its sector.[54] When Baylerein reported that his resources were still insufficient to 'stem the enemy onslaught', the Seventh Army committed Hauptmann Meissner's III Parachute Battalion.[55]

That same day, the paratroopers of Hauptmann Sauer's II Battalion were detected by the Americans and mauled en route to their assembly area. 'On account of the misconduct of several individuals, the approach march and concentration area of the II Battalion, 14 Para Regt were

---

50. Meindl, *B-401 II Parachute Corps*, p. 37.
51. Generalleutnant Fritz Bayerlein, *A-903 Pz Lehr Division (15–20 July 1944)* (Koenigstein: U.S. Army Historical Division, 20 May 1950), pp. 3–4.
52. See Map II 'First Army Front West of the Vire River 8–15 July 1944' in Blumenson, *Breakout and Pursuit*.
53. War Department, *St-Lo*, p. 100; Bayerlein, *A-903 Pz Lehr Division*, pp. 3.
54. 'Annex No. 1 to G-2 Periodic Report No. 21. Notes on the 5th Parachute Division,' 18 July 1944, 83rd Infantry Division, CG VII Corps, Box 3844 207.21 to 207.2.2 RG 407, NARA.
55. War Department, *St-Lo*, p. 100.

detected by the enemy, who proceeded to attack with artillery and fighter bombers,' wrote Major Herbert Noster, the regimental commander, on 15 July 1944:

> It therefore becomes the duty of all unit commanders to maintain the strictest front-line discipline especially in regard to camouflage. Special camouflage inspectors are to be appointed. Even when no enemy planes are overhead, all troops must move about under cover at all times. The violations are to be handled with ruthless disciplinary action for they endanger not only the individuals but the entire tactical commitment of our troops and the execution of our plans.[56]

The arrival of two battalions of the 14th Parachute Regiment was a mixed blessing for Panzer Lehr. Although their parachute infantry was sorely needed, both units were understrength and under-equipped, arriving without supporting artillery or anti-aircraft guns, further straining Panzer Lehr's already limited resources.[57]

Leutnant Otto Bernhardt, of the 5th Parachute Division's III Battalion, 14th Parachute Regiment, had arrived at the front after a strenuous march, lasting seven nights. Lack of motor vehicles meant that the men had to carry a heavy load of equipment the entire way as the 15th Parachute Regiment had done a few days earlier. The paratroopers dug in quickly, preparing for the inevitable American morning attack. When it came, the enemy infantry was accompanied by 'quite a few' tanks. The Germans fought them to a standstill. By the afternoon, Bernhardt was commanding the 9th and 10th Companies. All the company commanders in Hauptmann Joachim Meissner's III Battalion had been killed or wounded. A Knight's Cross recipient, Meissner had been one of the Fallschirmjager that had seized the Belgium fortress, Eben Emael in 1940. The Battalion Adjutant,

---

56. G-2 Periodic Report No. 22, 19 July 1944', 83rd Infantry Division, CG VII Corps, Box 3844 207.21 to 207.2.2 RG 407, NARA; For a roster of 5th Parachute Division officers in Normandy, see Erich Busch, '5. Fallschirmjäger-Division', Erich Busch, *Die Fallschirmjäger Chronik 1935– 1945. Die Geschichte der Deutschen Fallschirmtruppe* (Pozun-Pallas-Verlag, 1983), pp. 121–122.
57. Anthony Tucker-Jones, *Falaise: The Flawed Victory – The Destruction of Panzergruppe West, August 1944* (Pen & Sword Military, 2008), Chapter 4. 'Formidably Equipped – Panzer Lehr Panzer Division', Kindle.

Leutnant Witte, took command of the 11th and 12th Companies. The Intelligence Officer, Leutnant Illgner, took over as adjutant. Two days later the battalion had lost fourteen of the eighteen officers that had arrived at the front.[58]

The success of the American advance south to le Mesnil-Durand caused fresh alarm in the Seventh Army and was attributed to the poor performance of the newly committed units of the 14th Parachute Regiment. Their failure 'confirms our experience that newly committed troops which have not yet developed teamwork and are thrown together into heavy battle without having been broken in, suffer disproportionately heavy losses'. Seventh Army registered its disappointment over having to throw new units into battle immediately on their arrival in Normandy, undermining its ability to build up a reserve and, thus, limiting its operational and strategic options.[59] In the meantime, Oberstleutnant Kurt Gröschke's 15th Parachute Regiment had received replacements on 15 July, in the form of companies of 120 men each (divided into four platoons of three squads with one light machine gun per squad) from the 6th Company, 3rd Parachute Training Regiment, allowing it to fight on.[60] It seemed that everywhere they turned, the Americans found themselves battling Hitler's paratroopers.

According to an American intelligence estimate summarising the strength of the parachute formations serving with Bayerlein's Panzer Lehr Division, the 5th Parachute Division had almost 3,000 men on the lines by the middle of July. Of these 1,500 were from Major Meuth's 13th Parachute Regiment; 1,000 were from I and III Battalions of the 14th Parachute Regiment. The 2nd Parachute Reconnaissance Battalion had another 300 men, while a company of the 12th Reconnaissance Battalion had 150. In addition, the 3rd Parachute Division was represented by 200 men of the 1st Company, 5th Parachute Regiment. According to Bayerlein, however, only the paratroopers of the 5th Parachute Division's I and III Battalions were under the command of the Panzer Lehr. The II Battalion was the LXXXIV Corps reserve. The 13th Parachute Regiment had been subordinated to the 2nd SS-Panzer Division, while the men of the II Parachute Reconnaissance Battalion had been attached to the II Parachute Corps on 10 July. The 12th

---

58. Pisani, *Bocage*, pp. 281–284; Kurowski, 'Joachim Meissner', *Knight's Cross Holds of the Fallschirmjäger*, p. 147.

59. War Department, *St-Lo*, p. 100.

60. 'G-2 Periodic Report No. 22, 18 July 1944', 83rd Infantry Division, CG VII Corps, Box 3844 207.21 to 207.2.2 RG 407, NARA.

Reconnaissance Battalion was committed elsewhere. The paratroopers of the 3rd Parachute Division were not on the front lines of the Panzer Lehr Division positions, suggesting they were being held in reserve.[61]

These dispositions illustrate how Meindl's Fallschirmjäger were dispatched, in penny packets, to wherever the fighting was the fiercest to stem the tide until larger reinforcements could be sent. The result was a mish-mash of units thrown together all along the line, with even Fallschirmjäger formations intermixed. This meant that the men of the 5th Parachute Division were being fed piecemeal into battle and swept away by a growing firestorm of American artillery shells, mortar rounds and bombs. The Germans were running out of reinforcements and time. The Seventh Army knew another attack was coming but could do little to stave it off. Losses could not be replaced. Every unit was also hampered by the lack of motor vehicles, food, and even water, along with severe shortages of ammunition. Furthermore, a lack of fuel forced the Wehrmacht's ground forces in Normandy, already heavily reliant on horses, to expand the use of horse-drawn vehicles (as it had already done in Russia). Finally, air support from the Luftwaffe was non-existent, affecting both the combat and supply situations.[62]

On 17 July the 1st U.S and 2nd British Armies began large scale offensives from the St-Lô and Caen areas to force a strategic breakthrough. 'On 17 or 18 July 1944, the enemy attacked astride the Vire, toward St-Lô,' recorded General Meindl:

> There were more and more indications that this was a major attack with the main effort on the west bank of the Vire. Moreover, I did not believe that the unit on my left [LXXXIV Corps] would be able to cope with the situation. Consequently, I dispatched my only reserve, the 12th Reconnaissance Battalion, to Corps von Choltitz, on the condition that the battalion would be committed only on the St. Jean de Days–Hebecrevan–St. Lo road in order to secure the road from the north. The battalion was to cover my left wing (or west flank), as I expected an enemy breakthrough in the direction of Marigny and Canisy. It was the 12th Reconnaissance Battalion which stopped heavy enemy thrusts moving south from St. Jean de Days on about 20 July 1944.[63]

---

61. Bayerlein, *A-903 Pz Lehr Division*, pp. 1–3, 8.
62. War Department, *St. Lo*, p. 107
63. Meindl, *B-401 II Parachute Corps*, pp. 38–39.

Despite powerful air and artillery support, the American and British attacks failed to breakthrough. The American attack did succeed in pushing back the German 352nd Infantry Division on the left of the 3rd Parachute Division, exposing the latter's flank. 'This action was decisive in the battle for the city,' recorded General Schimpf:

> Therefore the 3 Fallschirmjäger Division retired its elements still holding out north of the St. Lo – Bérigny road to positions along the road and directly south of it. The constant battles and the reluctant heavy losses caused big gaps in the front lines, which would have made it possible for the enemy on 18 July to penetrate east of St-Lô towards the south and south-west. To the surprise of the Division, this did not take place. It seemed the enemy concentrated his activity exclusively on the town of St-Lô and these gaps were closed again during the night of 18 and 19 July.[64]

The defenders of St-Lô were now reaching the end of their strength. 'Losses in men and material were high during this six weeks of fighting that had to be endured without a break and during which losses were replaced only inadequately,' wrote Schimpf.[65] With the reliable and hard-fighting 3rd Parachute Division on the verge of collapsing from a lack of replacements, weapons, and ammunition, it was only a matter of time before the II Parachute Corps and entire Seventh Army followed.

General Hausser called OB West headquarters in the mid-afternoon to request permission to withdraw from the town to the heights just south of the town. The loss of Hill 122 and the attrition of German troops in the sector, which made it impossible for the II Parachute Corps to reestablish a viable defensive line north of the town, exposed St-Lô from the north. Furthermore, the advance of the U.S. 30th Division through Pont-Hébert to Rampan, the failure of a 15 July Panzer Lehr attack, and the mistaken notion that U.S. forces had crossed the river at Rampan to infiltrate the rear of the LXXXIV's Corps 352nd Infantry Division, all added up to the threat of an American encirclement east of the town from the west. Hausser indicated that combat outposts would be retained north of the town. The Seventh Army commander was told by Oberst Hans von Tempelhoff, to take whatever measures he deemed necessary. The OB West staff officer

---

64. Schimpf, *Operations of the 3 FS Div during the Invasion of France*, p. 18.
65. Ibid.

added: 'Just report to us afterwards that the enemy penetrated your main line of resistance in several places and that you barely succeeded in re-establishing a new line to the rear.' To further exacerbate the German situation in Normandy, Field Marshal Rommel, the Army Group B commander, had been attacked by an Allied plane on 17 July driving forward to visit the front. Seriously injured, he was replaced by Field Marshal Günther von Kluge later in the day, who was briefed on the situation around 2100 hours. By the time Army Group B passed Hausser's withdrawal request to OB West, it was too late for Kluge, unable to find any reinforcements for St-Lô, to reverse the order. Kluge reluctantly allowed Hausser to withdraw from the town. The II Parachute Corps' main forces retired that night, leaving strong combat outposts north of St-Lô.[66] 'The division fulfilled its mission,' reported General Wilke of his 5th Parachute Division, which was forced to fall back with the remainder of the LXXXIV Corps.[67]

On 18 July, the 29th Infantry Division attacked St-Lô for the last time. Its soldiers encountered only scattered German resistance, which held out to the end. 'To take it they had to root out and kill off the bitter-enders of the 3rd Parachute Division, fighting from every hole and corner, and stand off a massive armoured counter-attack,' recorded the U.S. XIX Corps World War II history.[68] By 19 July, the 29th Division had finished clearing the disfigured and lifeless town. It was relieved by the 35th Infantry Division. Between them, the two formations had lost 5,000 men killed, wounded, captured, and missing taking St-Lô. The U.S. First Army suffered 40,000 casualties, of which 90 per cent were infantrymen. Most of the casualties were caused by artillery and mortars. General Eisenhower later concluded that three factors made the Normandy campaign so tough. First and foremost was the 'fighting quality of the German soldier'. The other two were the nature of the terrain and the weather.[69]

Later, in the shadow of the 20 July assassination attempt on Adolf Hitler when all senior German generals were suspected of being complicit; and some were surprised and embarrassed by the speed with which the Americans had seized the town, the Seventh Army ordered II Parachute Corps to have the exhausted 352nd Infantry Division retake the town.

---

66. Zaloga, *St. Lô 1944*, p. 85; Blumenson, *Breakout and Pursuit*, pp. 168–169.
67. Wilke, *5th Parachute Division*, p. 8.
68. Captain Fredric E. Pamp, Jr., *Normandy to the Elbe, XIX Corps* (XIX Corps: Germany, 1945), p. 12.
69. Blumenson, *Breakout and Pursuit*, pp. 174–175.

Hausser refused Meindl's request for the 275th Infantry Division, which had just arrived in Brittany and was in Seventh Army reserve behind Panzer Lehr. The beleaguered 352nd Division counter-attacked, but, pummelled by U.S. artillery, was too weak to expel the Americans, who had moved rapidly into the town.[70]

According to General Meindl, it was he who, perhaps unwittingly, prompted General Hausser to abandon the town. Meindl had requested that his corps be allowed to move most of their troops out of St-Lô sector 3 to 5km south and south-west of the town as far as the Vire, leaving only strong rearguards in their present positions. 'We received no answer,' he remembered afterward. 'We remained as we were, and no order for a withdrawal was given.'[71] According to the II Parachute Corps commander, it was only after St-Lo had been abandoned by German forces that he learned from a Wehrmacht report that Seventh Army had evacuated the town without the enemy's knowledge and without a battle. 'I thought I was going to have a stroke, for now I definitely had to expect a rapid advance by enemy tanks on St. Lo,' he wrote:

I alerted the 352nd Infantry Division and the 3rd Parachute Division, as well as their artillery. Sure enough, about 1700 hours a strong armoured spearhead, followed by trucks full of infantrymen, came rolling down the road that leads into St. Lo from the north-west. The weak anti-tank defences were overpowered and crushed, and the newly formed reconnaissance battalion of the 352nd Infantry Division was annihilated in bitter street fighting north-east of and within St. Lo. The commander of this battalion, whom I had visited the day before and who was an able and experienced front line commander, fell in hand-to-hand fighting. St. Lo fell in a tragi-comical fashion, by a sudden attack (against our will) and by our own stupidity. Unfortunately, I was never able to determine the person responsible for forwarding my suggestion as an accomplished fact.[72]

The end of the Battle of St-Lô left many of the Seventh Army's units exhausted to a point where they could no longer be counted on for a sustained effort. None could be withdrawn from the front. The II Parachute

---

70. Ibid, pp. 173–174.
71. Meindl, *B-401 II Parachute Corps*, p. 40.
72. Meindl, *B-401 II Parachute Corps*, p. 40.

Corps lacked sufficient strength to maintain an MLR and advance combat outposts. LXXXIV Corps warned that it could not be counted on to stem any major attack. By keeping pressure along the entire Seventh Army, the First U.S. Army had not only prevented the Germans from regrouping but had also worn down their last immediate reserves for use against an American breakthrough. Enemy armour had been committed piecemeal and used up in the hedgerow battles and Wehrmacht strength along the entire Seventh Army sector was strained to breaking point.[73] The Americans estimated that the German troops facing the U.S. VII and VIII Corps numbered fewer than 17,000 men supported by fewer than 100 tanks. Those formations deployed against U.S. troops included the depleted 15th Infantry Regiment of the 5th Parachute Division, which had moved east of the Vire to provide a reserve for the equally exhausted 3rd Parachute Division in the St-Lô sector; the 6th Parachute Regiment augmenting the still-strong 2nd SS-Panzer Division; one regiment of the 5th Parachute Division to the east of the Périers area; and another understrength regiment of 500 paratroopers of the 5th Parachute Division defending with the Panzer Lehr Division. Captured letters and documents, as well as prisoner-of-war interrogations, indicated that the German soldier was weary of war and had no real hope of victory.[74] 'Every moment I expect deadly shrapnel,' read an unfinished letter found on the body of a fallen Fallschirmjäger at St-Lô. 'When one hears for hours the whining, whistling, and bursting of the shells and the moaning and groaning of the wounded, one does not feel too well. I almost lost my mind. I chewed up a cigarette, bit into the ground. The others acted just like me. Altogether, it was hell.'[75]

U.S. First Army was now commanding a powerful force of four corps, consisting of eleven full-strength infantry divisions and three armour divisions, poised for a major attack. Additional reserve divisions were available for later stages of the operation.[76] The time was ripe for Operation Cobra, the American breakout from Normandy.

---

73. War Department, *St-Lo*, p. 123.
74. Blumenson, *Breakout and Pursuit*, pp. 224, 227.
75. Hargreaves, *The Germans in Normandy*, p. 122.
76. Steven Zaloga, *Operation Cobra 1944. Breakout from Normandy* (Oxford: Osprey Publishing, 2001), p. 24.

Chapter 8

6th Parachute Regiment at Sainteny and Sèves Island

By the third week of July, the German Seventh Army was defending south of St-Lô with the II Parachute Corps in the east and the LXXXIV Corps in the west. II Parachute Corps' 3rd Parachute Division shielded the right of the corps' sector, its left wing on the St-Lô–Torigni-sur-Vire road. The remnants of the 352nd Infantry Division held the left, covering south of St-Lô–St-Thomas north of Courfalem–Canisy.[1] 'On about 20 July 1944, the enemy daily increased the pressure toward the south-east in order to push us farther away from St-Lô and to establish a line of communication through the town. Blanket bombing had buried all roads in the town and made them impassable,' recorded Meindl:

> At that time, I requested that the unit on my left return the 12th Reconnaissance Battalion, after it had repulsed several enemy attacks. I put this battalion on the boundary between the 3rd Parachute and the 352nd Infantry Divisions in order to block the road from St-Lô to the south-east. The II Parachute Corps had lost all hope of continuing a serious defence. Both of its divisions were at the end of their strength and, despite replacements, were never able to recover. Overall, any attempt to alter the overall situation was doomed to failure, as the picked troops had been worn down by continuous defensive fighting and the strategic reserves were too weak to achieve any decisive successes, particularly since the

---

1. See Map III 'The Battle of St. Lo (11–18 July 1944)' in Blumenson, *Breakout and Pursuit*; Meindl, *B-401 II Parachute Corps*, p. 40–41.

Luftwaffe was absent. Herewith began the actual holocaust of the once proud II Parachute Corps.[2]

The following day, the 5th Parachute Division was inserted on the line between Panzer Lehr and the 17th SS-Panzergrenadier Division.[3]

The period of 15 to 25 July was one of consolidation and regrouping for the Americans in France in preparation for execution of Operation Cobra. The attack was to be initiated by the VII Corps, with VIII Corps in support. Cobra called for a penetration of the German front, followed by an armoured exploitation to the south and west in the direction of Coutances. The point of breakthrough was a narrow front to the west of St-Lô, with the intent of opening a gap between Marigny and St-Gilles. This would permit the rapid passage of the armoured forces. Cobra would be preceded by 'saturation' bombing, intended to paralyze the Germans and facilitate the breakthrough. The VII Corps had under its command, the 1st, 4th, 9th and 30th Infantry Divisions and the 2nd and 3rd Armoured Divisions. VIII Corps, with the 83rd and 90th Infantry Divisions and 4th Armoured Division, was to attack the enemy from the north, delaying long enough to permit the effects of the VII Corps action to be felt, but not long enough to permit enemy withdrawal. Cobra was originally set for 21 July. However, bad weather forced a series of postponements until 25 July.[4]

'July, for the VIII Corps, had been a month of extreme opposites in fighting experiences,' recorded General Troy H. Middleton, the VIII Corps commander. 'The attack from 3 July to 15 July was characterised by slow, costly advance of foot troops against stubborn hedgerow defence. Casualties were high, and gains were measured in thousands of yards.' After twelve days of sustained combat at Mont-Castre and Beaucoudray, the 90th Infantry Division was an exhausted formation. According to the official U.S. Army history of the Normandy campaign: 'Less than six weeks after commitment in Normandy, the division's enlisted infantry replacements numbered 100 per cent of authorised strength; infantry officer replacements totalled 150 per cent. In comparison to the veterans who had fought in the hedgerows, the replacements were poorly trained and undependable, as soon became obvious in the division's

---

2. Meindl, *B-401 II Parachute Corps*, pp. 40–41.
3. Bayerlein, *A-903 Panzer Lehr*, p. 3.
4. Major General Troy H. Middleton, 'Report After Action against Enemy, 10 August 1944" www.90thdivisionassoc.org/afteractionreports/PDF/VIII%20AAR%2007–44.pdf, accessed on 27 February 2018.

new assignment.'[5] The 90th Division's next objective, in preparation for Operation Cobra and the U.S. First Army's breakout from Normandy, was a low hedgerowed mound of earth surrounded by swampland. Traversing the division's zone of advance, the island of dry ground held the village of St-Germain-sur-Sèves, near Le Closet and Sainteny. 'Possessing the island and across the Sèves River, the division would be in position not only to threaten Périers but also to get to the Périers–Coutances highway,' recorded U.S. Army historian Martin Blumenson.[6]

According to intelligence reports, only a weak German battalion held the island. However, it was well dug into the hedgerowed terrain, had good observation, and a superb field of fire. It was thought to be supported by several assault guns and a few light tanks. Artillery was tied into the strong point defences.[7] The report suggests a 90th Infantry Division doctrinal template or educated guess of what the Americans expected to find based on their previous experiences and growing knowledge of the German Army in Normandy.

Two miles long, half a mile wide and surrounded by swamps, Sèves Island had been more than normally isolated by the heavy rainfalls in June, which had deepened shallow streams along its north and south banks. Linking the hamlet of St-Germain to the 'mainland' was a narrow, tarred road from the western tip of the island. The Germans had destroyed the small bridge there, the only suitable site for engineer bridging operations. Several hundred yards away, a muddy country lane gave access to the island from the north, across a ford. How to cross level treeless swamps that offered no cover or concealment was the main problem for the American assault. Although a night attack seemed appropriate, General Landrum, the division commander, quickly abandoned the idea. 'With so many newly arrived replacements, he dared not risk the problem of control inherent in a night operation,' notes the official U.S. Army history.[8]

The Americans planned on compensating for the challenging terrain, the lack of tactical expertise among its commanders and NCOs, and its inexperienced soldiers with heavy fire support. As this was to be the only attack in progress in the VIII Corps sector, the attack was to be supported by all of VIII Corps Artillery and preceded by a preparatory bombardment. Furthermore, all non-participating infantry units would support the

---

5. Blumenson, *Breakout and Pursuit*, p. 201.
6. Ibid.
7. Ibid.
8. Ibid., pp. 201–202.

attack with direct and indirect weapons fire. However, after 17 July 1944, VIII Corps artillery was severely hampered by an extremely low ration of artillery and mortar ammunition imposed by the U.S. First Army to ensure sufficient stocks were available for VII Corps and Operation Cobra. According to General Troy H. Middleton, the VIII Corps commander, the allowance for most calibres was approximately one-fifth of a unit of fire.[9] The rationing of artillery and mortar ammunition lasted until the end of July. The 90th Infantry Division attack on Sèves Island was supported by three tank platoons from Company A, 712th Tank Battalion in the direct fire mode and three platoons from Company B in the indirect fire mode.[10]

Landrum selected the 358th Infantry Regiment to make the attack. The regimental commander, Lieutenant Colonel Christian E. Clarke, Jr., planned to attack with two battalions abreast on a narrow front of 2km, with each battalion advancing along one of the two roads to the island. Once on the island, the two battalions were to form a consolidated bridgehead. Engineers would then lay bridging so that tanks and assault guns could cross the Sèves and support the drive eastward to clear the rest of the island. Initially scheduled for 18 July, the operation was postponed several times until artillery ammunition problems were resolved. The attack was set for the morning of 22 July.[11] Considering all the challenges facing the 90th Infantry Division, the attack on Sèves Island was launched under great risk. Perhaps the Americans believed that the Germans were on the run and the island wouldn't be defended. If so, they were tragically mistaken.

Major von der Heydte's weary 6th Parachute Regiment, fighting alongside the battered 17th SS-Panzergrenadier Division and fresh tanks and panzergrenadiers of the newly arrived 2nd SS Panzer Division 'Das Reich', defended Sèves Island against the debilitated 90th Infantry Division. Both the parachute regiment and the Waffen SS panzer-grenadiers were subordinated to the 2nd SS-Panzer Division. Since the beginning of July, the paratroopers had suffered more than 1,200 casualties, more than a battalion's worth of men, leaving the regiment with the equivalent of two

9. Major General Troy H. Middleton, 'Report After Action against Enemy, 10 August 1944', www.90thdivisionassoc.org/afteractionreports/PDF/ VIII%20AAR%2007–44.pdf, accessed on 27 February 2018.

10. 2d Lt Stanley W. Seeley, 'After Action Report 712th Tank Battalion, July 44–March 45', p. 12. http://90thdivisionassociation.org/History/AAR/ PDF/712%20AAR.pdf, accessed on 27 February 2018.

11. Blumenson, *Breakout and Pursuit*, 'Chapter XI – COBRA Preparations, Kindle; Colby, *War from the Ground Up*, p. 138.

weak battalions.[12] The 17th SS-Panzergrenadier Division had lost 4,656 men killed, wounded, and missing.[13] By the third week of July, the Waffen SS division was just another debilitated and almost combat ineffective German formation. According to a Seventh Army report, it consisted of two 'weak' battalions, five 'exhausted' battalions, and a replacement battalion. Five light batteries made up the division artillery. The panzer force included five StuG III assault guns and ten self-propelled 75mm anti-tank guns. Seventh Army rated the 17th SS, which was now only 30 per cent motorised, as 'Capable of limited defence', the lowest of four readiness ratings assigned to German Army combat units.[14] A quarter of the 6th Parachute Regiment's casualties for the month occurred on 4 July, when the paratroopers, battling to stop two U.S. infantry regiments advancing down the Carentan–Périers road, had lost 300 men against the green U.S. 83rd Infantry Division south-west of Carentan near the small town of Sainteny.[15]

The 83rd Infantry Division had landed in Normandy only two weeks earlier, on 19 June 1944, its arrival in France delayed by a tremendous storm that pounded the Normandy beaches, sinking ships, destroying or damaging the Mulberries, and preventing the delivery of men, equipment and supplies to the Americans and British. 'This storm prevented the Division from landing for nearly a week on Omaha Beach,' remembered Captain Harry C. Gavelyn, commander of Company D, 331st Infantry

---

12. Assorted daily reports for July 1944 in M. Wind and H. Günther, *Kriegstagebuch. Götz von Berlichingen. 30 Oktober 1943 bis 6 Mai 1945* (München: Schild Verlag, 1993). Because the 6th Parachute Regiment was assigned to the 17th SS Panzergrenadier Division for most of June and July, casualty estimates were gleamed from regimental reports submitted to the division found in this volume; Otto Weidinger, 2-SS Panzer Division Das Reich, Vol 5. 1943–1945 (Winnipeg, Ca.: J.J. Fedorowicz Publishing Inc., 2012), p. 185.

13. M. Wind and H Gunther, *Kriegstagebuch: 30 Oktober 1943 bis 6 Mai 1945, 17. SS-Panzer-Grenadier-Division*, Report 483/44, 1 Aug 1944.

14. Antonio J. Munoz, *The Iron First Division. A Combat History of the 17th SS-Panzer Grenadier Division 'Götz von Berlichingen' 1943–1945* (Merriam Press, 1998), pp. 7–8.

15. Hans Stöber, Die Sturmflut und das Ende. Die Geschicht der 17. SS-Panzergrenadierdivision 'Götz von Berlichingen. Band I. Die Invasion (München: Schild Verlag, 2000), p. 130. The 6th Parachute Regiment suffered 50 killed and 250 wounded on 4 July 1944.

**General Schimpf, Commander of the 3rd Parachute Division, on
the battlefield.** The 3rd Parachute division was the backbone of the II
Parachute Corps in Normandy. A Bavarian, Schimpf had been awarded
the Iron Cross 1st and 2nd Cross in the First World War, where he fought on
the Western Front as an infantryman. The division commander expected
his men to live by his motto: 'a paratrooper dies in his foxhole'.

Fallschirmjäger of the 3rd Parachute Division captured by the 2nd Infantry Division on Hill 192. Fewer than 200 German prisoners were taken after the battle. Between 6 June and 25 July, General Schimpf's division suffered 6,053 casualties, including 153 officers and almost 6,000 enlisted. Many Germans, killed by American artillery, had to be dug out of holes and hedgerow emplacements. (U.S. Army)

3rd Parachute Division Fallschirmjäger at St-Lô with an early model FG-42. Developed specifically for the use of the Fallschirmjäger airborne infantry in 1942, the FG-42 was used in very limited numbers. Most of Hitler's paratroopers inFrance were armed with the Mauser Kar 98L carbine or the MP-40 submachine gun. A select few carried the G043 self-loading rifle or the MP-43, MP-44 or StG-44 assault rifles.(Author's Collection)

A-20 Havoc Bombers over France in 1944. American airpower proved decisive in the defeat of the Wehrmacht in Normandy. United States Army Air Forces unleashed some 12,000 aircraft during the Normandy campaign. (U.S. Air Force)

Paratroopers of the 3rd Parachute Division in defensive positions near St-Lô. Note the dead American soldier in the foreground. With the ever-reliable and hard-fighting 3rd Parachute Divisionon the verge of collapse from a lack of replacements, weapons, and ammunition, it was only a matter of time before the II Parachute Corps and the entire German Seventh Army followed. (Courtesy Steven Zaloga)

A U.S. heavy artillery piece hammers Wehrmacht positions in Normandy. Approximately 3,500 American guns pounded the Germans relentlessly. Neither airpower nor artillery alone, however, could win the battle for the Allies. U.S. infantry had to go in and root out the Germans. (U.S. Army)

Dead German paratroopers of General Schimpf's 3rd Parachute Division. The Fallschirmjäger in Normandy found themselves fighting a losing battle, as one depleted attacking American infantry division was pulled off the line and replaced by another, more capable one. Schimpf's elite division suffered some 9,300 casualties, including 151 officers, during the Normandy campaign. (U.S. Army)

An American column moves through a shattered St-Lô. The U.S. First Army suffered 40,000 casualties in Normandy by the end of the campaign; 90 per cent were infantrymen. Most were caused by German artillery and mortars. General Eisenhower later concluded that three factors made the Normandy campaign so tough. First and foremost was the 'fighting quality of the German soldier'.(U.S. Army)

Captured German paratrooper from the 3rd Parachute Division. According to one G.I. of the U.S. 2nd Infantry Division that battled Hitler's paratroopers at Brest: 'The hardest fighting the division had was when we met the German paratroopers in front of Brest. Those paratroopers were really tough. They had concrete pillboxes, stationary guns in concrete emplacements, a trench system, all protected by hedgerows.'(U.S. Army)

Dead German paratroopers and a destroyed Schwimmwagen from the 6th Parachute Regiment near Saintenay on 16 July. Von der Heydte's Fallschirmjäger suffered 3,000 casualties during the Normandy campaign. The regiment escaped the Falaise pocket with 1,007 paratroopers in tattered uniforms. All heavy weapons and supplies were left behind. (U.S. Army)

Sullen German paratroopers taken prisoner in the fighting for Brest. Even after their defeat in France, many of Hitler's surviving Fallschirmjäger never doubted that Germany would win the war. (U.S. Army)

General Bernhard Hermann Ramcke in captivity at Brest. Hitler was pleased with what Ramcke and his Fallschirmjäger had accomplished at Brest. Following the battle, the Führer promoted Ramcke to General der Fallschirmtruppe in absentia, awarding him the Swords and Diamonds to the Knight's Cross and elevating him to the ranks of the Wehrmacht's truly exalted. (Courtesy Mark Reardon)

The End. A captured Fallschirmjäger hides his face from the camera. Most of Hitler's paratroopers in Normandy were killed or wounded during the Normandy campaign. (Author's Collection)

Regiment, 'and made life miserable for everyone, both on the decks and below the decks.' Commanded by Major General Robert C. Macon, the 83rd Infantry Division was comprised of the 329th, 330th, and 331st Infantry Regiments and three artillery battalions. The 802nd Tank Destroyer Battalion and 453rd Anti-Aircraft Artillery Battalion were attached effective 1 July. After landing in Normandy, the 83rd Infantry took over defensive positions as part of the U.S. VIII Corps.[16] 'The 83d Infantry Division had not yet had any combat time and the proper technique of fighting in hedgerows had not been tried by this division,' recorded Captain Clarence P. Ziegler, an infantry platoon leader in the division. 'Infantry–tank team was a phrase unheard of until a few days before relieving the 101st Airborne Division, when the platoons were given three hours of infantry–tank team training. The division was quite up to strength although a few casualties were suffered while in the front line defensive position. Morale was high. The division was well-trained … and well supplied with ammunition and equipment. Only two of the regiments had received any patrol experience while the division was on line.'[17]

Since landing in Normandy, the Americans had learned to respect German Fallschirmjäger in general and the veterans of the 6th Parachute Regiment in particular. 'Everyone by this time was convinced of the toughness and battle experience of German paratroopers that we were attacking,' remembered Captain Harry C. Gavelyn, Company D, 331st Infantry Regiment. 'They were deadly shots and past masters at scouting and patrolling. They were tough soldiers and were battling us to a standstill and inflicting us with heavy casualties.'[18] The Americans had clearly underestimated the number, if not the fighting prowess, of the Fallschirmjäger and SS soldiers opposing them. The inexperienced soldiers of the 83rd Infantry Division charged into the fray, believing their preparatory artillery bombardment had decimated the Germans. 'In

---

16. Stanton, *World War II Order of Battle*, pp. 153–154.

17. Captain Clarence P. Ziegler, 'The Operations of the 2nd Battalion, 329th Infantry (83d Infantry Division) In the Attack Along the Road to Pôriers, 4 July 1944. (Personal Experiences of a Platoon Leader)', (Fort Benning Georgia: Infantry School, Advanced Infantry Officer's Course, 1949–1950), pp. 5–6.

18. Harry C. Gravelyn, *My Experiences as Captain of Company D, 331st Infantry, 83rd Division*, (Travelyn Publishing, 2016), Chapter 2. 'Normandy Campaign', Kindle.

the beginning there was a light-hearted mood, the new men watching a murderous American artillery barrage of German positions convinced the inexperienced troops that no one could possibly survive such a holocaust,' remembered E. Carver McGriff, a machine gunner in Company M, 357th Infantry Regiment. 'Then they jumped off.'[19] As the American troops advanced, they were cut to pieces by relentless enemy artillery, mortars, machine guns, anti-tank rounds, and tank fire. 'Mines added to the slaughter,' remembered McGriff. 'Before long the men of the 83rd had to retreat ...'[20] Failing in their first attack and suffering what McGriff called 'a horrifying' 1,400 casualties, the men of the 83rd Infantry Division persisted in their assaults over the next three days.[21] 'In the end, the American infantrymen pushed the Germans back, advancing more than a mile down the Carentan–Périers road and inflicting almost 500 casualties on the men of the 6th Parachute Regiment and 17th SS Panzergrenadier Division.[22] The 83rd Infantry Division suffered an additional 750 casualties. Only six German prisoners were taken.[23] By the end of the battle, one U.S. battalion, leading the attack, suffered 50 per cent casualties, including twenty-two officers and 540 men.[24] The Germans had inflicted almost three times the number of casualties they had suffered.

At Sèves Island, the 6th Parachute Regiment was deployed with three understrength parachute infantry companies abreast. The 9th Parachute Infantry Company, on the left, straddled the road to Périers. The 11th Parachute Infantry Company held the centre. The 7th Parachute Infantry Company defended the right. A forward machine gun outpost, guarding the road leading onto the island, occupied one of the few buildings on the island. In the week since they had moved onto Sèves Island, the men of the 6th Parachute Regiment had constructed a second defensive line 300 to 800m behind the main line of resistance in the event of an

---

19. E. Carver McGriff, *Making Sense of Normandy* (Inkwater Press: 2007), p. 109.
20. Ibid.
21. McGriff, *Making Sense of Normandy*, p. 109; Blumenson, *Breakout and Pursuit*, p. 84.
22. M. Wind and H. Günther, *Kriegstagebuch. Götz von Berlichingen*, Report 1174/44, July 4, 1944, p. 3.
23. Blumenson, *Breakout and Pursuit*, p. 83.
24. Headquarters 329 Infantry Regiment, 'Action Against Enemy', 8 August 1944, p. 3, https://83rdinfdivdocs.org /documents/ 329th/AAR/ AAR_329_JUL1944.pdf, accessed 28 February 2018.

American breakthrough. Although thinly manned, it was linked to the front line by connecting trenches. The paratroopers were supported by an understrength platoon of three tanks from 'Das Reich' 2nd SS-Panzer Regiment. The 3rd SS-Panzergrenadier Regiment 'Deutschland' and 4th SS-Panzergrenadier Regiment 'Der Fuehrer' defended on the right of the paratrooper regiment between Auxais and the Carentan–Périers road (inclusive). The remnants of the 17th SS-Panzergrenadier Division, combined into a single combat group, defended to the right of 'Das Reich'. Panzers from the 2nd SS-Panzer Regiment were positioned by battalions behind the individual infantry regiments and instructed to cooperate with those regiments. This positioning of armour battalions behind infantry regiments, to act as a mobile reserve for counter-attacks in the event of enemy penetrations, especially at the particularly vulnerable boundaries between defending units, was one of the lessons the SS panzer troops had learned fighting in Russia.[25] Available artillery support, in addition to the batteries of 'Das Reich', included three light batteries from the 17the SS-Panzergrenadier Division on the right and two light batteries from the 275th Infantry Division, along with one light battery from the 91st Air Landing Division on the left.[26]

Von der Heydte was especially pleased to be supported by 'Das Reich', whose combat efficiency he called 'far superior to that of the 17th SS Panzergrenadier Division.'[27] Commanded by SS-Gruppenführer and Generalleutnant of the Waffen-SS Heinz Lammerding, the 2nd SS-Panzer Division had been transferred from southern France, where it was being reconstituted after being hammered on the Eastern Front by the Red Army, to Normandy between the end of June and the beginning of July 1944. Lammerding was a recipient of the German Cross in Gold and the Knight's Cross, the latter awarded in April for his leadership of Kampfgruppe 'Das Reich' on the Eastern Front months earlier. According to an authoritative biography of the SS-General: 'Lammerding's skill and leadership placed the troops where the danger was most immediate. He was always to be found at the main point of the fighting, where he led daily counter-attacks. With his leadership it was possible to prevent a breakthrough in the corps

---

25. V der Heydte, *B-839 A German Parachute Regiment in Normandy*, pp. 30–32; See map 'Battle of Seves Island' – 22–23 July (as described by Sgt. Alexander Uhlig, German 16th Co., 6th Parachute Regiment),' in Colby, *War from the Ground Up*, p. 139.

26. Weidinger, *Das Reich*, p. 149.

27. von der Heydte, *B-839 A German Parachute Regiment in Normandy*, p. 31.

area until he could launch his main attack.'[28] Now Lammerding and his elite division, fighting alongside Hitler's Fallschirmjäger, were expected to prevent an American breakthrough in Normandy until the Wehrmacht's panzer divisions were ready to counter-attack. Encountering a series of French Resistance, SAS, and SOE delaying actions en route to Normandy, the men of the SS division reacted violently. Their reprisals culminated in the massacre of 642 French men, women, and children at Oradour-sur-Glane on 10 June 1944. The mission of 'Das Reich' and the 6th Parachute Regiment read: 'The front is to be firmed up by a counter-attack with armoured support between St-André-de-Bohon and Sainteny.'[29]

Among the largest and most powerful Wehrmacht combat formations in France and one of the few panzer divisions sent to fight the Americans in Normandy, 'Das Reich' was a powerful addition to the German defensive line. On 1 July the division recorded a personnel strength of 17,283. However, only 11,195 personnel were sent to Normandy. By the third week of July, 'Das Reich' was lavishly equipped (by German standards in Normandy), with thirty-seven Panzer IVs, forty-one Panzer V Panthers and twenty-five StuG III assault guns. Additionally, the elite division had 227 armoured halftracks. The SS division also arrived in Normandy with twenty-two towed artillery pieces, along with six self-propelled 105mm Wespe light field howitzers and five self-propelled 150mm Hummel howitzers. Twenty-one heavy anti-tank guns were also combat ready.[30] It is clear why the Americans considered 'Das Reich' to be one of the best panzer divisions in the German Army.[31] 'The division's unit commanders and troops were well trained and experienced in combat. Their equipment was excellent,' marvelled von der Heydte. The 2nd SS-Panzer Regiment consisted of a panzer regiment of two battalions and a StuG III battalion, rather than the single assault gun battalion of the 17th SS Panzergrenadier Division. 'However, the main difference was not in organisation but in the quality of the officers,' enthused the paratrooper major. 'Most of the unit commanders up to and including the regimental commanders had several years of combat experience and those up to and including company

---

28. Mark C. Yerger, 'Heinz Lammerding', *Waffen-SS Commanders. The Army, Corps and Divisional Leaders of a Legend. Kruger to Zimmermann* (Schiffer Military History, 1999), p. 75.
29. Weidinger, *Das Reich V 1943–1945*, p. 149.
30. Zetterling, '2. SS-Panzer Division 'Das Reich', *Normandy 1944*, pp. 323–325.
31. See note in von der Heydte, *B-839 A German Parachute Regiment in Normandy*, p. 32.

commanders had sufficient knowledge of tactics to enable them to fill their posts satisfactorily. In this division one frequently came across men of a type probably best described as 'mercenary' or 'legionary'. Von der Heydte and his paratroopers looked upon 'Das Reich's penal company, consisting of men convicted of minor military or political offences, as the best unit in the entire division.[32]

Of great importance to the commander of the 6th Parachute Regiment was the 'Das Reich' artillery regiment of four battalions, which would be supporting his parachute infantrymen. 'The artillery of the 2nd SS-Panzer Division was particularly good,' recorded von der Heydte. 'Perfect observation facilities, for which the commander of the 6th Fallschirmjäger Regiment had constantly and fruitlessly struggled with the artillery command of the 17th SS Panzergrenadier Division, were taken for granted in the artillery of the 2nd SS-Panzer Division.' According to U.S. Army sources, the weakness in the command of the artillery that were present in almost every other SS division did not exist in the 2nd SS-Panzer Division. Von der Heydte called cooperation between his parachute infantry and the 2nd SS-Panzer Division's artillery 'outstanding', adding 'requests made by the infantry, even if they involved only such matters as noise deception, were always taken into consideration.[33] The combination of elite German paratroopers and SS-panzer and panzergrenadier troops, backed by excellent and plentiful tanks and artillery, spelled trouble for the Americans.

Like the 90th Infantry Division it was facing, the 6th Parachute Regiment was filled with many new, untested replacements, having received some 1,000 men after the battle of Carentan. A large number, as many as 800, were killed or wounded in a short period of time.[34] 'The main reason for this was their lack of experience,' reported a German Seventh Army 14 July report. 'Troops must first be trained by experienced soldiers behind the line. However, present conditions cannot be altered just yet, as we have no more reserves.' The 3rd Parachute Division alone had suffered 4,064 casualties by 12 July.[35] Many of the 6th Parachute Regiment's replacements had arrived without uniforms or weapons.

---

32. von der Heydte, *B-839 A German Parachute Regiment in Normandy*, pp. 30–31.
33. von der Heydte, *B-839 A German Parachute Regiment in Normandy*, pp. 30–32.
34. Wood, *Army of the West*, p. 140.
35. Ibid.

'About a third of them didn't even have a steel helmet, over half had ripped footgear, their training and morale were even worse than it had been with the original regiment,' wrote the ever-critical von der Heydte. 'Among the replacements were many young boys around 17 or 18 years old, that had absolutely no combat experience and had basically been brought into the military directly from the school benches. There were no well-trained Fallschirmjäger, whom one could send into battle without concern,' remembered Corporal Franz Hüttich. 'There was no evidence in their behaviour of training or jump school. We had to teach the boys everything, and because we were constantly deployed in combat, they had to learn very quickly if they weren't going to fall in battle.' Hüttich went on to note that there were men in the once elite regiment that hadn't held a weapon in years; 'they had voluntarily signed up for the Fallschirmjäger troops after hearing the persuasive talks of the recruiters. Some had been threatened with deployment to the Waffen-SS, because the ranks of the fighting troops urgently needed to be filled up.'[36]

Each of von der Heydte's companies had approximately thirty to forty men. Since Carentan, he had reorganised his regiment so that battle-experienced paratroopers fought alongside inexperienced new replacements. A newly formed 16th Company had been created out of the bicycle platoon and the regimental combat platoon (headquarters security guard), allowing the regimental commander to place more of his men on the front lines. The new platoon was commanded by Obergefreiter Thiel, who had been decorated with the Iron Cross First Class for his efforts earlier in the Normandy campaign.[37] Unlike the 90th Infantry Division in the upcoming battle, the 6th Parachute Regiment had had an opportunity to recover from the mauling at Carentan and provide some combat experience to what remained of the new replacements. As no other U.S. combat operations were occurring in the immediate vicinity of Sèves Island, the Germans, like the Americans, would be able to concentrate all their artillery within range in support of von der Heydte and his 6th Parachute Regiment to meet the American attack. This, too, boded poorly for the Americans.

The 90th Division launched its assault with the 1st and 2nd Battalions of the 358th Infantry Regiment at 0630 hours on 22 July. Poor visibility grounded both the fighter-bombers that were to conduct the preparatory air strikes and the artillery observation aircraft that were vital to the

---

36. Griesser, *The Lions of Carentan*, pp. 125–126.
37. Ibid., p. 127.

success of American combat operations in Normandy. Although of great volume, the artillery preparation was unobserved. The men of the 90th Infantry Division believed, mistakenly, that the bombardment had done 'much damage' to the defenders.[38] After the war, survivors from the 6th Parachute Regiment stated that the American artillery had fired over the German positions, failing to inflict any casualties.[39] The bombardment alerted the paratroopers to an imminent attack, causing them to send up flares all along the line. 'When we attacked, the enemy machine gun and artillery fire was the thickest we had ever seen,' remembered Major William J. Falvey, the 358th Infantry Regiment's S-2 (intelligence officer).[40] 'Immediately the preparation lifted at 0630 the Boche began the most intense and sustained counter preparation fire that the division had experienced to date,' reported General Landrum in his after-action report.[41] 'The artillery was like hail,' recorded Falvey. 'The 1st Bn could not move forward one inch because its line of departure was impossible to cross.'[42] One battalion of the 90th Infantry Division not participating in the attack sustained forty-two casualties from enemy shelling. American counter-battery fire proved ineffective.[43] The German heavy artillery fire, which began at H-Hour and continued throughout the day, disrupted and disorganised the assault echelons from the outset and, according to Landrum, foredoomed to failure what he believed had been a well-planned and well-coordinated attack.[44]

The entire attack had been premised upon the rapid movement of the leading waves across the barren approaches to Sèves Island and the quick overrunning of its first line of defence. Due to the tardiness in reaching the Line of Departure, the assault as conceived was never launched. Once aware of the American point of attack, the Germans shifted troops to

---

38. Colby, *War from the Ground Up*, p. 138.
39. See Note in Colby, *War from the Ground Up*, p. 140.
40. Colby, *War from the Ground Up*, p. 140.
41. '90th Infantry Division After Action Report', July 1944, p. 27, http://90thdivisionassociation.org/History/AAR /Regtl /358/358%20 AAR%2007%20July%201944.pdf, accessed on 27 February 2018.
42. Colby, *War from the Ground Up*, p. 140.
43. Blumenson, *Breakout and Pursuit*, 'Chapter XI – COBRA Preparations', Kindle
44. '90th Infantry Division After Action Report', July 1944, p. 27, http://90thdivisionassociation.org/History/AAR /Regtl /358/358%20 AAR%2007%20July%201944.pdf, accessed on 27 February 2018.

the southern bank of the stream to oppose the attackers, mortaring and machine gunning the troops. 'The assault companies,' lamented General Landrum … were pinned to the ground and, notwithstanding the heroic actions of their leaders, remained immobile throughout the afternoon.'[45] A small lodgement had been seized by 1100 hours. However, the troops subsequently withdrew to allow their Sherman tanks to suppress the buildings on the island. Two hours later, B and C Companies from the 1st Battalion established themselves on the island. They were, however, unable to expand their small bridgehead.[46] 'Owing to the fact that the main line of resistance was thinly manned, approximately one enemy battalion succeeded in penetrating this line and holding out for one night in a group of farm buildings after the gap in the line was closed again,' remembered von der Heydte.[47] In the meantime, German mortar, artillery, and machine gun fire blocked all efforts by the engineers to construct a vehicular crossing. The existing road to the island was held by paratroopers, supported by panzers, holding the far approach. Attempts by the 2nd Battalion, 358th Infantry Regiment, to cross were unsuccessful, with only one company making the crossing. Unable to advance or retreat, the few men on the island hunkered down, waiting to be reinforced and resupplied.[48] A platoon of Sherman tanks attempting to cross over to the island was unable to do so due to a combination of the mud and concentrated enemy fire. During the fight, one tank was destroyed by a German 75mm anti-tank gun, probably from one of the panzers defending the island.[49]

At 2000 hours, German paratroopers in two-company strength, reinforced by tanks, struck the Americans of the 1st Battalion on the flank under cover of an intense artillery bombardment. According to the 90th Infantry Division report on the battle: 'The attack was firmly repulsed at dusk, but its weight and fury had reduced the bridgehead to a scant 300 yards depth south of the stream. An all-around defence was established,

---

45. Ibid.
46. Ibid.
47. Von der Heydte, *B-839 A German Parachute Regiment in Normandy*, p. 32.
48. '90th Infantry Division After Action Report', July 1944, p. 28, http://90thdivisionassociation.org/History/AAR /Regtl /358/358%20 AAR%2007%20July%201944.pdf, accessed on 27 February 2018.
49. 2d Lt. Stanley W. Shelly, 'After Action Report 712th Tank Battalion, July 44–March 45,' p. 12. http://90thdivisionassociation.org/History/AAR/ PDF/712%20AAR.pdf, accessed on 27 February 2018.

covered by all available artillery, pending the arrival of reinforcements in men and equipment.'[50] During the first day's fighting, the 358th suffered almost 200 casualties, including twelve officers. The loss of these leaders no doubt further handicapped American efforts to defend, let alone take, Sèves Island. Adding to the difficulties of the 90th Infantry Division, a dense fog overhung the area, rendering American airpower impotent. To make matters worse, the Sèves River overflowed its banks and became unfordable in most spots. The fog and flooding, together with the continuous German artillery and mortar fire that hammered both banks, negated resupply. By first light there was still no tank crossing and only a handful of ammunition had reached the American troops stranded on the island.[51] American tanks continued to support the infantry with direct and indirect fire. However, the Germans were strongly entrenched, with their artillery falling heavily on infantrymen and tankers alike. According to after action reports, the two companies of the 712th Tank Battalion supporting the attack may have fired as many as 1,000 main gun rounds.[52]

Unbeknown to the Americans, elements of two companies from the 1st Battalion, 358th Infantry Regiment (estimated at some 300 men by the Germans), had penetrated the 6th Parachute Regiment's main defensive line, establishing themselves at the critical boundary between the 9th and 11th Parachute Infantry Companies, which were defending the left and centre of von der Heydte's position. Due to his heavy losses in the past weeks, Major von der Heydte turned to the only part of the regiment available for a counter-attack, Oberfeldwebel Alexander Uhlig's 16th Company. Because the regimental commander had previously designated Uhlig's company for 'special deployment', it stood ready for battle near the command post.[53] Von der Heydte had picked the right man for the job. The twenty-five-year-old Uhlig was a veteran of the General Göring Regiment, having joined the 4th Battalion in 1937. On 1 April 1938, after earning his parachutist–rifleman certificate, he was assigned to the 1st Company, 1st Parachute Regiment, in Stendal, where he took part in the

---

50. '90th Infantry Division After Action Report', July 1944, p. 28, http://90thdivisionassociation.org/History/AAR /Regtl /358/358%20 AAR%2007%20July%201944.pdf, accessed on 27 February 2018.

51. Ibid.

52. 2d Lt. Stanley W. Shelly, 'After Action Report 712th Tank Battalion, July 44–March 45', p. 12. http://90thdivisionassociation.org/History/AAR/ PDF/712%20AAR.pdf, accessed on February 27, 2018

53. Greisser, *The Lions of Carentan*, p. 130.

formation of the regiment. Uhlig saw action in Poland and Norway, where he was captured, but soon freed. In August 1943 he received the Iron Cross for flying supply missions to German forces in Africa. Uhlig joined Major von der Heydte's 6th Parachute Regiment on 1 March 1943 as it was being formed. He was made a platoon leader in the 8th Company and later took command of the 16th Company after its commander was killed.[54]

Von der Heydte gave this first-generation Fallschirmjäger and combat veteran complete freedom of action, the right to subordinate paratroopers from other companies, and the assignment to push the Americans back over the Sèves so that the former main line of resistance could be restored. 'Whenever possible, I was supposed to bring two or three captives along so that we could learn about the details of the [American] regiment, their units and their strength,' remembered Uhlig. 'We marched off on foot towards the area of our mission. We only carried light weapons with us (rifles, pistols, submachine guns, hand grenades and rifle grenades), and thus we were well equipped for the close combat we were expecting. Because of [the] enemy's ground-attack aircraft, which had control of the air space, we made slow progress.'[55] About 1300 hours, Uhlig's understrength company was bombarded with mortars, wounding and injuring four men. Two men were detached to take them back to the nearest aid station. 'The terrain north of the Sèves-St Germain road was occupied by the enemy in a breadth of 800m,' he remembered. 'To the east of Closet I encountered a blocking position of 9./FJR 6. Between the two positions, our whole main line of resistance was in American hands. Unfortunately, we weren't just dealing with a single combat patrol, but with a whole unit of more than 300 men. With my few people, a frontal attack against the enemy... did not seem promising. Therefore, I decided to attack the enemy's flank in the wing where his numbers were spread thinnest, i.e. his right flank near Sèves.'[56] Uhlig's company crouched and crawled behind the hedgerows toward Sèves, along the whole of the American breach without being detected. At 1800, the paratroopers began their flank attack. 'It surprised the enemy, who certainly must of have been counting on a different direction of attack,' recorded Uhlig. 'Within the next three hours the enemy was pushed back around 350m in close combat, and so they lost about half of their ground. During this battle we lost none of 16./

---

54. Kurowski, 'Alexander Uhlig', *Knight's Cross Holders of the Fallschirmjäger*, p. 255.
55. Greisser, *The Lions of Carentan*, p. 131.
56. Ibid., pp. 131–132.

FJR 6.' This was the attack the Americans reported as having taken place at 2000 hours. Fighting ceased after darkness fell. With the return of his litter bearers, Uhlig's company had a strength of four NCOs and twenty-four enlisted men. The Germans had failed to take any prisoners.[57]

Afterward, Uhlig heard the Americans digging in. 'He was probably preparing a defence for the next morning against a surprise attack from the same direction as earlier,' he remembered. 'That gave me the idea of surprising him again; so instead of attacking the position he was currently reinforcing, we would attack his newly formed flank. For that I would need reinforcements.'[58] Uhlig spoke with the commander of the 2nd SS Panzer Regiment, who promised to support the attack with three tanks. Additional support came from the commander of the 2nd Battalion, 6th Parachute Regiment, Hauptmann Mager, who reinforced the 16th Company with an NCO and 15 enlisted paratroopers, equipped with two heavy machine guns capable of firing 1,300 rounds per minute. These he positioned north-east of the Sèves on a sunken road, where they could see the whole Sèves lowland and had a completely free field of fire. 'Thus, it was possible to block any retreating enemies or enemies trying to move behind us,' calculated Uhlig. 'My assignment to the group was: to build and camouflage the machine gun position in the remaining hours of night. They did not have permission to fire during my morning attack … They were free to fire only on retreating or advancing enemies.'[59]

'On 23 July at 0730 hours, it was absolutely still,' remembered Uhlig. 'Low-lying cloud cover had appeared that prevented the enemy ground-attack planes from engaging. Three panzers waited on the streets toward St-Germain at the Sèves town exit.' The 16th Company stood ready to march from their old position across from the Americans. Uhlig had an NCO assign six men to every tank. The attack was supposed to start at exactly 0800 by firing all weapons from the road running north-west. After that, the panzers were supposed to drive forward, with the groups assigned to them following. However, the SS panzer commanders rejected Uhlig's plan. 'For this kind of attack, the complicated plan left them too open to enemy tank-killing units,' he wrote. Uhlig changed the plan, ordering his three groups of parachute infantry to attack in front of the panzers. Shortly before 0800, the panzers advanced.[60] 'The firefight began

---

57. Ibid., p. 132.
58. Ibid., pp. 132–133.
59. Ibid., pp. 132–133.
60. Ibid., p. 133.

and suddenly, almost the exact minute, the American artillery unleashed a heavy barrage on the area behind us,' recorded Uhlig. 'The fire gradually shifted back to our initial position and came closer and closer to us. We were forced to attack, so to speak.'[61]

According to American reports, German mortar and artillery fire intensified at 0830, the harbinger of an impending attack. Shortly after 0900 the enemy, 'in considerable strength', according to General Landrum, attacked both flanks of the isolated American battalion.[62] 'During the pandemonium, our opponents disappeared into their foxholes,' observed Uhlig. 'Because of this we could storm forward and so escape the artillery fire.'[63] Panzers operating with both attack groups made deep penetrations as U.S. bazooka teams were picked off by the paratroopers. However, a panzer on the left soon broke down, while another on the right was immobilised under a collapsing roof in Closet. 'Nevertheless, we made progress,' recorded Uhlig.[64] At about 0930, the Germans launched a frontal attack, breaking through the lines into the battalion command post area.[65] 'Certainly the enemy had not realised how inferior our numbers were, because the first US soldiers surrendered themselves,' wrote Uhlig. 'Others tried to withdraw through the Sèves lowlands.' At this moment, the concealed machine guns opened fire, cutting off the return path. 'In the sunken road on the south-eastern edge of the Sèves lowlands, we drove the opponents together and began to take prisoners ... Around 1100 the battle was successfully concluded,' noted Uhlig.[66] The U.S. 1st Battalion commander, Lieutenant Colonel Albert L. Seebert (one of the 90th Division's few remaining original battalion commanders) ordered his men to stop firing and surrender. Some refused to do so and attempted to fight their way out. Few succeeded.

'Worn by fatigue, decimated in strength and bewildered by the success of the German attack, the battalion broke and began withdrawing to the northern bank of the river,' reported General Landrum. 'Many men swam the water gap and reached our lines safely.' The 90th Infantry Division

---

61. Ibid., p. 133.
62. Colby, *War from the Ground Up*, p. 141.
63. Greisser, *The Lions of Carentan*, p. 133.
64. Ibid., p. 133.
65. Colby, *War from the Ground Up*, p. 141.
66. Greisser, *The Lions of Carentan*, p. 133.

reported eleven officers and approximately 200 men captured.[67] The Germans reported taking 234 prisoners, including the battalion commander and eleven officers.[68] In an entry on the battle of Sèves Island, Seventh Army commander, General Paul Hausser, gave credit for 308 American captives at Le Closet, including twelve officers, to the 2nd SS-Panzer Division 'Das Reich', which he had formerly commanded.[69] According to historian John Colby, who served in the 90th Infantry Division during the war and has researched its campaigns intensively, the total number of surrendering U.S. troops came to eleven officers and 254 men. Colby adds that on 23 July another sixty-nine were killed and 104 wounded.[70] U.S. Army Historian Martin Blumenson notes that the 90th Infantry Division suffered a total of 100 killed, 500 wounded and 200 captured during the two days of fighting.[71] The 6th Parachute Regiment suffered few casualties at Sèves Island.

According to General Landrum, the Battle of Sèves Island had been a costly failure, 'shattering as it had 2 battalions of infantry'. Landrum attributed the failure of the attack to the lack of supporting attacks by the entire U.S. First Army along the front, that might have drawn some of the German artillery away from the 90th Infantry Division; weather conditions; the failure to achieve surprise at the beginning of the American attack; and the lack of combat experience among half of his troops who went into battle.[72] Blumenson asserts that the main reason for the 90th Infantry Division's failure at Sèves was the presence of so many inadequately trained replacements. 'The 90th Division had not had enough time to fuse its large number of replacements into fighting teams.'[73] The U.S. Army infantry division commander and historian gave little credit for the American defeat to an elite band of Fallschirmjäger, supported by a handful of panzers from an equally elite band of SS tankers, that had

67. '90th Infantry Division After Action Report', July 1944, p. 29, http://90thdivisionassociation.org/History/AAR /Regtl /358/358%20 AAR%2007%20July%201944.pdf, accessed on 27 February 2018.
68. Greisser, *The Lions of Carentan*, p. 234.
69. Hausser, *A-974 Normandy. Seventh Army*, p. 30.
70. Colby, *War from the Ground Up*, p. 144.
71. Blumenson, *Breakout and Pursuit*, p. 204.
72. '90th Infantry Division After Action Report', July 1944, p. 29, http://90thdivisionassociation.org/History/AAR /Regtl /358/358%20 AAR%2007%20July%201944.pdf, accessed on 27 February 2018.
73. Blumenson, *Breakout and Pursuit*, p. 205.

attacked aggressively and skilfully, making maximum use of terrain, the night, and the equipment available to them.

American efforts to seize Sèves Island were discontinued. On 27 July, following the opening of Operation Cobra, the Germans withdrew from the island. Sergeant Alexander Uhlig was captured by soldiers of the 90th Division on 30 July. The ever-intrepid paratrooper was commanding a delaying force that was outflanked by the 357th Infantry Regiment.[74] Uhlig would be awarded the Knight's Cross on 29 October 1944 for his leadership at Sèves Island.[75] The last casualty of the battle was the man held responsible for failing to seize it. On 31 July, General Middleton relieved General Landrum, replacing him with Major General Raymond S. McLain.

On 23 July 1944 at 2345 hours, Major von der Heydte sent his report on the battle to his parent unit, the 2nd Parachute Division. 'Oberfeldwebel Uhlig led the operation to repair the breach,' he wrote. 'With a combat team of only 30 men and support of one Panzer, they predominantly destroyed an American battalion (I./358.). 234 unwounded prisoners were taken, including a battalion commander and 11 officers. According to capture papers available to the regiment, the 358th Regiment, that stood ready south of Gonfreville before the attack, was supposed to break through the German main line of resistance east of Sèves and then swing east and take the area around St. Germain.'[76] Von der Heydte's report prompted Max Pemsel, Seventh Army Chief of Staff, to write: 'The almost incredible victory achieved by twenty paratroopers with one tank against an American battalion which had broken through and of which five hundred enlisted men and thirteen officers were captured, occurred because the actual strength of the Americans was at first underestimated, the attack was launched audaciously in spite of the uncertainty of the situation, the field of vision was obscured, and the first large-scale use of Panzerfausts in house-to-house fighting had a significant effect on morale.'[77] Writing about the battle of Sèves Island after the war, von der Heydte noted: 'With certain exceptions, the fighting on both sides was invariably gallant and fair, at least in the 6th FS Regiment's sector.' At

---

74. Colby, *War from the Ground Up*, p. 144.
75. Kurowski, 'Alexander Uhlig', *Knight's Cross Holders of the Fallschirmjäger*, p. 255.
76. Greisser, *The Lions of Carentan*, p. 136.
77. See note, von der Heydte, *B-839 A German Parachute Regiment in Normandy*, p. 33.

different times, the Americans, after severe fighting, proposed a truce in order to make possible the collection of wounded men from no man's land; such a truce was then scrupulously observed by both sides. Once, when about ten medical non-commissioned officers, who belonged to the U.S. infantry division commanded by General Macon, were searching for wounded men and lost their way in the Meautis area and happened to get behind the German main line of resistance into the vicinity of a battalion command post, they were returned to their division by the commander of the 6th FS Regiment. On the other hand, American forces, as far as they were able, always replied to inquiries concerning the fate of wounded men. Frequently, wounded men were exchanged in the forward line.[78]

In its battles at Sainteny and Sèves Island against the 83rd Infantry and 90th Infantry Divisions, the 6th Parachute Regiment had once again shown what elite Fallschirmjäger, well led, well supported, and ensconced behind defensive terrain, were capable of accomplishing. It was a lesson playing out across Normandy, as the German Army and the Waffen-SS struggled to hold terrain against an ever growing and powerful U.S. Army and Air Corps. Senior Wehrmacht officers sensed that they were on the verge of being overwhelmed, if not by U.S. infantry, then by American artillery and airpower. By 23 July, the Wehrmacht in Normandy had suffered almost 117,000 casualties, including more than 2,700 officers and more than 110,000 NCOs and enlisted soldiers, along with some 3,800 Russian volunteers. The total number of replacements since 6 June was 10,078 men, or just 9 per cent of total losses. According to Army Group B reports, replacements for the SS panzer divisions had been particularly heavy and were urgently needed.[79] A 23 July 1944 Army Group B report notes:

> The battle potential of the infantry is being especially undermined by the artillery and mortar fire, which the enemy is putting up in hitherto unknown quantity, using a tremendous amount of ammunition (20:1), even for small reconnaissance raids, and for the large attacks this is increased to a 30-hour long pounding. The effect on morale of facing an enemy equipped with such superior weapons is especially bad when the commanders are killed, and the units become mixed up in the desperate attempts to close the gaps.[80]

---

78. von der Heydte, *B-839 A German Parachute Regiment in Normandy*, p. 33.
79. Wood, *Army of the West*, p. 126.
80. Ibid., pp. 141–142.

Realising it was only a matter of time before the Americans broke out of Normandy, Field Marshal von Kluge, Army Group B commander, warned Hitler: 'The psychological effect on the fighting forces, especially the infantry, of such a mass of bombs, raining down on them with all the force of elemental nature, is a factor which must be given serious consideration … Consequently, the troops have the impression that they are battling against an enemy who carries all before them.'[81] General Hausser recommended measures to be taken. These included moving up mobile reserves and additional reinforcements, especially mortar brigades and heavy artillery; increasing the supplies of munitions and fuel to the front in express trains; deploying additional anti-aircraft guns to protect bridges and railways; and sorties by the Luftwaffe to combat American artillery and combat aircraft.[82] But the time was past for most of these measures.

The bulk of the German Army's and Waffen SS's mobile panzer and motorised divisions in France were tied down against the British at Caen and thus unable to reinforce the Seventh Army.[83] Furthermore, reinforcements from Germany were forced to run a gauntlet of ruined roads and shattered bridges under constant air attack to reach the front. Having emasculated the Luftwaffe, Allied air power ensured that any reserves sent forward reached the front lines in a battered state. Once they entered battle, Wehrmacht units were pounded again and again by U.S. airpower and artillery. It was these, Hausser recognised, that were causing the greatest casualties among the German Army in Normandy. 'Casualties caused by tanks and infantry were less severe,' he told the Americans after the war.[84] All that was left for the Wehrmacht and Hitler's paratroopers in Normandy was to fight on in the hopes of containing the Americans and preventing a breakout. As Field Marshal von Kluge told his commanders and staff at a meeting on 21 July 1944: 'We must hold our ground, and if nothing happens to improve conditions, then we must die an honourable death on the battlefield.'[85] Kluge expected the next Allied offensive to begin shortly near Caen. He could not have been more mistaken.

81. Ibid., p. 144.
82. Ibid., pp. 142–143.
83. Generaloberst Paul Hausser, *ETHINT 48. Seventh Army in Normandy* (September 1945) (U.S. Army Historical Division, September 1945), p. 7.
84. Hausser, *ETHINT 48. Seventh Army in Normandy*, p. 6.
85. Wood, *Army of the West*, p. 145.

Chapter 9

2nd Parachute Division at Brest

While the II Parachute Corps and the 6th Parachute Regiment were fighting for their lives in France, the 2nd Parachute Division's battle was just beginning. Following the breakthrough at St-Lô and the drive southward, General George Patton's U.S. Third Army's advance was so rapid that the Wehrmacht was unable to implement its defensive plans. Led by the U.S. VIII and XII Corps' 4th and 6th Armoured Divisions, which made good use of their absolute air supremacy, the motorised infantry of the 8th, 83rd and 80th Infantry Divisions struggled to keep up with the fast-moving tankers. The American armour division benefited also from the weakness of Wehrmacht forces in front of them and French Resistance guides as they overran or bypassed Wehrmacht forces trying to stem their progress.

The VIII Corps' mission was to capture the bocage-covered Brittany peninsula, with its excellent road network but extremely rough and compartmented terrain. The plan called for the 6th Armoured Division, followed by the 83rd Infantry Division, to proceed west through the centre of the peninsula in two or more columns and capture Brest with all possible speed. 'Although there were, in total numbers, more enemy troops in the Brittany peninsula, including the many ports, than there were in the whole attacking U.S. VIII Corps, the speed of our advance and the maneuverability of our forces left the Germans bewildered, never sure just where we were,' wrote Brigadier General Brenton G. Wallace, a senior staff officer of George Patton, in his first-hand account of the U.S. Third Army in the war. 'As a result, they were divided into isolated groups, surrounded, their supplies and communications cut off, and gradually were forced to succumb one by one or were left to 'wither on the vine'. Later they were either killed by the French Maquis or had to surrender to these French patriot forces.'[1]

---

1. Maj. Homer H. Hammond, 'The Operations of the 6th Armoured Division in the Brittany Peninsula' (Ft. Benning, Georgia: The Infantry School

There was little that German forces could do to stem the American blitzkrieg flowing out of Avranches. In the end, the OKW resorted to concentrating whatever ad hoc units it could find or create at locations that would afford them the opportunity for long-term defence. Accordingly, the Führer ordered his commanders to hold the ports of St-Malo, Brest, Lorient, and St-Nazaire, and defend these cities to the bitter end. 'The fortresses which had not been attacked were urged to conduct a more aggressive warfare,' recorded Major Percy Schramm, keeper of the German High Command War Diary. 'This order was observed as far as possible but could not be carried out to the fullest extent since the bulk of the garrisons had no infantry training and anti-tank weapons were lacking.' The brief Wehrmacht stand at Rennes, the ancient capital of Brittany, was short-lived. The city was encircled by the 8th Infantry Division with elements of the 4th Armoured Division. St-Malo was reduced by Major General Robert C. Macon's 83rd Infantry Division in a matter of weeks. Bypassing St-Malo and pushing west through the Brittany peninsula, Major General Troy H. Middleton's VIII Corps, led by the 6th Armoured Division, made rapid progress until they approached Brest.[2]

As it advanced southward towards the port, the 6th Armoured Division's Combat Command A ran head-on into the German 2nd Parachute Division at Huelgoat, yet another major junction some 20 miles east of Daoulas. The division was part of General der Artillerie Wilhelm Fahrmbacher's XXV Corps, which was responsible for the defence of the Brittany peninsula. Fahrmbacher had only three divisions to stem the tide of the American advance. The 266th and 343rd Infantry were both static divisions, understrength and with few heavy weapons and little to no mobility. Generalleutnant Karl Spang's 266th Division had sent a mobile kampfgruppe to fight in Normandy with the 352nd Infantry Division at the beginning of the Allied invasion. That battle group had taken all

---

Officers – Advanced Course, 1946–47), pp. 5–6; Bretton G. Wallace, *Patton and His Third Army* (Military Service Publishing, 1948), p. 43.

2. Colonel Theodore W. Parker Jr. and Colonel William J. Thompson, *Conquer. The Story of the Ninth Army 1944–1945* (The Battery Press, 1947), pp. 2–3; Major Wade Hampton, 'A Proposed Doctrine for the Attack of a Built-Up Area' (Fort Leavenworth, Kansas: U.S. Army Command and General Staff College, 1966), p. 17; Schramm, *B-034 The OKW War Diary. The West*, p. 146; Oberst Rudolf Kogard, *MS # B-427 The Battle in France in 1944. Events in Western Brittany, especially Within the District of the Brest Fortress* (U.S. Army Historical Division, 19 March 1947), p. 29.

the unit's motor transport vehicles and most of its heavy weapons with it. The division's strength at Brest was between 5,000 and 6,000 men. Generalleutnant Erwin Rauch's 343rd Division had a strength of more than 11,000 personnel, but few motor vehicles and some 1,200 horses. It was better equipped than the 266th in crew-served and heavy weapons, possessing three dozen French and Russian 155mm and 76.2mm artillery pieces and most of the mortars and machine guns it was authorised. The artillery, however, was static and the unit possessed few anti-tank guns.[3]

The heart of Fahrmbacher's corps and defence of Brest was General-leutnant Hermann Bernhard Ramcke's 2nd Parachute Division. Hitler and the commander of the German XXV Corps placed a great deal of faith in it. Subordinated to the German 343rd Infantry Division after the American breakthrough at Avranches, the paratroopers had been ordered to screen westward and stall the advance of U.S. forces from the area of Landerneau–Monts d'Arrée. The delay would provide German forces at Brest with time to strengthen the fortresses' defences by transferring artillery and other heavy weapons from the coast. The combination of Fallschirmjäger and the restricting terrain at Carhaix and Huelgoat should have slowed the American advance long enough for the defenders of Brest to complete their task of preparing the city for a prolonged defence. The paratroopers were ordered to avoid any major combat engagements that would decrease their striking power. The intent was clear – an economy of force mission that delayed the Americans while ensuring the survival of the elite paratroopers and their tremendous defensive potential.

The 2nd Parachute, however, was far from ready and still in the process of rebuilding following its mauling in Russia and its arrival back in Germany earlier in the year. By the end of July 1944, the remainder of the division was still understrength and lacking many of the major weapons systems. Authorised 10,813 personnel, it had 7,389 available, including 162 of the 306 officers mandated. The 2nd and 7th Parachute Regiments were all understrength, as was 2nd Parachute Engineer Battalion and the 2nd Parachute Signals Battalion. The parachute engineers had only 42 per cent of its authorised personnel. The division was short 1,088 trucks, 350 motorcycles, 266 passenger cars, 242 machine guns, eighty mortars and fifty-six anti-tank guns, and thus lacked mobility and heavy firepower. Only the I Battalion, 2nd Parachute Artillery Regiment, with twelve 105mm LG-42 recoilless rifles, was with the division at Brest. Its other two artillery

---

3. Zetterling, '266.Infanterie Division,' and '343.Infanterie Division', *Normandy 1944*, pp. 247–248, 270–271.

battalions were at the artillery school in Luneville in eastern France. Its anti-aircraft battalion had lost most of its equipment fighting with the II Parachute Corps in Normandy.[4] According to a U.S. Ninth Army report: 'The parachute division was an elite of the German Army [sic], but it was estimated that loses without corresponding replacements had reduced the parachutist strength in its infantry companies to about thirty-five per cent of the normal.'[5]

On the eve of the battle of Brest, Ramcke was still waiting for the arrival of most of his vehicles, supply units and heavy anti-tank weapons. Furthermore, the 2nd Parachute Division had been ordered to send another parachute battalion (the 6th Parachute Regiment was already fighting in Normandy), along with a detachment of regiment staff, to the Normandy front. 'The regimental staff, led by the ever cheerful and fearless Lt. Col. Rolchewski, was expected to gather scattered parts of the 5th Paratroop Division into new battle units,' wrote Ramcke.[6] Finally, even as he prepared to battle the Americans, veteran Fallschirmjäger such as Oberleutnant Alfons Bialetzki, were being diverted from Ramcke's division to bolster Luftwaffe field divisions on the Eastern Front. Bialetzki was already a recipient of the Iron Cross First and Second Class, the Infantry Assault Badge, the Wound Badge in Silver, and two Tank Destruction strips, all for his earlier service on the Eastern Front. He would go on to earn the Knight's Cross and the Close-Combat Clasp in Gold in Russia, one of only ninety-eight men in all of the Wehrmacht to do so.[7] The 2nd Parachute Division would thus fight the Americans short not only four of its nine parachute infantry battalions and most of its heavy weapons, but also bereft of many combat-seasoned paratroopers. Fortress Brest would make up the shortages in heavy weapons. However, its second-class soldiers were no substitute for Ramcke's elite Fallschirmjäger.

One of the units encountered by the 6th Armoured Division's Combat Command B (CCB) was the 2nd Parachute Regiment, 2nd Parachute Division. 'The drive to Brest was gathering momentum now, the race that

---

4. Hermann Bernard Ramcke, *Fallschirmjäger Damals und Danach* (Frankfurt am Main: Lorch-Verlag, 1951), p. 13; Zetterling, '2. Fallschirmjäger-Division,' *Normandy 1944*, pp. 214–215.
5. Nicholas, et. al., *Conquer*, pp. 2–3;
6. Ibid., p. 42.
7. Florian Berger, 'Oberleutnant der Reserve Alfons Bialetzki', *The Face of Courage. The 98 Men Who Received the Knight's Cross and the Close-Combat Clasp in Gold* (Stackpole Books, 2011), Kindle.

was to tax the endurance of brawny men and sturdy vehicles was on in earnest,' recorded Sergeant Joseph D. Buckley of CCB's 50th Armoured Infantry Battalion. 'However, the enemy offered only scattered resistance until the column approached Carhaix, and here the Nazis indicated an intention to offer determined opposition to our progress.'[8] A road junction 30 miles east of the entrance to the Crozon peninsula, it was an ideal location for waylaying the road-bound Americans. Carhaix was held by a German force of about 2,000 paratroopers who had destroyed all local bridges and were prepared to defend the city.[9]

Oberst Hans Kroh commanded the 2nd Parachute Regiment. A veteran of Crete, North Africa with the Ramcke Brigade, and the Eastern Front, the highly decorated regimental commander had been awarded the Knight's Cross in August 1941, while commanding I Battalion, 2nd Parachute Regiment; the German Cross in Gold in December 1942; and the Oak Leaves to the Knight's Cross in April 1944 as commander of 2nd Parachute Regiment in Russia. Kroh and his Fallschirmjäger were prepared to do battle with the Americans to slow their progress toward Brest.[10] 'Of all the commanders, who ever wore the helmet of the German parachute forces he was one of the bravest and most resourceful combat leaders and that truly means something,' wrote Generalmajor Bernhard Hermann Ramcke.[11] Leutnant Erich Lepkowski was a typical example of the junior leaders serving under Kroh. The twenty-five-year-old native of Geisen in East Prussia had volunteered for the Fallschirmjager, quickly becoming a jack-of-all-trades. Lepkowski trained as a combat engineer, skier, driver, radio operator, and even a locomotive driver. He joined the 2nd Parachute Regiment in 1941, participating in the airborne assaults on the Corinth Canal and Crete, where he was awarded the Iron Cross First Class. Later, he served on the Eastern Front (twice), where he was wounded in the eye by shrapnel his first tour.[12]

---

8. Sergeant Joseph D. Buckley, *A History of the 50th Armoured Infantry Battalion* (self-published, 1945), Chapter. 3. 'Driving Through Brittany', http://super6th.org/50thAIB/DrivingBrittany.html.
9. Maj. Gen. Robert W. Grow and Clyde and J. Burk, *Combat Record of the Sixth Armoured Division* (Germany: Sixth Armoured Division, 1945), p. 15.
10. Kurowski, 'Hans Kroh', *Knight's Cross Holders of the Fallschirmjäger*, p. 125.
11. Hermann Bernhard Ramcke, *Fallschirmjäger. Brest and Beyond 1944–1951* (Shelfbooks, 2016), p. 28.
12. Franz Kurowski, 'Erich Lepkowski', *Infantry Aces. The German Soldier in Combat in World War II* (Stackpole Books, 2005), pp. 187–238; Kurowski, 'Erich Lepkowski', *Knight's Cross Holders of the Fallschirmjäger*, p. 137.

The French Resistance informed Major General Robert Walker Grow, commander of the U.S. 6th Armoured Division, of the presence of Ramcke's troops at Carhaix. Intent on reaching Brest before the Germans could organise their defences, Grow declined battle with Hitler's paratroopers and instead bypassed the town. The 6th Armoured Division was moving so fast that Grow radioed Patton to inform him that he would be in Brest by 5 August. That day, Allied heavy bombers made the first heavy air strike against the port. On 7 August, Carhaix was evacuated by the Germans with the paratroopers reaching Brest by way of the Crozon peninsula.[13] .

After bypassing Carhaix, the 6th Armoured Divisions CCA and Reserve Command encountered Oberstleutnant Erich Pietzonka's 7th Parachute Regiment on the high ground around Huelgoat, south-east of the Monts d'Arrée in the middle of the Brittany peninsula. The thirty-eight-year-old regimental commander was a veteran Fallschirmjäger and a combat-seasoned officer. Following parachute training in July 1940 he was appointed as commander of the II Battalion, 2nd Parachute Regiment, 2nd Parachute Division. On 26 April 1941 he had parachuted into the Corinth Canal with his battalion, sustaining serious injuries during the operation. He re-joined the battalion and fought with it at Volkhov and Mius on the Eastern Front in 1942–43, earning the German cross in Gold. He later commanded the 2nd Parachute Regiment during the Wehrmacht's occupation of Rome and then returned again to Russia, battling the Red Army at Zhitomir and Kirovgrad. Pietzonka assumed command of the 7th Parachute Regiment in December 1943.[14]

Although Ramcke proposed withdrawing the 7th Parachute Regiment for fear of encirclement, Generalleutnant Rauch of the German 343rd Infantry Division rejected the proposal, pointing out that preparatory measures in Brest were still far from completed and more time was needed. Twelve hours later, the encirclement of the regiment was reported. Rauch ordered Pietzonka and his men to fight their way out and back to the fortress. In the meantime, a stiff battle ensued with the 6th Armoured Division's CCA committing tanks, infantry and artillery to overcome the German resistance and move through Huelgoat. Hours later, the Reserve Command, also attempting to bypass the town, plunged headlong into a deep defile in the woods east of Huelgoat, where it came under intense artillery and small arms fire. The column, however, was unable to leave

---

13. Grow and Burk, *Combat Record of the Sixth Armoured Division*, p. 15.
14. Kurowski, 'Erich Pietzonka', *Knight's Cross Holders of the Fallschirmjäger*, p. 171.

the road due to the steep banks on either side. Dismounted armoured infantrymen, supported by artillery, forced the Fallschirmjäger to fall back into the town. Unable to move forward, the vehicles of the Reserve Command reversed their direction of march, extricated themselves from the defile, and broke contact with Ramcke's paratroopers. Six precious hours had been lost in the process.[15]

Although the Americans had extricated themselves from Huelgoat, the 6th Armoured Division spent three days attacking Monts d'Arrée. Using Panzerfausts and Panzerschrecks at close range, Pietzonka and the Fallschirmjäger of 7th Parachute Regiment claimed to have destroyed thirty-two tanks, forcing the Americans to call off their attacks and bypass the hard-fighting German paratroopers. 'With the energetic assistance of Col. Pietzonka, I directed the defensive action from the Commna heights,' recorded Ramcke. 'By repeatedly moving our few truck-drawn anti-tank guns from one threatened sector to the other, we were able to destroy quite a number of tanks.'[16] Both Erich Pietzonka and Oberfeldwebel Adolf Reininghaus, a platoon leader in 7th Parachute Regiment, would be awarded the Knight's Cross for their actions.[17]

According to the 6th Armoured Division's history, the German paratroopers, who had been reinforced with anti-tank guns and artillery pieces, managed to knock out only two medium tanks and one half-track and kill eight Americans. U.S. forces reported killing twenty Germans and taking another 100 prisoners. The 7th Parachute Regiment's defence of Huelgoat delayed the American columns for hours, rather than days. 'What enemy was encountered usually fought stubbornly and well with his available personnel and equipment and our rapid progress was only made possible by our superiority in strength,' notes the 6th Armoured Division official history of Combat Command B.[18] Engagements such as these were cumulative and, along with rearguard actions by other

15. Hammond, 'The Operations of the 6th Armoured Division in the Brittany Peninsula', pp. 15–26.
16. Ramcke, *Fallschirmjäger. Brest and Beyond*, p. 44.
17. Kurowski, 'Erich Pietzonka', and 'Adolf Reininghaus', *Knight's Cross Holders of the Fallschirmjäger*, pp. 171, 181; Franz Kurowski, *Jump into Hell: German Paratroopers in WWII* (Stackpole Books, 2010), p. 316.
18. Hammond, 'The Operations of the 6th Armoured Division in the Brittany Peninsula', p. 15: Commanding General 6th Armoured Division, *Unit History. Combat Command B, 6th Armoured Division* (Headquarters Combat Command B, 22 August 1944), pp. 3–4, 6.

Wehrmacht units and the presence of obstacles, such as blown bridges and mines, succeeded in delaying the 6th Armoured Division's advance toward Brest by forty-eight hours. This provided the defenders with the time needed to emplace heavy weapons and troops and build a viable defensive shield. More importantly, the majority of both 2nd and 7th Parachute Regiments were able to make their way back into Brest and prepare themselves for its defence.[19]

By 3 August U.S. VIII Corps troops were at Pontivy, catching the German XXV Corps staff by surprise. Two days later, armoured spearheads had reached the outskirts of Brest. Short of artillery, the Americans waited for it to arrive, while planning a coordinated attack on the city beginning at dawn on 9 August. On the early morning of 8 August, 6th Armoured Division G-2 (Intelligence Officer) and an interpreter entered the city in a quarter-ton truck under a white flag to present the German commander with a demand for the surrender of Brest. 'The United States Army, Naval, and Air Force troops are in a position to destroy the garrison of Brest,' wrote the 6th Armoured Division commander, in a letter to the Wehrmacht commander dated the same day. 'This memorandum constitutes an opportunity for you to surrender in the face of these overwhelming forces … and to avoid the unnecessary sacrifice of lives. I shall be very glad to receive your formal surrender and make the detailed arrangements any time prior to 1500 this date.' According to an officer of the 6th Armoured Division. 'The German general was polite but refused to consider surrender.'[20]

Grow's troops prepared to attack the following day in a south-westerly direction with its two combat commands abreast (CCA on the right and CCB on the left) and the Reserve Command following. The division G-2 estimated that an enemy force of at least 3,000 German soldiers, including at least one regiment of 2nd Parachute Division, guarded the outer defence of Brest along a line running from St-Renan–Gouesnou–Guipavas. These defences consisted of a large number of previously prepared positions, including concrete pillboxes, fox holes, anti-tank guns and minefields, all covered by registered artillery fire. Road blocks covered all the approaches to the city. Bridges and buildings had been prepared for demolition. It was believed that the city itself had the same types of defences as the outer line. 'Important intersections and CPs [Command Posts] were well

---

19. Hammond, 'The Operations of the 6th Armoured Division in the Brittany Peninsula', p. 27.
20. Ibid, pp. 19–20.

prepared for defence and the city was covered by artillery from the points of land across the Rode de Brest as well as from the naval arsenal across the estuary from Brest proper,' noted the intelligence report.[21]

As U.S. units shifted into their attack positions, the Germans in Brest began pouring in concentrated and accurate artillery fire on the Americans, inflicting heavy casualties on CCA and destroying many vehicles. Additionally, the paratroopers of the 2nd Parachute Division sallied from their defensive positions, attacking the vulnerable logistics and support formations and being repulsed only after an intense firefight. To make matters worse for the U.S. force, powerful small arms, mortar and artillery fire broke out to their north-east, heralding a surprise attack by the German 266th Infantry Division. The attack was triggered when the division commander, Generalleutnant Karl Spang, and his staff accidentally drove their vehicles into the rear of a U.S. artillery position and were captured. Spang's soldiers attempted to liberate their commander from the Americans, setting off a major battle. U.S. forces had earlier bypassed the division at Morlaix. It was now trying to fight its way into Brest.

The American attack on the city was cancelled. The following morning the 6th Armoured Division did an about face and launched a full-scale attack on the German 896th, 897th, and 898th Infantry Regiments around Plouvien and Bourg-Blanc. Supported by its artillery and U.S. Air Force fighter-bombers, which repeatedly strafed the exposed and hapless Wehrmacht soldiers, the 6th Armoured Division managed to badly damage the division. The Germans suffered 1,100 casualties, including 230 officers and men killed, 70 wounded, and 800 captured. The dead included General Spang and most of his staff. U.S. soldiers also captured or destroyed 200 vehicles and twenty anti-tank guns and artillery pieces.[22] 'The 266th Division was completely destroyed,' recorded the 6th Armoured Division's combat history.'[23] The statement was far from

---

21. Clyde J. Burk and Cyrus R. Shockey, *Combat Records of the 6th Armoured Division* (Germany: 6th Armoured Division, 1945), p. 15.

22. Commanding General 6th Armoured Division, *Unit History. Combat Command B, 6th Armoured Division*, p. 5: Mitcham, '266 Infantry Division', *German Order of Battle, Volume One: 1–290 Infantry Divisions in WWII* (Stackpole Books, 2007), p. 314.

23. Lieutenant Colonel Ernest W. Mitchell, et. al., *Combat History of the 6th Armoured Division in the European Theatre of Operations, 18 July 1944–8 May 1945* (6th Armoured Division: William E. Rutledge, Jr., 1945), p. 24.

accurate. Although the 266th had indeed lost most of its officers and vehicles and many of its heavy weapons, as many as 4,000 to 5,000 of the division's soldiers survived the battle, making their way into Brest.[24]

Meanwhile, the defenders of Brest attacked the rear elements of the 6th Armoured Division, trying to assist their comrades. An American petrol dump was raided by 150 Fallschirmjäger of 2nd Parachute Division, who destroyed 5,000 gallons of fuel before being driven off. Throughout the remainder of the day the unit logistics formations were shelled, with ammunition and more petrol destroyed by an unidentified enemy column moving in from the north. American P-51 fighter-bombers strafed and bombed the enemy column to destruction. At the same time, the lead elements of the 8th Infantry Division were arriving. The 6th Armoured Division planned another attack on Brest. On 12 August, however, the division was ordered to leave one Combat Command to contain the city and to proceed to Lorient on another mission. The 6th Armoured Division had suffered some 600 combat casualties and lost fifty armoured fighting vehicles, more than sixty other vehicles, and eleven artillery pieces in its advance from Avranches to Brest and the attack on the city. It had captured 3,715 Germans and killed hundreds of others.[25]

At about the same time, a crisis had arisen among the Fallschirmjäger that demanded immediate action. Paratroopers from the II Battalion, 7th Parachute Regiment who had managed to escape encirclement at the hands of the Americans reported that 130 of their captured comrades were being held in a Brasparts schoolhouse and guarded by French Resistance forces. The French sent two prisoners to Ramcke demanding that he surrender Brest within two days or his Fallschirmjäger would be shot. Ramcke approved a surprise attack to free the German paratroopers. It would be led by 'the best combat team leader of the 2nd Fallschirmjäger Regiment,' according to Ramcke, Leutnant Erich Lepkowski. Fallschirmjager in trucks led by armoured cars quickly penetrated the French lines at night, assisted by a diversionary attack, reaching Brasparts, 40 km behind the lines. Overpowering the French guards, they loaded their liberated

---

24. Zetterling, '266.Infanterie Division', *Normandy 1944*, p. 248. According to Zetterling, about 5,000 to 6,000 men remained with the division in Brittany after the departure of a Kampfgruppe to Normandy, leaving 4,000 to 5,000 men after the loss of some 1,000 to the U.S. 6th Armoured Division.

25. Burk and Shockey, *Combat Records of the 6th Armoured Division*, p. 15: Hammond, 'The Operations of the 6th Armoured Division in the Brittany Peninsula', p. 28.

comrades into the vehicles and fought their way back through now alerted companies of French Resistance forces. Lepkowski and his men suffered only three casualties and brought back forty French prisoners. 'I knew you would do it – Oberleutnant Lepkowski,' Ramcke told him, replacing his lieutenant's shoulder boards with those of a senior lieutenant. 'I congratulate you on being promoted from the ranks for bravery in the face of the enemy.' On 22 August Lepkowski was once more summoned by Ramcke, who handed him a radio message that had just come in from the German High Command. 'In recognition of his heroic actions in the southern sector of the Eastern Front, Leutnant Erich Lepkowski is hereby awarded the Knight's Cross of the Iron Cross.' 'Lepkowski, this decoration is well-deserved,' Ramcke told him. 'But it's not for your special action here at Brest and your breakout. For that you have been recommended for the Oak Leaves.'[26]

VIII Corps, with the 2nd, 8th and 29th Infantry Divisions, was responsible for the reduction of Brest. It would also control the 6th Armoured Division. Due to the pause in operations against the city, U.S. forces would not be prepared to recommence their offensive operations until 18 August, almost a week later. It was later learned that the weakest defences at Brest at the time were at the entrances from the north-east, the attack sector assigned to CCA. Had it reached its assigned strike positions on 7 August and attacked the next morning, there is a good possibility it would have penetrated the defences of the city. The Americans had probably missed their best chance to take one of their important objectives in all the war on the run.[27]

When the Wehrmacht had swept across western France in 1940, Brest was one of the plums that fell to the Germans. According to the Ninth Army Report of Operations: 'The excellent deep-water roadstead, which made it the largest land-locked harbour in Europe, was vitally needed by the Allies.' Brest was France's fourth largest naval port in terms of annual peacetime capacity, capable of handling 5,160,000 tons a year. In comparison, Rochefort handled 5,630,000, Boulogne 5,400,000 and Cherbourg 5,300,000 tons. In Brest's magnificent harbours, the Kriegsmarine was able to develop their most important submarine

---

26. Ramcke, *Fallschirmjager. Brest and Beyond*, pp. 70–71; Kurowski, 'Erich Lepkowski, *Infantry Aces*, pp. 241–244.
27. Hammond, 'The Operations of the 6th Armoured Division in the Brittany Peninsula', pp. 21–22, 27.

bases, which had withstood all Allied attempts to knock them out from the air.'[28]

Old Brest alone would have been a tough nut to crack. The city, which was surrounded by an ancient wall 30ft high and 15ft thick and protected by a dry moat, spanned both sides of the Penfeld River and was studded with numerous fortifications. These were formidable enough, but the Germans had spent almost four years expanding and improving them to protect their vulnerable submarines from Allied bombers. Extensive construction work had resulted in enormous submarine pens surrounded by additional facilities housing shore batteries with heavy artillery and anti-aircraft guns protected by extensive concrete defensive positions and minefields. According to a U.S. VIII Corps Artillery estimate, 'Fortress Brest' was composed of many strong points, most of which were built around anti-aircraft guns or searchlight positions, coast defence guns and old French forts. Between these strong points were many weapons positions, varying from holes in the hedgerows to reinforced concrete casemates for light anti-tank guns and armoured machine gun turrets.'[29] One of the most imposing strong points at Brest was the Lochrist or 'Graff Spee' Battery, which consisted of four 280mm howitzers in permanent emplacements, three of which permitted a 360-degree traverse.[30]

The U.S. VIII Corps controlled four infantry divisions: 2nd, 8th, 29th, and 83rd. Three formed an arc around the port city, with the 29th Infantry on the right (west), the 8th Infantry Division in the centre, and 2nd Infantry Division on the left (east). This arch stretched from the Conquet peninsula around to the Élorn River east of Brest proper. Another two brigade task forces, consisting of infantry, armoured cavalry, tank destroyers and combat engineers, extended the arc further to the south, isolating the Crozon peninsula south of Brest. Their mission was to prevent the Germans from infiltrating back onto the peninsula from either Crozon or Brest. The 83rd Infantry Division provided flank protection to the south and east and contained German forces at St-Nazaire and Nantes.[31]

---

28. Parker and Thompson, *Conquer*, p. 23; Schramm, *B-034 OKW War Diary. The West*, p. 144.

29. 'Report on the Artillery with VIII Corps in the Reduction of Brest, 22 August–19 September 1944', (VIII Corps: October 16, 1945), p. 23. See http://cgsc.contentdm.oclc.org/cdm/ref/collection/p4013coll8/id/52.

30. Ibid, pp. 23–25.

31. Parker and Thompson, *Conquer*, pp. 25–27.

VIII Corps Artillery consisted of five group headquarters, an observation battalion and fifteen artillery battalions. It was equipped with medium 105mm and 155mm howitzers and heavy 155mm guns, 8in guns and howitzers, and 240mm howitzers. This was in addition to the twelve battalions of 105mm and 155mm howitzers assigned to the 2nd, 8th, and 29th Infantry Divisions. After the commencement of the attack, these were supplemented by another two battalions of 4.5in guns, a battalion of 240mm howitzers, a field artillery observation battalion, and a field artillery brigade headquarters. In all, Americans would bring thirty howitzer and gun battalions to bear on the Germans at Brest.[32]

Initially the XIX Tactical Air Command, operating with the US Third Army, was assigned the mission of supporting the U.S. Ninth Army in the Brest battle and along the Loire. On 5 September, eleven groups of medium bombers, reinforced by heavy bombers of the Royal Air Force and both heavy bombers and fighter-bombers of the United States Eighth Air Force, conducted a heavy air bombardment of the port city. Later, during the battle, the XIX Tactical Air Command would be replaced by the XXIX Air Command. It controlled four fighter-bomber groups.[33] The combination of American air power and artillery support would prompt one German paratrooper to recall: 'There was always something gurgling or whistling through the air – bombs from above, or shells from the countryside. No matter where you were in Brest, in the front lines or in a downtown street, it was never safe to be more than a few yards from cover.'[34]

In addition to 2nd Parachute and 343rd Infantry Divisions, along with the decimated 266th Infantry Division, the defending garrison included a collection of battle groups comprising all manner of personnel, including a static coastal garrison and various odds and ends of Army and Navy formations which had been trapped by the advancing American forces. The defenders even utilised members of the customs service and the Kriegsmarine's meteorological service in their desperate attempt to hold out.[35] A 29th Infantry intelligence report, dated 21 August 1944, estimated that the Germans had 16,500 to 20,000 troops defending Brest. Of these, 8,500 were believed to Army troops. The remainder belonged to the other services. 'A prisoner captured from 7th Parachute Regiment

---

32. Joseph Balkoski, *From Beachhead to Brittany: The 29th Infantry Division at Brest, August–September 1944* (Stackpole, 2008), p. 23.
33. Parker and Thompson, *Conquer*, pp. 29–30.
34. Balkoski, *From Beachhead to Brittany*, p. 131.
35. Parker and Thompson, *Conquer*, p. 27.

states that food and water are critical, and morale is low,' recorded the report, continuing. 'A question exists as to whether or not the will to resist will continue when a show of strength is made by us and when the natural inclination of the naval and marine garrison not to fight a ground battle penetrates the command.'[36] The French Resistance was telling the Americans that the German garrison at Brest consisted of between 40,000 and 50,000 personnel, or more than twice the number given in U.S. intelligence reports before the battle.[37]

The Brest fortress bristled with artillery, including guns in fixed emplacements, coastal defence weapons and anti-aircraft guns with calibres ranging from 20mm AA guns to 280mm coastal defence weapons. VIII Corps intelligence estimated that the Germans had some eighty-six artillery batteries consisting of 320 guns in the Brest area. In addition, there were believed to be another 330 heavy, medium, and light AA weapons, which would probably be used in the ground support role against American infantry and armoured vehicles. VIII Corps artillery officers believed that, except for specialised large-calibre coastal artillery pieces, shortages of artillery ammunition for the myriad of foreign (non-German) guns would hamper the defenders.[38]

In command of the Brest fortress was the fifty-five-year-old Ramcke, a legendary Fallschirmjäger. He was considered one of the toughest and bravest German soldiers of the war. Ramcke had, almost single-handedly, turned the tide of battle at Crete in 1940 in favour of the Germans, snatching victory from the jaws of defeat when he led a 'Do or Die' assault that captured Malame airfield and broke the British defences. Ramcke was a recipient of the Knight's Cross with Oak Leaves and the Iron Cross 1st and 2nd Class, each with a bar (indicating a second award); the Imperial Prussian Distinguished Service Cross; the Baltic Cross 1st and 2nd Class; and the Wound Badge in Gold. All had been awarded during his time as a sailor in the German Imperial Fleet and the Marine Assault Battalion in Flanders in the First World War. He had also won a battlefield officer's commission during that period. Ramcke, who had qualified for his Fallschirmjäger wings at the age of fifty-one, became the first commander of the newly formed 2nd Parachute Division in February 1943, leading it

---

36. Balkoski, *From Beachhead to Brittany*, p. 130.
37. Ibid.
38. 'Report on the Artillery with VIII Corps in the Reduction of Brest, 22 August–19 September 1944, p. 5; Parker and Thompson, Conquer, pp. 1–2, 20.

to Russia, where it was decimated in bitter fighting. He was placed back in command of the division during the battle for Normandy in anticipation of the hard battle ahead.[39] General der Panzertruppe Wilhelm Ritter von Thoma, once the commander of the famed Afrika Korps, characterised Ramcke as a 'fervent Nazi [who] boasted loudly about his division and his activities. Above all, he didn't let anyone forget that he was the only one who could work something out and he was the one who had the experience required.'

Ramcke had received his marching orders for Brest from the commander of the German First Parachute Army, Generaloberst Kurt Student, at Student's headquarters in Nancy on 12 June, almost a week after the beginning of the Allied invasion.[40] The commander of 2nd Parachute Division was not happy with his new assignment, believing that defending a static position was not the best use of Hitler's elite Fallschirmjäger. 'However bad things looked,' he admitted later, 'I was a soldier and had to fight.' Still, he understood exactly what Hitler expected of him and had no intention of letting the Führer down. 'There was nothing for me to do but by all means defend the town of Brest until the last shot had been fired and only to surrender to the Americans after it had been reduced to ruins. This is a fortress commander's duty.'[41]

Ramcke arrived in Brest on 9 August. He assumed command of the fortress from Oberst Hans von der Mosel two days later. Ramcke's orders from Hitler were clear. In his address to his soldiers he made it known to all that he intended on carrying them out to the fullest: 'Faithful to the oath we have sworn to the Führer, people, and the Fatherland, and safeguarding the traditional honour of the German soldier, we are going to defend the Fortress Brest to the last grenade, committing our very lives; and shall cede this important port to the enemy only as a pile of ruins.'[42] Ramcke recognised that his mission was 'to hold the fortress as long as possible, to tie down a substantial enemy force in order to reduce

---

39. Kurowski, 'Bernhard Hermann Ramcke', *Knight's Cross Holders of the Fallschirmjäger*, p. 175; Hildebrand, 'Bernhard Hermann Ramcke', *Die Generale der deutschen Luftwaffe*, Band 3, pp. 76–79; Neitzel, ed., General der Fallschirmtruppen Bernhard Ramcke', *Tapping Hitler's Generals*, p. 309.
40. Kurowski, *Jump Into Hell*, pp. 314–315; Hildebrand, 'Kurt Student', *Die Generale der deutschen Luftwaffe 1935–1945*, Band III, p. 363.
41. Neitzel, 'Document 39', *Tapping Hitler's Generals*, p. 107.
42. Ibid., p. 26.

the burden on the hard-pressed German front in the west', and, in the event the Americans should succeed in capturing the fortress, to ensure that 'all facilities of military value' were 'so thoroughly destroyed, that the harbour could not be used for a long time'.[43]

The new commander strove to impose his will to win on all his soldiers, not just his Fallschirmjäger. Shortly after assuming command, he brought four high-ranking officials and officers up for trial by courts martial and had another six men shot for defeatist talk, going over to the enemy and desertion. 'I had them all shot after I called up representatives from each unit – 300 men in all [to witness the executions]. After that there was order.'[44] A captured Fallschirmjäger later told his American captors before the battle that a senior German officer had been dismissed from Fortress Brest because 'he didn't believe Brest could be defended and wanted to surrender'.[45]

Never one to waste time, Ramcke led an attack on the village of Gouesnou, 8km north-west of Brest, on 9 August with the aim of opening the road, leading north via Plabennec toward Brest, for a column of the 266th Infantry Division. Ramcke quickly assembled 7th Parachute Regiment with two anti-tank platoons armed with Panzerfausts and Panzerschrecks and supported by a battery of army artillery from the fortress and two navy anti-aircraft batteries. The village, defended by American infantry and dug-in tanks, was quickly taken following an artillery barrage. The German attack, however, bogged down at the northern limits of the village as the Americans pounded it with artillery and launched their own counter-attack. The Fallschirmjäger went to ground, burrowing into the hedgerows 'like foxes', according to Ramcke. In the end, the prodigious use of artillery, mortar and tank fire by U.S. forces forced the Germans back.[46] One suspects Ramcke's actions were intended as much as for instilling an offensive spirit into the defenders of Brest as improving the tactical situation.

Ramcke split the Brest area into two defensive sectors divided by the Penfeld River. The Crozon and Daoulas peninsulas to the south were placed under the 343rd Infantry Division. Roughly two battalions of the 266th Infantry Division defended Le Conquet. The German main defensive effort was on the city of Brest, north of the river, and the surrounding

---

43. Ramcke, *Fallschirmjäger. Brest and Beyond*, pp. 56, 60.
44. Neitzel, 'Document 108', *Tapping Hitler's Generals*, pp. 193–194.
45. Balkoski, *From Beachhead to Brittany*, p. 23.
46. Ramcke, *Fallschirmjäger. Brest and Beyond*, pp. 52–55.

area. Ramcke positioned the 2nd Parachute Regiment around Chateaulin; 7th Parachute Regiment around Sizun, responsible for the Monts d'Arrée heights; 2nd Parachute Engineers at Douarnenez Bay; and II Battalion, 7th Parachute Regiment with 2nd Parachute Anti-Tank Battalion (with only four guns) north and north-east of Brest.[47] The ad hoc battle groups formed by Ramcke provided the defenders with more troops than Colonel Hans von der Mosel, the Brest fortress' original commander, had originally planned for, allowing the Germans to push positions past the old fortifications into the surrounding hedgerow country. The main line of resistance was established on a line Plouzane–Guilers–Guipanas. The new extended line was based on a system of strong points consisting of anti-aircraft positions, old forts and earthworks. The second line of defence was placed on the outskirts of the city, using prominent buildings as strong points. The Germans made maximum use of the extensive network of tunnels in the city. Tunnels were employed as hospitals, headquarters and troop shelters, and were used to facilitate movement of troops from one section of the city to another in comparative safety.[48]

The failure of the Americans to follow up their attacks earlier in August provided Ramcke and his men with the time they needed to prepare their defence of Brest. 'We had no illusion about Brest being a last stand,' remembered the Fallschirmjäger commander. 'Every man was fully aware of the gravity of our situation, but every man was also convinced that the enemy formation engaged here would take the pressure off the front lines of the western theatre and that the bombs and shells dropped on us would not hit our beloved homeland. Emboldened by the determination to carry out their duty to the last even in this gruelling and hopeless situation, the garrison went into battle in a spirit of solidarity that extended from the oldest commander to the youngest paratrooper, rifleman, sailor and dock worker.'[49]

By 19 August the soldiers of the U.S. 2nd Infantry Division had arrived on the Brittany peninsula. Four days later they were followed by the G.I.s of the 29th Infantry Division. However, priorities elsewhere deprived the VIII Corps of the supplies it needed to launch a robust and sustained attack against the now well-prepared defenders. On 25 August General

---

47. Ibid., pp. 36–37.
48. Ramcke, *Fallschirmjäger. Brest and Beyond*, p. 68; Hampton, 'A Proposed Doctrine for the Attack of a Built-Up Area by a ROAD Division', pp. 26–27.
49. Ramcke, *Fallschirmjäger. Brest and Beyond*, p. 66.

Middleton hurled his corps at Brest, only to discover that promised supplies would not arrive. The VIII Corps commander also had to inform his disappointed divisions and regiments that the ground attack missions that had been promised by the Ninth U.S. Air Force had been cancelled without any explanation. The lack of solid intelligence on the location of German formations caused the cancellation.[50]

The VIII Corps attack commenced at 1300 hours after a one-hour artillery barrage with the 2nd, 8th and 29th Infantry Divisions advancing against the city's strong outer defences from the east, north and west respectively.[51] American GIs quickly learned that, as in Normandy, the hedgerows gave the Germans the upper hand, allowing them to open fire unseen from virtually point-blank range before switching to another well-hidden position. The defenders waged a skilled delaying action, buying time for their main line of resistance to prepare, while inflicting as many casualties as possible. Still, by the third day of the attack, soldiers of the 29th Infantry Division had penetrated the enemy's defence at Keriolet. They were immediately set upon by the Fallschirmjager of 7th Company, 2nd Parachute Regiment. A savage battle ensued. The two sides had clashed before outside of St-Lô and the Germans wanted revenge. 'The fight inside the position became a personal, hand-to-hand action fought for the most part with rifles and grenades inside buildings, along zig-zag trenches and in underground dugouts,' writes historian Joseph Balkoski. The Americans prevailed, driving out the German defenders and capturing forty-three prisoners. However, accurate artillery fire and repeated counter-attacks took their toll on the Americans. 'The position changed hands two or three times,' remembers Fallschirmjäger Rudolph Müller. The Americans, however, could not hold on for more than an hour since our counter-attacks dislodged them each time.' In the end, the G.I.s left unscathed were forced to abandon the position, while those that were wounded were captured. 'An odor of decaying flesh spread rapidly because the days were really hot,' recalled Müller, 'and we could not bury the dead as the slightest noise provoked American fire.'[52]

By 30 August, VIII Corps units had cleared the Daoulas peninsula south of Brest of German troops. Elements of the 29th Infantry Division had seized

---

50. Blumenson, *Breakout and Pursuit*, p. 636; Balkowski, *From Beachhead to Brittany*, p. 33.
51. Williams, *The United States in World War II. Special Studies. Chronology 1941–1945*, p. 256.
52. Balkoski, *From Beachhead to Brittany*, pp. 48–49.

the top of Hill 103, a commanding feature in the Brest defences. A company of Fallschirmjäger from 2nd Parachute Regiment were ordered to 'get the hill at all costs'. They failed to do so but retained the eastern slope. Afterward, a 29th Infantry Division intelligence report described the paratroopers as 'the toughest' enemy unit at Brest. The following day General Middleton was forced to suspend operations and regroup due to a lack of supplies, especially of artillery ammunition. However, VIII Corps had completed the encirclement of Brest. It was not until 7 September that the corps was provided with sufficient stocks of ammunition to permit the resumption of a sustained full-scale attack.[53] Although large scale U.S. ground operations came to a halt, the Americans pounded Brest around the clock with air and artillery, inflicting heavy casualties and demoralising the defenders. A direct hit on one German artillery position detonated 3,000 rounds of artillery, blowing the position 'sky high', according to a survivor, who was captured. 'The explosion was terrific, tearing a crater 30ft deep and at least 50ft wide,' he told the Americans. 'A nearby gun went up at least 60ft into the air.' Other captives called the U.S. fire 'heavy' and 'very accurate' and 'effective', noting that it was causing 'many casualties' and preventing them from accessing the wells that provided Brest and the defenders with fresh drinking water.[54]

By 1 September, most of the German artillery and flak positions had been wiped out. 'The enemy had not reached the improved Main Line of Resistance at any point until 5 September,' noted the OKW War Diary. 'However, the anti-aircraft positions and some pockets of resistance in the main positions had been knocked out by carpet bombing.' According to Major Schramm, of the ninety-six navy flak guns, only two were still in use. Schramm writes that the Wehrmacht had already suffered significant casualties before the last phase of the battle of Brest had even begun, recording that between 8 August and 5 September the German defenders had already sustained almost 8,000 battle casualties, including 838 killed, 3035 wounded and 3,944 missing. A large part of these were, of course, the soldiers of the 266th Infantry Division. According to the OKW War Diary: 'The 2nd Parachute Division suffered the greatest number of casualties.'[55]

53. Balkoski, *From Beachhead to Brittany*, p. 74; Blumenson, *Breakout and Pursuit*, p. 636; Williams, *The United States in World War II. Special Studies. Chronology 1941–1945*, pp. 257, 260.
54. 'Report on the Artillery with VIII Corps in the Reduction of Brest, 22 August–19 September 1944', pp. 61–62.
55. Schramm, 'Report by the Commander dated 5 September 1944', B-034 *OKW War Diary. The West*, pp. 148–149.

The final battle of Brest began at 1000 hours on 8 September. Three U.S. divisions surrounding the city, attacking simultaneously following a twenty-minute artillery preparation. There was little room for large-scale manoeuvring. Even small unit movements were difficult. The terrain was studded with steel rail obstacles, which were well wired. Coastal guns of up to 14in (350mm) covered the land approaches. The Americans were committed to a head-on attack against a stubborn enemy that was well entrenched. Resistance was stiff during the first day, particularly on the Conquet peninsula and in the Recouvrance area. North and north-east of the city gains of up to half a mile were achieved. The Germans used every device at their disposal to maximise casualties among the attackers. According to the Ninth Army historian: 'Pillboxes and strong points were hotly defended, and mines and booby traps were used in great numbers.' For the first time in this area, the Germans used 'Goliath', a cable-controlled demolition vehicle or 'tracked mine', capable of carrying up to 125lbs of high explosive. These miniature tanks could be used for multiple purposes, including destroying tanks, disrupting dense infantry formations and the demolition of buildings and bridges.[56] The defenders of Brest were not particularly impressed with their U.S. infantry opponents. One Fallschirmjager remarked: 'They struck us as extremely cautious, unwilling to venture forward without thorough reconnaissance and artillery bombardment.'[57] Perhaps. But the Americans, supported by their overwhelming air supremacy and artillery, continued to grind forward inexorably, even against the dogged determination of the paratroopers of 2nd Parachute Division.

On 9 and 10 September fighting continued in much the same pattern. On the Conquet peninsula, the 29th Infantry Division, despite heavy resistance, secured the surrender of the commanding officer of the troops in their area on the 9th, although mopping up operations met fierce opposition. Isolated German forces refused to acknowledge their commander's surrender and gave up as individuals only after another day of fighting. The last German defenders were cleared from the Conquet peninsula on 10 September. In the Recouvrance area, however,

---

56. Office of the Chief of Ordnance, 'Cable Controlled Demolition Vehicle Goliath – BI', *Enemy Ordnance Material (German)* (Office of the Chief of Ordnance, 1 March 1945), p. 40; Alexander Lüdeke, 'The Remote-Controlled Demolition Carrier', *Weapons of World War II* (Bath: Parragon, 2013), p. 178.
57. Balkoski, *From Beachhead to Brittany*, p. 129.

the division made little or no progress. By 9 September the 2nd and 8th Infantry Divisions had pressed forward nearly a mile and were well into the built-up area of the city. 'The advance, which squeezed the life from the encircled fortress, was not made down the streets of the city but rather through the buildings, block by block,' notes the Ninth Army history. 'Pillboxes, positions dug in at intersections and small embrasures cut in the buildings at street level permitted the enemy to sweep the streets with such intense fire as to deny their use to the attacker.' Avoiding the fire-swept streets, cemeteries, parks and railway yards, the infantry and engineers advanced methodically, blasting their way through the buildings and assailing the defenders from the bottom floor. The Germans made maximum use of the extensive network of tunnels under Brest, using them not only to facilitate the movement of troops but also as shelters for the exhausted defenders, headquarters and hospitals. Despite the fact that the German paratroopers were monitoring U.S. radio transmissions and anticipating enemy attacks before they were launched, they could still not prevent the Americans from tightening their hold.[58]

'Until September 10th the 2nd Fallschirmjäger-Division had been able to assert itself at the outer defensive line,' recorded Ramcke. 'Following weeks of heavy defensive combat, the Division now withdrew to the main battle line, which was held by the fortress defence forces. The paratroopers' high hopes to be relieved by these units for a few days' rest would not be answered, however. Many sections of the main battle line were already shattered by saturation bombing, artillery bombardment and ceaseless attacks by fighter bombers. The fortress troops ... consisting of mostly older age groups unaccustomed to combat, had already taken many casualties. Thus, the paratroopers had to man the main defensive line.'[59] On 11 September, the two U.S. infantry divisions advanced another half a mile, while the 29th Infantry Division in the Recouvrance sector still made little progress.[60]

In Brest, the old wall and moat that surrounded the medieval fortress in the centre had now been reached. The moat was some 45 to 60ft wide and some 18 to 45ft deep and, in general, followed the contour of the fortress wall. The wall varied from 25 to 45ft in height. It was strongly defended and initial efforts to scale it were repulsed. All entrances were blocked,

---

58. Parker and Thompson, *Conquer*, pp. 31–32; Ramcke, *Fallschirmjäger. Brest and Beyond*, p. 77.
59. Ramcke, *Fallschirmjäger. Brest and Beyond*, p. 78.
60. Parker and Thompson, *Conquer*, pp. 31–32.

and the Germans were firmly entrenched along the wall and on top of it. American efforts to breach it with heavy and super-heavy 8in and 240mm howitzers proved unsuccessful. While the upper portion of the wall was breached in several places, the lower part, forming the rear wall of the moat and hence defiladed from direct artillery fire, remained undamaged. With the Conquet peninsula cleared and Brest penetrated as far as the old wall, the Americans decided to withdraw the 8th Infantry Division and recommit it on the Crozon peninsula. There was simply not sufficient room for two divisions to manoeuvre east of the Penfeld River. Additionally, the presence of the 8th Infantry Division on the peninsula prevented large numbers of German troops from escaping the city through Crozon, where Task Force A was having difficulties containing strong enemy resistance. Accordingly, the 8th Infantry Division withdrew 1,000 yards on the night of 11–12 September and prepared to make the move. By 13 September, the 29th Infantry Division had replaced the 8th Infantry Division. The 29th had also taken Forts Keronroux and Portzic, west of the city, and stood before Fort Montbary, the toughest of the strong points. In the meantime, the 2nd Infantry Division was still battling the enemy at the walls of the old fortress. On that day General Ramcke reported that 'resistance had been given up in the centre of the city'[61]

On 13 September, General Middleton, VIII Corps commander, sent a staff officer to Ramcke demanding the surrender of the city. Middleton outlined the German defenders' position as hopeless and urged Ramcke as a professional soldier, to surrender the city. 'Your soldiers have fought a valiant fight. Some 10,000 men are now prisoners. You know your own losses,' wrote Middleton. 'You have hence performed your duty to your country to the utmost.'[62] Under orders from the Führer himself to hold the city to the last man and seeking further glory and recognition for himself, Ramcke refused with a simple: 'I decline your proposal.'[63] Middleton ordered his soldiers to 'enter the fray with renewed vigor', adding 'let us take them apart and get the job finished.'[64]

The following day, Ramcke, preparing for the inevitable final assault on Brest, had thousands of leaflets printed addressed to his 'Soldiers of Fortress Brest' instructing them that if 'after heroic resistance we have to

---

61. Parker and Thompson, *Conquer*, pp. 32–33; Schramm, *OKW War Diary. The West*, p. 149.
62. Ramcke, *Fallschirmjäger. Brest and Beyond*, pp. 81–82.
63. Ibid., p. 82.
64. Parker and Thompson, *Conquer*, p. 33.

surrender to the numerical superiority of the enemy, it must be done in an honourable way'. In one of his typically racist and anti-Semitic rants worthy of Adolf Hitler, the Luftwaffe general wrote: 'It must be expected that these inferior elements in the American Army will disobey [the Geneva Convention] and, obeying their base instincts, will mistreat defenceless POWs, just as much as the coloured vassals of England have done in innumerable cases. [You will oppose] such treatment, in contradiction to existing laws, with your pride as a member of a nation of ancient culture and of the glorious German race.'[65]

The last phase of the battle for the fortress had begun. 'Surrounded by burning buildings, inundated by rolling artillery barrages and shells raining from grenade launchers, under fire from bombs and guns of low-flying fighter-bombers, individual concentrations of resistance defended themselves to the last round ... Even the underground sewers were used for combat by both sides,' recalled Ramcke. 'Thick clouds of back and yellow smoke, mixed with waves of toxic phosphorus fumes wallowed over the fortress, hung in the streets, penetrated bunkers and dugouts and weighed heavily on the lungs of defending forces.'[66] From 14 to 16 September the Americans made little progress in the city. Led by the 2nd Parachute Division's Fallschirmjäger, the defenders continued to fight skillfully and zealously. 'The German defence was desperate, and their use of the build-up city was particularly effective,' records the Ninth Army history. 'Fort Montbary withstood terrific punishment before it finally capitulated to the 29th Infantry Division on the afternoon of the 15th.' Some 200 to 250 German troops defended the old French fort, which had earth-filled masonry walls 40ft thick and was surrounded by a moat 40ft wide and 15ft deep. Its gun positions, facing to the north-west, were protected by minefields composed of 300lb naval shells equipped with pressure-sensitive fuses. The use of British flame-throwing 'Crocodile' tanks and white-phosphorus grenades turned the tide of battle in favour of the Americans. According to the US Ninth Army: 'It was a bloody battle and only eighty Germans remained alive to be finally taken prisoner.'[67] For their part, the defenders of Brest knew the end was near. Some scribbled the word 'Brestgrad' on the walls of their pillboxes, alluding to the catastrophe suffered by the German Sixth Army at Stalingrad the previous

---

65. Balkoski, *From Beachhead to Brittany*, p. 218.
66. Ramcke, *Fallschirmjäger. Brest and Beyond*, pp. 78–79.
67. Parker and Thompson, *Conquer*, pp. 33–34.

year.[68] By 16 September the Americans had succeeded in penetrating into the city of Brest itself, which was a heap of rubble.

On 16 and 17 September, American artillery maintained a continuous and murderous fire into an area only 900 yards wide paralleling the waterfront, and into the walled city itself. German resistance deteriorated rapidly. On 17 September, the 29th Infantry Division broke through the Recouvrance defences and occupied the entire area west of the Penfeld River. On the same day, the 2nd Infantry Division breached the fortress walls in two places, allowing its soldiers to pour into the fortress itself. Meanwhile, the 8th Infantry Division had moved another 3 miles to the west of the Crozon peninsula, steadily reducing the area that the defenders of Brest might have hoped to occupy for a last stand.[69] The Germans on the Crozon peninsula continued to hold out. By 18 September, U.S. soldiers had penetrated the defences there as well. Although Hitler had ordered General Ramcke to be flown out of the beleaguered city, the Führer's orders could no longer be carried out.[70]

On 18 September Brest finally fell to the Americans. The 2nd Infantry Division completed the capture of the fortress and cleared the area east of the Penfeld River, while the 29th Infantry Division completed mopping up the area west of the river. Among those captured were Generalmajor Hans von der Mosel, Chief of Staff of the Brest fortress garrison; Oberst Hans Kroh, commander of the 2nd Parachute Division; and Rear Admiral Otto Kahler of the Kriegsmarine. General Ramcke had escaped to the Crozon peninsula. He was captured the next day when the 8th Infantry Division finished clearing the area. According to British intelligence reports, his bunker, the last to surrender, contained a vast store of cognacs, liquor, enormous quantities of food and other plunder, including a complete dinner set.[71] On 20 September the battle of Brest ended when a small pocket of German defenders on the Pont Croix peninsula, across the bay to the south of Crozon, was finally eliminated.[72] Major Percy Schramm recorded in the German High Command War Diary: 'At 2000 hours on 19 September all resistance in Brest had ceased.'[73]

---

68. Balkoski, *From Beachhead to Brittany*, p. 217.
69. Parker and Thompson, *Conquer*, p. 34.
70. Schramm, *B-034 OKW War Diary. The West*, p. 149.
71. Neitzel, ed., 'General der Fallschirmtruppen Berhard Ramcke', *Taping Hitler's Generals*, p. 309.
72. Parker and Thompson, *Conquer*, pp. 34–35.
73. Schramm, *B-034 The OKW War Diary. The West*, p. 149.

The US VIII Corps captured 37,888 prisoners at Brest. Approximately 20,000 of these were combat troops, including naval personnel. The remainder were described as 'civilians who had been put in uniform and armed to assist in the defence'. An American officer observing the line of surrounding German troops noted: 'No Stalingrad or Bataan, this; no starving, disease-ravaged skeletons doomed to a fate as terrible as the one from which they had just escaped. Instead, the men Hitler had ordered to defend Brest to the death were well-fed, clean-shaven and well-turned out.'[74] Among the captured Germans were almost 6,000 that had been wounded in Brest proper and another almost 2,000 wounded in Recouvrance, attesting to the intensity of the fighting. From 5 to 20 September, U.S. Ninth Army casualties totalled 2,952, including 436 killed and 2,286 wounded. Hermann Ramcke and his Fallschirmjäger, however, had held Brest long enough to deny the Americans and their British allies the working port that they so desperately needed to resupply their growing armies. Ramcke wrote:

> The sea Brest Fortress was now in enemy hands. With an enormous investment of armament and vastly superior forces, the opponent would only gain a worthless pile of rubble. All harbour facilities were thoroughly destroyed … When the thunder of the last rounds faded over the bay and smouldering ruins of Brest we felt in our hearts that we had carried out our duty as soldiers in a hopeless stand.[75]

The Americans agreed with Ramcke. 'It was bitterly ironical that the port for which this bloody campaign had been waged was rendered entirely useless in the talking and proved valueless as a port to the Allies throughout the war,' notes the Ninth Army history. 'In fact, the terrific destruction brought upon Brest by the desperate resistance of its trapped German defenders was the worst suffered by any major city of the invasion up to that date and left the French nation with the difficult decision as to whether it was even worthwhile to rebuild the city in the same location.'[76]

Before marching into captivity, his American captors allowed Ramcke to address a few words to his assembled Fallschirmjäger:

---

74. Balkoski, *From Beachhead to Brittany*, p. 287.
75. Ramcke, *Fallschirmjäger. Brest and Beyond*, p. 86.
76. Parker and Thompson, *Conquer*, p. 35.

The battle of Brest was difficult. Some of you will question the reason for this long hopeless resistance. But every shell dropped on us, every grenade launched at us and every burst of machine gun fired at us was therefore not directed at our beloved homeland. As soldiers, we obey. As you now begin your journey into captivity, you can do so with your heads held high, knowing you have fulfilled your duty as soldiers. Should you be forced, against international law, to work against our German nation in making weapons, then you know what to do; what you make with your hands, you knock down with your backside. Although our Fatherland must face a bitter, hard future, you will see that there are limits to what the enemy can do to us. In this hour, we think of our loved ones at home. God protect our people and Fatherland, which we greet with our last 'Sieg Heil'.[77]

Ramcke's paratroopers responded enthusiastically with a standing ovation and the cry 'Papa Ramcke!' 'This heartfelt farewell from my soldiers, given not to flags and the sounding trumpets of a thunderous ceremony, was the deeply moving finale of my 44 years of being a soldier,' he recalled fondly.[78]

Hitler was pleased with what his paratroopers had accomplished at Brest. It was exactly what he had expected of them in Normandy. Following the battle, he promoted Ramcke to General der Fallschirmtruppe in absentia, awarding him the Swords and Diamonds to the Knight's Cross and elevating him to the ranks of the truly exalted. Only three other Luftwaffe officers had or would receive that honour by the end of the war.[79] Oberst Hans Kroh was promoted to generalmajor in absentia and awarded the Swords to his Knight's Cross with Oak Leaves on 12 September for his role as the commander of the 2nd Parachute Division.[80] Oberstleutnant Erich Pietzonka was promoted to the rank of oberst in absentia and awarded the Knight's Cross for his actions as commander of the 7th Parachute Regiment on 5 September and the Oak Leaves to the Knight's Cross for his regiment's tenacious defence of the

---

77. Ramcke, *Fallschirmjäger Damals und Danach*, pp. 74–75; Ramcke, *Fallschirmjäger. Brest and Beyond*, p. 89.

78. Ramcke, *Fallschirmjäger. Brest and Beyond*, p. 89.

79. Kurowski, 'Bernhard Hermann Ramcke', *Knight's Cross Holders of the Fallschirmjäger*, p. 175.

80. Kurowski, 'Hans Kroh', *Knight's Cross Holders of the Fallschirmjäger*, p. 125.

Brest fortress on 16 September.[81] Other Fallschirmjäger Knight's Cross recipients for the battle of Brest include Oberstleutnant Karl Stephan Tannert, Deputy Commander of the 2nd Parachute Regiment; Major Reino Hamer, commander of the I Battalion, 7th Parachute Regiment; Major Siegfried Joseph Gerstner, commander of the II Battalion, 7th Parachute Regiment; Oberleutnant Georg Rupert Jacob, commander of the 1st Company, I Battalion, 7th Parachute Regiment; and Oberfeldwebel Adolf Reininghaus, platoon leader in the 14th Company, 7th Parachute Regiment. All followed their commander into captivity.[82] The unfortunate Erich Lepkowski never received the Oak Leaves to his Knight's Cross promised by Ramcke for his daring raid to liberate 130 Fallschirmjäger from the French Resistance.

The number of Knight's Crosses awarded to the 2nd Parachute Division at Brest and its heavy casualties attests not only to the intensity of the fighting, but also to the fanatical and effective resistance put up by Ramcke and his men. Perhaps the best testimony to their skill and tenacity as soldiers comes from a senior U.S. commander and a lowly U.S. Army infantryman who participated in the battle. 'In the 2nd Parachute Division of the German Army [sic], you have met the best,' General Middleton told the soldiers of his VIII Corps. 'You will meet no better troops in your future battles.' Private First Class Aurele J. Michaud of the 2nd Infantry Division's 9th Infantry Regiment remembered after the war: 'The hardest fighting the division had was when we met the German paratroopers in front of Brest. Those paratroopers were really tough. They had concrete pillboxes, stationary guns in concrete emplacements, a trench system, all of it protected by hedgerows.'[83]

---

81. Kurowski, 'Erich Pietzonka', *Knight's Cross Holders of the Fallschirmjäger*, p. 171.
82. Kurowski, 'Karl Stephan Tannert', 'Major Reino Hamer', 'Siegfried Josef Gerstner', 'Georg Ruperet Jacob', 'Adolf Reininghaus', *Knight's Cross Holders of the Fallschirmjäger*, pp. 239, 77, 67, 101, 181.
83. Balkoski, *From Beachhead to Brittany*, p. 344; Carleton B. Clyma, ed., *Servicemen's Commemorative Booklet Volume I. No. 9. Connecticut Men of the Second Division* (Office of the Governor of Connecticut: August 1945), p. 8.

Chapter 10

From Cobra to Falaise and Germany

On the morning of 25 July, six fighter-bomber groups of the U.S. Ninth Air Force, some 600 aircraft, attacked German forward positions along and beyond the St-Lô–Lessay road, dropping 300 tons of bombs, many filled with napalm. As they completed their task, three United States Army Air Corps bombardment divisions, 1,503 heavy bombers of the U.S. Eighth Air Force, flew in wave after wave for three hours dropping 3,400 tons of explosives and fragmentation bombs along the Périers–St-Lô road in an area 7,000 yards long by 2,500 yards deep. Finally, 396 medium- bombers of the U.S. Ninth Air Force continued to attack targets just south of the main bombed areas for another hour, dropping 130 tons of high explosive and more than 4,000 fragmentation bombs. Altogether, nearly 3,000 aircraft had joined in carpet bombing the battlefield in preparation for the infantry attack that was to follow.[1]

The attacks decimated Panzer Lehr, killing some 1,000 men and wiping out all but a dozen or so panzers.[2] 'It was hell,' remembered General Bayerlein. 'The planes kept coming overhead like a conveyor belt, and the bombs carpeted down ... My front lines looked like a landscape on the moon, at least seventy per cent of my personnel were out of action – dead,

1. Major L.F. Ellis, *History of the Second World War. United Kingdom Military Series. Victory in the West. Volume I. The Battle of Normandy* (The Naval & Military Press, 2004), p. 381; Blumenson, *Breakout and Pursuit*, pp. 228–229; Stephen Darlow, *D-Day Bombers. The Stories of Allied Heavy Bombers during the Invasion of Normandy* (Stackpole Books, 2004), pp. 229, 231.
2. Hargreaves, *The Germans in Normandy*, p. 167.

wounded, crazed or numbed. All my front-line tanks were knocked out.'[3] Bayerlein reported to OB West that his division, which had lost its organic infantry, along with most of its assault guns and tanks, had ceased to exist as an organised unit. The carpet bombing, which ruptured the German lines, also demolished much of the 5th Parachute Division. Following the heavy bombers, squadrons of Lockheed P-38 Lightnings and Republic P-47 Thunderbolt fighter-bombers returned, roaming the battlefield in packs of up to two dozen aircraft, strafing all known or suspected German positions and hunting down individual tanks and soldiers. 'Several companies of the 5th Para Division that had tried to withdraw to the north in the direction of Marginy were entirely destroyed by Lightnings, pursuit planes, and bombers,' remembered Medical NCO Walter Klein, who was serving with Kampfgruppe Heinz, attached to Panzer Lehr, near Marigny, 6 miles west of St-Lô. Klein had attended five Fallschirmjager of the 5th Parachute Division, wounded by bomb splinters. 'The effect was devastating; all our anti-aircraft guns and artillery were destroyed,' he remembered. 'Tanks which had tried to get away were destroyed by pursuit planes. When a wave of planes had passed, one could hear the crying of the wounded and shouting for help of medical personnel ... Worse than the loss of weapons was the effect the attack had on our morale.'[4]

The carpet bombing was followed by a major U.S. VII Corps offensive, starting with the 4th, 9th and 30th Infantry Divisions supported by Sherman tanks, artillery and more fighter-bombers. For Cobra, the U.S. First Army threw six divisions, numbering about 70,000 men, more than 660 tanks, 3,000 aircraft and 43 battalions of artillery (some 650 guns) at the German Seventh Army. General Hausser defended with fewer than 35,000 men and about 80 armoured fighting vehicles.[5] Still, the initial U.S. attack encountered stiff resistance from pockets of surviving German infantry supported by handfuls of tanks. These included a kampfgruppe of the 5th Parachute Division, probably from 14th Parachute Regiment, that had escaped the worst of the bombing and was holding a sector east of Panzer Lehr against the U.S. 2nd Infantry Division.[6] However,

---

3. Darlow, *D-Day Bombers*, p. 231.
4. Medical NCO Walter Klein, *MS # A-910. Bombing and Operation Cobra* (Headquarters United States Arm Europe: Historical Division, 1954), p. 2.
5. Tucker-Jones, *Falaise: The Flawed Victory*, Chapter. 2. 'The Road to Falaise', Kindle.
6. Steven Zaloga, *European Theatre of Operations 1944. Panzergrenadier versus US Armoured Infantryman* (Oxford: Osprey Publishing, 2017)

according to Klein, even these succumbed to American pressure and were captured.[7] One parachute company that had begun the day with thirty-five men ended it with just five.[8] By the late afternoon of 25 July, General Hausser counted seven penetrations of the Lessay–St-Lô defensive line. The following morning, as German defences began to collapse, the U.S. 2nd and 3rd Armour Divisions, along with the 1st Infantry Division, exploited the breakthrough, capturing Marigny and advancing 7 miles. Having broken out of the restricting bocage and assisted by dry and clear weather, American forces advanced rapidly.[9]

By 27 July, Meindl and his II Parachute Corps were holding on the flank of the southward American advance. The 12th Parachute Reconnaissance Battalion, under Hauptmann Goestche, had held the crossroads at Le Mesnil Hermann against an advancing U.S. armour spearhead for twenty-four hours, destroying a half dozen Sherman tanks. Still, it was not enough to plug the gap left by the decimated Panzer Lehr division. The 13th Parachute Regiment had also been devastated at Marigny, with one battalion reduced from 800 to 100 men. Hausser order two panzer divisions to strike at the American front from II Parachute Corps' threatened flank. The decision prompted Meindl to jump into his staff car and make his way to the Seventh Army Headquarters, pursued by American fighter-bombers the entire way. Upon reaching the headquarters, he unloaded on Field Marshal Günther von Kluge's son, a General Staff lieutenant colonel, who had passed on his father's order to hold: 'The time has come when Normandy can no longer be held,' Meindl told the younger Kluge. 'It cannot be held because the troops are exhausted. The main reason for this is holding out in hopeless positions, and even now all we hear are orders to "hold"' All that's left for the grenadiers to do is to lie down and sacrifice their lives. It's heartbreaking to have to stand by and watch.'[10] The combat-seasoned and ever-candid Meindl was correct. By 30 July, the U.S. 4th Armoured Division had seized Avranches. On 1 August, General George Patton's U.S. Third Army was activated and the U.S. First Army was redesignated the 12th Army Group.

7. Klein, *A-901 Bombing and Operation Cobra*, p. 3.
8. Hargreaves, *The Germans in Normandy*, p. 167.
9. Blumenson, *Breakout and Pursuit*, pp. 228–229, 248, 254–255; Zaloga, *Operation Cobra*, p. 11.
10. Paul Carell, *Invasion! They're Coming!* (Schiffer Military History, 1995), pp. 245–247; Hargreaves, *The Germans in Normandy*, p. 171.

By the beginning of August, the morale of a great many German soldiers in Normandy had collapsed. A corporal, decorated with the German Cross in Gold for having destroyed five Russian tanks with anti-tank mines on the Eastern Front, told Klein: 'This is no more a war here in Normandy. The enemy is superior in men and material. We are simply sent to death with insufficient arms. Our High Command doesn't do anything to help us. No airplanes, insufficient ammunition for our artillery.' He concluded: 'Well, for me, the war is over.' A severely wounded infantryman from the medical NCO's company said: 'This piece of iron that hit me should have hit the Führer's head on 20 July and the war would already be over.' Another comrade told Klein: 'I don't care for anything. Two of my brothers were sacrificed in Stalingrad and it was quite useless. Here we have the same movie.' As Klein moved toward his command post, a wounded Fallschirmjager from the 5th Parachute Division and veteran of almost every campaign grabbed the young medical orderly. 'Don't you know it's no longer a battle here in Normandy?' he told Klein. 'We're led like lambs to the slaughter. Our Supreme Command has left us in the lurch.'[11] Klein, who was later captured by the Americans, noted that his patients did not consider the American infantryman as particularly energetic or brave.[12]

On 1 August, OB West reported that four American armour and eight infantry divisions were trying to envelop the II Parachute and XXXXVII Panzer Corps, which were retreating to the southern bank of the Vire, to open the road to Paris.[13] Between 3 and 7 August, American forces advanced through Rennes, Vannes on Quiberon Bay and Lorient. On 5 August the U.S. 83rd Infantry Division attacked the German garrison at St-Malo. By 6 August, the Wehrmacht and Waffen SS in Normandy had lost 3,630 officers and 151,487 non-commissioned officers and men, including 14 general officers and more than 200 unit commanders.[14] Only 30,000 men had arrived to replace losses in the west with another 10,000 on their way to the front.[15]

On the night of 6 August, Hitler's forces launched Operation Lüttich, the German counter-attack at Mortain to restore the situation in Normandy. The Wehrmacht hurled three panzer divisions, two infantry divisions, five panzer and infantry kampfgruppe and 150 tanks and assault guns at the

---

11. Hargreaves, *The Germans in Normandy*, pp. 166–167.
12. Klein, *A-901 Bombing and Operation Cobra*, pp. 4–5.
13. Schramm, *MS # B-034 The OKW War Diary. The West*, p. 74.
14. Ibid, p. 63.
15. Blumenson, *Breakout and Pursuit*, p. 516.

Americans, seeking to stem the U.S. Third Army's advance into Brittany, reach the coast around Avranches and eliminate the gains made by the U.S. First Army during Operation Cobra. By 13 August, dug-in American infantry of the 30th Infantry Division, supported by tanks, artillery and air strikes, had defeated Hitler's final offensive in France. 'The counter-attack by our own tanks against Avranches was naturally a failure,' recorded General Meindl, who had experienced Allied air supremacy first-hand. 'And the distrust of the troops toward their leaders grew from day to day. This could be noted from the questions asked by my NCOs, who spoke to me quite openly on the subject.'[16]

On 7 August, the First Canadian Army, reinforced with a British infantry division and armoured brigade and a Polish armoured Division, some 85,000 men, launched Operation Totalize, from positions 3 miles south of Caen toward Falaise against the I SS Panzer Corps. The offensive was supported by more than 1,000 RAF bombers, which dropped 5,000 tons of bombs on German defensive positions, 720 artillery pieces and 600 tanks. By 9 August, the Allied attack had penetrated 5 miles into the German positions. The Canadians were soon joined by the British Second Army, which pushed forward slowly, but inexorably, bringing the Wehrmacht in France to the edge of crisis. [17] A week later, on 14 August, the First Canadian Army, reinforced with a Polish armoured division and a British armoured brigade, attacked again, launching Operation Tractable. This daylight attack was aimed at enveloping Falaise, held by the 12th SS-Panzer Division and remnants of four German infantry divisions.[18] The offensive opened with 800 Royal Air Force heavy bombers striking Wehrmacht positions along the front. Despite fierce German resistance, some 300 Canadian, British, and Polish tanks and infantry pressed forward relentlessly, breaking into Falaise on 16 August and clearing it by the next day.[19]

---

16. Meindl, *MS # A-923 Northern France 25 July to 14 September 1944* (Koeningstein: United States Army Historical Division, 20 May 1946), p. 24.

17. Blumenson, *Breakout and Pursuit*, pp. 480–481.

18. Ellis, *Victory in the West*, p. 430; Angelo Caravaggio, *21 Days in Normandy. Maj. Gen. George Kitching & the 4th Canadian Armoured Division* (Pen & Sword Military, 2016), Chapter. 'Tractable', Kindle edition.

19. Colonel C. P. Stacey, *The Canadian Army 1939–1945. An Official Historical Summary* (King's Printer: Ottawa: 1948), pp. 202–203; Ellis, *Victory in the West*, pp. 430–431; Caravaggio, *21 Days in Normandy*. Chapter. 'Tractable', Kindle.

On 15 August, more than 151,000 American and French troops with 21,400 tanks, tank destroyers and trucks, invaded southern France. They were supported by some 75,000 French Resistance personnel. Operation Dragoon (initially Operation Anvil) would grow to encompass more than 575,000 men, including British and Canadian soldiers.[20] 'As soon as the crisis had reached its peak in northern France, the enemy landed at the southern French coast, which had previously been weakened through the withdrawal of troops to such an extent that a crisis also developed quickly at the Nineteenth Army,' recorded Major Percy Schramm in the OKW War Diary. 'Its effect was felt far beyond the limits of the combat sector.'[21] The Germans were now fighting for their lives in France against an immense Allied force on three fronts. Hitler is reported to have lamented: 'The 15th of August was the worst day of my life.'[22]

The Allies advanced rapidly on all fronts, sweeping the disorganised and fleeing Wehrmacht before them. 'The battle had now changed to mobile warfare whose swiftness possibly surpassed that of 1940,' recorded the OKW War Diary.[23] The remaining German forces in France found themselves surrounded on three sides in a pocket extending from Nécy in the north-west to north of Argentan – south-east to Mont Ormel – to Hill 239 approximately 2.5km south of Les Champeaux. As the ring closed around them, the Fallschirmjäger of the II Parachute Corps found themselves at the western end of the pocket with the German Seventh Army – the farthest from salvation. Squeezing the pocket from the north, east and south were a host of American, British, Canadian, French, and Polish formations intent on closing the bag and annihilating the German forces inside. 'The enemy now only exerted pressure slowly against our front. We heard about it all from the crews of the supply vehicles – sometimes the news they brought was the truth, but more often than not, it was completely garbled, but we did learn of the success of the enemy

20. Jeffrey J. Clarke and Robert Ross Smith, *United States Army in World War II. The European Theatre of Operations. Riviera to the Rhine* (Washington, D.C: Centre of Military History, 1993), pp. 42, 92; Anthony Tucker-Jones, *Operation Dragoon: The Liberation of Southern France 1944* (Pen and Sword, 2010), p. 92.
21. Schramm, *B-034. The OKW War Diary. The West*, p. 99.
22. F. Gilbert, ed., *Hitler Directs His War* (New York: O.U.P., 1950), p. 102; See also Ellis, *Victory in the West*, p. 431.
23. Schramm, *B-034. The OKW War Diary. The West*, pp. 60–61.

in the plains of France,' remembered General Meindl. 'And again, the II Parachute Corps was the one to have its nose stuck furthest into the enemy and it was from that time onward that the danger of encirclement from the right and the left continued to increase. The attacks from the region of Caen gained ground more and more quickly. And to me, at any rate, it was clear that the enemy had chosen the grandiose solution and meant to cut us all off from France.'[24]

Combat on the Seventh Army front now assumed the nature of delaying action, with Wehrmacht units fighting to gain time and avoid annihilation. The Germans sought to lure the Allies into time-consuming reconnaissance and deployment for attack, before retiring to the next defensive position during the night. In this manner, the Seventh Army continued to resist, withdrawing weak formations steadily eastward. For once, Hitler authorised further withdrawals. Where the situation was favourable, German units counter-attacked the overextended and disorganised Allies. On 16 August, for example, tanks of the 2nd SS and 116th Panzer Divisions attacked U.S. 90th Infantry Division roadblocks at the village of Le Bourg-St-Léonard, opening the planned German withdrawal to the Seine. Intense fighting continued for more than twenty-four hours.[25]

'An attempt must ... be made in collaboration with our neighbours to avoid encirclement by a strong retreat movement in depth carried out at night,' General Hausser informed his II Parachute Corps commander. 'Our first destination will be east of the Orne.' The Seventh Army commander then asked: 'How far do you think the II Parachute Corps can be expected to get in one night?' 'The retreat itself presents no difficulties to the Corps,' responded Meindl, 'provided we are given the fuel and spare tires which we need so urgently for all our vehicles, and if the paths of retreat are clearly defined, because we are now getting a bit cramped for space!'[26] Meindl added that the panzer formations would have to cover II Parachute Corp's right flank. Hausser then asked his dependable subordinate whether he thought he could get his corps behind the Orne River. Meindl answered in the affirmative. He proposed moving his corps in two echelons in three great night marches. The first echelon included the 9th Parachute Regiment, the 15th Parachute

24. Meindl, *A-923 Northern France*, p. 24.
25. Blumenson, *Breakout and Pursuit*, pp. 516–517, 525.
26. Meindl, *A-923 Northern France*, p. 24.

Regiment and the 12th Artillery Battalion. The second included the 5th and 8th Parachute Regiment.'[27] Meindl wrote:

> We managed to get the units of the II Parachute Corps behind the Orne with difficulty. After that the whole plan went to pieces. The batteries were unable even to change their position. The supplies promised by the Seventh Army failed to appear. They couldn't be brought up in the daytime, on account of the enemy fliers and in the night the roads were so congested that it was impossible then too. It was the panzer formations which were to blame for this. They took up all the available space on the roads without a thought for anybody else and there were only a few roads available. A few days later both the Commander in Chief and myself had a sample of this totally selfish type of unit behaviour when we attempted to travel back to our new command post further to the rear. The chaos on the roads was already proof of the coming catastrophe. I myself had been careful to send the main columns of the II Parachute Corps to the rear of the danger zone some weeks before. But we had the greatest difficulty in getting even the most essential elements back to the rear on single motor trucks. Even the ambulances and fuel trucks could hardly move through the undisciplined stream of 'semi-soldiers'. And the strange thing was that it was not only large supply columns and repair trucks from the tanks which were moving along the roads from the 12th of August onward, but complete tank units which, a few days before, were supposed to require repairs before they could be moved! I discerned already the first signs of an overall panic.[28]

By 17 August the main body of the II Parachute Corps stood behind the Orne with combat posts, supported by a few guns, still holding out north and south of Tourailles. Meindl recorded:

> We were obliged to stop with the staff of the 3rd Parachute Division, located just where we had been brought to a halt and this had its advantages. It gave me the chance to see for myself on the spot, early on the morning of 18 August, how our flanks were

---

27. Ibid., pp. 24–25.
28. Ibid., p. 26.

being squeezed in from the north and to proceed accordingly. Unfortunately, on this day my new commander of the 12th Artillery Battalion, Captain von Koenitz, a capable ordnance officer and first-rate pilot, was killed.[29]

In the early hours of 18 August, the II Parachute Corps was provided with a supply of vehicles. 'There was a good deal of air reconnaissance,' remembered Meindl:

The noises of the trucks moving along all the available roads penetrated even to the mill where we were, although it was located in a depression and not easy to reach. Nothing special happened on our own front, but the din of fighting could be heard along all of our right flank. There was much noise and confusion in the ranks of the rear echelons and artillery, portions of which streamed into our sector. In our own neighbourhood we could hear tank guns firing from the direction of Nécy and Le Mesnil Guérard. Further to the east we could recognise the sound of infantry and strong machine gun fire mingled with artillery fire. There was some routine reconnaissance in the air above us. I ordered Generalmajor Schimpf to move his command post further south, nearer to that of the Corps. I then got into my own 'bomber-dodger' and took a road at an early hour, which the Commander in Chief had told me about, through the woods to Montabard, and ordered the Corps' staff to move from the post they had set up there on the previous day to La Lande, to a group of farm buildings nestling in a hollow, some 1.5km north-east of Villedieu-lès-Bailleul. I ordered our radio station to move about 1.5km north of there.[30]

The command post of the German Seventh Army was set up in a quarry at Villedieu, with subordinate command posts all squeezed together inside the ever-shrinking ring. The only passable road remaining, from Trun running to the north-east, was completely dominated by the Allies. 'Since early morning of that day the motorised troops were raising clouds of dust and pushing against one another on the congested roads,' recalled Meindl. 'It was enough to make one tear one's hair out and ask oneself

---

29. Ibid., pp. 26–27.
30. Ibid., p. 27.

if the drivers had gone off their heads completely and were hastening to place themselves in the view of the enemy planes as targets until they went up in blazes!'

> There was hardly any anti-aircraft artillery on our side. Unlike us, the Army troops did not let fly at the enemy planes with rifle and MG-42 machine guns, which we had done very successfully in the past. The first thing I did now was to establish a circle with a radius of 1,000 meters around my command post, so as not to be betrayed by the troops gone completely wild. The most varied of marching groups now overtook one another and got hopelessly mixed up together. After eleven years as a front line officer I had been through some very peculiar adventures, but the formation of the encircling pocket of Falaise on 19 and 20 August will always rank among the most dreaded memories of my not uninteresting life as a soldier. It is only in such a situation that one finds out who is really a soldier and who only a militarist, who belongs to the brave and who to the bosses and cowards and even traitors![31]

That afternoon Meindl found Hausser at his command post. 'Here, the first thing I learned was that the 'Das Reich' SS-Panzer Division and several others had already been sent to the rear to lend us a hand!' recorded Meindl. 'From the outside! In other words, we were good enough to be left inside the ring! I put a black mark in my mind against the Commander in Chief for this, but kept my thoughts to myself and contented myself with the announcement that with us, everything had gone off according to plan, but that we hadn't a drop of gasoline left in the tanks of the mobile artillery and as it couldn't change its position and if the ring was drawn tighter the guns would have to be blown up and the heavy gear left behind.'[32] Hitler and the German High Command were concerned with ensuring the survival of the Third Reich's elite panzer divisions for the later defence of Nazi Germany.

By the morning of 19 August, the Seventh Army was encircled in the vicinity of Trun in the north-east, Flers in the west, and Argentan in the south-east. Inside the pocket were the commanders, staffs, and troops of two armies (Seventh Army and Panzer Group Eberbach); four corps (LXXXIV Infantry, LXXIV Infantry, XXXXVII Panzer, and II Parachute);

---

31. Ibid., p. 28.
32. Ibid., pp. 28–29.

five panzer divisions (1st SS, 10th SS, 12th SS, 2nd and 116th); and nine infantry divisions (3rd Parachute, 84th, 89th, 271st, 276th, 277th, 326th, 353rd and the 363rd).[33] Meindl recorded:

> At about 0700 hours I received a visit from Oberstgruppenführer Hausser. So early? A bad sign! One look at his face was enough to tell me what was wrong. I greeted him with the words: 'Well, the lid's shut tight now!' Which means, I suppose, that we'll have to try and shove it open again! 'Yes,' he replied. 'That's just what I've come to talk to you about. We've seen it coming for a long time!' 'Good!' I said. 'We'll do it! But how we're to do it, I shall decide. Nobody's going to tell me how to do this.' (Up until then our suggestions had always agreed.) After reflecting for a bit and making a few marks on my map I put forward the following proposal:
>
> 1. So far as we had been able to ascertain up until then, there was still a small gap in the ring south of Coutances and another at Magny on the Dives. We didn't know how things were going at St. Lambert and Chambois. The eastern bank of the Dives, too, had not been reconnoitered. But for paratroopers the Dives River constituted no sort of hindrance.
> 2. The 3rd Parachute Division would divide into two wedges and without firing a shot would steal forward like Indians with the aid of the compass south of Coutances–Magny, past the mill 1km south-east thereof and onto the heights of Coudehard, and there they would form a front facing west and keep the four to five kilometer gap open.
> 3. To aid this, the parachute regiment would be withdrawn through the ranks of their left and right-hand neighbours and move back to position for attack in small groups into the wood here west of Montabard. Rear commandos would stay by the troops withdrawing until early on the morning of 20 August and then come on later with the covering regiment of the division.

---

33. Generalmajor Rudolf Christoph Freiherr von Gersdorff, *MS # B-727 The Campaign in Northern France* (U.S. Army Historical Division: Allendorf, September 1946), p. 47.

4. I recommended that the position on the Orne be withdrawn to the heights of Montabard on the night of 19 August so that the divisions here might be able to follow on the heels of the 3rd Parachute Division through the gap at Coudehard eastward.

5. The artillery should stay where it was. It should use up what ammunition it had during the day and join us as a personnel unit with its rear covering regiment (presumably the 8th Parachute). Single anti-tank and 8.8 cm antiaircraft cannon, so far as fuel was available, should be brought along.

6. Only light assault equipment would be carried along. The maintenance sections would follow later, most likely on 20 August, through St. Lambert.

7. During the attack, not a word was to be uttered, not a glim to be shown, no noise to be made! No fighting before it grew light. Any resistance, any obstacles, were to be gone around. The goal would be the heights of Coudehard. Every man was to keep close to his neighbour. The units would move in rows. Every leader must keep the point, the goal, and his own particular mission in his own head.

8. I myself would take part in the attack with the most forward patrol company so as to be able to make fast decisions on the spot. There would be no radio activity, no advance elements.

9. Our troops would move forward from the ready position in the wood here at La Lande at 2230. If the enemy was not too thickly pressed together we should do it and I recommended that the Army staff follow on the heels of the breakthrough of the paratroopers.[34]

Hausser agreed with Meindl's proposal and assigned the II Parachute Corps the 353rd Infantry Division, which Meindl employed as a third wedge south of his 3rd Parachute Division at St-Lambert-sur-Dive. The Fallschirmjager would break through 2km south-east of Trun. The 5th Parachute Regiment would advance on the right, north-west of St-Lambert. The 9th and 15th Parachute Regiment would advance on the left, 1km south-east of Hill 107. The 8th Parachute Regiment was designated the rearguard.[35] At the same time, the panzer divisions near Argentan were ordered to break through south of the II Parachute Corps.

---

34. Meindl, *A-923 Northern France*, pp. 30–31.
35. von Gersdorff, *B-727 The Campaign in Northern France*, pp. 52–53.

They were not to start before 2400 hours. Finally, a radio message was sent to the 2nd SS-Panzer Division outside the ring, instructing it to attack from outside the ring in the direction of Trun to divert attention away from the II Parachute Corps.[36] Meindl remembered:

> Yes, a solemn sort of feeling possessed us, a desire to show that a paratrooper was not so easily to be taken in the net! The arduous nature of the operation was clear to us all! I expected the greatest difficulty to occur on the eastern bank of the Dives and I thought to myself 'If we manage to get through at this point, then we've done it!' The encircling ring was now notably thicker and deeper, and the critical moment arrived only when we reached the heights of Coudehard. Our covering regiment to the rear (8th Parachute Regiment) was to assemble itself there with its front facing west and await the arrival of the other divisions of the Army between Trun and St. Lambert on 20 August. Luckily, on the afternoon of 19 August enemy air activity immediately above our sector was not very great. The enemy had shifted the centre of gravity of attack more to the east (a bad sign for us). Enemy artillery fire waxed from hour to hour and the batteries came nearer and nearer. Everything and everybody pressed toward the centre of the ring.[37]

The situation inside the pocket was bleak. 'Hundreds upon hundreds of vehicles that had been put out of action by enemy fire, untended wounded, innumerable dead, characterised a battlefield in a manner rarely seen throughout the entire war,' remembered Colonel von Gersdorff, the Seventh Army Chief of Staff.'[38] By 19 August, the escape route was just 5 miles wide and the rapidly shrinking pocket measured just 7 miles by 6 miles. Still, Meindl's paratroopers were at the forefront of the fighting everywhere, leading the way forward. In one case, a German paratrooper colonel and a handful of paratroopers fought alongside the last few Tiger tanks of SS-Panzer Abteilung 102 near Chambois, knocking out British Churchill tanks with Panzerfausts and forcing their way through Allied troops. Under constant pressure from the German paratroopers within the pocket, the Poles were forced to relinquish control of some of the roads,

---

36. Meindl, *A-923 Northern France*, pp. 31–32.
37. Ibid.
38. von Gersdorff, *B-727 The Campaign in Northern France*, p. 53.

allowing up to 4,000 Fallschirmjäger with a handful of tanks from the 2nd SS-Panzer Division to escape.[39]

Before moving out, General Schimpf gave his Fallschirmjäger a pep talk aimed at raising their spirits and reinforcing discipline. 'There is no reason for concern about the situation. It is rumoured that the division is encircled by the enemy. All rumours of this kind are false,' he stressed. Technically, Schimpf was correct. The Allies had yet to close the pocket at Falaise. 'The Army, British or American, which can encircle or capture our division does not exist!' he told his men, seeking to raise the morale of his exhausted soldiers. 'It is certain that we will finish this war victoriously. And it is just as certain that the glorious 3rd Fallschirmjäger Division will never cease to fight and will do its duty unvanquished to the end of the war. Whoever thinks or speaks differently will be slapped across the face.' Schimpf was calling for iron discipline in the face of adversity and impending catastrophe. If the men of the division were to be saved, it would only be through unflinching obedience to orders, sacrifice, and rapid movement. Despite his admonitions, there was indeed great reason for concern. The Allies were pressing on all sides and the ring around them was closing.[40]

By 2225 hours the men were assembled. Five minutes later the first German patrols 'glided forward like shadows into the dark night' remembered Meindl.

> They had to keep close up to one another so as not to lose touch. The Commander in Chief had come into the assembly area with a small staff and entrusted himself to the cleverness of the paratroopers. I inserted his staff into my group of the Corps' staff at the end of the most forward company of the 9th Parachute Regiment (Major Stephani).[41]

'The mist stank of death and gunpowder 'recalled Fallschirmjäger Johann Bornett. 'We were still being shelled and my ears could no longer bear the screams and the misery of the wounded, calling for stretcher bearers. I knew there weren't any left.'[42]

---

39. Tucker-Jones, *Falaise*, Chapter 15. 'Falaise – The Killing Ground', Kindle.
40. Meindl, *A-923 Northern France*, pp. 32–33.
41. Meindl, *A-923 Northern France*, p. 33.
42. Hargreaves, *The Germans in Normandy*, p. 209.

Meindl wrote:

> At about 2315 hours we felt the first directed fire, coming from a tank. As was usual at night time, the cone of fire of the machine guns lay too high. Luckily, the enemy was only shooting off illuminating shells. This enabled us to find the spots not being fired on and creep through. We lost time whenever a star shell lit up the landscape as, of course, we had to lie low until it got dark again. The enemy artillery had grown a bit alarmed and were pasting the area where we had been a short while before with shells, although by this time only the 8th Parachute Regiment was lying low in their foxholes. And as we were now close to the enemy tanks we were no longer interested in the artillery fire. We didn't think they would be likely to fire on their own buddies. We made a detour, only to come up against other enemy tanks after having moved a distance of about 300 meters in a small hollow. Again, we turned aside, this time to the south. We came up close to where the enemy was letting off well-placed fire with 2 cm. cannon and the commander of the 3rd Parachute Division was badly wounded in the leg. After the division had been fed and cared for I took over command of it.[43]

General Schimpf was wounded immediately after the paratroopers began their attack on Hill 107, forcing General Meindl to assume command of his division.[44] Due to the large number of disparate groups that had gotten mixed up and the wounding of General Schimpf, the 9th Parachute Regiment lost contact with the rest of the division. Hausser and Meindl and some paratroopers proceeded on their own. 'We shall find the others at the Dives River,' Meindl told himself:

> We crept through innumerable hawthorn hedges covered with barbed wire and dodged around some tanks at the roadside, arriving at the Dives River about 1230 hours. While looking for a fordable spot we ran up against [Major] Stephani again, who had found a shallow spot south of the mill mentioned previously. It was a nasty job getting the whole crowd across the stream without lights, noiselessly.

---

43. Meindl, *A-923 Northern France*, p. 33.
44. von Gersdorff, *B-727 The Campaign in Northern France*, p. 54.

The eastern bank was covered with blackberry bushes and was steep in the bargain. The enemy tanks positioned just behind the bushes, three of them on a small mound, clear against the sky. And now we tried to steal past them to the south. There was no time to be lost now if we hoped to get past the tanks while it was still dark. I stole around the three tanks with those at the head of the group but suddenly we were discovered by one that we hadn't seen in front of us and its crew opened fire on us from a distance of thirty meters. I threw myself flat on my face with a few of the others in a potato field, while the company behind us ran straight in a 'dear' corner. The enemy tanks all opened fire on the fleeing Germans, but their fire was too high and went over our heads. But now behind us to the right there started a mad shooting match on the part of the enemy infantry in St. Lambert. Presumably this was directed at the 344th Infantry Division, which was supposed to cross the river just there. And as the tank fire flew about a meter over my head I crept and crept along with my people, centimeter by centimeter along a deeper furrow in the field, eastward. Fifteen paratroopers and a first lieutenant among us managed to get behind the tanks. It was the third row we had come through![45]

Meindl and his men heard the tank crews radioing one another:

Then, all of a sudden, other tanks opened fire. They must have been standing along the edge of the heights, to the rear. Their fire was likewise directed toward St. Lambert. I myself saw two of them, positioned at separate houses on Hill 117 (the north-east part of the slope). And now I and my men turned off eastward in the direction of Hau de Foulbec (a stream) slinking along the hedges. Behind me, in St. Lambert, the noise of infantry fire increased. A house in St. Lambert caught fire and blazed up, enabling us to see the lay of the land somewhat. We moved along the depression formed by the bank of the stream under cover of houses. We heard single tanks rolling past. On the bridge over the stream we saw tank tracks, made about three hours previously. We darted across the bridge and dived again into the cover of the bushes, making for the houses. Here, we came upon some dead

---

45. Meindl, *Northern France*, p. 34.

horses yoked to shot up German vehicles, about three days old, from the stench! Victims of the fighter-bombers![46]

The escaping Germans were forced to clamber over fences to escape. 'It might have been the 15th Parachute Regiment that was being shot at,' remembered Meindl:

> By this time, it had grown so light that it was getting clear enough for us to be shot at, misty, and we felt very warm. All of us (we had been joined by other paratroopers by this time) were absolutely dead beat! We had to plunge in up to the neck for the second time in the water. Our saviours, the hedges of Normandy, which we had cursed so fluently, had by this time covered us with scratches and torn our clothes to ribbons. But so far they had saved us for the umpteenth time! At about 0430 hours I heard the sound of tanks again, moving presumably along the road from Coudehard to Trun. The noise of the battle on the left of us grew in intensity. But onward![47]

A light rain began to fall, hindering Allied aircraft and ground observation. 'It was very welcome to us!' remembered Meindl, as the group reached Coudehard in the early morning. 'As the noise of the guns to the left of the road died away we counted twenty enemy tanks rolling forward … and watched them roll past at about a distance of 150 meters along a road toward a small hill beginning to stand out more and more clearly.'[48] The tanks were from Major General Stanislaw Maczek's 1st Polish Armoured Division. The group remained covered and concealed for several hours, listening to the sounds of battle, artillery, anti-tank guns, and machine guns firing, all around them. Meindl again:

> Toward 0900 hours the first of the tanks on Hill 252 grew more violent. In my opinion, they showed a touch of nervousness. On the right, to the south, the fire of our own machine guns had almost died away. Suddenly I caught sight of some paratroopers moving across a part of the ground lit up by the sun's rays in attack formation. I put two fingers in my mouth and let out a

---

46. Ibid., p. 34–35.
47. Ibid., pp. 35–36.
48. Ibid., p. 36.

sharp whistle as we used to do on the training grounds at home, and when they turned their heads in my direction I waved them urgently into the bushes. I heard the voice of the leader of the group call out softly 'Oh! It's the old boy'. I damned his stupidity under my breadth! When this lot reached us, I handed over to him the care of the paratroopers with me, whose numbers had now swollen considerably, and enlightened him as regards the tanks on the height, which could not now be attacked frontally. I pointed out the possibility of encirclement to the north. He was an experienced fighter and he took my meaning at once. He was able to tell me where the Commander in Chief had been and where he now was most probably. But where Stephani's regiment might now be he was unable to tell me. That morning they had assembled some tank units and sent a curtain of tank fire all around and only moved back when the anti-tank defence began to make itself strongly felt.[49]

Meindl ordered his men to prepare for an encircling attack northward against Hill 252, 'Tank Hill' as he called it, overseeing the positioning of available artillery and anti-tank guns, while trying to avoid enemy fire. At 1130, as he and his men moved along the St-Lambert road and reached the West Wall at Coudehard near Hill 137, they encountered General Hausser with elements of the 15th SS Das Führer Regiment of the 2nd SS-Panzer Division. 'I enlightened the Chief on the situation on the dominating heights and explained to him my plan to take the position to the north,' he recorded. 'The Chief told me he had made contact with a tank division, which had returned in the meantime to the slopes of Mont Ormel and meant now to attempt a breakthrough there. He told me he intended to join in with them and take part in the breakthrough. I, he said, was to do all I could to make the breach wider, so that we could all make our way through. "We shall do all in our power!" I said. "Our strength has been diminished greatly because of the strenuous night attack and our efforts of the previous week. But we'll do it! What is worrying me is how we are to get the wounded through."'[50]

Hauser and Meindl were soon joined by more German tanks leading Fallschirmjager from the 9th and 15th Parachute Regiments. Meindl remembered:

---

49. Ibid, pp. 37–38.
50. Ibid, pp. 37–39.

Both at and inside Coudehard the artillery first came at us from three directions the whole day through and at times rose to great intensity. And I noted with chagrin that the continuous stream of vehicles of every type and description from the Army divisions were being handled without the slightest trace of discipline, just like the first lot I had seen previously, the occupants with fear in their eyes and cowardliness in their hearts.

And although they could plainly see and hear that the enemy guns were sweeping the road and firing toward Coudehard, they still pressed forward like madmen toward the command heights of Coudehard. I had never seen anything so silly in my life except on manoeuvres! Here one saw the Communication Zone [rear area] troops from France, who hadn't known what war was for the past three years. The vehicles were simply sacrificed, although there was plenty of good cover off the roads, even against enemy planes! It was a pitiful sight, not to be described in words! Dissolution and panic! And in between them, my paratroopers, with contempt in their eyes, fulfilling their duties in an exemplary way! In tatters, in many cases wounded, dead beat and starving, but despite all still carrying their weapons, very often two or three, still on the job, ready to help one another at need. And this other pack! Displaying nothing but crass and cowardliness! Many decent men from the Army and the SS, who had lost touch with their own units, really lost touch, still holding on to their weapons, came and wanted to join us, saying they wanted nothing to do with the heap of cowardly curs and 'tea doilies' (as we called them). Unnumbered was the pack of rascals, however, who had no thought in mind other than to dash forward with their hands stuck above their heads, ready to surrender abjectly! All they had with them was their steel helmets, bread-satchels, and overcoats, most of them with a blanket as well. I could tell what they were long before they came near me, whether they faced me or had their backs turned to me, by their shuffling gait, the hanging, drawn in heads, slinking along always close to the ditches at the side of the road, ready to throw themselves flat on their faces if a grenade exploded 500 meters away from them! And, unfortunately, some officers among them![51]

51. Ibid, pp. 39–40.

Meindl's distain for panic-mongers in uniform was balanced by his new-found admiration of the Seventh Army commander:

> How manly, on the other hand, had been the conduct of the Commander in Chief. He'd gone through all the hardships of night attack, often enveloped in heavy machine gun fire! Here, the sheep had been clearly separated from the goats, the real from the 'phony' soldiers! An immeasurable contempt swelled in our hearts. I felt burning shame at the thought of the impression such scoundrels would make when they fell into enemy hands. What an impression they would give of the German soldier! An impression not justified! For the first time I now understood how WAR was the worst possible way of breeding the best type of human being. How the best blood was lost and the poorest retained.[52]

With tank support from the 2nd SS-Panzer Division, the Germans succeeded in taking the heights east of Coudehard at about 1630 hours. Thirty minutes later, German motor columns were rolling eastward. 'Unfortunately, a lot of them were chased by enemy planes and shot up in flames,' wrote Meindl. 'I was only able to keep a narrow gap free with the few men I had assisting me, a gap of about 2 or 3 kilometers wide. By taking some prisoners we confirmed the presence of a Polish armoured division.'[53] At 1900 hours the II Parachute Corps was able to evacuate the seriously wounded out of the pocket, including General Schimpf, with the aid of a hastily thrown together Red Cross column bearing large white flags with a red cross sewn on them. 'Not a shot was fired at them,' remembered Meindl, 'and I recognised, with thankfulness in my heart, the chivalrous attitude of the enemy, after the hail of fire which had been descending on our heads a little while before. After the ugly scenes I had witnessed that day, the nobility of our enemies made me forget for a moment the nastiness of it all and I offered thanks in my heart in the name of the wounded.'[54]

The Germans did everything they could to escape the Falaise pocket. Allied pilots reported a large proportion of Wehrmacht vehicles, even tanks, carrying Red Cross flags and emblems. 'It was obvious that it was

---

52. Ibid, p. 40.
53. Ibid, p. 40.
54. Ibid, pp. 40–41.

merely a ruse to avoid having their transport attacked,' recorded Major General Sir Francis de Guingand, General Montgomery's Chief of Staff. 'The decision was to avoid attacking them, for it was thought that the Germans in their present mood might well take reprisals against our prisoners and wounded. A difficult decision, but probably the right one.' Among those misusing the Red Cross were the Fallschirmjäger of the 3rd Parachute Division.[55]

The news that there was a way through at Coudehard spread like wildfire inside the ring, attracting a rush of stragglers that swept through the gap from nightfall until the morning of 21 August, when traffic dried up completely. Meindl recorded:

> Both General Straube and Generalmajor Dettling of the neighbouring corps had arrived beside me, having made their way on foot.[56] They wanted to join up with me for whatever was now to occur. Colonel Liebach had also arrived on the scene at about 0100 hours with the portion of the regiment which had been fighting the whole day through at the Dives River. He gave me a picture of the state of the troops trapped inside the ring.
>
> The majority, even the officers, had declined to attempt to get out of the trap. They considered it a hopeless project! I believed he had to witness worse scenes that I had had to during the day! I handed over control of the remainder of the 3rd Parachute Division. I sent officers off on bicycles into the ring to let them know inside what was happening and what was now to be expected. And an armoured reconnaissance battalion, the covering force for the panzer division, came up and announced that nothing was following behind them. I waited another three hours and managed to get the last of the wounded away. And

---

55. Tucker-Jones, *Falaise*, Chapter 15. 'Falaise – The Killing Ground', Kindle; According to a captured officer of the Colonel Sieback's 8th Parachute Regiment, Schimpf's 3rd Parachute Division often violated the Red Cross insignia in Normandy, in some instances transporting ammunition in ambulances. See 'Information secure in Intelligence Report 6824 ID (MIS) X-142 on file in the Office of CPM Branch MIS, RG 153 War Crimes Office', 'Richard Schimpf' undated, NARA, College Park, Maryland.

56. General der Infanterie Erich Straube was the commander of the LXXIV Armeekorps; Generalleutnant August Dettling was the commander of the 363rd Infantry Division.

then I decided to move back with the paratroopers as soon as it grew light, for I knew it would not be possible to keep the gap open for another whole day.[57]

On 19 August Polish, Canadian and British forces linked up with the American 90th Infantry Division at Chambois, closing the Falaise Gap. The line, however, was thinly held and German soldiers continued to pour eastward. General Heinrich Eberach, the commander of the Fifth Panzer Army, replaced the wounded General Paul Hausser, who had been shot through the jaw, as commander of the German Seventh Army. Rainy weather kept Allied aircraft on the ground on 20 and 21 August, facilitating German attempts to escape from the pocket.[58] 'The pouring rain and the sound of the wind drowned any noise from the marching feet,' wrote a relieved Meindl. 'My young one [Meindl's son, Klaus] and his infantry made up the front with myself, with two tanks bringing up the rear, so that we should not be surprised and run down by enemy tanks. Up till 0500 we kept the gap open, then when the tail end had come through, it closed again. It was with a heavy heart that I found myself on the retreat at this time. The rain, still pouring down in streams, enabled us to continue our march by daytime.'[59] Some 8km outside the ring, near Champosoult, the last remnants of the II Parachute Corps and Seventh Army encountered the 2nd SS-Panzer Division in defensive positions. Meindl was told that a steady stream of men, including paratroopers, without weapons or motor vehicles, had been pouring to the rear throughout the night. An assembly point for the II Parachute Corps was established at Neuville-sur-Touques, where the men would be collected and sent ahead into Germany.[60]

'I knew nothing of the whereabouts of my chief assistants, my Chief of Staff and my G-3 [Operations Officer], whom I had lost sight of at the tank line by the Dives River, nor of the 9th Parachute Regiment under Stephani or the 5th Parachute Regiment under Becker,' remembered Meindl:

After I had rested a bit from the strain of the march on foot and the efforts of the past night I left General Straube and Generalmajor Dettling to the care of the regimental command post and got

57. Meindl, *A-923 Northern France*, pp. 41–42.
58. Wood, *Army of the West*, p. 177; Tucker-Jones, *Falaise*, Chapter 15. 'Falaise – The Killing Grounds', Kindle
59. Meindl, *A-923 Northern France*, p. 43.
60. Ibid., p. 43.

inside the amphibious car allotted to me by the Commander in Chief and with it chockfull of companions set off along the Corps' road back to Orville.

It was touching to me to see how I was greeted on the road by my paratroopers whom I passed. It was as if the 'boys' (as I called the paratroopers) had no enemy chasing them. Unfortunately, there was no member of the 'propaganda company' on the scene to maintain an honest enthusiasm coming from the heart. I am not ashamed to confess that tears rose to my eyes when I saw this spirit of gratitude glowing in the eyes of my 'boys'. They might have looked like a pack of ragged tinkers, but their glance was bright and proud, despite their exhaustion. If any of us ventured to sit down for a minute we fell at once into a deathlike sleep, from which we were hardly to be roused. I saw this for myself when my 'young one' and I went around at 0230 hours and wakened them all quietly, as to get ready for the march again. I wakened my son first of all, stood him on his feet, and wished him a 'Happy Birthday' as it happened to be for him that morning, and then got him to give me a hand to wake up the others. The Command General himself went around awakening his men! And it proved such a job to get the men awake that in spite of the downpour both my son and myself were pouring with sweat before we got through.[61]

Only the task of constantly checking on his soldiers, running in circles and the heavy rain kept the exhausted Meindl from falling asleep.

Colonel Blauensteiner, Meindl's Chief of Staff, arrived in Orville around midday. He had taken charge of the 9th Parachute Regiment at Coudehard after major Stephani had been mortally wounded. Later, no trace of the brave officer was found. Colonel Blauensteiner had led an attack on the heights south-east of Coudehard with portions of the 5th and 9th Parachute Regiment, breaking through shortly afterwards. At the same time, German tanks had attacked eastward south of the 9th Parachute Regiment. By the evening of 21 August, Meindl had collected a few exhausted Fallschirmjager from 3rd Parachute Division east of Orville. He established communications with the Seventh Army, who ordered him to march his men to the Seine River in two night marches and assemble at three ferrying sites on the banks and wait for transportation to the other

---

61. Ibid., pp. 43–44.

side, south of Rouen. The 2nd SS-Panzer Division once again covered the II Parachute Corps' retreat.[62]

'During the night of 22 August, we reached the area of Beaumesnil, south-east of Bernay, then, continuing the march, we got as far as the woods south-west of Louviers. We were shielded by fog during these night marches,' wrote Meindl. 'The units had to wait to be taken across for several days, there was such a crush waiting to get over. We had no losses at this time, but I think other units lost a devilish lot of men.'[63]

Meindl and his small corps staff managed to cross on 24 or 25 August east of Louviers. 'From the columns present, everything in the way of fighting men, NCOs, weapons and vehicles were withdrawn, so as to raise a little the fighting ability of the regiment,' he recalled:

> Heavy weapons were completely lacking, nor could they be procured. All the supply dumps were exhausted, and the homeland was not in a condition to send us anymore.
>
> The 3rd Parachute Division and the 12th Artillery Battalion had no fighting value whatsoever after they got back across the Seine. There were, however, so many fighting men and NCOs present that we could have set up another division after they had been trained and equipped, if that had been possible. I therefore suggested to the Army and the Army Groups that these remnants of the various regiments could be conveyed back to Germany as quickly as possible, so that they could be rested and reassembled and trained, all the more insomuch as the remaining units were not in a fit state and lacking heavy weapons as they were, to fight a battle with an enemy operating almost exclusively with tanks. And the loss of experienced leaders was grievous![64]

Escaping with Meindl and the wounded Generaloberst Paul Hausser were three division commanders and 300 staff officers, regimental commanders and other officers, and 5,000 men.[65]

Combat in Falaise ended on 22 August, when all surviving German troops in the pocket surrendered. The efforts of the XLVII Panzer and II SS Panzer Corps aided the escape of approximately half the troops originally

---

62. Ibid., p. 45.
63. Ibid., p. 45.
64. Ibid., pp. 45–46.
65. Lucas, *Das Reich*, p. 148.

caught in the pocket. Although many support units remained intact, a significant number of combat formations suffered tremendous losses in men and equipment. According to Allied sources, the Americans, British and Poles killed an estimated 10,000 Germans and captured another 40,000 to 50,000.[66] Between 20 and 23 August some 20,000 to 40,000 German soldiers escaped the Falaise Gap, taking with them approximately 100 tanks and artillery pieces.[67] Bad weather prevented the Allies from cutting them off before they reached the Seine, allowing eighteen German ferries, operating around the clock, to evacuate Hitler's soldiers over the river. By 24 August, as many as 25,000 vehicles of all types had made it across.[68] A British Operational Research Section from General Montgomery's 21st Army Group later found more than 3,000 vehicles and artillery pieces around Falaise, including 344 tanks, self-propelled guns and other armoured vehicles, 2,447 trucks and cars and 252 towed guns.[69]

On 28 August the High Command in the West ordered all units of the II Parachute Corps back to the Cologne and Wahn area in Germany for rest and reconstitution. There, they would be brought back up to strength with paratroopers from General Kurt Student's German First Parachute Army. 'At this time our entire strength would be about 2,500 or 3,000 men, of which only about 500 or 600 were fighting men,' recorded Meindl. 'The Corps Staff and troops rolled off in the direction of Cologne–Wahn on 29 August. I myself reported to Sepp Detrich of the Army Group in Rouen and believed that at least now we would be spared from any further senseless orders! With the Chief I had to travel to Nancy, so as to receive orders for the setting up of the 3rd Parachute Division and so on, from the High Command of the Army there.'[70] By the beginning of September 1944, the remnants of the II Parachute Corps had reached the Cologne–Wahn area in Germany. Meindl lamented:

> I learned to my horror that as soon as I had gone, the 3rd Parachute Division had been held back by General Krause, Sepp Detrich's Chief of Staff, and ordered back over the Somme as a covering force for the panzer formations! Hardly motorised at all, scarcely

---

66. Ellis, *The Battle of Normandy*, pp. 447–448; Blumenson, *Breakout and Pursuit*, pp. 557–558.
67. Blumenson, *Breakout and Pursuit*, p. 555.
68. Wood, *German Army of the West*, p. 227.
69. Ellis, *The Battle of Normandy*, p. 448.
70. Meindl, *A-923 Northern France*, p. 46.

fit for use against infantry formations, and completely useless against tanks, this brave company of men, the like of whose valour I had never seen in the whole of France, had now been thrown back recklessly into the melee.

By this, the 3rd Parachute Division was condemned to be surrounded on 3 or 4 September while acting as a covering force for the 'doughty' tank formations, and therewith had taken the last step on the road to their martyrdom! Valuable, irreplaceable human material was thus sacrificed in this senseless way through the fatuousness and fear of a higher officer (in this case at least not by the Highest Command). No more than 100 or 150 officers and men managed to make their way singly through Belgium and France, chased for their lives like hares the whole time, and got back to Cologne and reported there. Among them were only two officers, 1st Lieutenants Becker and Croeschke.[71]

The remnants of the 3rd Parachute Division, along with two infantry battalions of the 6th Parachute Division and a few heavy-calibre weapons, were among the fragmentary units, stragglers, depot personnel and a host of miscellaneous troops with little ammunition, fuel or communications that were bombed and strafed from the air, ambushed by Resistance groups, attacked by Allied armoured spearheads, and finally encircled near Mons.[72] The retreating German convoy, miles in length and numbering as many as 30,000 troops, stumbled into American roadblocks and was thrown into confusion and virtually annihilated by the U.S. 3rd Armoured and 1st Infantry Divisions, which together captured some 27,000 Germans. 'Their organisation shattered and without proper communication, this huge force blundered into the road blocks of General Rose's armour during the early morning hours of September 3,' notes the 3rd Armour Division history of the war. 'Many Jerry soldiers came in and surrendered willing enough, but there were others, like groups of paratroopers who attempted to blast through a 36th Armoured Infantry road block to rescue general officers. After a short, sharp fight they were all killed, wounded or captured.'[73] Among the prisoners were three Wehrmacht generals,

71. Ibid., p. 47.
72. Blumenson, *Breakout and Pursuit*, pp. 683–684.
73. Sergeant Frank Woolner, et. al., *Spearhead in the West: Third Armour Division 1940–1941* (Darmstadt: Third Armour Division, 1946), Chapter: 'Northern France & Belgium', Kindle edition.

including General Rudiger von Heyking, commander of the 6th Parachute Division. Heyking told the Americans that the Germans had been caught completely by surprise. He had been erroneously advised that there was a 15-mile gap south of Mons. After so much hard fighting in Normandy, the 3rd Parachute Division ceased to exist in Belgium, along with the recently committed 6th Parachute Division.[74]

The 3rd Fallschirmjager Division, however, would live on. 'In Cologne an attempt was made to pick out from the swarm of stragglers, men out of hospital, and others, a nucleus for the new 3rd Parachute Division,' remembered Meindl:

> We did our best to collect something dependable in human material despite the great losses sustained by the units. We tried to scrape up enough equipment and so on to fit them out. All such work, which had until now proceeded smoothly and fairly quickly, now seemed to make no progress at all. The sacrifice of the last remnants of the 3rd Parachute Division now took a heavy toll on us! The number of really experienced soldiers we could gather together was frighteningly small! So far as numbers went the 3rd and 5th Parachute Divisions, along with the Corps troops in Normandy and throughout France, would have lost about the authorised strength of some two parachute divisions in the battles fought from 6 June to 14 September and on 4 September 1944 (Mons Pocket) without mentioning the whole of the heavy equipment of two divisions. It might be true that the II Parachute Corps had more than fulfilled all that had been expected of it, but at what a price! And all of this as a consequence of the hopelessly dilettante and completely incompetent assessment of front line conditions by higher authorities with not the faintest notion of the real conditions reigning there, a state of affairs for which all the highest authorities were to blame![75]

The Eugen Meindl who escaped the Falaise pocket with his son was not the same man who had fought at Normandy. 'When Eugen Meindl staggered back to his Fallschirmjäger in Nancy, his staff noticed their leader had changed,' records historian Richard Hargreaves. 'Gone was

---

74. Woolner, *Spearhead in the West*, Chapter: 'Northern France & Belgium', Kindle edition.
75. Meindl, *A-923 Northern France*, p. 48.

the "well-known iron discipline", in its place "loud emotional outbursts" aimed at the impossible demands of the supreme command. Meindl would fight on to the war's end, but never again with the same ferocity.'[76]

But the war was far from over. Even before the end of the battle of Falaise, the Third Reich had begun reconstituting old formations, especially its valuable panzer divisions, and assembling new ones, along with a host of new tanks, artillery and aircraft to defend the Netherlands and Germany. Among the new formations were a multitude of airborne units, including seven parachute divisions (7th, 8th, 9th, 10th, 11th, 20th and 21st) and parachute anti-tank units. By early September, the First Parachute Army had been subordinated to OB West under Field Marshal Model and was defending a sector in Holland from the coast to Maastricht, where it would meet the advancing Allied armies. The Americans and British would find themselves facing new Fallschirmjäger formations, as well as the already familiar II Parachute Corps, 6th Parachute Regiment and the reconstituted 3rd and 5th Parachute Divisions at Arnhem and the Ardennes. There would be no respite for Hitler's Fallschirmjäger, who would be called upon, once again, to meet the Allies in battle and stop their advance into Nazi Germany.

---

76. Hargreaves, *The Germans in Normandy*, p. 218.

Conclusion

By the end of the Normandy campaign, the Wehrmacht in France had been shattered. 'The German Seventh Army and the Fifth Panzer Army had been decisively defeated,' reported General Dwight D. Eisenhower, the Supreme Allied Commander, in his report to the Combined Chiefs of Staff, 'and into the debacle had been drawn the bulk of the fighting strength of the First and Fifteenth Armies.'[1] Captured German documents from senior headquarters revealed that the Wehrmacht in France had been taken almost completely by surprise with regard to not only the timing and location of the Allied landings, but also by the unprecedented Allied superiority on land, sea and air. Wehrmacht command reports stressed the 'careful planning and preparation' of the Normandy landing operations, noting that Allied reconnaissance and intelligence preparation had been so thorough that landing troops had maps showing all defensive installations, strong points, obstacles and armed minefields, 'even omitting dummy minefields'. The Germans were surprised by the 'new and improved' types of landing craft and equipment, 'concrete-filled ships' and 'pre-fabricated pylons' for the artificial Mulberry harbours. The reports stressed that the landings had been rehearsed on the English coasts, allowing Allied troops to carefully train on their special tasks on terrain like Normandy's, while American and British paratroopers had studied models of their objectives. Wehrmacht officers were impressed with how strictly secrecy and surprise were safeguarded, noting: 'The timing and place of the Normandy landings definitely took the defenders by surprise.' Furthermore, the strong preparatory air attacks that preceded the landings against coastal and inland targets 'and even the home theatre' threw the entire German supply and communications net

---

1. Eisenhower, *Report by the Supreme Commander to the Combined Chiefs of Staff*, p. 50.

'into confusion'.[2] According to other documents: 'In their first advance the Allies pressed boldly inland, attacking artillery positions still intact but simply bypassing strong points not yet out of action.' Counter-attacks cost the Germans heavy losses and were smashed by tanks and the fire of heavy naval guns. The extremely accurate fire of the warships eliminated every important target and individual heavy weapons and made the movement of strategic reserves 'impossible within the range of their guns' (20 miles inland). 'Cooperation between Allied air and ground forces was complete.' High praise was paid by the commander of the German 6th Parachute Regiment, Major Friedrich von der Heydte, to the 'marksmanship of the American parachute and airborne troops'.[3]

The same reports addressed the Wehrmacht's weaknesses at Normandy. They noted that German troops in the coastal defence areas were suffering from overstrain since 'for weeks before the invasion they had been working every daylight hour building field works'. They also highlighted that the commander of the German 6th Parachute Regiment, Major von der Heydte, complained that his company commanders were 'not equal to their battle tasks, so that regimental and battalion commanders had to supervise the execution of their orders themselves'. These comments certainly put the commander of 6th Parachute Regiment in a somewhat different light than that in which he presents himself in his post-war manuscripts. Regarding equipment, German front line troops, including Meindl's paratroopers, found their close-combat anti-tank weapons deficient. The Panzerfaust was characterised as 'inaccurate', while the Püppchen was called 'too heavy and immobile'. Only the 88mm Panzerschreck was praised as 'effective'. But there were not enough of these weapons available to make a difference.

Regarding tactical shortcomings, the German reports stressed that when Allied tanks broke through onto the roads leading inland, 'there were no emergency barriers or engineers to improvise such' and that the Luftwaffe 'was entirely absent' from the battle. Finally, regarding leadership, the reports note: 'Responsible German commanders did not draw the same lessons from invasion experiences. Some thought strategic reserves and attached artillery should be located further forward and

---

2. Headquarters Twelfth Army Group, 'Annex 6 to Twelfth Army Group Weekly Intelligence Summary, No. 18. German Views on the Normandy Landings', *Weekly Intelligence Summary No. 18. For Week Ending 9 December 1944* (Office of the Assistant Chief of Staff G-2, 12 December 1944), p. 1.
3. Ibid, pp. 1–3.

employed to strengthen defensive fire, whereas others stressed that defence should be conducted not in a single line but in depth and so reserves must be held in the rear. Still others see the salvation of defence in strong points, to be held to the last if cut off.'[4]

General der Panzertruppen Heinrich Eberbach, commander of Panzer Group West, placed the blame for the Wehrmacht's defeat at Normandy on the failures of Hitler's Supreme Headquarters, the Luftwaffe, the German supply services and the Führer's neglect of the German Seventh Army from 1941 to 1944. Hitler had failed to provide his army groups and armies with 'the necessary authority for independent action,' complained Eberbach after the fact. 'All decisions, despite clear reports from the front, were drawn up in the Supreme HQ and based on illusions, not on intimate knowledge of the situation, actual estimates of the condition and efficiency of the German and American divisions, and of the situation in the area of supplies.' Eberbach went on to add that the failure to subordinate the air forces and the navy to Army Group B left 'very large reserves' of men and motor vehicles in branches where they could not be used. And he added that Hitler had erred by 'using up the panzer divisions at the front, instead of holding them for counter-attacks, with the exception of Avranches'.[5]

Eberbach gave the Allied air forces the chief credit for the German defeat in Normandy. 'Their successes were obtained through choking off the delivery of services in the communications zone (railway stations, bridges, etc.) and in the combat area (making movements impossible during daylight hours except during period of bad weather).' He went on to note: 'The losses of panzers from lack of gasoline were larger than those destroyed by all kinds of enemy armaments put together.' The commander of Panzer Army West stressed that American and British bombers 'had a big effect on morale and material', as did the use of aircraft in the close support role, especially rocket-firing RAF Typhoons, 'especially against panzer units'.[6] Finally, Eberbach praised U.S. armour divisions for their success through 'proper commitments, deep breakthroughs, quick and resolute actions' and 'attacks into deep flanks and into the rear of the army'. He added that the American armour formations were 'correctly organised and had a great number of tanks'. And he praised U.S. armour personnel as 'well trained,' noting: 'The fine achievements of the Americans' tanks

---

4. Ibid, p. 4.
5. Eberbach, *A-922 Panzergruppe Eberbach*, pp. 34–38; For Eberbach's 'Reasons for the German Defeat' see Mitcham, *Panzers in Normandy*, pp. 160–163.
6. Eberbach, *A-922 Panzergruppe Eberbach*, p. 37.

must be appreciated because the Sherman tank, considering its armaments and armour, is not quite equivalent to the German Tiger and Panther.' As for American artillery, he stressed that only its high expenditure of ammunition made it as effective as it was. In the end he emphasizes that it was Allied airpower that played the greatest role in shattering the Wehrmacht in Normandy. 'I estimate the percentage of casualties to the German soldiers due to enemy aircraft was 50 per cent; due to enemy tanks, 20 per cent; to artillery, 20 per cent; and to infantry, 10 per cent.'[7]

After the war, General Meindl provided his U.S. captors with the reasons why he believed the Wehrmacht was defeated in Normandy. 'We did not have sufficient strategic reserves for a successful counter-attack against the beachheads.' Other critical factors included the lack of an air force; the lack of a well-functioning system of support; the lack of clear combat instructions pertinent to the situation to replace Hitler's 'Hold Fast' order, 'a handicap,' stressed Meindl, 'which made things easier for the enemy; the daily increase in the use of heavy equipment by American forces and the drop in U.S. casualties, resulting in a decrease in German heavy equipment and increase in casualties. Furthermore, according to the II Parachute Corps commander, as the American forces gained combat experience, their morale increased, while German morale decreased. 'The enemy had complete freedom of action,' wrote Meindl, 'as we launched very few attacks. Moreover, time was working solely in favour of the attacker.' In Meindl's opinion, what was needed operationally and tactically was a mobile defence 'so that our forces would not be exposed to the enemy's heavy attack weapons unnecessarily'. At the strategic level, Meindl concluded: 'The logical decision would have been to evacuate France for the defence of the Homeland.'[8] Like most Wehrmacht commanders at Normandy, Meindl blamed the overwhelming Allied preponderance in material for the German defeat, failing to mention the fighting prowess of U.S. forces, which outfought his paratroopers in a number of engagements. And he never addressed how the Wehrmacht would have overcome the Allies' air supremacy to conduct their mobile defence.

Using German archival documents, Swedish historian Niklas Zetterling records that OB West suffered almost 35,500 casualties in June (including

7. Eberbach, *A-922 Panzergruppe Eberbach*, p. 38. Most modern historians and front line soldiers of that era would disagree given artillery and mortar fire accounted for eighty per cent of losses in all armies.
8. Meindl, *B-401 II Parachute Corps (Dec 1942–25 Jul 1944)*, p. 18.

some 5,000 killed and 16,000 missing) and another 105,000 casualties in July (including some 11,000 killed and 55,000 missing).[9] In the meantime, OB West received 27,125 replacements. Of these, only 10,078 reached the front lines.[10] According to German Seventh Army Chief of Staff Oberst Rudolph-Christoph Freiherr von Gersdorff, four German infantry divisions were completely 'annihilated' at Normandy. Six other divisions, including the 5th Parachute Division (along with II Parachute Corps' 17th SS-Panzergrenadier and the 352nd Infantry Divisions) 'were so badly worn out that their fighting qualities were reduced to those of weak combat groups'. The same was true of the 6th Parachute Regiment and the regimental troops of three other divisions sent to reinforce the Normandy front from Brittany. All the other units, including the 3rd Parachute Division, had suffered 'severe losses' in personnel and equipment that could not be replaced. 'In this connection,' recorded Gersdorff (a key anti-Hitler conspirator who would rise to the rank of generalmajor and be awarded the Knight's Cross before the end of the war), 'it is important to note that almost all annihilated and seriously mauled Wehrmacht units had been committed against the American invasion army.' Gersdorff went on to denigrate the German soldiers who fought in Normandy in 1944, noting that they compared poorly with those who had manned the Wehrmacht between 1939 and 1942, or even those still fighting on the Eastern Front in 1944. 'This does not preclude the fact that the units employed on the west front, above all the panzer and Fallschirmjager divisions in view of their composition in respect to personnel, accomplished most excellent combat feats and displayed a maximum devotion to duty and readiness for combat.' He added that, in some cases, units whose personnel and material were 'good' (panzer, panzergrenadier, Fallschirmjäger) had the disadvantage of having only recently been organised or rehabilitated. 'On the whole,' he concludes, 'all these units were wasted one by one in unfeasible missions through inappropriate commitment by the Supreme Command.'[11]

Major von der Heydte's 6th Parachute Regiment was the first Fallschirmjäger formation and among the first Wehrmacht units in Normandy to encounter the Americans in combat and experience first-hand

---

9. Zetterling, 'German Losses in Normandy', *Normandy 1944*, p. 77.
10. Wood, *Army of the West*, p. 126.
11. Generalmajor Rudolf Christoph Freiherr von Gersdorff, *MS # B-722 The Campaign in Northern France 25 Jul 1944–14 Sep 1944* (U.S. Army Historical Division, 1946), pp. 4–8; Dermot Bradley, et. al., 'Rudolf-Christoph

U.S. air and naval superiority (in the form of naval artillery), along with American employment of large parachute and glider formations, which landed all around the Fallschirmjäger. The 6th Parachute Regiment defended St-Côme-du-Mont and Carentan without respite from 6 to 10 June against American paratroopers of the 101st Airborne Division attacking from multiple directions. As a result, the German paratroopers suffered heavy casualties. Less than two days later, with less than a day of rest, von der Heydte and his regiment were committed to an ill-planned and poorly resourced counter-attack, destined to fail without any air and insufficient artillery support or sufficient combat power against a superior force, resulting in even more losses. Afterward, the 6th Parachute Regiment was assigned a sector where it could recoup its losses and integrate replacements, while reinforcing the 17th SS-Panzergrenadier Division. Having integrated its new replacements and recovered from the trauma of almost a week of intense combat, von der Heydte's understrength Fallschirmjäger regiment held Sainteny and Sèves Island, supported by tanks and panzergrenadiers of the 2nd SS-Panzer Division 'Das Reich' against determined, but ill-conceived, attacks by the U.S. 90th and 83rd Infantry Divisions. Having avoided being demolished during Operation Cobra, von der Heydte's parachute regiment was the only German Fallschirmjäger formation to survive the Normandy campaign relatively intact as the result of the scruples of its commander, unwilling to sacrifice himself or his men to delay the Americans for another day or two. The 6th Parachute Regiment experience in Normandy was proof that, well-supported with tanks and artillery, the Fallschirmjäger could be expected to hold their ground, but not indefinitely without a steady flow of replacements and ammunition. One can only imagine what von der Heydte and his men might have accomplished had they been supported by the Luftwaffe.

The 3rd Parachute Division defended the approaches to St-Lô and then the city itself, first against the U.S. 2nd Infantry Division, and then the 29th Infantry and 30th Infantry Divisions from the middle of June until the middle of July in positional warfare. Constantly attrited by American bombs, artillery, mortars, and incessant infantry attacks, the 3rd Parachute Division lost more than a third of its authorised strength by mid-July, making it necessary to attach the 5th Parachute Division's 15th Parachute Regiment to make up some of the losses. Whenever possible,

---

Freiherr von Gersdorff', *Die Generale des Heeres 1921–1945* (Osnabrück: Biblio Verlag, 1996), pp. 259–260.

General Schimpf's men counter-attacked aggressively, usually succeeding in throwing back their U.S. attackers and delaying further American offensives. However, the lack of reserves limited both the size and frequency of the German counter-attacks, especially later, as the division lost more and more paratroopers in battle and the size of its regiments and battalions diminished.[12] Though chronically short of artillery (the 3rd Parachute Division was initially supported by a single artillery battalion after arriving in Normandy), the Fallschirmjäger made excellent use of the terrain and all their supporting weapons, especially their StuG III assault guns, 88mm anti-tank artillery pieces and portable anti-tank weapons, such as their Panzerfausts and Panzerschrecks. But, like the 6th Parachute Regiment before it, the 3rd Parachute Division found itself fighting a losing battle as one depleted attacking American infantry division was pulled off the line and replaced by another fresher and more capable one. By the third week of July, Meindl's most elite parachute division had suffered more than 6,000 casualties. And yet, for Schimpf and his men, there was no relief. The few who escaped Falaise were thrown back onto the front lines to stem the American advance at Mons, unbeknown to General Meindl.

General Wilke's 5th Parachute Division was fed piecemeal, regiment by regiment, into the Normandy battle with the 15th Parachute Regiment fighting at Mont-Castre against the U.S 90th Infantry Division. The Americans were supported by thirteen artillery battalions. The Fallschirmjäger failed to retain the high ground against the relentless ground attacks and artillery barrages, which threatened at times to overwhelm them. The 5th Parachute Division suffered such heavy losses that it was almost rendered ineffective as a fighting force. Later, the 13th Parachute Regiment reinforced the depleted 17th SS-Panzergrenadier Division. The 14th Parachute Regiment reinforced the weakened Panzer Lehr Division, itself redeployed from the Caen sector to face the Americans because of the tremendous losses suffered by German Seventh Army infantry divisions. The 15th Parachute Regiment reinforced the depleted 3rd Parachute Division. The heroism and sacrifice of the paratroopers of the 5th Parachute Division was never recognised by their fellow Fallschirmjager nor by the German High Command, which denigrated their performance. The men of the 15th Parachute Regiment and the 5th Parachute Engineer Battalion never received the credit they deserved for their skilled and

---

12. Generalleutnant Richard Schimpf, *MS # B-020 Fighting of the 3rd Parachute Division During the Invasion of France from June to August 1944* (U.S. Army Military History Institute, November 1989), p, 19.

tenacious defence of Hill 122 and Mont-Castre. Without their sacrifices, the German line would have collapsed much sooner than it did. Many of the Fallschirmjager of the 5th Parachute Division disappeared beneath a deluge of bombs during the opening phase of Operation Cobra. Others, stunned by the carpet bombing, surrendered to U.S infantry divisions in the first days of the American breakout from Normandy.

After Major von der Heydte's 6th Parachute Regiment, his parent unit, General Ramcke's 2nd Parachute Division, was the most fortunate. Supported by plenty of artillery, anti-aircraft artillery and ammunition and ensconced in the hills surrounding Brest and then in the city itself, Ramcke and the Fallschirmjäger of the 2nd Parachute Division made the Americans of the U.S. 6th Armoured Division and 2nd, 8th and 29th Infantry Divisions (supported by thirty artillery battalions, eleven medium bomber groups, and four fighter-bomber groups) pay dearly for their capture of the fortress. That U.S. forces would capture Brest was never in question. But the Americans expected to end up with a harbour that could be put back into working order rapidly to support their offensive against Nazi Germany. Instead, Ramcke and his men succeeded in delaying them long enough to reduce the harbour facilities to rubble. In the words of the U.S. Ninth Army history of the battle, Brest was rendered 'entirely useless' by the Germans.[13] Some 38,000 Germans were captured at Brest, including Ramcke and all that remained of the 2nd Parachute Division. Most had survived the ordeal and ended up in prisoner of war camps in the United States. Ramcke's last stand at Brest ensured that the Americans were unable to support their advance into Germany logistically and bought valuable time for the Germans to move new units into the Netherlands and the West Wall.

Rüdiger von Heyking's ill-fated 6th Parachute Division, which was still in the process of forming (and sending a regiment to the Eastern Front) when the Allies landed in France, managed to send a single kampfgruppe to bolster German defences against General George Patton's U.S. Third Army after the American breakout from Normandy. These were quickly overrun and annihilated.[14]

Despite their superior leadership, training, and armaments, Hitler's paratroopers in France fared little better than their less elite infantry counterparts in the Normandy bocage. Between 1 July and 10 September 1944, the II Parachute Corps' troops suffered 1,529 casualties, including

---

13. Parker and Thompson, *Conquer*, p. 35.
14. Zetterling, '6. Fallschirmjäger-Division,' *Normandy 1944*, pp. 223–224.

176 killed, 776 wounded, and 577 missing.[15] These figures include losses for the 12th Parachute Assault Gun Battalion (about 600 personnel) and the 12th Parachute Reconnaissance Battalion (of approximately 750 personnel).[16] The ever-reliable and hard-fighting 12th Reconnaissance Battalion of the II Parachute Corps was just west of the Dives River when it was finally surrounded in the Falaise pocket.[17] The more fortunate 12th Parachute Assault Gun Brigade, which had done such stellar work in Normandy, managed to cross the Seine River with 60 per cent of its original manpower in combat formations and 90 per cent manpower for its support elements.[18]

On 31 August 1944, Eugen Meindl was awarded the Oak Leaves to his Knight's Cross for his inspirational and untiring command of the II Parachute Corps in Normandy and France and for leading the breakout at Falaise. He was the 564th recipient of that honour. Meindl would go on to command the reconstituted II Parachute Corps for the duration of the war. His paratroopers would be rushed to the Nijmegen area of the Netherlands in September 1944 to counter Allied Operation Market Garden as part of General der Fallschirmtruppe Kurt Student's First Parachute Army. Meindl and his Fallschirmjäger would go on resisting the British and Canadian advance into Holland tenaciously, only laying down their arms after the Third Reich had capitulated to the Allies. On 8 May 1945, Meindl would be awarded the Swords to the Knight's Cross of the Iron Cross, this time in his capacity as Commander of the II Parachute Corps, the 155th recipient to do so. Captured on 25 May 1945, Eugen Meindl spent more than two years in Allied prisoner of war camps. He died on 24 January 1951 in München.[19]

---

15. Zetterling, 'II. Fallschirmjäger Korps', *Normandy 1944*, p. 151.
16. Zetterling, 'Fallschirm-Aufklärungs Abteiling 12' and 'Fallschirm-Sturmgeschütz Brigade', *Normandy 1944*, pp. 166, 203; According to George Nafziger, the 1944 German assault gun brigade were battalion-sized formations with three batteries and numbered approximately 1,500 personnel. George Nafziger, 'Sturmgeschütz (Abteilung) Battalions/Sturmgeschütz Brigades', (Unpublished).
17. Zetterling, 'Fallschirm-Aufklürungs Abteiling 12', *Normandy 1944*, p. 166.
18. Zetterling, 'Fallschirm-Sturmgeschjütz Brigade 12', *Normandy 1944*, p. 203.
19. Hildebrand, et. al., 'Eugen Meindl', *Die Generale der deutschen Luftwaffe*, pp. 372–373.

The 6th Parachute Regiment suffered 3,000 casualties during the Normandy campaign. Attached to the 353rd Infantry Division after it escaped the Falaise pocket, it received orders on 7 August to move to Nancy for refitting and did so with its 1,007 remaining paratroopers.[20] According to von der Heydte, his men lacked heavy weapons and supplies and were clothed in tatters. 'After a few days of rest at Dreux ... the regiment was transferred in motor vehicles to Nancy,' remembered the regimental commander. Von der Heydte failed to report to his superiors the establishment of an assembly point at Alencon for minor casualties and stragglers of the regiment. 'There was great danger that the higher Army authorities would learn of this secret assembly of men by the regiment and that those who had been collected at Alencon would again be sent to the front and thrown into battle which had become meaningless,' explained von der Heydte. This action earned him the condemnation of Oberst Max Pemsel, the former Chief of Staff of the German Seventh Army. 'The regimental commander was still in command of sixty men and, as a result of his orders, found more than one thousand "stragglers" belonging to his regiment when he arrived at Alencon,' recorded Pemsel. 'None of the divisions which were being drained of their last resources at the front had such numbers at their disposal at this time. It is furthermore incomprehensible that the regimental commander incorporated into his regiment "stragglers" who naturally had been attracted by the news that the regiment was to be transferred to the zone of the interior instead of turning them over, in accordance with regular procedures, to the collection points for stragglers,' continued Pemsel. He concluded with the following: 'A curious feature is that the regimental commander equipped his forces by making large-scale purchases on the French black market.'[21]

Considering the commitment and complete destruction of the 3rd Parachute Division at Mons resulting from the order of German Army commanders, von der Heydte's actions were reasonable. His regiment, like 3rd Parachute Division, belonged not to the Army but to the Luftwaffe High Command and the First Parachute Army, and could not be committed again without the permission of the commander of the Luftwaffe. Furthermore, when the shock suffered by von der Heydte at the almost total annihilation of his 1st Battalion at Hell's Corner is considered, his desire to save the remainder of his regiment is understandable. Von der

---

20. Zetterling, 'Fallschirmjäger Regiment 6', *Normandy 1944*, p. 165.
21. von der Heydte, *A German Parachute Regiment in Normandy*, p. 46.

Heydte and his 6th Parachute Regiment would fight again in the Ardennes in December 1944 during the Wehrmacht's last major offensive of the war.

Despite the criticisms against him, Major Dr. Friedrich August Freiherr Von der Heydte was promoted to oberstleutnant on 1 August 1944 and mentioned in German High Command communiqués for his leadership during the fighting in Normandy. He was assigned to set up the Army's new parachute school in Aalten. On 18 November 1944 he received the Oak Leaves to the Knight's Cross. On 8 December 1944 he formed and took command of Battle Group von der Heydte, which parachuted into the Ardennes during the night of 17 December to facilitate the movement of the Sixth SS Panzer Army westward. Wounded during the fighting, he was captured by the Americans on 24 December. Von der Heydte was transferred to the British facility for senior Wehrmacht officers at Trent Park 23 February 1945. He was assessed by his captors as 'genuinely anxious to cooperate with the Allies to bring the war to an end'. He provided a great deal of information on the German paratroopers and their part in the Ardennes counter-attack. During his time in captivity he authored several lengthy manuscripts on his 6th Parachute Regiment in Normandy, Holland and the Ardennes. Von der Heydte was never tried for war crimes, even though he was recorded, while at Trent Park, admitting to having shot dead American prisoners in Normandy when his 6th Parachute Regiment needed to cross a river and the prisoners would have hampered their progress. In 1951 he became a Professor for Civil and International Law at the University of Mainz. He also served in the Bundeswehr, becoming a brigadegeneral der reserve in 1962. He was one of only two German officers to receive that distinction. From 1966 to 1970, von der Heydte served as a member of the Bavarian State Parliament and as a member of the Christian Social Union. He remained involved with the Fellowship of 6th Fallschirmjäger Regiment, founded by Second World War veterans of the unit. Friedrich August Freiherr von der Heydte died in Aham, Landshut, in 1994 after a long illness.[22]

The II Parachute Corp's most elite formation, 3rd Parachute Division, was singled out for special recognition and praise by the Wehrmacht High Command. 'The breaking-out of the Falaise pocket, during which the 3rd Parachute Division distinguished itself above all, remained one of the great feats of the campaign,' recorded Major Percy Schramm in

---

22. Neitzel, ed., *Tapping Hitler's Generals*, p. 55. Von der Heydte was released on 12 July 1947; Kurowski, *Knight's Cross Holders of the Fallschirmjäger*, pp. 95–96.

the OKW War Diary, 'the second opportunity, which presented itself to the enemy during the retreating movements when an entire army could have been cut off, was thwarted by this division.'[23] Schimpf's division was one of the most severely damaged German formations in the fighting at Normandy. Between 6 June and 12 July the 3rd Parachute Division suffered 4,064 casualties. Between 1 July and 4 September the division suffered 2,561 men killed in action, 7,248 wounded and 16,370 missing in action. As these figures exceed the authorised strength of the division it can be assumed that the unit either received replacements during the fighting in Normandy or that the figures also represent casualties of attached formations not organic to the division. Historian Niklas Zetterling notes that many German divisions fighting in Normandy were described as destroyed in the battle, observing correctly that, many times, these statements were exaggerated. 'For this division,' writes Zetterling, 'the word destroyed might, however, be more appropriate.'[24] Zetterling estimates that up until the breakout, the 3rd Parachute Division suffered some 11,000 casualties, the second highest for any division-size formation fighting in Normandy.[25] According to Eugen Meindl, the last remaining elements of the formidable and hard-fighting division were destroyed at the Mons pocket between 3 and 4 September 1944.[26]

Historian Fritz Roppelt provides a more detailed breakdown of 3rd Parachute Division's casualties between May and August 1944. According to Roppelt, the division suffered ten casualties in May 1944, 2,085 in June, 3,845 in July and 3,385 in August for a total of more than 9,300 personnel killed, wounded and missing. This figure includes 151 officers. Hardest hit was the 5th Parachute Regiment, which lost 3,067 men between June and August 1944, including fifty-one officers. Next was the 9th Parachute Regiment, which lost 2,610 men, including fifty-two officers. Finally, came 8th Parachute Regiment which suffered 1,919 casualties in the same period, including thirty-four officers. The division staff, combat support and combat service support battalions and regiments lost another 1,399 men. Hardest hit of these was the 3rd Parachute Engineer Battalion, which lost 349 men in June alone, fighting on Hill 192, and the 3rd Parachute Reconnaissance Company, which suffered 284 casualties in the

---

23. Schramm, *The OKW War Diary. The West*, p. 113.
24. Zetterling, '3. Fallschirmjäger Division', *Normandy 1944*, p. 218.
25. Zetterling, *Normandy 1944*, p. 79.
26. Meindl, *A-859 II Parachute Corps*, p. 5. Neither Meindl nor General Scimpf describe how exactly the division was destroyed.

three-month period. Taken together, these losses were indeed debilitating. However, Roppelt goes on to note that the 3rd Parachute Division received some 5,000 replacements during the battle for Normandy, confirming Zetterling's assertions.[27]

Schimpf's badly battered 3rd Parachute Division was hastily rebuilt in the Netherlands from excess Luftwaffe personnel with 'woefully inexperienced' officers and men. In November OB West committed the 3rd Parachute Division near Aachen, where it once again fought the American Army as it attempted to drive through the north-eastern edge of the Hürtegen Forest. By mid-December, the German Fifteenth Army reported that the division had been so diminished in fighting strength that it was 'incapable of any offensive action'. Understrength or not, the German High Command threw the 3rd Parachute Division into the Ardennes Offensive, Hitler's and the Wehrmacht's make or break assault aimed at splitting the British and American Allied line, capturing Antwerp, destroying four Allied armies and forcing the Western Allies to negotiate a peace treaty favourable to Hitler and the Third Reich. During the intense fighting that raged from 16 December to 25 January, the once elite Fallschirmjager suffered grievous losses with many killed and wounded.

In recognition for his efforts, Generalleutnant Richard Schimpf, who had been severely wounded in the leg on 20 August 1944 leading the breakout from the Falaise Pocket and had to be carried out by his men, was awarded the Knight's Cross on 6 October 1944. After recovering from his wounds, he returned to command the 3rd Parachute Division on 11 January 1945, replacing the unit's caretaker commander, Generalmajor Walter Wadehn. After the withdrawal of the 3rd Parachute Division from the Ardennes following the failure of the German offensive there in December 1944, Schimpf also assumed command of the 85th Infantry Division at the Roer. At the end of February, 3rd Parachute Division relieved remaining elements of the 85th Infantry Division. Part of General der Panzertruppe Hasso von Manteuffel's Fifth Panzer Army, Schimpf and his paratroopers were engaged in delaying the Allied advance on Germany. On 8 March 1945, Schimpf and the remaining Fallschirmjäger of 3rd Parachute Division were captured near Bad Godesberg. Schimpf remained in Allied captivity until December 1947 when he returned home to Germany. In 1957, he entered the Bundeswehr,

---

27. Roppelt, *Der Vergangenheit auf der Spur*, pp. 691–695. My thanks to Lieutenant Colonel (Retired) Mark Reardon for providing me with this information.

Germany's post-war armed forces, and joined the West German Air Force, serving as generalmajor and commander of Military District III until his retirement in 1962. Richard Schimpf died on 30 December 1972 in Düsseldorf.[28]

Casualty estimates for 5th Parachute Division are difficult to assess as the unit, with 12,836 men prior to the Allied landing at Normandy, was never deployed as an organic whole, but rather parcelled out to reinforce various other formations. Generalleutnant Gustav Wilke estimates that the 15th Parachute Regiment alone suffered 70 per cent casualties between 15 June and 15 July 1944. Additionally, two battalions of 14th Parachute Regiment lost 50 per cent of their personnel and equipment on 23 and 24 June each when they were subjected to heavy aerial attacks. Wilke goes on to note that during the remainder of the Battle of Normandy each battalion lost another 25 per cent of its remaining personnel. Among them were two regimental commanders and two battalion commanders from a single regiment. What little remained of the division, fewer than 250 men, according to Wilke, was then subordinated to the II Parachute Corps. According to a German Army High Command estimate, the division had approximately 4,000 men left on 1 September 1944. Thus, the 5th Parachute Division may have lost as many as 8,000 men in the fighting in Normandy, ranking fifth among all German divisions in Normandy for the number of casualties suffered.[29]

Moved to the Bitburg area and placed under the command of Oberst Ludwig Heilmann, a Knight's Cross and German Cross in Gold recipient, the 5th Parachute Division was reconstituted with cadre and fillers from Holland and Germany. It fought once more alongside the 6th Parachute Regiment and the 3rd Parachute Division during the Ardennes Offensive. After the Americans turned the tide and started driving back the Wehrmacht and SS, Heilmann was able to lead the division out of encirclement, securing for himself a promotion to generalmajor. Nonetheless, by the end of January, the 5th Parachute Division had suffered such heavy casualties that it ceased to exist. Trapped with survivors of the 5th Parachute Division in the Falaise Pocket, Generalleutnant Gustave Wilke managed to escape, leading a kampfgruppe to safety. He formed the 9th Parachute Division in the Stettin area in December 1944, although this formation contained

---

28. Dixon, 'Richard Schimpf', *Luftwaffe Generals*, pp. 191–192; Schimpf, *B-020c Ardennes Campaign*, p. 1; Schimpf, *020d Rhineland Campaign*, p. 2.
29. Zetterling, '5. Fallschirmjäger Division', *Normandy 1944*, pp. 221–222. Zetterling calls the OKH estimate 'overly pessimistic'.

very few actual paratroopers and was a Fallschirmjäger division in name only, a phenomenon increasingly more common toward the end of the war. Wilke led the division in fierce fighting at Stargard, Stettin and the Küstrin Bridgehead in Pomerania. He was then ordered to form the 10th Parachute Division in Austria. Although it never reached more than kampfgruppe strength, this unit fought well against the Russians in the Danube Valley before being transferred to Czechoslovakia in the final days of the war. Wilke surrendered with his command in Iglau in May 1945. He was released from captivity in July 1947 and returned home to Germany. He died in Oberstdorf on 14 March 1977.[30]

The 2nd Parachute Division ceased to exist at Brest. It suffered some 7,550 casualties (including 162 officers) as the entire unit (minus the 6th Parachute Regiment and 2nd Parachute Anti-Aircraft Battalion fighting in Normandy) was killed, wounded, missing, or mostly captured at Brest.[31] Ramcke and the bulk of his men would spend the remainder of the war, and several years beyond, in American and British prisoner of war camps. Ramcke spent from 27 September 1944 to 10 March 1945 at Trent Park in England. In captivity he was described by British intelligence officers as 'inordinately vain' and with 'a most extensive knowledge of distorted history; ambitious, ruthless yet naïve, an opportunist'. He remained a fervent admirer of Hitler and an unrepentant anti-Semite, telling his fellow captives: 'One day history will say the Führer was right in recognising the great Jewish danger threatening all nations and in realising the Jewish Communist threat to Europe from the east.' During his imprisonment he made no bones to his British captors about the fact that he had been determined to win the highest decorations during the war and he described to them how he recommended his subordinates for high decorations knowing well that the German High Command would have to recommend him for a higher award than they received. Awarded the Swords and Diamonds to the Knight's Cross for his defence of Brest, his last act before being captured was to send a message to Hitler recommending himself for the award of an estate.[32]

Ramcke spent the next year as a POW in Camp Clinton, Mississippi. He was one of the 3,000,000 prisoners of war held by the Allies during and after the war. Some 425,871 of these, including 371,683 Germans, were

---

30. Dixon, 'Gustav Wilke', *Luftwaffe Generals*, p. 222.
31. Willi Kammenn, *Der Weg 2.Fallschirmjäger-Division*, p. 91.
32. Neitzel, 'Document 61', and 'General der Fallschirmtruppen Bernhard Ramcke', *Tapping Hitler's Generals*, pp 130, 309.

held in camps within the continental United States.[33] On 25 December 1945 Ramcke wrote a letter to Mr. Byron Price, a former reporter and editor who had been President Roosevelt's Director of Censorship during the war. After the war, Price was the ranking American member of the United Nations Secretariat. In that letter POW No. 18878, Hermann Ramcke, expressed his grief at the 'utter collapse of my Fatherland and its hopeless future' and protested at the 'cruel treatment of a completely defenceless nation'. He then proceeded to give Mr Price a lesson on German history followed by a laundry list of complaints on his life in an American POW camp, including 'the stopping of all correspondence between the prisoners of war and their families after the hostilities have ceased'; the fact that German prisoners of war 'were officially informed that they would continue to be regarded as such and treated accordingly, even after the end of the war'; a cut in food rations during the months May to October 1945 'to an extent that, on the average, all the prisoners lost 25–41 pounds in weight and can hardly stand on their legs while working hard on the Mississippi project'; the 'complete deprivation of tobacco and cigarettes from May to June' followed by 'the cutting of tobacco rations from then on until December to 2 oz. a week'; the 'deprivation of all luxuries and objects of daily use, as well as refreshments, who's lack was particularly felt in the hot summertime and in a climate to which the prisoners are not used to'; and finally, 'prohibition of all sports and games for a period of four weeks'. He concluded his letter by writing: 'I feel I am called upon to let you know on this Christmas Day about the feelings of the German prisoners of war, who, as a result of short-sighted measures, are put into a mood and attitude constituting a danger to general cooperation in the work of reconstruction and preservation of peace in the Western and Christian world.'[34] Ramcke's U.S. war crimes file, some 244 pages, is filled with letters he wrote to American political and military leaders in an attempt to extricate himself from his imprisonment. Most are a mixture

---

33. Judith M. Gansberg, *Stalag U.S.A. The Remarkable Story of German POWs in America* (New York: Thomas Y. Crowell Company, 1977), pp. 1, 13.

34. For a short synopsis of Ramcke's complaints while at Camp Clinton see Ramcke, *Fallschirmjäger Damals und Danach*, p. 90; for an English translation of his letter see 'Letter Hermann Bernard Ramcke, General i/c Parachute Troops, last Command of the fortress of Brest, P.O.W. No. 18878 Camp Clinton, Mississippi to Mr. Byron Price, The Capitol', Washington D.C. dated December 25, 1945' at www.kilroywashere.org/004-Pages/JAN-Area/04-D-Jan-POW-Ramcke.html.)

of moralising, self-justification, arrogance and unrepentance. Some are pleading in nature.[35]

According to his own account, Ramcke escaped from Camp Clinton on the morning of New Year's Day 1946 and made his way to Jackson, Mississippi, where he bought stamps at a local drug store and mailed his letter at the post office. In his dyed paratrooper's uniform and wearing a German naval jacket, he enjoyed a leisurely breakfast of eggs and ham, pancakes with syrup, and two cups of coffee, for which he paid 40 cents, bought himself several cigars, and then spent the next several hours reading the latest newspapers in the lobby of the Grand Heidelberg Hotel and exchanging New Year's greetings with passers-by. Afterward he caught a train back to Clinton and then crawled back into Camp Clinton, returning before the evening headcount. 'The supervising officer omitted the evening roll call,' he remembered afterwards. 'I could have stayed out the whole night.' Once the camp commander was informed by Senator Price of Ramcke's letter, the former paratrooper general, who writes that he was next planning an escape to South America, was moved to Camp Shelby and put into detention on only bread and water.[36]

In December 1946 Ramcke was handed over to the French to be tried for war crimes. He spent his time in captivity soliciting assistance against the French charges from the former American corps and divisions commanders that fought him at Brest. Surprisingly, most wrote letters of support praising the behaviour of Ramcke and his paratroopers during the battle and opining that he was not guilty of the alleged crimes. Ramcke, however, had been recorded admitting to some of his crimes, including arson, while in British captivity at Trent Park. It is unclear if these recordings were provided to the French. On 21 March 1951 he was sentenced to five years' imprisonment for war crimes at Brest, including hostage taking, murder of civilians, looting, intentional burning down of private residences and use of French persons for war work contrary to international law. He was released on 23 June 1951 for time served while awaiting trial. He published a second book in 1951, *Fallschirmjäger. Damals und Danach (Paratrooper. Then and Now),*

---

35. See U.S. War Department War Crimes Office, Judge Advocate General's Office, 'Hermann Bernard Ramcke' Record Group 153, Stack Area 270, Row 22, Compartment 11, Shelf 1 Box 82, File 100–852, NARA, College Park, Maryland.
36. Ramcke, *Fallschirmjäger Damals und Danach*, pp. 94–97.

completing the life story he began in his first book in 1943. He died of cancer in Kappeln, Germany, on 5 May 1968.[37] Hermann Ramcke was, without a doubt, a fervent Nazi, an egomaniac, a racist and anti-Semite. He remained to the end one of Hitler's most dedicated, reliable and hardest-fighting paratroopers.

Only a battlegroup of the 6th Parachute Division, consisting of the 21. Fallschirmjäger-Lehr Regiment [21st Parachute Demonstration Regiment], 1st Battalion of 6th Parachute Artillery Regiment, and Schwere Werfer Abteilung 21 [21st Heavy Rocket Launcher Artillery Battalion] fought at Normandy. These was sent to bolster German defences against General Patton's armoured spearhead. On 12 August the kampfgruppe was reportedly located in the area of L'Aigle–Moulins, well east of the area where elements of the German Seventh Army were surrounded. It appears to have remained in that area until the breakout from the Falaise pocket. By early September, the kampfgruppe, which had been reduced to two infantry battalions and a few heavy-calibre weapons, had been pushed back to Mons, Belgium by the First U.S. Army. Harassed from the air, ambushed by Resistance groups, attacked by Allied armoured spearheads and finally encircled near Mons, the paratroopers, with little ammunition, fuel, or communications, blundered repeatedly into American roadblocks, were thrown into confusion, and almost annihilated. Only a few of those caught at Mons escaped.[38] 'The 6th Parachute Division engaged in Normandy at the beginning of the invasion had been completely annihilated by the end of August 1944 during the heavy fighting which took place in the area roughly between the Seine and Amiens,' recorded Generalmajor Rudolph Langhaeuser (who commanded 6th Parachute Division from November 1944 until May 1945), in his history of the unit. 'No remnants of any consequence were left of these fighting units which would, later be used as seasoned cadre for a subsequent reorganisation. The new organisation was effected in October 1944 in Holland in the area of Assen-Mepel-Coevorden.'[39]

---

37. Neitzel, ed., 'General der Fallschirmtruppen Bernhard Ramcke', *Tapping Hitler's Generals*, p. 309.

38. Von Heyking, *A-956 Kampfhandlungen Nordfrankreich 1944. Der 6.Fallschirmjäger-Division*; von Heyking, *A-898 Kampfhandlungen in Nordfrankreich 1944 der 6.Fallschirmjäger-Division. II*; Blumenson, *Breakout and Pursuit*, pp. 498–500, 503, 575–578, 671, 683.

39. Langhaeuser, *B-368 Einsatz und Kampf der 6. Fallschirm-Jaeger-Division*, p. 1.

Generalleutnant Rüdiger von Heyking, commander of the 6th Parachute Division, was captured by the British at Mons on 3 August 1944. He was transferred to the British prisoner of war camp for senior Wehrmacht officers on 26 August and was held there until May 1945. In captivity he was described as 'quite friendly' and 'cooperative' in his attitude toward Allied officers. 'He thinks the war is definitely lost,' noted one British intelligence report, 'and is disillusioned and disgusted by the commands of Higher HQ.' Von Heyking was transferred to a prisoner of war camp in the United States in May 1945. He was repatriated in June 1947 and died on 18 February 1959 in Bad Godesberg.[40]

40. Neitzel, ed., 'Generalleutnant Rüdiger von Heyking', *Tapping Hitler's Generals*, pp. 298–299; 'Rudiger von Heyking,' in Hildebrand, et. al., *Die Generale der deutschen Luftwaffe*, Band 2., pp. 83–84.)

Appendix A

German – Allied Rank Equivalents

German	Allied
Generalfeldmarshall	Field Marshal
Generaloberst	General of the Army
General	Lieutenant General
General der Artillerie	Lieutenant General of Artillery
General der Infanterie	Lieutenant General of Infantry
General der Fallschirmtruppe	Lieutenant General of Paratroopers
General der Panzertruppe	Lieutenant General of Panzer Troops
Generalmajor	Major General
Generalleutnant	Brigadier General
Oberst	Colonel
Oberstleutnant	Lieutenant Colonel
Major	Major
Hauptmann	Captain
Oberleutnant	First Lieutenant
Leutnant	Lieutenant
Fahrenjunker	Officer Candidate
Oberfeldwebel	Master Sergeant
Feldwebel	Technical Sergeant
Obergefreiter	Corporal
Gefreiter	Acting Corporal

German Parachute Formations in Normandy 1944

1st Parachute Army	Generaloberst Kurt Student
II Parachute Corps	General der Fallschirmtruppe Eugen Meindl
2nd Parachute Division	Generalmajor Hermann Bernhard Ramcke
• 2nd Parachute Regiment	Oberstleutnant Hans Kroh
• 6th Parachute Regiment	Major Friedrich August Freiherr von der Heydte
• I Battalion	Hauptmann Emil Preikschat
• II Battalion	Hauptmann Rolf Mager
• III Battalion	Hauptmann Horst Trebes
• 7th Parachute Regiment	Oberstleutnant Erich Pietzonka
3rd Parachute Division	Generalmajor Richard Schimpf
• 5th Parachute Regiment	Major Karl Heinz Becker
• 8th Parachute Regiment	Oberstleutnant Ernst Liebach
• 9th Parachute Regiment	Major Kurt Stephani
5th Parachute Division	Generalmajor Gustav Wilke
• 13th Parachute Regiment	Major Wolf Werner Graf von der Schulenburg
• 14th Parachute Regiment	Major Herbert Noster
• 15th Parachute Regiment	Major Kurt Gröschke
6th Parachute Division	Generalmajor Rüdiger von Heyking
• 16th Parachute Regiment	Oberstleutnant Gerhart Schirmer
• 18th Parachute Regiment	Oberstleutnant Helmut von Hoffmann

Appendix C

Strength of German Airborne Formations at Normandy Beginning of June 1944 (Approximate)

First Parachute Army	10,000
II Parachute Corps	3,363
2nd Parachute Division (-)	6,631
6th Parachute Regiment	3,457
3rd Parachute Division	17,420
5th Parachute Division	12,253
6th Parachute Division (-)	10,000
Total	63,000 +

Bibliography

Primary Sources

'After-Action Report, 1944. Phase V – Capture of St. Lo', 29th Infantry Division, *World War II Unit Histories & Officers*, p. 1., www.maryland military history.org/ files/AftActRpt-29ID-44–07.pdf.

'After Action Report, July 1944, 90th Infantry Division', *90th Infantry Division History & Research, http://www.90thidpg.us/Research/90thDivision/ History/AAR /july44.html*

'After Action Report, July 1944', 115th Infantry Regiment After Action Report', *World War II Unit Histories & Officers*, p. 1., www.unithistories. com/units_ index/default.asp?file=../units/115th%20Inf.Reg%20 AAR%20july%201944.htm

'After Action Reports, Action Against Enemy, 13 July 1944', 116th Infantry, *World War II Unit Histories & Officers*, p. 2., www.unithistories.com/ units_index/default. asp?file=../units/116th%20Inf.Reg%20AAR%20 july%201944.htm.

'Annex No. 1 to G-2 Periodic Report No. 21. Notes on the 5th Parachute Division', 18 July 1944, 83rd Infantry Division, CG VII Corps, Box 3844 207.21 to 207.2.2 RG 407, NARA.

'G-2 Periodic Report No. 22, 18 July 1944', 83rd Infantry Division, CG VII Corps, Box 3844 207.21 to 207.2.2 RG 407, NARA.

'G-2 Periodic Report No. 22, 19 July 1944', 83rd Infantry Division, CG VII Corps, Box 3844 207.21 to 207.2.2 RG 407, NARA; For a roster of 5th Parachute Division officers in Normandy, see Erich Busch, '5. Fallschirmjäger-Division'.

Headquarters 329th Infantry Regiment, 'Action Against Enemy', 8 August 1944, p. 3, https://83rdinfdivdocs.org /documents/ 329th/AAR/ AAR_329_JUL1944.pdf.

'Report 143. Rudolph, Entler, Cpl, 11th Co, 5th Prcht Regt, FPN L50510', Tactical Interrogation Report, IPW Team 60-B, 134th INF, 3 Aug 1944,

134th Infantry Regiment, www.coulthart.com/134/ipw-index-44–8. htm

'Report on the Artillery with VIII Corps in the Reduction of Brest, 22 August–19 September 1944', (VIII Corps: October 16, 1945), p. 23. See http://cgsc.contentdm.oclc.org/cdm/ref/collection/p4013coll8/id/52

'Tactical Interrogation Report No. 30, Annex No. 1 to G-2 Periodic Report No. 30, 27 July 1944', RG 407 VII Corps, 207.21 to 207–2.2, 17 June 1944, Box 3844, NARA.

Generalleutnant Fritz Bayerlein, MS # A-903 Pz Lehr Division (15–20 July 1944) (Koenigstein: U.S. Army Historical Division, 20 May 1950).

Colonel Ernst Blauensteiner, MS # B-261 II. Normandy 6 June–24 July 1944 (U.S. Army Historical Division, October 1946).

General der Infanterie Guenther Blumentritt, MS # B-283 Evaluation of German Command and Troops (U.S. Army Historical Division, 25 March 1966).

Generalmajor Freiherr Treusch Buttlar-Brandenfells, MS # B-672 OB West (U.S. Army Historical Division, 5 December 1947).

Captain Henry L. Calder, 'The Operations of the 2nd Battalion, 23rd Infantry (2nd Infantry Division) in the Attack on Hill 192, West of Berigny, France 12–16 June 1944 (Normandy Campaign)' (Fort Benning, Georgia: Advanced Infantry Officers Course, 1949–50).

'Casualty Appendices to Hill 192 Combat Interviews (13–18 June [sic] 1944)', 2nd Infantry Division Combat Interviews, RG 407, NARA.

'Battle Casualties Zone of Combat Continental Europe in Compliance with WAR-41940', 26 May, Attention SPXOM from General Lee to General Eisenhower E33677; Msg CM-IN-14997', 18 June 1944; Msg CM-IN-19242', 23 June 1944; Msg CN-IN 592, 1 July 1944, Historical Reference Collection.

Commanding General 6th Armoured Division, Unit History. Combat Command B, 6th Armoured Division (Headquarters Combat Command B, 22 August 1944).

Combined Services Detailed Interrogation Centre (C.S.D.I.C), Special Interrogation Report (S.I.R) 350 KP/4120 (M/A) 'Gerf. Abledinger', KP/4506 (M/A) 'Gefr. Toschka', RG 165, NARA II.

C.S.D.I.C., S.I.R 651 'Report on Information obtained from PW DE/21042 (M) Ostubaf REINHARDT, Comd 1st Bn, SS PGR 37 captured North of Saintenay 7 July 1944'.

C.S.D.I.C., S.I.R 834 KP/43677 O/Fw Leyendecker, 'German Paratroop Formations', 6 August 1944, RG 165, NARA

C.S.D.I.C, S.I.R 1055 CS/480 Uffz Deiser 'The Parachute Army, 14 September 1944', RG 165, NARA II

Charles D. Curley, *How a Ninety Day Wonder Survived the War. The Story of a Rifle Platoon Leader in the Second Indianhead Division During World War II* (Ashcraft Enterprises, 1991).

Generalmajor Rudolf Christoph Freiherr von Gersdorff, *MS # B-727 The Campaign in Northern France* (U.S. Army Historical Division: Allendorf, September 1946).

Harry C. Gravelyn, *My Experiences as Captain of Company D, 331st Infantry, 83rd Division* (Travelyn Publishing, 2016) Kindle.

Maj. Homer H. Hammond, 'The Operations of the 6th Armoured Division in the Brittany Peninsula' (Ft. Benning, Georgia: The Infantry School Officers – Advanced Course, 1946–47).

Generaloberst Paul Hausser, *ETHINT 48. Seventh Army in Normandy (September 1945)* (U.S. Army Historical Division, September 1945).

MS# A 974 Normandy. Seventh Army from 29 June to 24 July 1944 (U.S. Army Historical Division: Koenigstein, 16 August 1950).

Oberst Friedrich August Freiherr von der Heydte, *MS # B-839 6th Parachute Regiment* (1 May–20 August 1944) (U.S. Army Historical Division, 1 July 1954).

General Rüdiger von Heyking, *MS # A-956 Combat Operations of the 6th Parachute Division in Northern France in 1944* (U.S. Army Historical Division, 17 June 1950).

'History of the VII Corps for the Period 1–31 July 44 (Report after action against the enemy)', pp. 10–11, RG 407, NARA.

HQ British Army of the Rhine, *Notes on the Operations of 21 Army Group 6 June 1944–5 May 1945* (1 September 1945).

HQ First U.S. Army, 'After Action Report. 6 June 1944–1 August 1944', RG 407, Box 1823, File 101-.03 A/A Report, NARA, College Park, Maryland.

Medical NCO Walter Klein, *MS # A-910. Bombing and Operation Cobra* (Headquarters United States Arm Europe: Historical Division, 1954).

Oberst Rudolf Kogard, *MS # B-427 The Battle in France in 1944. Events in Western Brittany, Especially Within the District of the Brest Fortress* (U.S. Army Historical Division, 19 March 1947).

Lieutenant Colonel D. C. Little, '105mm Howitzer Battalion in Attack of a Position, Hill 192, Normandy, 11 Jul 44', (Fort Leavenworth, Kansas: Command and Staff College, 1946–47).

E. Carver McGriff, *Making Sense of Normandy* (Inkwater Press: 2007).

General der Fallschirmtruppen Eugen Meindl and Generalleutnant Richard Schimpf, *ETHINT 78. 3rd Parachute Division in Normandy. An Interview with Eugen Meindl and Richard Schimpf* (U.S. Army Historical Division, January 17, 1946).

General der Fallschirmtruppen Eugen Meindl, 'Combat Procedures Against Numerically and Materially Superior Opposing Forces,' dated 26 June 1944 in 'G-2 Periodic Report, 182100 July 1944, 35th Infantry Division,' CG VII Corps, RG 407, 207-21 to 207-2.2, Box 3844, NARA.

MS # A-923 Northern France 25 July to 14 September 1944 (Koeningstein: United States Army Historical Division, 20 May 1946).

MS # B-401 II Parachute Corps (Dec 1942–24 Jul 1944) (United States Army Historical Division, May 1946).

Major General Troy H. Middleton, 'Report After Action against Enemy, 10 August 1944', www.90thdivisionassoc.org/afteractionreports/PDF/VIII%20AAR%2007-44.pdf.

Lieutenant Colonel Frank T. Mildren, 'The Attack of Hill 192 by the 1st Bn, 38th Infantry (2nd Division), July 11, 1944, (Normandy Campaign)' (Fort Leavenworth, Kansas: School of Combined Arms, 1946–1947).

Navy Department Library, 'Generaloberst Alfred Jodl, German Army', *Oral History World War II Invasion of Normandy (1944)*, at www.history.navy.mil/library/online/normandy_jodl.htm.

Office of the Chief of Ordnance, 'Cable Controlled Demolition Vehicle 'Goliath – BI', *Enemy Ordnance Material* (German) (Office of the Chief of Ordnance, 1 March 1945).

Max Pemsel, *MS # B-763 The Seventh Army in the Battle in Normandy* (U.S. Army Historical Division, March 1948)

Martin Poppel, *Heaven and Hell. The War Diary of a Paratrooper* (Sarpedon Publishing 1996).

Hermann Bernard Ramcke, *Fallschirmjäger Damals und Danach* (Frankfurt am Main: Lorch-Verlag, 1951).

Fallschirmjager. *Brest and Beyond, 1944–1951* (Shelfbooks, 2016).

Generalleutnant Richard Schimpf, *MS # B-020 Fighting of the 3rd Parachute Division During the Invasion of France from June to August 1944* (U.S. Army Military History Institute, November 1989).

MS # B-020a Normandy Campaign (6 June–24 July 1944) (U.S. Army Historical Division).

MS # B-541 Operations of the 3 FS Div during the Invasion in France Jun–Aug 1944 (US Army Historical Division, 22 April 1947).

Major Percy Ernst Schramm, *MS # B-034 OKW War Diary (1 April–16 December 1944)* (U.S. Army Historical Division, 31 December 1947).

Colonel C.P. Stacey, *The Canadian Army 1939–1945. An Official Historical Summary* (King's Printer: Ottawa: 1948).

2nd Lieutenant Stanley W. Seeley, 'After Action Report 712th Tank Battalion, 3 July 1944, July 1944–March 1945' (Headquarters 712th Tank Battalion: 20 August 1944).

John Robert Slaughter, *Omaha Beach & Beyond. The Long March of Sgt. Bob Slaughter* (Zenith Press, 2009).

Lieutenant General Hans Speidel, *Invasion 1944. The Normandy Campaign from the German Point of View* (New York: Paperback Library, 1968).

Colonel Henry G. Spencer, *Nineteen Days in June 1944* (Henry Grady Spencer, 2014) Kindle.

Captain Paul R. Steckla, 'The Operations of the 3rd Battalion, 358th Infantry, 90th Infantry Division in the Battle of Foret de Mont-Castre, France, 10–12 July 1944 (Normandy Campaign)' (Fort Benning, Georgia: The Infantry School, 1947–1948).

War Department, *Special Series No. 7 Enemy Airborne Forces* (Military Intelligence Services, December 2, 1942)

Special Series No. 14. German Infantry Weapons (Military Intelligence Division, May 25, 1943);

TM-E 30-451 Handbook on German Military Forces (Washington, D.C: Military Intelligence Division, September 1943).

Order of Battle of the Germany Army February 1944 (Washington D.C: Military Intelligence Division, February 1944).

Company Officer's Handbook of the German Army (31 March 1944) (Military Intelligence Division, 31 March 1944).

'German Anti-Tank Weapons'. *Intelligence Bulletin* (Military Intelligence Service, November 1944), Vol. III. No. 3.

'Germany's Rocket and Recoilless Weapons', *Intelligence Bulletin*, (Military Intelligence Service, March 1945) Vol. III, No. 7.

'101st Airborne Division', *Order of Battle of the United States Army World War II. Divisions* (Paris: Office of the Theatre Historian, 20 December 1945).

American Forces in Action Series. St-Lo (7 July–19 July 1944) (Historical Division, 21 August 1946).

Generalleutnant Gustav Wilke, *MS # B-820 5th Parachute Division (6 June– 24 July 1944)* (United States Army Historical Division, undated).

M. Wind and H. Günther, eds., *Kriegstagbuch 30 Oktober 1943 bis 6 Mai 1945, 17. SS Panzer-Grenadier-Division 'Götz von Berlichingen'* (München: Schild Verlag, 1993).

Major Dick Winters, *Beyond Brand of Brothers. The Memoirs of Major Dick Winters* (New York: Berkley Publishing Group, 2006).

Oberstleutnant Fritz Zieglemann, *MS # B-432 History of the 352 Infantry Division* (U.S. Army Historical Division, undated).

MS # B-433 352nd Infantry Division (7 June 1944) (U.S. Army Historical Division, undated).

Captain Clarence P. Ziegler, 'The Operations of the 2nd Battalion, 329th Infantry (83d Infantry Division) In the Attack Along the Road to Périers, 4 July 1944. (Personal Experiences of a Platoon Leader)', (Fort Benning Georgia: Infantry School, Advanced Infantry Officer's Course, 1949–1950).

Secondary Sources

Thomas Anderson, *Sturmartillerie: Spearhead of the Infantry* (Oxford: Osprey Publishing, 2016) Kindle.

The History of the Panzerwaffe, Volume 2: 1942–1945 (Oxford: Osprey Publishing, 2017) Kindle.

Joseph Balkowski, *From Beachhead to Brittany: The 29th Infantry Division at Brest, August-September 1944* (Stackpole, 2008).

Mark Bando, *101st Airborne. The Screaming Eagles at Normandy* (MBI Publishing Company, 2001).

Vanguard of the Crusade: The 101st Airborne Division in World War II (Casemate Publishing, 2012).

Florian Berger, *The Face of Courage. The 98 Men Who Received the Knight's Cross and the Close-Combat Clasp in Gold* (Stackpole Books, 2011) Kindle.

Georges Bernage, *3–9 juillet 1944 Objectif La Haye-du-Puits* (Heimdal 2013).

Objective Saint-Lô. 7 June 1944–18 July 1944 (Pen & Sword Military, 2017).

Edmund Blandford, *Two Sides of the Beach. The Invasion and Defence of Europe in 1944* (Castle Books, 2001).

Martin Blumenson, *United States Army in World War II. The European Theatre of Operations. Breakout and Pursuit* (Washington, D.C: Centre of Military History, 1989).

Horst Boog, et. al, *Germany and the Second World War. Volume VII. The Strategic Air War in Europe and the War in the West and East Asia, 1943–1944/45* (Clarendon Press, 2015).

Robert Bowden, *Fighting with the Screaming Eagles. With the 101st Airborne From Normandy to Bastogne* (Casemate, 2010).

Dermot Bradley, Karl-Friedrich Hildebrand, Markus-Rövekamp, *Deutschlands Generale und Admirale. Teil IV Die Generale des Heeres 1921–1945. Die militärischen Werdegänge der Generale, sowie der Ärzte, Veterinäre, Intendanten, Richter und Ministerialbeamten im Generalsrang*, Band I-VII (Osnabruck: Biblio Verlag, 1993–2004).

Omar N. Bradley, *A Soldier's Story* (Henry Holt And Company: 1951).

John Buckley, ed., *The Normandy Campaign. Sixty Years On* (London: Routledge, 2006).

Sergeant Joseph D. Buckley, *A History of the 50th Armoured Infantry Battalion* (self-published, 1945).

Clyde J. Burk and Cyrus R. Shockey, *Combat Records of the 6th Armoured Division* (Germany: 6th Armoured Division, 1945).

Erich Busch, *Die Fallschirmjäger Chronik 1935–1945. Die Geschichte der Deutschen Fallschirmtruppe* (Pozun-Pallas-Verlag, 1983).

Angelo Caravaggio, *21 Days in Normandy. Maj. Gen. George Kitching & the 4th Canadian Armoured Division* (Pen & Sword Military, 2016).

Paul Carell, *Invasion! They're Coming!* (Schiffer Military History, 1995).

Centre of Military History, *Regimental Study No. 1. The Carentan Causeway Fight* (Historical Manuscripts Collection 2, File No. 8-3.1 BB1 (Washington: Fort McNair).

Regimental Study No. 2. The Fight at the Lock (Historical Manuscripts Collection 2, File No. 8-3.1 BB2 (Washington: Fort McNair).

Regimental Study No. 3. 506 Parachute Infantry Regiment in Normandy Drop (Historical Manuscripts Collection 2, File No. 8-3.1 BB3 (Washington, Fort McNair).

The U.S. Army Campaigns of World War II. Normandy (Washington, D.C; 1994).

Robert M. Citino, *The Wehrmacht's Last Stand. The German Campaigns of 1944–1945* (University of Kansas Press, 2017).

Jeffrey J. Clarke and Robert Ross Smith, *United States Army in World War II. The European Theatre of Operations. Riviera to the Rhine* (Washington, D.C: Centre of Military History, 1993).

Elbridge Colby, *The First Army in Europe 1943–1945* (Nashville: The Battery Press, 1969).

John Colby, *War from the Ground Up. The 90th Division in WWII* (Eakin Publications, 1991).

Wesley Frank Craven and James Lea Cate, *The Army Air Forces in World War II. Vol. 3, Europe: Argument to V-E Day* (Office of Air Force History, 1983).

Stephen Darlow, *D-Day Bombers. The Stories of Allied Heavy Bombers during the Invasion of Normandy* (Stackpole Books, 2004).

Alejandro de Quesada, *MP 38 and MP 40 Submachine Guns* (Oxford: Osprey Publishing, 2014).

Henry L. deZeng IV and Douglas G. Stankey, *Luftwaffe Officer Career Summaries Section: Section L-R* (April 2017) at www.ww2.dk/LwOffz%20 L-R%202017.pdf.

Jeremy Dixon, *Luftwaffe Generals: The Knight's Cross Holders 1939–1945* (Schiffer Publishing, 2008).

Captain Michael Doubler, *Busting the Bocage: American Combined Arms Operations in France 6 June–31 July 1944* (Pickle Partners Publishing, 2013) Kindle.

Major L.F. Ellis, *History of the Second World War. United Kingdom Military Series. Victory in the West, Volume I. The Battle of Normandy* (London: HMSO, 1962).

General Dwight D. Eisenhower, *Report by the Supreme Commander to the Combined Chiefs of Staff on the Operations in Europe of the Allied Expeditionary Force* (Washington, D.C.: Centre of Military History, 1994).

Rudi Frühbeißer, *Opfergang deutscher Fallschirmjäger. Normandie – Ardennen* (Eigenverlag 1966).

Judith M. Gansberg, *Stalag U.S.A. The Remarkable Story of German POWs in America* (New York: Thomas Y. Crowell Company, 1977).

Ian Gardner, *Airborne. The Combat Story of Ed Shames of Easy Company* (Osprey Publishing, 2015).

Ian Gardner and Roger Day, *Tonight We Die as Men. The Untold Story of the Third Battalion 506 Parachute Infantry Regiment from Toccoa to D-Day* (Oxford: Osprey Publishing, 2011) Kindle.

Jonathan Gawne, ed., *Lessons Learned in Combat: D-Day and Beyond* (Ballacourage Books, 2013), Kindle.

Lessons Learned in Combat: Normandy Paratroopers (Ballacourage Books, 2014), Kindle.

F. Gilbert, ed., *Hitler Directs His War* (New York: O.U.P., 1950).

Donald L. Gilmore, ed., *U.S. Army Atlas of the European Theatre in World War II* (New York: Barnes & Noble, 2004).

Donald Graves, *Blood and Steel. The Wehrmacht Archive: Normandy 1944* (London: Frontline Books, 2013) Kindle.

Maj. Gen. Robert W. Grow and Clyde and J. Burk, *Combat Record of the Sixth Armoured Division* (Germany: Sixth Armoured Division, 1945).

Major Wade Hampton, 'A Proposed Doctrine for the Attack of a Built-Up Area' (Fort Leavenworth, Kansas: U.S. Army Command and General Staff College, 1966).

Richard Hargreaves, *The Germans in Normandy* (Stackpole Books, 2006).

Gordon A. Harrison, *United States Army in World War II. The European Theatre of Operations. Cross Channel Attack* (Washington: Centre of Military History, 1989).

B. H. Liddel Hart, *The Rommel Papers* (New York: De Capo Press, 1953).

Karl Friedrich-Hildebrand, *Die Generale der deutschen Luftwaffe 1934–1945*, Band I–III (Osnabruck: Biblio Verlag, 1990–1992).

Major General Anthony Farrar-Hockley, *Student* (New York: Ballentine Books, 1973).

Volker Griesser, *The Lions of Carentan. Fallschirmjager Regiment 6, 1943–1945* (Casemate Books, 2011).

Willi Kammann, *Der Weg der 2. Fallschirmjägerdivision* (München: Schild Verlag, 1998).

George Koskimaki, *D-Day with the Screaming Eagles* (Casemate, 2011).

Franz Kurowski, *Knights of the Wehrmacht. Knight's Cross Holds of the Fallschirmjäger* (Schiffer Publishing, 1995).

Infantry Aces. The German Soldier in Combat in WWII (Stackpole Books, 2005).

Jump into Hell: German Paratroopers in WWII (Stackpole Books, 2010).

James Lucas, *Das Reich. The Military Role of the 2nd SS Division* (London: Cassell, 1991).

Alexander Lüdeke, 'The Remote-Controlled Demolition Carrier'. *Weapons of World War II* (Bath: Parragon, 2013).

French L. MacLean, *Quiet Flows the Rhine. German General Officer Casualties in World War II* (Fedorowicz, 1996).

2000 Quotes from Hitler's 1000-Year Reich (Schiffer Military History, 2007).

Luftwaffe Efficiency & Promotion Reports for the Knight's Cross Winners (Schiffer Military History, 2007).

Unknown Generals. German Corps Commanders in World War II (Biblioscholar, 2012), Kindle.

S. L. A. Marshall, *Night Drop. The American Airborne Invasion of Normandy* (Boston: Little, Brown and Company, 1962).

Alexander McKee, *Caen. Anvil of Victory* (London: Souvenir Press, 1984).

Chris McNab, *MG 34 and MG 42 Machine guns* (Oxford: Osprey Publishing, 2012).

German Automatic Rifles 1941–1945. Gew 41, Gew 43, FG 42 and StG 44 (Oxford: Osprey Publishing, 2013).

Lieutenant Colonel Ernest W. Mitchell, et. al., *Combat History of the 6th Armoured Division in the European Theatre of Operations, 18 July 1944–8 May 1945* (6th Armoured Division: William E. Rutledge, Jr., 1945).

Vince Milano and Bruce Conner, *Normandiefront: D-Day to Saint-Lô Through German Eyes* (The History Press, 2012).

David Miller, *Fighting Men of World War II. Allied Forces Uniforms, Equipment & Weapons* (Chartwell Books, 2011).

Fighting Men of World War II. Axis Forces: Uniforms, Equipment & Weapons (Chartwell Books, 2011)

Samuel W. Mitcham, Jr., *German Order of Battle, Volume One: 1–290 Infantry Divisions in WWII* (Stackpole Books, 2007)

Antonio J. Munoz, *The Iron First Division. A Combat History of the 17th SS-Panzer Grenadier Division 'Götz von Berlichingen' 1943–1945* (Merriam Press, 1998).

George Nafziger, *The German Order of Battle. Infantry in World War II* (Greenhill Books, 2000).

The German Order of Battle. Waffen SS and Other Units in World War II (De Capo Press, 2000).

Sönke Neitzel, ed., *Tapping Hitler's Generals. Transcripts of Secret Conversations 1942–1945* (Frontline Books, 2007).

Captain Fredric E. Pamp, Jr., *Normandy to the Elbe, XIX Corps* (XIX Corps: Germany, 1945).

Colonel Theodore W. Parker Jr. and Colonel William J. Thompson, *Conquer. The Story of the Ninth Army 1944–1945* (The Battery Press, 1947).

Arve Robert Pisani, *Bocage. The Battle for Normandy* (Aperture Press, 2018).

Leonard Rapport and Arthur Norwood, Jr., *Rendezvous with Destiny. History of the 101st Airborne Division* (Konecky & Konecky, 1948).

Mark Reardon, *Defending Fortress Europe. The War Diary of the German 7th Army in Normandy 6 June to 26 July 1944* (The Aberjona Press, 2012).

Walter M. Robertson, *Combat History of the 2nd Infantry Division in World War II* (The Battery Press, 1980).

Fritz Roppelt, *Der Vergangenheit auf der Spur: 3 Fallschirmjäger Division. 1943–1945* (Roppelt, 1993).

Gordon L. Rottman, *US World War II Parachute Infantry Regiments* (Oxford: Osprey Publishing, 1990).

Panzerfaust and Panzerschreck (Oxford: Osprey Publishing, 2014).

Friedrich Ruge, *Rommel in Normandy. Reminiscences by Freidrich Ruge* (London: Presidio Press, 1979).

Shelby L. Stanton, *World War II Order of Battle* (New York: Galahad Books, 1984).

Hans-Martin Stimpel, *Die deutsche Fallschirmtruppe 1942–1945. Einsätze auf Kriegsschauplätzen im Osten und Westen* (Hamburg: Verlag E.S. Mittler & Sohn, 2001).

Hans Stöber, *Die Sturmflut und das Ende. Die Geschicht der 17. SS-Panzergrenadierdivision 'Götz von Berlichingen. Band I. Die Invasion* (München: Schild Verlag, 2000).

Telford Taylor, *March of Conquest: The German Victories in Western Europe 1940* (New York: Simon and Shuster, 1958).

Georg Tessin, *Verbänd und Truppen der deutschen Wehrmacht und Waffen-SS im Zweiten Weltkrieg 1939–1945*, Band I (Osnabrück: Biblio Verlag, 1979).

Leroy Thompson, *The M1 Garand* (Oxford: Osprey Publishing, 2012).

Anthony Tucker-Jones, Falaise: *The Flawed Victory – The Destruction of Panzergruppe West, August 1944* (Pen & Sword Military, 2008) Kindle.

Operation Dragoon: The Liberation of Southern France 1944 (Pen and Sword, 2010).

Major General J. A. Van Fleet, *Tough Ombres. The Story of the 90th Infantry Division* (Stars and Stripes, 1944).

Karl Venltzé, *German Paratroopers. Uniforms and Equipment 1936–1945. Volume II: Helmets, Equipment and Weapons* (Berlin: Zeughaus Verlag, 2016).

Gilberto Villahermosa, *Hitler's Paratrooper. The Life and Battles of Rudolf Witzig* (Frontline Books, 2010).

Bretton G. Wallace, Patton and His Third Army (Military Service Publishing, 1948).

Otto Weidinger, *2-SS Panzer Division Das Reich, Vol 5. 1943–1945* (Winnipeg, Ca.: J.J. Fedorowicz Publishing Inc., 2012).

Mary Williams, *U.S. Army in World War II. Special Studies. Chronology 1944–1945* (Washington, D.C: Centre of Military History, 1994).

Ernst Martin Winterstein and Hans Jacobs, *General Meindl und seine Fallschirmjäger. Vom Sturmregiment zum II Fallschirmjägerkorps 1940–1945* (Braunschweig, 1970).

Sergeant Frank Woolner, et. al., *Spearhead in the West: Third Armour Division 1940–1941* (Darmstadt: Third Armour Division, 1946).

James A. Wood, ed., *Army of the West. The Weekly Reports of German Army Group B from Normandy to the West Wall* (Stackpole Books, 2007).

Mark C. Yerger, *Waffen-SS Commanders. The Army, Corps and Divisional Leaders of a Legend*, Vol. II (Schiffer Military History, 1999).

Steven Zaloga, *Operation Cobra 1944. Breakout from Normandy* (Oxford: Osprey Publishing, 2001).

   The Devil's Garden. Rommel's Desperate Defence of Omaha Beach on D-Day (Stackpole Books, 2013).

   European Theatre of Operations 1944. Panzergrenadier versus US Armoured Infantryman (Oxford: Osprey Publishing, 2017).

   Saint-Lô 1944: The Battle of the Hedgerows (Osprey Publishing, 2017).

Niklas Zetterling, *Normandy 1944. German Military Organisation, Combat Power and Organisational Effectiveness* (J.J. Fedorowicz Publishing, 2000).

Index